The Present Moment

The Present Moment

A DAYBOOK OF CLARITY AND INTUITION

Penney Peirce

CONTEMPORARY BOOKS

Library of Congress Cataloging-in-Publication Data

Peirce, Penney.
    The present moment: a daybook of clarity and intuition/ Penney Peirce.
        p.   cm.
    ISBN 0-8092-2475-5
    1. Intuition (Psychology) 2. Intuition (Psychology)—Problems, exercises, etc.
    I. Title.
BF315.5.P455   2000
153.4'4393—dc21   99-088335
                                                                  CIP

Cover design by Kim Bartko
Cover photograph by Sandra Davis
Interior design by Diane Jaroch Design

Published by Contemporary Books
A division of NTC/Contemporary Publishing Group, Inc.
4255 West Touhy Avenue, Lincolnwood (Chicago), Illinois 60712-1975 U.S.A.
Copyright © 2000 by Penney Peirce
Printed in the United States of America
International Standard Book Number: 0-8092-2475-5
00 01 02 03 04 05 LB 19 18 17 16 15 14 13 12 11 10 9 8 7 6 5 4 3 2 1

For my parents,
Skip Peirce and Mid Peirce,
without whom I would have no present moments

CONTENTS

Acknowledgments

I didn't know what I was getting myself into when I decided to do a daybook! It seemed simple enough—straightforward, cleanly structured. But this format held different challenges from an ordinary book. I quickly found I could not easily make up 365 stories out of my own imagination and that relationships were important in the creation of such a piece. Often, just as I had exhausted my own ideas and sat wondering where the next one would come from, I'd get an unsolicited E-mail or the phone would ring, and it would be someone who'd seen my first book and wanted to chat. Unknowingly, that person would provide the content I needed. I am grateful—to the very process of writing this kind of book with this particular theme—because I was tricked into learning how exquisitely the universe does meet our needs. I intellectually understood it before, but now I *know*.

I want to thank the many people who reached out to help me, both knowingly and unwittingly. Deep gratitude goes to Marcus True, Karen Harvey, David Finch, Myfanwy (Mo) Lloyd-Tabb, Lisa Dickson, Diane Budo, Carol Adrienne, Larry Leigon, Donna Hale, Colleen Mauro, Karla McLaren, Lorraine Anderson, Cynthia Schmidt, Camilla Jewell, Stacy Brice, Cameron Hogan, Jon Driscoll, Allen Hicks, Kevin Kemper, David Newlin, Marilyn Mackey, Henry Smiley, Rod McDaniel, Jaye Oliver, Monica Suder, S'arka Felligiova, Pam Kramer, Carolyn Franklin, Suzie Daggett, Melanie Mulhall, Pam Van Orden, Becky Blanton, Marlane Miller, Peter Martin, Max Wellspring, Barbara Garro, Lisa Yoshimi Vogt, Yoshie Usuba, Masako Watanabe, and the many, many clients who have shared their lives with me. In many cases I have used pseudonyms to respect the privacy of contributors. Thank-you also to the people who sent interesting anecdotes from the Internet. I have used a couple that I felt were particularly moving. In addition, I want to thank my agent, Sheryl

Acknowledgments

Fullerton, for her clear mind and ongoing encouragement and my editor, Erika Lieberman, for her openness and spirit of cooperation.

My immediate family—Mid, Skip, Paula, Allan, Valerie, and Julia—have been unflagging in their support, providing material and inspiration through the high quality of their morals, sensitivity, intellectual feedback, heart, and humor. You are priceless.

A word about God, while I'm expressing appreciation. For many years, I wouldn't say the word *God* because I wasn't sure what I meant by it and didn't want to buy into any dogmatic belief system. I have now relaxed and am comfortable reverting to this simple term. When I use it I refer to a transcendent experience, not an old man with a long white beard. The God Experience is whatever we need it to be and evolves as we do. I love this Great Consciousness because it keeps emptying me of everything I thought was real and replacing it with an understanding that's even more real.

Foreword

What priceless experiences stand out in your life? Looking at a special sunset? Laughing uproariously through a hilarious play? Embracing your beloved after a long absence? An experience I treasure was reading Penney Peirce's first book, *The Intuitive Way*. I, too, teach others how to cultivate their intuitive abilities and was interested in sampling other teaching approaches. I opened her book intending to read for an hour before meeting a few friends. When I glanced at the clock, ninety minutes had passed. Then the electricity unexpectedly went out in my house. The book was so engrossing that I continued to read by candlelight until the last page was finished in the wee hours of the morning. It was truly the most exciting book on intuitive development I had ever read. Penney is a consummate teacher.

The book you are now holding is every bit the precious gem her first book was. As you read through *The Present Moment* and digest each day's thought, you will receive amazing nuggets of truth and insight. *The Present Moment* is most assuredly a tool to further your intuitive development, open the gateway to your soul, and put you in touch with your inner wisdom.

Intuition is metaphoric and often speaks through pictures and symbols. As I write this, my mind receives the image of a Hoberman sphere, an amazing transforming globe that I use in classes and discussions to demonstrate how the intuitive spark brings power and scope to the mind. This sphere consists of interlocking pieces that allow it to expand and contract. You can pull on any part and the entire sphere extends in volume ten times. This is what your consciousness will do as you work through *The Present Moment*. By the time you reach the last page, you will have considerably expanded the power of your mind.

Dr. Jonas Salk frequently said, "The intuitive mind tells the thinking mind what to do next." When I taught a course in a master's in management program called "Integrating Intuition and Logic for Managers," I asked the students to interview upper- and midlevel managers about how they used intuition in their decision-making processes. The students were amazed to discover that every person they talked to used intuition in some form. Like the managers interviewed by my students, you, too, are intuitive, whether you realize it or not. The challenge is to be aware of your own wisdom and be able to use your intuition regularly and reliably in all your endeavors. You will be more balanced and have much greater clarity when you use both your intuition and your logic.

Intuitive ability can be likened to one big muscle running throughout your body. This muscle needs to be exercised daily to be kept in shape. This reminds me of the old joke about "How do you get to Carnegie Hall?" And the answer is, of course, "Practice, practice, practice." *The Present Moment* shows you how to practice and exercise that intuition muscle. By setting the intention to use this book on a daily basis, you are making a commitment to work with self-development in an optimal way. Focusing on each day's affirmation and exercise will help you develop a heightened awareness of your body and your surroundings, which will strengthen your intuition. You'll be guided to pay attention to the insights and creative ideas whispering softly in your ear. In addition, your days will fill with a greater sense of joy, peace, and vitality.

Perhaps today's unprecedented fast pace and the overwhelming amount of information flowing through our lives has caused you untold stress. Perhaps you're experiencing burnout from shouldering too many responsibilities. Is the window to your mind wide open, allowing too many ideas to roll into play? Perhaps your mind meanders unceasingly from one thing to another, making you feel either hyperactive or apathetic. Learning to be centered, mindful, and intuitive is the best way to cut through this veil of confusion, clarify your priorities, and get back in balance.

The most magnificent gift I can give myself, truly, is to focus on one project or idea at any given moment. I feel an actual sense of relief (or is it joy?) as I bring each thing consciously to completion. *The Present Moment* offers you the luxury of doing this by focusing on one theme daily and letting the nuances of the lesson unfold throughout the day. You can slow down and embrace each theme, becoming mindful of how the principles that you are learning are vividly alive in your world.

An exquisite storyteller, Penney draws on personal experiences and the adventures of her clients, friends, and family to illustrate the principles of heightened perception that she weaves throughout the book. The anecdotes and poems are sometimes humorous, sometimes touching, sometimes highly practical. Stories are powerful teaching tools because they activate intuition; you will notice how feelings and pictures from your own life bubble up in your imagination as you read her stories. I also appreciate that Penney helps us retrieve wisdom from the practices of other cultures.

It really is exhilarating and energizing to observe and experience our world in the present moment as Penney suggests. Much emotional debris is accumulated when we fret about past deeds or ruminate about the what-ifs of the future. The potential for vibrantly learning about ourselves and the world is heightened when we focus on the here and now. *The Present Moment* will help you discover how you truly feel and eradicate the ghosts of how you *should* feel. You will soon become the expert on your own reality rather than relying on others to shape your opinions and constructs.

I leave you with a last thought from Eleanor Roosevelt: "The purpose of life is to live it, to reach out eagerly and without fear for newer and richer experiences." This beautiful and useful book will give you all the tools you need to live fully and have a rich, adventurous life.

MARCIA EMERY, PH.D.

To the Reader

*The soul can be experienced by releasing the familiar
and safe, by the constant renewal and expression
of our presence in the world, and by the moment-to-moment
attention we give to daily life.*
—BENJAMIN SHIELD, PH.D.

Faster and Faster, but Are We "There" Yet?

I have a friend who is a Buddhist priest/cabinetmaker/poet
living in New Mexico. Lately we've been exchanging letters as a kind of creative spiritual practice. Mine are filled
with humorous sagas of my book tour, my work in Tokyo,
and computer and Internet snafus combined with details of
my struggling vegetable garden which was stunted by the
El Niño weather. His, in contrast, are Zen-simple, recount-
ing horseback rides across wide-open mesas, the smell of
rain and juniper in the desert evening, with an occasional
burst of passion. I can see him out on his horse, atop a rise
with a 360-degree view, exclaiming to the wispy dragon
clouds above, "I want to say, 'Let us cast off the veil of
belief that keeps us centered in our narrow biography; let
us enter the dreamtime of souls and be gods and goddesses, Buddhas and birds, animals and stars!'" His reality
is a baseline that I gratefully tune in to when mine becomes
too flooded with the chaos and shallowness of urban life.

Living and working much of the time in bustling cities,
I can't help but notice that something is happening to us,
individually and culturally, that may never have happened
before, at least not with such promise of conscious recognition. Life is accelerating. *We* are accelerating. Everything is increasing, from the speed of our modems, to the
number of phone calls we receive, to the number of hours
we feel we must stay awake to handle all the tasks at hand.
We're aware of a massive amount of complexity these
days. Even the pitch of our stress levels seems screechier,

whinier. Thankfully, the inner frequency level of our thoughts and feelings is also rising, making us yearn for a higher kind of experience, a more noble, spiritual quality to our relationships and work. It may seem we're about to blow apart from the velocity of our rocketing lives, but perhaps the speed is actually guiding us toward a threshold where we'll be propelled into a vast, harmonious, super-conscious universe. It's encouraging that so many of us are now hungering for heart, soul, and purpose in life.

In our information-overloaded society, it's easy to deify the sources of incoming information. We tend to place authority in the outside world, in the experts who speak the loudest or portray themselves most audaciously. We hear so many competing voices that we've become distracted, fragmented, pressured, and rushed. As a result, our health and our humanity are at stake. A high-level executive I spoke with recently told me she had been trying to reach her company's computer consultant for two weeks. She'd left five messages but nobody returned her calls. Exasperated, she left an insistent, angry message and finally got a response. The man explained the poor service by saying, "You never seemed angry in any of your previous messages, so I figured you really didn't need help that badly."

Where is our common sense? What's happening to our standards? Why are we treating each other so disrespectfully, even in the most innocent arenas of life? By going so fast, we're losing touch with our bodies and nature, where the wisdom of our souls resides. We're up in our heads or in cyberspace using willpower to survive the onslaught of mental data. The more "heady" we get, and the more diversity we feel compelled to keep track of, the less heart we seem to have. It's ironic that the faster we go, the slower our progress, both physically and spiritually. How long can we keep up the pace? It seems we're approaching the time when we can no longer process the quantity of discrete facts and tasks with our linear, logical minds even with the help of computers. Our logic is a poor vehicle; it's simply not broad enough to contain the vastness of the new world that is now being born. This new reality is based on a greater number of dimensions of awareness: a *collective superconsciousness*.

To know this world of the future, we must learn to maximize our perceptions and integrate our intuitive, "direct knowing" *with* our logic. We must drastically shift the way we think. The fact that we have a chance to come together first within ourselves and then with one

another and the earth, to consciously know more and
more as one mind, one heart, one great body—this is the
opportunity of an eon. How can we do it? The answer
lies in the present moment.

---

*Intuition is notoriously clever and happens most when we
shift our rational mind into an unfocused state.
It is the wellspring of our creativity, our guidance, and our
ability to take the road less traveled—more often than not
leading us to our heart's desire.*
—CAROL ADRIENNE

Intuition: Knowing at the Speed of Light

In my first book, *The Intuitive Way: A Guide to Living
from Inner Wisdom*, I detailed the process of intuition
development, which I believe is the fastest path to the
experience of soul and enlightenment. Intuition is a doorway to the divine and helps us achieve the kind of wholeness, integration, and communion that leads to the shift
of awareness that will reveal our future reality. With its
quality of knowing from within rather than observing
from without, intuition is immediate; it is perception at
the speed of light.

Writer and filmmaker Phil Cousineau says, "In a world
moving at hyperspeed, where so many of us are anxious
because of the rate of change, the soulful move is the
move toward contemplating the source of things deeply
rooted in eternity, the things that always are. . . . If all we're
trying to do is keep up with change, I think we lose the
momentum of our soul's journey." Intuition is the key to
perceiving those things deeply rooted in eternity; it is the
perception of the soul. To develop intuition and be capable
of expanded perception . . . we must first slow down,
narrow our fields of vision, and pay attention to what is
right in front of our nose.

In *The Present Moment: A Daybook of Clarity and Intuition*, my intention is to help you find the intuitive doorway to your soul's inner wisdom. By practicing some
simple habits of centered attentiveness, you will easily and
consistently be able to hear the guidance that comes from
the still, small voice within. In *The Intuitive Way* I outlined a process of growth that took ten weeks. Here I want
to help you focus for a whole year on one simple thought
and action per day that will increase your sense of spirit,

presence, and meaning in life. Each day you'll concentrate on an affirmation and a short exercise designed to heighten your connection with your body, your intuition, and the world around you. These exercises will help you tap into your deepest, most real source of guidance and supply. *The Present Moment* will help you find inner wisdom in 365 different yet simple ways.

The affirmations and exercises are based on universal principles that can help you be more fully aware of life. Some of the themes underlying the daily practices in *The Present Moment* come from tenets of Buddhism, Christianity, and other major religions. Others I've plucked from my own experience of what empowers us to be more intuitive. Described below are the key ideas that will keep you focused and aligned for the year—so you can reap the greatest benefit from your own precious string of jewel-like present moments.

Be aware of your masculine nature;
But by keeping to the feminine way,
You shall be to the world like a canyon,
Where the Virtue eternal resides,
And go back to become as a child.
—LAO-TZU

Value the Feminine Mind

Most of us need a little help and encouragement or some sort of excuse to slow down, pay attention, and shift gears from the masculine mind to the feminine mind. The masculine mind is the linear, action- and goal-oriented, will-based part of our awareness. The feminine mind is the part of our consciousness that quietly notices, appreciates, includes, and experiences connections and oneness. Our feminine, or yin, awareness allows us to exhale, drop down into our body, take the pressure off, and feel knowledge rather than collect it, analyze it, categorize it, and memorize it. By using our mind in a soft, nonambitious way, we are magically ushered into an inspired state where personal insights and global visions give themselves to us willingly. Just as we cannot hold water in a clenched fist, the soul's wisdom cannot be realized with a mind that is driven and anxious. Our feminine awareness allows us to commune with knowledge, to be in a cocreative friendship with the process of our life, and to be so directly connected with what we perceive that we lose the sense of relatedness and actually *become* what we're observing.

Working with this book can provide you with the excuse you need to enter your feminine awareness. By taking in the ideas presented here day by day, you'll be gently guided into a new way of living and knowing, one based on receiving the love and wisdom in the presence that's everywhere around you and within you. My Buddhist friend in Santa Fe writes in his latest letter, "I'm really in no way trying to analyze events, dreams, or waking realities, not trying to reshape things into some second or third reality that my intellect likes better. I seem to live more fully by not trying to abstract meaning. It's like suddenly finding your way out of the canyon and riding up onto the mesa; the great circle of the horizon engulfs and swallows your mind in a single small gulp and all you can say is—Oh, yes!"

See how nature—trees, flowers, grass—grows in silence?
See the stars, the moon, and the sun—how they
move in silence?
We need silence to be able to touch souls.
—MOTHER TERESA

Enter the Silence

We are overwhelmed visually with myriad television channels, videos, movies, books, magazines, newspapers, E-mail, websites, and catalogs hawking everything from Southwest clothing to fancy gadgets for the world traveler. That visual stimulation becomes auditory stimulation as we translate the images into our own internal language, explaining what we see to ourselves. Add to that the actual auditory stimuli of phone calls, voicemail, pager messages, talk radio, audiotape lectures, music and song lyrics, even our on-line service that cheerfully exclaims, "You've got mail!" If you live in the city or suburbs, you're also dealing with noise from traffic, neighbors, and solicitors ringing your doorbell to give you the latest pitch.

How, then, are we to hear the still, small voice? Most of us are even catapulted from sleep by an alarm. When do we find quiet? When we finally get time to sneak off for a long hot bath, we probably read a book or magazine at the same time; there is an urgency to squeeze just one more task into any free time we find. And yet the quiet voice of our soul is always ready to give us insights and interesting, purposeful things to do. We just have to be simple and silent to hear it.

It's so vital that we create a new habit of dropping down, quieting down into the body's intuitive awareness. By shifting away from our predominant visual mode of perceiving and paying more attention to the auditory, we actually drop closer to the body's primal perception, in which we experience a more direct connection with life. By cultivating an awareness of silence then listening for the first sounds—the normally inaudible messages emerging from that core place—your intuition is likely to wake up enthusiastically as if from a long winter's nap.

In my many years of using intuition to sense the underlying patterns in people's lives and then finding the most accurate words to describe the subtle insights, I've learned to listen for that inner voice, that faintest of whispers. One of the most important skills in developing accurate intuition is the ability to tone down our domineering, talk-addicted mind, which arrogantly thinks it knows how the world works without ever observing what's happening in the freshly occurring present moment. To know clearly, we must learn to observe neutrally, and true observation can only take place with a silent mind. Experiencing the purity of silence is the prerequisite to knowing the beauty of the songs made by all living things and the particular sound of our own soul's narrative. Ironically, by slowing down and listening for one insight at a time, we end up knowing more, and more instantaneously.

Mind is the forerunner of all actions.
All deeds are led by mind, created by mind.
If one speaks or acts with a corrupt mind, suffering follows,
As a wheel follows the hoof of an ox pulling a cart.
Mind is the forerunner of all actions.
All deeds are led by mind, created by mind.
If one speaks or acts with a serene mind, happiness follows,
As surely as one's shadow.
—BUDDHA

Practice Skillful Perception

In *The Present Moment* you'll have an opportunity to practice a variety of principles of "skillful perception." But what is skillful perception? Buddhist philosophy, much

like the channeled, metaphysical Christian writing called
A Course in Miracles, encourages us to be conscious about
the choices we make, to use our awareness to see love and
connectedness not separation and fear. If we use our perception skillfully, we complete the karma (partial understanding or beliefs we hold about life based on fear) that
was generated in our near and distant past and don't create
any new blockages for ourselves or others. In other words,
we commit to add love and truth to the world instead of
contributing to the reality of pain and suffering. Your
choice for love is an act of love.

When I committed to my spiritual path, I made a practice out of a few simple ideas. I made an agreement with
myself to be honest and not judge, blame, or punish people. In no way did I become a saint, but by highlighting
these intentions it was easier to catch myself when I
drifted over the line and haul myself back on course.
Then I tried to look past people's outer personalities and
fear-based behaviors to the soul inside. I would say to
myself, "The light in me sees and knows the light in you."
I checked my thoughts and actions constantly by asking
myself, "What would Jesus, Buddha, Mary, Chief Seattle,
the Dalai Lama, or Mother Teresa do in this situation?"
Or, "If they were watching me right now, what would
they think?" Or, "If they were guests in my home, or
serving me at the lunch counter, or fixing my computer,
how would I treat them?" Or, "If I were dying right now,
scanning through my life in my final 'life review,' what
would I wish I'd done differently? Was I loving enough?
Conscious enough? Courageous enough?"

At some point we *will* face our judgment day, but how
interesting and valuable to make each day the judgment
day and have our own soul be the fair judge. In ancient
Egypt, it was believed that after death a person's heart
would be weighed on a scale against the Feather of Truth.
A heavy heart meant not enough love to balance with
clarity. I remember hearing author Dannion Brinkley tell
the story of how, in his near-death experience as he went
through his life review, he not only saw what a jerk (his
word) he'd been, he actually felt the effect of his actions
on others, experiencing himself through *their* perceptions.
It shocked him, and, after he came back to his body, he
vowed to become the kind of person others would feel
glad to know.

*The grace to be a beginner is always the best prayer for
an artist. The beginner's humility and openness lead to
exploration. Exploration leads to accomplishment. . . .
The stringent requirement of a sustai-ned creative life is the
humility to start again, to begin anew.*

—JULIA CAMERON

Return to Beginner's Mind

Zen Buddhism has a term, *shoshin*, which means "beginner's mind." All successful Zen practice, be it meditation, the reading of a sacred text, or the expression of an art form, must start with this innocent openness, or the "original attitude." For us to know the wisdom of our souls, we must not approach our own inner "oracle" with any preconceived or polarized ideas. We must be like a child, sincerely interested and open to any insight and experience. Writing teacher and Buddhist Natalie Goldberg says, "We never graduate from first grade. Over and over, we have to go back to the beginning. We should not be ashamed of this. It is good. It's like drinking water; we don't drink a glass once and never have to drink one again. We don't finish one poem or novel and never have to write one again. Over and over, we begin. This is good. This is kindness. We don't forget our roots."

In Zen, the beginner's mind is also what is called the "original mind," which includes everything inside itself, and is always rich, sufficient, and ready. Shunryu Suzuki, a Japanese Zen master, said, "In the beginner's mind there are many possibilities; in the expert's mind, there are few. In the beginner's mind there is no thought, 'I have attained something.' All self-centered thoughts limit our vast mind. When we have no thought of achievement, no thought of self, we are true beginners. Then we can really learn something. The beginner's mind is the mind of compassion. When our mind is compassionate, it is boundless. Then we are always true to ourselves, in sympathy with all beings, and can actually practice."

As you work with the affirmations and exercises in *The Present Moment*, pretend you've never heard of each concept before. "What I am given is what I need." "My body knows exactly what it wants." "Anything worth doing is worth doing well." "My soul moves my mind." What is your fresh take on each thought? Sometimes I pretend I'm from another planet just learning about what goes on here on earth, like in the scene from the movie ET: The Extra-Terrestrial, where the little boy is giving ET a tour of the toy shelf in his bedroom. He's explaining what his various toys do in rapid-fire succession, and, as he comes to a giant Mr. Peanut with little feet on the bottom, he says something like: "This is a peanut. You wind it up and it walks." Still wide-eyed, ET makes his little acknowledging "ahhhrr" sound, and they move on to the next item.

The Way is round, a vast emptiness,
nothing lacking, nothing left over.
Only because you choose and reject
does it cease to be so.
View the ten thousand phenomena as equal
and all will revert to naturalness.
The very basis of their being wiped out,
impossible to rate one above another!
—SENG-TS'AN

Embrace "Nothing Special"

To be fully aware in the here and now, you'll have to give up voting on the kind of perceptions, feelings, and reality you want to encounter. Do you only want to experience pleasant things? If so, you'll miss the tremendous amount of intuitive insight and deep understanding that are so often cloaked in discomfort. The shadowy as well as the illuminated part of life holds amazing revelations. When I do life readings for people, I begin with a bit of numerology. More often than not, when I tell someone that they're in a "five year," for example, they respond, "Is that bad?" Or when I say that a cycle they had in their youth will repeat at age fifty-one, they say, "Is that good?" Instead of being able to understand the potentially self-expanding concept I am about to relate, they freeze up, their whole reality having just reduced itself to a concern over right and wrong. Writer Anne Lamott says, "The villain has a heart, and the hero has great flaws."

Jon Kabat-Zinn, Ph.D., explains, "Zen has an expression, 'nothing special.' When you understand 'nothing special,' you realize that everything is special. . . . It's how you see, it's what eyes you're looking through, that matters. Are you looking through eyes of wholeness, or are you looking through eyes of fragmentation?" To hold fixed opinions about what is real or good fragments you just as surely as splitting your attention among too many ideas at once. A Tibetan Buddhist teacher, the Maha Siddhi Saraha, said, "Those who believe in existence are stupid like cattle; but those who believe in non-existence are still more stupid."

---

*The moment one gives close attention to anything,
even a blade of grass, it becomes a mysterious, awesome,
indescribably magnificent world in itself.*
—Henry Miller

Develop Mindfulness: The Art of Attention

It's amazing and totally magical when you discover that whatever you pay attention to comes alive! In my intuition training I have people hold up a finger and stare at it, slowly concentrating on the ridges of the fingertip, then the fingernail set into the skin, the blood pulsing through the capillaries, the tissues vibrating with nerve force, the bone running through the center. We move down the finger, section by section, including every component in our awareness, then go on to the other fingers, including them in our attention as well, and also putting attention *into* the parts we're noticing. Suddenly everyone gets it. Their whole hand is vibrating like a buzz saw! And the other hand, which was being ignored, feels dull and relatively lifeless. "Wow! My mind did all that?" they say. I tell them the life force was already there—it was their attention that was elsewhere. Lack of attention produces lack of life.

As you learn to enter the present moment and place your attention consciously on, then in, your experience, you'll first need to practice the art of "be here now," or being with what is, the way it is, without wanting or needing to change anything. If you want to change something, let that very thought be just another element in the way it is. You don't need to *do* anything right now; you don't need to comment about what's happening. Just be involved in existence. Ram Dass says, "The thinking mind is always *thinking* about things—it's always one thought from where the action is. It's far out to realize that when you're completely identified with your thinking mind, you're totally isolated from everything else in the universe." I also like what Irish poet and Celtic scholar John O'Donohue says, "We are sent into the world to live to the full everything that awakens within us and everything that comes toward us. Real divinity has a passionate instinct for creativity and the fully inhabited life."

Every life is made of a string of moments, each filled consciously with attention and presence, each one with its own dignity and wisdom. One of the greatest acts of love we can undertake is to grant each moment its own unique and precious identity, just as we do with newborn babies. Let the moment educate you as you join it, let it give itself to you, nurture, love, and embrace you. As you place your attention on something, allow yourself to fully sink into it. Keep paying attention, keep merging with it. As you do, the thing you're paying attention to will seem to notice you! You have called it to life, awakened the field around it from its nap. Perhaps this is why so often when you think of someone strongly, it is likely that he or she will contact you. Or why, when you stare at a dozing dog, it may suddenly lift its head and glance your way.

Mindfulness practice is about being awake in the moment. You can start in any still moment. Are you sitting, reading a magazine? Or looking at your hair in the mirror? Stop your mind's momentum and feel life. Notice all your senses, notice what your mind is thinking and suspend your thoughts. Just notice, feel, include, and appreciate existence as it's occurring. Then sink in deeper. What do you notice *now*? Make a small movement—turn a page in your magazine, comb your hair in slow motion. Be fully aware of the increments of the movement and enter the flow of the movement. Feel yourself going through the action; feel the consciousness of the page as it is turned, the hair being touched by the comb, the comb's reality as it passes over the head. Become the movement itself. As you do, you'll realize that any flow, any process, is conscious. Then enter a bigger, more complex movement; pay attention to how you have an entire conversation with a friend, how you exercise at the club or drive to work. Stay in each momentary phase of the process and notice as much as possible. Zen has a saying, "*Talk when you talk, walk when you walk, die when you die.*" When you give your present moment your total interest, you'll be surprised how much it gives back to you.

My goal in *The Present Moment* is to help make meditation a continuous part of your ordinary life, not just something you do first thing in the morning or at the end of a long day. We can meditate all day, eyes open, as we're involved in business meetings, or going out on a date, or having an argument. Eventually, we can aim for twenty-four-hour consciousness, becoming mindful even of what we do in our dreams. Jon Kabat-Zinn, who teaches mindfulness at the Stress Reduction Clinic at the University of Massachusetts Medical Center, says through mindfulness practice people discover that they're actually only alive in this moment and that they *can* affect the quality of their lives. "If I can relate to *this moment* with integrity, and then *this moment* with integrity, and then *this moment* with integrity, wakefully, then the sum of that is going to be very different over time, over mind moments that stretch out into what we call a life, than a life lived mostly on automatic pilot, where we are reacting and being mechanical and are therefore somewhat numb."

---

*Man is a chaos . . . but within this chaos is a wonder-eye:
God Himself, the Being of Beings who manifests Himself in
particular beings as the Eye of Eternity. . . .*
—JACOB BÖHME

*And I entered and beheld with the eye of my soul, above the
same eye of my soul, above my mind, the Light Unchangeable.*
—ST. AUGUSTINE

Keep Thine Eye Single

The beauty of a daily practice such as the one offered in *The Present Moment* is that you can have the luxury of a single theme to explore. You can play with the idea that it's really OK to pay attention to one thing at a time. How refreshing! There is just one you, with just one view, in each moment.

First, get centered. That means it's time to reel in your projections, all those lines you've cast out into the world. Bring your point of attention inside your skin. Perceive from inside your body. Look out from the centermost point in your head and feel outwardly from the center of your heart, from the center of each cell. Learn to feel the focus of complete attention. Then, as you view your moment, look with the eye of your soul. It's simple. There is only one insight, one message, one experience, one consciousness, and one self in any one moment. There is no future, there is no past, there is nowhere else to be.

We learn through this singularity to see through the polarities and illusions of the outer world. As spiritual teacher Sri Aurobindo said, "The torment of the couch of pain and evil on which we are racked is (God's) touch as much as happiness and sweetness and pleasure. It is only when we see with the eye of the complete union and feel this truth in the depths of our being that we can entirely discover behind that mask too the calm and beautiful face of the all-blissful Godhead, and in this touch that tests our imperfection, the touch of the friend and builder of the spirit in man."

Within the circles of our lives
we dance the circles of the years,
the circles of the seasons
within the circles of the years,
the cycles of the moon
within the circles of the seasons,
the circles of our reasons
within the cycles of the moon.
—WENDELL BERRY

Go with the Flow

I watched a friend, a skilled martial artist, gather his energy and awareness and pull into a poised stance, hands up and slightly separated in front of him, balanced perfectly on one foot, the other raised and resting easily in the air. He waited this way for what might have been a minute or an eternity, then the raised foot led the way and he stepped into a river of energy. I could almost see it, this stream of fluidity, this current of liquid fire. It enveloped him, moving through his body with lightning speed, guiding him through a complex sequence of silky smooth mercurial movements. He was a tiger, then a water bird, then a snake. The flow consumed him entirely and, when it finally released him and flowed off in another direction, he sat on the ground, almost dizzy, as his personality slowly returned to his body. Later that evening as we walked past a gnarled cherry tree, he stopped. Silently he stared at the forked trunk and twisted branches. Then his hands and arms began to snake their way up through the air, turning gracefully and sensually. "I often do this," he said, "as part of my practice. I enter the flow of the tree; I follow the path of its growth."

Since feeling the power of his focus and almost seeing the real currents of energy my friend was tapping into, I have been much more conscious of the streams of action, the flowing of the process, that I have stepped into at any given moment. Wherever you are right now, you are in a stream, too. Your currents are carrying you, moving through you, possessing you, informing you. By staying in the present moment and trusting the wisdom of the process itself, your expression can be inspired, beautiful, and effortless. Wayne Dyer talks about the importance of knowing your soul by entering the state of "flow." He says that in this state all distractions are gone. "The difference between being in and out of flow is the difference between knowing God and knowing *about* God."

Part of going with the flow is realizing that we are all part of nature, and nature operates according to universal principles. When we act in alignment with those principles, life greases the wheels. When our fixed beliefs get in the way, life grinds, sputters, and stalls. For example, one of nature's principles is that at the end of every cycle of creativity, when the final result has manifested, there is a normal period of disengagement. There must be a time to rest and renew. It's OK to feel blank, frivolous, or unmotivated for a while. This is necessary in the scheme of things to allow us to be repatterned and reinspired for the next cycle of creation. Yet we usually resist this part of our experience because we mistake it for laziness or, even worse, loss of control. By resisting this natural step, we create pain and disturbance. Go with the flow means embrace what comes next no matter what predetermined notions you may have about it. If you think your next career move should be a logical extension of what you've been doing for the past ten years, reconsider. The river of life that's running through you may want to veer to the extreme left and take you on a pilgrimage to Nepal, or make you take acting classes, or quit your job and go back to school for a master's degree in social work. Why limit your options?

To be able to know what the flow wants to do for you and with you, you'll have to stay loose. That means give up your fixations! Where in your life are you stuck, repeating behaviors or story lines like a broken record? What issues trigger avoidance, resistance, refusal, or hostility in you? What habits do you find hard to break? To what, or to whom, are you addicted? What roles, beliefs, styles, or possessions do you strongly identify with—so that losing them would feel life-threatening? To be in the flow, you may need to surrender any part of your life that has become too static, paralyzed, precious, or protected. As our lives continue to accelerate, we'll get progressively drained if we attach ourselves to any form or definition for too long. Here's the new mantra: "Anything is possible!"

With love, even the rocks will open.
—HAZRAT INAYAT KHAN

Express Loving-Kindness

Brian Weiss, M.D., reminds us, "There are several things we can do to stay in touch with our soul. The most important is to go within. . . . The purpose is to remind yourself of your true nature, which is that of a spiritual being. . . . As you find your true nature, you find that you are really a being of love. And when you think about it you see that everyone else is too. So besides meditating, practice acts of love." By living in the present moment, you'll discover many joy-producing truths. One is that your real nature is one of innate harmony. Another is that love is the core experience, or subtle substance of which you and all things are made; it is the glue that holds the continuous field of the universe together. By placing your attention in the now, you will also be forced to become aware of things you've felt uncomfortable about, that you've denounced as unworthy or bad, and that your conscious mind may have suppressed. How can you remain loving in the face of these rising monsters?

Pema Chödrön, a Tibetan Buddhist nun, talks about how when we begin a spiritual practice we often think we'll improve ourselves—and how that idea in itself is a subtle aggression against who we really are, as if there could be any unworthy parts of us, not created by God. She says the practice of loving-kindness must first begin by befriending ourselves, who we are right now, just as we are. And that if you could see a video of yourself at the end of each day, "You would wince quite often and say 'Ugh!' You probably would see that you do all those things for which you criticize all those people you don't like in your life, all those people you judge. Basically, making friends with yourself is making friends with all those people too." Loving-kindness is first about accepting your whole, surprising, gifted, and flawed self.

By making an agreement with yourself to experience love and express love, you ask to see that all things in life are connected and similar—and subsequently you experience that you are in some way like everything else and are connected to it all and that you cannot act on anything in the world without affecting yourself. Act lovingly and your own sense of self increases. Act fearfully or hatefully and your life becomes stunted. If you despise a part of yourself, you wound others to a similar degree. If you reject certain kinds of people, you handicap yourself to the same degree.

Leo Tolstoy said, "It is within my power to serve God or not to serve him. Serving him, I add to my own good and the good of the whole world. Not serving him, I forfeit my own good and deprive the world of that good, which was in my power to create." Yet perhaps the idea of giving and receiving love is really just an illusion; how can we give or receive what we already have in such abundance, that which is our very ground of being? Can we possibly squeeze any more love into the spirit of love that already creates us millisecond by millisecond? I think all we can do is know that we are love, that love fuels every motive and shapes every thought, action, and result. Love even fuels fearful, angry, victimy, and controlling thoughts. Thich Nhat Hanh prays, "Please call me by my true names, so I can hear all my cries and my laughs at once, so I can see that my joy and pain are one. Please call me by my true names, so I can wake up, and so the door of my heart can be left open, the door of compassion."

After accepting your whole self, loving-kindness is about practicing the golden rule. Treat other people as you would have them treat you. You are your brother and sister's keeper; they are yours. As you practice this premise, you naturally begin extending your definition of "brother" and "sister." Soon you feel kinship with animals, plants, rocks, the landscape. I saw naturalist and writer Barry Lopez recently, and he said that landscape is such a powerful force in our spiritual growth because it is through our basic involvement with the land that we come to develop not the "I-it" relationship but the "I-Thou" relationship. For without reverent care, the land does not give back. It comes alive and nurtures us in proportion to the love we give it and thus teaches us how to relate to each other. When you're being mindful and present, throwing litter onto the street feels the same as eating food that clogs your arteries. Severely trimming a tree is like having someone cut off your arm instead of clipping your fingernails. Driving your car when it needs a tune-up is like going to work with pneumonia. Lama Govinda said, "Reality is infinite relationship."

A more subtle level of the loving-kindness practice is attending to the quality of your thoughts and words—and even to the deeds that no one sees. As you experience the truth of our interconnectedness and feel that there really is just one mind running throughout all of life, it becomes evident that thoughts have real force and that there are no secrets. Your negative, gossipy words will reach the person you're talking about, no matter how far away you are, just as surely as your innermost complaining thoughts will cut through time and space and affect the mood of the person at whom they are aimed. I am reminded of a scene from the movie *Always* in which Richard Dreyfuss, who has just died and become an entry-level spiritual guide, is experimenting with his new ability to get a message through to a living person. He comes up behind a mechanic who is cheerfully whistling and sweeping and whispers something like, "What are you smiling about? Don't you know what a silly-looking guy you are?" The man's face clouds over; he stops and looks worriedly at his reflection in the rearview mirror of a van. We all have the ability to lighten the load for others or add to their burdens just by the way we think, speak, and act in our private moments.

As soon as you notice the slightest sign of indifference,
the moment you become aware of a loss of a certain seriousness,
of longing, of enthusiasm and zest, take it as a warning.
You should realize your soul suffers if you live superficially.
—ALBERT SCHWEITZER

Live a Life of Inquiry

While we are alive in bodies, I think we are meant to be dynamic, moving then resting both in body and in mind. Our minds are meant to ask ten million questions, then answer them. In between all the talking we get to experience the healing silence. How else can we have creativity? The search is not meant to be frenetic, nor are we to accept our lot with lazy vacuousness. We're here to learn, grow, and evolve. Like children, who start asking questions as soon as they can speak, we as adults naturally want to continue the quest. It is through awe and wonder that our minds are guided to ask the important questions, those that propel us onward in our evolutionary journey. Someday we'll grow beyond questions and answers, beyond the fascination to know, and we'll merge totally with that higher awareness that simply *is*. Until then, it's helpful to make an art form of asking questions. Everything and everyone you look at contains questions and answers. Every experience you have can be seen as symbolic of a more fundamental reality, or a lesson, or a message from your soul. Why not entertain and educate yourself by heightening your curiosity?

Contemplation, examination, and seeking: these are actually our active relationships with the unknown. And the unknown is just the unrealized next level of our identity. When the unknown knocks on the door, you'll be drawn to ask, "Why did I narrowly escape that serious accident on the highway today? What is the hidden meaning of the dream I had last night? What's the real reason behind my string of dominating girlfriends? What is the message in the barn owl's hoot?" Writing teacher Natalie Goldberg says, "If you can write a question, you can answer it. When you are writing, if you write a question, that is fine. But immediately go to a deeper level inside yourself and answer it in the next line. 'What should I do with my life?' I should eat three brownies, remember the sky, and become the best writer in the world."

Man has no Body distinct from his Soul;
for that called Body is a portion of Soul
discerned by the five Senses, the chief inlets of Soul.
—WILLIAM BLAKE

Trust Your Body: Home of Your Soul

Let me tell you a secret, a cosmic joke. It is an irony so obvious yet hidden for centuries by the longing for some kind of heaven. *When your mind and body become one, you see that your soul, your own personal heaven, is right here!* Not above, not in the future, not in the abstinence from "lowly" human experience nor in vows of poverty, but in our core physical and emotional nature. Soul, or superconsciousness, interpenetrates and composes all of space and form and our whole personality. It's only the separation of mind from body that gives us the experience of fear or "hell," the void. Your soul's guidance springs effortlessly and continuously from your body.

In intuition development, the first skill to develop is the ability to discern your body's subtle first cues, what I call the truth and anxiety signals. Your ancient reptile brain is constantly monitoring the environment, assessing whether situations and people are safe or dangerous. Pay attention to the expansion of energy, thought, and emotions, which feel like enthusiasm or anticipation, and you'll know what your soul wants to do next. Notice the contraction of energy, thought, and emotions that leave you cold, make you numb, or create a knot in the pit of your stomach—and you'll know what to avoid. If you can learn to discern these signals at the earliest possible point, when they're still subtle vibrations in your body, you'll save an incredible amount of time and grief.

The next skill to develop when opening your intuition is the ability to receive messages through all five of your senses: smell, taste, touch, hearing, and vision. This is perception filtered through the midbrain. Learn to make decisions based on how you imagine a new job might taste, for example, or what kind of sound it would make over time. Get the scents of potential employees—do they reek of self-loathing, or do they radiate the freshness and optimism of a spring day? If a prospective romantic partner were an animal, what might he be? And what does it mean to you that he seems like a hawk? If the person's physical body had a texture, would it be silky, gritty, sticky, or liquid? If her inner energy had a feel, might it be different from the physical one? Perhaps hot, prickly, sluggish, or jerky? What about the dream you had this morning? What does that volcano, or the flying carpet, or the forest of telephone poles symbolize about your life process right now? Do you experience how the smell of the toast you burned is related to the screech of brakes you heard in the intersection, and how that is like the dream you had of falling, and that is like the heartburn you got after lunch? Alan Watts said, "I have the image of the senses being terms, forms, or dimensions, not of one thing common to all but of each other, locked in a circle of mutuality. Closely examined, shape becomes color, which becomes vibration, which becomes sound, which becomes smell, which becomes taste,and then touch, and then again shape."

Pay attention to your body. Your intuition rises; it percolates up directly into your conscious mind, straight from your cells. The first intuitive messages occur as attraction or repulsion, then they come as a whiff, a flavor, a hue, a texture, a tone. It is only later in the process that your sensory impressions turn into visions, acquire meaning, and are locked in temporarily by definition and language. You don't need to wait that long to know.

The first draft is the child's draft, where you let it all pour out and then let it romp all over the place. . . .
If one of the characters wants to say, "Well, so what, Mr. Poopy Pants?," you let her. No one is going to see it. If the kid wants to get into really sentimental, weepy, emotional territory, you let him. Just get it all down on paper, because there may be something great in those six crazy pages that you would never have gotten to by more rational, grown-up means.
—ANNE LAMOTT

Imagination Is Your Ally

You'll notice as you start working through *The Present Moment* that a number of the exercises focus on creativity and imagination. To get good results from your intuition, you must trust the delivery system that brings you ideas. Your imagination is your intuition's delivery system; it makes full use of all your senses as well as handing you ancient planetary secrets from your cellular memory and higher, more geometric patterns of knowledge from other dimensions. The more fluid your imagination, the wider the range of ideas and inspiration it can deliver. Maybe you think your imagination will carry you away, that it's like a wild pony just itching for trouble. That's probably because you haven't let it out to run and kick up its heels in the big pasture for a long time.

Children live quite happily and harmoniously with their imaginations totally intact, and they are naturally engaged with the real world in a very intense and spiritual way because of it. When my niece Valerie was four, we were riding in the back seat of my sister's car along one of the ridges east of Denver. To the west, the sun was just breaking through some storm clouds as it set over the Rockies. The sky was glowing with neon pinks and lavenders, sun rays streaming dramatically toward earth. "Look over there, Val," I pointed, "isn't that beautiful?"

She looked up from her coloring book, in which she was furiously scribbling, and rendered me speechless when she replied, "Oh, yes! Doesn't that look just the way it did when God created the world?" Julia Cameron says, "People frequently believe the creative life is grounded in fantasy. The more difficult truth is that creativity is grounded in reality, in the particular, the focused, the well observed or specifically imagined."

It is by paying attention to the symbols and sensations, the recurring themes and preoccupations in your dreams, fantasies, and synchronicities that you will start to hear the voice of your soul. Make use of the imaginative data that comes to you by interpreting it, creating with it, entertaining others with it, or allowing it to heal your wounds; imagination is one of life's greatest, most direct, most impactful gifts.

I find you in all these things of the world
that I love calmly, like a brother;
in things no one cares for, you brood like a seed;
and to powerful things you give an immense power.

Strength plays such a marvelous game—
it moves through the things of the world like a servant,
groping out in roots, tapering in trunks,
and in the treetops like a rising from the dead.
—RAINER MARIA RILKE

Respect the Authority in Yourself and Others

When I was writing *The Intuitive Way*, I needed a section that would address the idea of keeping our agreements with ourselves, of not resisting our own internal authority. I looked up the word *authority* and found that it really means the creative force, which naturally wants to expand as soon as it is activated by having attention placed on it. When you grant yourself authority, energy expands from your center and *you* have creative power. When you recognize or invest authority in other people or in an organization or idea, energy increases and expands from *that* source, and then your mother, your boss, the church, the IRS, or whomever you gave the authority to has the creative power. If you are caught in the belief that you can have only half of reality at a time, you'll be susceptible to dominator-victim behavior patterns, and these are the biggest killers of heart and the natural flow of our love—and probably of our bodies, too.

Here's how it works: if you see authority in yourself and not in anyone else, you'll jump into the role of leader. You'll be original and excellent and so good at what you do that no one will help you. After all, you're the expert. This leads to isolation, martyrdom, and bitterness. Being the sole authority can also create a messiah complex, in which you scoff at the incompetence and unconsciousness of others and feel a need to control, save, direct, or even punish the "less fortunate ones." So in the end, seeing authority only in yourself leaves you alone, unsupported, and cynical. On the other hand, you may have little sense of self; then you'll see authority externally, in celebrities, cultural heroes, your spouse, your personal trainer, or your religion, and sooner or later you'll become resentful at having to emulate or obey some outside source or some rule that you feel at odds with because you aren't being recognized reciprocally. The person, idea, or organization you grant authority to will eventually dominate you and you'll become a victim, either succumbing to resignation or fighting for recognition. Both extremes can ultimately lead to violence against yourself or others.

And yet, if you realize that you are the one who recognized and bequeathed the authority in the first place, then *you* are the true authority, the creator, the one who says what or who is powerful in your life. Acknowledge first your own authority as the Perceiver. What you see is what you get. Place your attention inside yourself and you'll feel the divine power there. Place your attention outside yourself and you'll feel the divinity there. It's the same creative force, the same authority, running throughout. Why not see authority everywhere? If you can simultaneously grant authority to yourself and to others, to the inside and the outside world, you'll easily slide into the realization that all life forms have an equal voice and are worthy. Then there is no outside authority to resist, no need to fight to be yourself or save the suffering masses.

As a person with authority, you learn that every choice you make determines the quality of your life. You have free will to perceive a situation as adding to you and offering an opportunity for expansion, or threatening you, subtracting from your happiness and blocking your path. The experience of your life is entirely up to you. And yet, you do not live in a vacuum and cannot go it alone. Your thought processes are influenced by people you know and don't know in this world and the nonphysical worlds as well. We're all making choices constantly, and we play off one another both consciously and unconsciously. The path you take to work each day is determined by when you and everyone else leaves home, which cars are driving in which lanes, how fast they are going, and a variety of other outside factors. Each day your commute is different and new, even though you take the same route. Part of being in the present moment is learning to enjoy this cocreated quality of our lives and at the same time make authentic choices.

Gone, inner and outer,
no moon, no ground or sky.
Don't hand me another glass of wine.
Pour it in my mouth.
I've lost the way to my mouth.
—RUMI

Your Inner and Outer Worlds Are Correlated

After you invest authority everywhere, it's easier to grasp the idea that your world is actually continuous; there is no gap between the form that is you and the form that is the air, and the form that is another person, or a pickup truck, or a stray cat, or the garbage you throw out. In fact, the pickup truck is an aspect of you. The garbage is a part of your bigger body. You are a jewel with countless facets. With all these options, you have a very large arena in which to live. Life can be anything and come from anywhere. It can originate as a thought, feeling, or impulse inside your mind or as an event or action in the world of form. It all still comes from the soul. If a flow of life begins inside, look immediately for its correlating event, expression, or symbol in your outer life. If you think, "I feel restless and agitated today," notice the world. Are people cutting you off as you drive? Did you overhear a loud argument between strangers, or is your dog whining a lot when you leave him in the backyard? Your inside and outside selves are always doing the same thing. You and the world are one.

If a flow begins outside as an event, look internally for the corresponding idea. If your husband suddenly informs you that he's in love with someone else, that he needs to get on with his life and wants a divorce, you might say,

"This is unfair! Why is this happening to me?" But listen inside. Maybe your soul is really saying, "I'm ready to move on in *my* life. I want increased creativity, more power, and a greater challenge." You and the world are one. Look for similarities and metaphors. The more interplay between your inner and outer selves, the more at home and at peace you'll be in your life.

The ability to see the universe from different perspectives
may be a reflection of the different vantage points of perception
of our subtle energetic vehicles of expression, such as
the astral, mental, and causal bodies.
—RICHARD GERBER, M.D.

You Are a Multidimensional Being!

You are much more complex than you appear on the surface. If you could see yourself from a clairvoyant's point of view, you'd look something like an egg-shaped onion with layers of energy and consciousness progressing from a relatively dense inner core outward and upward. Each layer takes up more time and space and vibrates at a higher frequency. If the layers were colors, you'd look like a rainbow. If you perceived yourself auditorily, you'd sound like do-re-mi-fa-so-la-ti-do. If you could feel the different bodies, they might progress from something like sandpaper to silk to a cool, soft breeze. If you imagine that your conscious mind is like the zoom lens on a camera, then you can imagine opening or closing your view, zooming in and out through the available territory, taking various snapshots along the way at whatever focus fascinates you.

The tight focal length of the physical body is just one of many realities to which you have access. You are habituated to this one, but, when you dream at night or meditate or daydream, you are opening your lens and taking in a wider view. When your lens zooms out, you may become aware of emotions or patterns of thought or of the deep-seated intentions of your soul's purpose for your life. The farther you zoom out, the less you'll feel like a finite personality, restricted to linear time and space or cause and effect. Your energy will seem freer, you'll seem to move faster, and knowledge will be more instantaneous and direct. The higher the frequency of consciousness, the more connectedness and belonging you'll feel and more knowledge and purpose will be shared among many. When you use your intuition to sense what's underneath the physical reality, you're opening your zoom lens for the wider view.

In *The Present Moment* you'll have many opportunities to stretch beyond the small physical focus, to glimpse what you're doing at the other levels of your being. You, the soul, are active in every dimension of yourself all the time, but your conscious mind is so acclimated to the tight focus of this three-dimensional world that you simply forget to look up and out for the extended view. That's why, when you get busy in another dimension while you're awake, it often seems like you space out or leave your body. You can learn to stay centered and actually bring back the memories of what you're doing in that other dimension. The present moment is expandable! Your reality can contain any amount of self, any amount of knowledge. You are actually a very big and fascinating situation!

Let's have a merry journey, and shout about how light
is good and dark is not. What we should do is not
future ourselves so much. We should now ourselves more.
"Now thyself" is more important than "Know thyself."
Reason is what tells us to ignore the present and live in the
future. So all we do is make plans. We think that
somewhere there are going to be green pastures. It's crazy.
Heaven is nothing but a grand, monumental instance
of future. Listen, now is good. Now is wonderful.
—MEL BROOKS

How to Use This Book

So the one supreme desire of the mystic comes to be,
to merge the consciousness of both the world and of himself in
the consciousness of God . . . , (and) to realize the unfelt
natural presence of God in creation, by entering into
a personal relationship with the concealed Presence
which is the Source of being.
—EVELYN UNDERHILL

I began by introducing the idea that we, our lives, our
knowledge, our emotions, even the vibrations of the earth
itself are accelerating, so we have an opportunity to experience a kind of perceptual, spiritual transformation. By
developing intuition and mindfulness, you will find your
particular path into the direct experience of your soul.
Your path may be quite different from the paths of other
people. The idea here is not to look so much for the right
form but to be directly connected to your own source of
guidance and live it day to day. Be human, be real, be all
of who you are and adapt as the flow carries you. As
Ralph Blum says in his book on the rune oracle, the goal
is to "live an ordinary life in a non-ordinary way." So to
experiment with this fullness and directness, you can use
The Present Moment in a variety of ways, depending on
your mood, time constraints, and level of seriousness.

There is no particular order to the ideas presented in
this daybook. There is no weekly or monthly structure
nor any particularly astrological organization of themes.
You may sense a soft connection to the seasons, but there's
no need to pay it too much conscious attention. Your
body will make the themes relevant for you. What you'll
encounter is a string of days with an emphasis on universal
themes that will be pertinent any time you think of them,
in any year.

An Oracle Practice

You can open *The Present Moment* to any page and read the message on any day. Concentrate on the affirmation and exercise for that day, read the anecdote, and stimulate your thinking to stretch into new possibilities. You can use this book to help solve problems, get specific guidance, or change your mood. For example, today I was worrying about how I would finish all the tasks that have to be completed before I leave for an upcoming trip. I opened the manuscript for *The Present Moment*, and my eye fell on a sentence that began, "The hand is connected to the soul . . ." I let that trigger the next thought I needed. What came to me was that my hand knew what it wanted to do first, then next, then after that. I simply let my hand stretch out and touch the thing it wanted to do as if it had its own brain. It reached for the telephone, and after that it reached for the dishes that needed to be put away, and after that it went to the front doorknob on its way out to the steering wheel of my car on its way to find an object it wanted at the hardware store.

You may find that some element of an anecdote provides just the insight you need, and the affirmation and exercise are incidental. One of my friends, reviewing an early draft of this manuscript, told me that reading the story about Roger Housden's comical and humbling spiritual journey to St. Catherine's Monastery in the Sinai helped her put a personally humiliating experience in perspective. After almost two years of not entertaining and being chided by her friends, she planned a dinner party and made a stunning array of food. That evening people called to cancel at the last minute with a variety of excuses, and only two friends showed up. She made the best of it and served them the fabulous dinner. But her two friends talked almost exclusively to each other all night, and she could hardly get a word in edgewise. So she cleared the dishes, served dessert, cleared those dishes, made coffee, cleared those dishes, and eventually bid her friends adieu. She felt like hired help instead of a gracious hostess. Reading the anecdote, she realized that instead of receiving the glorious praise and warm fuzzies she had expected, her dinner party had provided her with a perfect chance to get to the heart of giving, to feel what it's like to give with no strings attached, for her own joy in generously performing each small task.

A Creativity Practice

Try skimming through the pages and see which theme jumps out at you each morning. Then jot down key ideas on an index card and carry it with you for the day, making notes on the card as you notice interesting vignettes, conversations, or omens. You might keep all the cards in an envelope and go back later and put them together into an interesting piece of writing or a painting. Or use them to stimulate themes for a magazine collage. You can write a poem or a haiku every day, prompted by the daily focus. You can use the ideas as fodder for a creative writing practice, such as Natalie Goldberg's ten-minute timed writings or Julia Cameron's morning pages. Or you can keep a sketchbook instead of a diary and draw a picture or a symbol each day.

A Process Practice

You might read the entries in order and see if a process emerges and your life starts making more sense. Even superficial contact with the concepts can align you and make your life smoother and more conscious. Maybe you'll be like me with good intentions to take my vitamins yet distracted most mornings by important destinations and other goals instead. If you miss a day, it's OK. But if you stray from your intent, get back on track as soon as you can and note the theme you missed. Was there anything significant about that particular theme? Perhaps there is something about it you might be subconsciously resisting. Aligning with, intensifying, and recognizing a process that's ongoing in yourself is a matter of regularity, of consistently checking in with your inner observer. It's like a twenty-four-hour radio station. The station is broadcasting continually with interesting programming and guests, but if you haven't turned on your radio and tuned in to the appropriate frequency, and if you don't listen long enough, you'll never quite understand the richness of a month's or a year's worth of programming on even one one-hour talk show.

A Journal Practice

You'll receive the most value from *The Present Moment* if you keep a journal, loyally document your daily observations, and let them weave organically into a yearly process.

Why not go ahead and commit to the full program? Take the days in their natural order, one by one. Be willing to go slowly, consider the daily themes deeply, and train your attention to develop the mindfulness habit. Use the affirmations, exercises, and anecdotes to stimulate your awareness of what a day can *really* bring when you stay alert. You might enjoy the ritual of giving yourself the little daily assignment, paying attention to how the theme manifests that day, then writing about it that night or the next morning in your journal.

If you don't notice the daily theme being addressed in your external reality, sit down with your journal, be quiet, and let your inner reality provide the message. Let the affirmation trigger some direct writing in which you take dictation from your inner mind, word by word, without jumping ahead and second-guessing what's trying to be said and without stopping to read back over what you've written. Try writing as the voice of your infant self, your future self, your inner male or female self, your cheerleader, or your critic. By writing this way, you'll often receive surprising, accurate guidance from your inner cast of characters and from your mysterious, no-nonsense internal source of truth.

One of my students wrote the following in her journal, triggered by "I am vibrating with life!"

Last night I jumped up in the middle of a video and rearranged the living room furniture. I just couldn't stand it the way it was. A few days ago I spontaneously rearranged my closets; moved the things I use regularly to the spots where I can easily reach them. It had been a small unconscious tension I'd lived with for years. This morning I can feel a stream of entertainment inside me somewhere, wanting to break out of this hypnotic sleep state I've been in for months. I've been in suspended animation, like I'm on a long voyage through outer space, floating weightlessly in my bed capsule programmed to be restimulated in several years when we "get there."

I'm at a coffee place this morning, among other weekend newspaper readers and journal writers, bombarded by the kind of jazz that disconnects all the pathways in my brain and makes me want to attack someone like an inbred Doberman. I AM vibrating with life— yes, I am—and I know at some level it must be positive and creative!! I saw a documentary on a highly productive soul singer who gets up at 4 A.M. and fills her day with meaningful projects and side businesses. But life for me is still thick and somnambulistic with lots of cleaning and maintenance, videos, novels, coffeehouses, baths, and shopping.

You don't always have to agree with what the affirmation says. Some days you may feel contentious, lazy, or blurry. Write about how those sensations relate to the theme of the day. Write about the opposite of the day's theme or what blocks you from experiencing it fully. Or write: "If I *were* vibrating with life I'd . . ."

Sometimes you'll find that an insight about the day's theme comes the next morning as you're about to move on to the new idea. Another of my students woke up with a dream that he realized pertained to the previous day's focus. He had been trying to get insight about the idea, "The earth is my mother." Here's what he wrote about his dream that night:

I'm hiking in some red sandstone mountains and I find a place where there are waterclear crystals imbedded in the rock. They are huge! I reach down and pull on one and it comes out easily. I get very excited and kind of greedy. I pull out three really big ones. I want to take more and fill up all my pockets, but some tourists start flooding into the area, and I don't want to see them, or have them discover the treasure, so I have to leave. I can't get any more crystals and part of me is sad. But I have the biggest, clearest one in my coat pocket in my right hand. I feel rich and special.

When he thought about the dream, he realized there were many "jewels"—talents and knowledge—that had been freely given to him and that what he already possessed was very powerful—and all he needed right now. He could stop his limitation thinking and emotional hoarding, use what he had, and encourage others to discover some of the treasures that this world and the body hold for them. It would feel good to feel generous; there are plenty of riches to go around.

On occasion, one day's focus may actually launch you into an expanded exploration of that theme that may go on for a week or more as though a big bubble has popped, freeing some unruly but liberating feelings that need to be understood. Keep writing about it, even as you continue with the next day's focus, and the next day's. Braid your themes and insights together as you go along.

A Group Practice

Your life process can be clarified and accelerated not only when you commit to working with a journal but also when you share your ongoing experience with a support

group. When other people are committed to listen to you
and truly hear your unique observations, you'll feel validated, and your life will take on a glowing, heightened
psychic weight. As you commit to hear and validate
the others in the group, you'll receive great benefit from
their creative, totally individual responses to the same
daily issues and themes. As you see the validity and
beauty of others' ways of being, you'll start to respect
their inner purposes, their particular paths in life and the
many wonderful ways that we make sense of the world.
This then helps you respect your own way even more.

As a group synthesis evolves, you'll experience how
each person becomes an aspect of you, their process an
aspect of your process, their life a part of your life, their
soul contributing to your soul. Even if someone bothers
you, let that person be a relevant influence in your process
and see how their input moves you to your next important insight. If you judge yourself or others negatively,
simply use it as a lesson in what doesn't work. So if this
interests you, why not form a support group? Or expand
the activities of a group you already belong to to include
a discussion of your weekly or monthly mindfulness
process?

---

*I have realized that the past and future are real
illusions, that they exist only in the present, which is
what there is and all that there is.*
—ALAN WATTS

Oh, how daily life is.
—JULES LAFORGUE

The Present Moment

January

January 1

I invite you to make a clear agreement with yourself to pay thorough and detailed attention to everything today and all through the year. No one has to know you're doing it. It can be a secret that requires no explaining or justifying. This is an action you do for your own pleasure, and you share it only with your own idea of the Creator. I invite you to give your word today that you will pay absolute attention to your soul and body. Vow solemnly to give yourself and others, even the inanimate objects of the world, what you complain that *you* don't get: loving, unbiased attentiveness. Vows are powerful. In a vow you invest your vitality in a life-enhancing endeavor. You focus it and bring it into reality.

VOW: a solemn pledge, especially one made to God or a god, dedicating oneself to an act, service, or way of life.

SOLEMN: from *sollennis*, yearly, hence religious (from annual religious festivals); done according to ritual; sacred in character; deeply earnest; arousing feelings of awe.

To make a successful agreement to improve the quality of your perception, it's important that you realize there is no outside authority to resist. You are your own master teacher, and it is the authority of your perception that makes life meaningful to you. What you find fascinating holds the ultimate authority. So as you begin the year, get fascinated with what's right in front of your nose, within arm's reach. Write out the following contract with yourself and sign it:

"I, _____ , COMMIT TO TRUST AND PAY ATTENTION TO THE SUBTLE INSIGHTS, FEELINGS, HUNCHES, AND EXPERIENCES I HAVE EACH DAY. I AGREE TO PARTICIPATE FULLY IN THE PROCESS OF CONSIDERING THE DEEPER MEANING IN EVERYTHING I NOTICE AND FIND THE WISDOM IN MY OWN LIFE PROCESS. I VOW TO KEEP MY AWARENESS IN THE PRESENT MOMENT AND IN MY BODY AND TO LIVE AN AUTHENTIC LIFE."

I vow to pay attention and interpret my view with love.

Today, practice feeling that God is getting a chance to see the world through your eyes. Let the divine force direct your perception. Paying attention can be a form of service to yourself and the world.

**I know
what is on
purpose
for me,
and I know
what
I love.**

*Today, as you
begin your year,
instead of making
resolutions, write
about what's
important to you.
When you focus
on what you love
to do, how you
like to feel,
and what you're
excited about,
you'll find it's
easy to make
clear statements
of intent from
your soul.*

Carol Adrienne, author of *The Purpose of Your Life*, tells how, as she was getting ready to go on a tour to promote her new book, she couldn't crystallize the key points and sound bytes she would need for radio interviews and lectures. She invited a friend, a management consultant and innovative thinker, to help her get focused. Instead of diving into the daunting task of analyzing her book and extracting the golden nuggets, he asked her a simple question: "What interested you this morning?" Relieved that his question was something so immediate and personal, she quickly replied, "I saw an article in the newspaper about a man in Italy who was helping manifest significant positive changes in his community even though he wasn't a high government official."

"What interested you about that?" her friend asked. "Well," she replied, "maybe it's because I'm about to go to Italy to do some presentations." "OK," he said, "and what else interested you about that article?" "I just love the idea of an ordinary person being able to do something that seems so improbable and to make such a great contribution."

"That's interesting," he said. "Why is that idea so important to you?" Carol thought a moment and replied, "That man was living from his passion, and look what he was able to do!" "What's important to you about living from passion?" her friend asked. "You have to live from your passion if you want to find and manifest your life purpose!" she exclaimed, her enthusiasm rising. "I'm just realizing that what gives *me* passion is getting information to people so they can make a contribution and feel like they're living their truth. I love sparking people into life!" Suddenly, Carol was totally clear and not at all worried about what to say to her audiences. She was centered in the place of her soul's main intent and her body's joy, and she knew everything she needed would flow easily from there.

January 3

Shari is self-employed and works alone in her home office. She talks about how easy it is to think she must do everything herself and work extra hours. Without the camaraderie of the typical office atmosphere, she often feels isolated; and without the advantages of a big corporate budget and expensive equipment, she is hypervigilant about cost-cutting measures. It's hard for Shari to relax.

We spoke about this sort of dead-end state of mind, where we can't remember our original motivating enthusiasm. I suggested playing hooky during a workday. After all, everyone loves getting away with something. Doing something totally private and frivolous, or sensual and artistic, something that doesn't have the slightest chance of making money is definitely the kind of forbidden fruit we'd all secretly like to pluck.

When we next spoke, Shari said she'd been overwhelmed coordinating the pieces of a new marketing campaign. Her head was resounding with "shoulds." Somehow, her mind drifted to the new batch of photographs she had just picked up from the drugstore, and she sat down with a cup of tea to look at them. They were of a vacation she'd taken, and the colorful scenery made her feel nostalgic. On impulse she went to her hall closet and dug out the box of photos she'd taken over the last ten years. She felt compelled to look at the images of her friends and relatives and the beautiful places she had visited. As she pored over them, she got another impulse—to run out and buy some photo albums and put together a collage of images. She'd create one album for her European holidays and one to chronicle the growth of her nieces and nephews! For the rest of the day and on into the evening, she cut, pasted, and arranged experiences from her past.

As Shari worked, she lost track of time and became absorbed by the juxtaposition of ideas, images, moods, and memories. Something inside her felt like it was being rearranged and reconnected as well. The next day, without any effort, she had a new interest in her work. As she thought about how to market her service, she immediately got an image for a flyer. By trusting her natural desires, Shari had allowed herself to feel the fullness of her own creativity, which, when allowed to flow in one area, overflowed into other areas as well.

My body, mind, and soul come together when I trust my enthusiasm.

Do only what has "juice" for you today, and notice how you lose track of time and feel more whole, happy, and full of energy. You may be surprised how being "selfish" can open your creativity and solve problems effortlessly.

Things happen when I focus my intent.

Get clear about something you have conviction about manifesting today. Make a commitment to complete it by the end of the day. When you stay in touch with your intention as you work, you'll notice how effortless and fun the process can be.

It took five years to produce my first book. I disgorged ideas and shaped them into chunks. The pieces changed and the interconnections grew. Eventually the parts flowed into a process that made sense. Elated, I showed it to colleagues. "You have three books here! Go back and break it down," they said. So I chopped. Now I had three outlines and had to decide which one to start with. I went back to my colleagues. "This is the most timely," one said. "This is the most personal, and you want people to know who you are," another voted. "Start with a high-concept idea and make a big splash," said a third. I wrote a proposal for the timely idea, sent it to agents, waited six weeks for replies, and was unanimously turned down. Then I tried the personal theme and waited another year as I was turned down for not being known well enough. Finally a successful author advised me, "Write the first book based on your most basic material, what you have a track record with." I wrote yet another proposal and sent my intuition handbook, based on my intuition training, to a publisher I was sure would want it. I waited breathlessly for a month for another polite rejection letter. After that, my drive to write dwindled. Even so, when people asked what I was doing, I'd unflaggingly say, "I'm writing a book." But was I?

Idly, I showed what I had to a freelance editor who thought it needed work but had great potential—*and* she had time to commit to the project. This meant putting cold hard cash on the line, which made me think, "If I invested in myself, would I be a good investment?" It was show time.

"When was the last time you took a risk?" I asked myself. *Too long!* "What's the riskiest and most attractive idea you can think of?" *Writing!* "If you don't do it, how will you feel?" *I won't be proud of myself.* "So are you going to do it?" *Absolutely!* Within a month, I had an agent, an editor, and a revised package to submit to publishers. In three more months, I had an advance and a contract. By the end of the year, the manuscript was complete.

Sometimes intention comes in dribs and drabs doled out over time. Yet when our soul's purpose finally saturates the body, creating motivation and conviction, the final outcome occurs swiftly and surely.

January 5

I am typing at my desk when I remember to notice what's going on just below the surface of my mind. What am I aware of right now? What am I supposed to be noticing now? I hear the tortured whining of the dog next door, left alone this afternoon by his people. The sound has a disturbing emotional tone, and I realize that, though I'd been trying to tune it out, it has been affecting my body's comfort level for the past hour. I want to go out and yell at the dog. As I entertain this fantasy, I am appalled with myself. An insight comes to me then: how we so often want to punish people who are weak or in pain because we don't want to have to feel the same way. *Stop it, control it, any way you can—even if it's by force!* I resolve, once again, to let go of punishing behaviors in myself.

Then another insight comes. There's a part of me making the same noise inside, whining and lonely, pining for loved ones who may never return. I am that dog; somewhere deep within I am protesting about a similar condition in my life over which I have no control. I relax and let myself be alone today, let life be out of control, let myself just enjoy the sunshine, the twittering birds, the cars honking in the distance, and, yes, even the sad song of my little friend next door. Strangely, the whining stops. Maybe he's worn himself out. Maybe he's finally dozing, head on paws, also enjoying the sun, breeze, birds, and distant noises. Maybe my accepting him, even in his pain, has soothed him in a way that's so immediate it's miraculous.

My soul gives me things to think about.

Ask yourself as often as possible today, "What am I supposed to be noticing now?" What comes to mind? Trust what you get and listen further for the insight your soul wants you to receive. Your soul's insights come easily and smoothly, without struggle.

January 6

**My world
is full of
similarities.**

*Practice seeing
the connections
between ideas
today. What
caused you to
think what you're
thinking now?
How is the
butterfly outside
your window like
something in
your work?
Have several
people expressed
similar senti-
ments to you
today? Your
intuition increases
when you create
links between
things.*

Marilyn Mackey, who teaches tai chi and intuition classes in Dallas, told me she has started teaching children how to use intuition for information retrieval by having them simply focus on something they'd like to know, then use their imaginations any way they want to get words, pictures, or feelings. She was working with two ten-year-old boys one day and asked them if they could retrieve the names of her twin nieces, who lived on the East Coast. After some quiet time, the first boy said, "Is it Jessica?" The second boy said, "Is it Jennifer?" And Marilyn verified that indeed the girls were named Jessica and Jennifer!

She later overheard them talking. The first boy said, "I kept seeing that tree outside, and I just was drawn into it, and somehow it helped me get the answer." The second boy said, "Well, I was drawn to the cross on the wall, and that made me think of God, and that helped me get the answer." Then he thought some more and said, "You know, you went to the tree, and the tree is connected to nature. And I went to God, and God is connected to nature. So we must have gotten our answers from the same place!"

January 7

A walking meditation: I slow down and become my foot. I hear it chatting quietly with the earth. I feel each step as it comes home. I walk full-footed, fat-footed, flat-footed; even pressure, step, place, lift, step, place, lift, step. Now I am wobbling, stepping on the side of my foot. I'm seeing flowers bloom up underfoot as I lift, and after a trail of four or five, they disappear with the inattentiveness of my mind. But if I remain alert, might I leave long trails of blossoms across the world? Step, place, lift, step, place, lift. I cross paths now with a tiny tree frog, part lime green, part burnt sienna, and I lift, place, and carry her in cupped hands covered by green knit gloves. What does my loving human-hand energy do to her tiny heart and feet and brain and eyes? She sits perfectly still for a long while as I concentrate on step, place, lift, step, place, lift. I am a body, I am feet, fully connected with the heart of this hill, with this cool, wet spring ground.

Suddenly she's full, she's had enough, tries for an exit, bounding forward, pushing her tiny nose into the V my fingers make. Maybe I've changed her forever with humanness, perhaps for the better, perhaps not. I place her gently in a clump of rattlesnake grass, a million tree frog miles from her last home, and I walk on. I am a body, missing the impression of the tree frog's life, feeling now too giant and alone. Have I ruined a pristine form of God by interfering? Or been transformed forever myself by a deity as big as my fingernail? Are we both shuddering now, shaking the new information down into our cells? Step, place, lift, step, place, lift, step, place, lift, breathe; be blank, breathe; be life.

**My body
is alert and
aware.
I am my body.**

Whenever you say "I" today, imagine your body is speaking. From your point of view as a body, notice what captures your attention, what choices you want to make. Your body moves naturally, harmoniously, and helps you understand how simple your life really is.

January 8

People benefit from my point of view.

Speak your truth today, with kindness. Contribute a differing idea; say why something doesn't work for you; give someone some truthful positive feedback; play the devil's advocate.

One of the hardest things to do is share an uncomfortable truth with a friend or family member. Often our tendency is to keep things to ourselves, try to change our attitudes, take a walk, take a vacation, or go into therapy. Sometimes a letter is as close as we can get to direct communication because of the emotion involved.

The most difficult communication I ever made was to my mother. I had been working for years on healing the emotional pain from my childhood. I was also diligently working on my spiritual life, trying to see the soul in others and the good sense in all that happens. I had a positive attitude, and my communication to my mother was intended to bring light to a habitual role I had felt compelled to play; I felt I was responsible for keeping her happy. I did not blame anyone. I saw clearly that I had been loved, but I wanted my family relationships to be more *freely* loving and creative. I wrote a fifteen-page tome to her, rewrote it fifty times, literally sweated and cried and had anxiety attacks. I tore it up many times. I put it into an envelope but couldn't send it. It sat on my desk for weeks. Finally I sent it. And her reaction was as I'd expected—she was mortally wounded and hardly talked to me for several years.

Gradually we became friends again. But we never spoke about my letter. I understand how shocking it was for her, and how she had very little idea what I was talking about since she was not particularly oriented toward psychology and self-examination. In spite of the long, strained silence and the pain I seemed to cause, my experience of my family eventually felt lighter, and I was more able to be myself.

I had broken the taboo about speaking personal truth and cracked through a suffocating pattern of self-sacrifice my family had accepted for generations. Now there was a new possibility. I sense that the risk I took in speaking up helped my mother later to speak up for herself in various ways, which brought her to the self-fulfillment she is now having in her late seventies.

January 9

Native American people inspire us in their reverent praise and knowledge of the earth. One Navaho song goes:

> The Earth is beautiful
> The Earth is beautiful
> The Earth is beautiful
> Below the East, the Earth, its face toward the East,
> the top of its head is beautiful
> Its legs, they are beautiful
> Its body, it is beautiful
> Its chest, it is beautiful
> Its breath, it is beautiful
> Its head-feather, it is beautiful
> The Earth is beautiful

Chief Seattle once said, "Every part of this soil is sacred in the estimation of my people. Every hillside, every valley, every plain and grove, has been made holy by some sad or happy event in days long vanished. Even the rocks, which seem to be voiceless and dead as they swelter in the sun along the silent shore, thrill with memories of stirring events connected with the lives of my people. And the very dust upon which you now stand responds more lovingly to their footsteps than to yours, because it is rich with the blood of our ancestors and our bare feet are conscious of the sympathetic touch."

The earth is my Mother.

Be aware of and grateful to the ground as often as possible today. Your very knowledge of how to survive comes from below.

I choose silence.

Stop your internal dialogue for as long as you can, as often as you can today. Let your mind be like a soft muscle—totally relaxed. After a period of blankness, what is the first thought that emerges from the unknown? True messages have a better chance of making themselves known after a time of quiet.

I did a twenty-four-hour vision quest some years ago on Mt. Shasta, California. I sat for what seemed like forever and watched the mountain peak and its dancing lenticular clouds, the circuit of the sun and moon, and the multitudinous forms of nature in the pine needles under me, the trees above me, and the air all around me. I alternately wrote in my journal and meditated. I could only quiet my busy, thought-generating mind for about a minute at a time before I became distracted from my silence by the abundance of life teeming in that remote setting. I wrote, "Being in nature is exhausting, if I pay attention. The varieties of life compete raucously, even as it all coexists and ebbs and flows so smoothly. But this noise is only an illusion to be penetrated with yet more attention. Perhaps the commotion is due to the smallness of my mind and its prehistoric habit of knowing one thing at a time, from the outside rather than from within.

"Now: the second visit from the hummingbird, whizzing closely past, vibrating my left eardrum. Now a third pass. He stops to hover. What message does he bring? He reminds me that inside his buzz, under his wildly beating heart lies the silent sound of the life forms. It's hard to hear it, though, in the grating calls of the katydids oscillating between the far sides of the forest. As I drifted off a moment just now in a nap, I was awakened suddenly by a woman's voice in my head saying, 'You have to be quick.'"

After another long lull, I continued to write. "The real work of enlightenment must come from the heart. A stillness in the heart reaches far, forever. It connects us to infinity, which is just our enlightened self. A quiet in the mind is what allows the extension of the heart's awareness, what helps us recognize the 'rest' of ourself. It lets us think without words, experience pure sensation without description. It gives us permission to be aware without asking questions. Another step toward peace. Words slow us down. Maybe that's what she meant by 'You have to be quick.'"

January 11

Ellen had been in a difficult marriage to a wealthy man, and it had taken her a long time to realize she needed to end it and discover her own interests, talents, and life work. In the process of her individuation, Ellen realized she'd always had a strong interest in the environment and animals; she decided she'd like to work to protect endangered species and ecosystems. By taking the risks involved in speaking her truth, Ellen entered that wonderful synchronous state of being where the whole universe seemed to conspire to support her. She found herself writing articles for magazines and sitting on the boards of several wildlife organizations with well-known leaders in the field. She said incredulously, "I don't know what I'm doing here!" I told her she had stepped into her destiny and that made her highly recognizable to other people with the same destiny.

Ellen said that since she'd made these life-changing decisions, synchronicity and omens had increased dramatically in her life. She dreamed repeatedly of certain symbols, especially of turtles and a vertical spiral. On a recent dive trip, she saw an inordinate number of sea turtles and a beautiful waterspout skittering across the surface of the ocean. Then she met a new man, and, in the air around his head, she swears she saw neon arrows blinking on and off, pointing insistently toward him. She discovered they had many things in common, and their work for the environment seemed to dovetail uncannily.

Next, her conversation turned to money. She told me how a friend had shown her some old Roman coins, and she loved holding them. "You could just feel how many people had held these! They contain such a rich history! So I bought a few. And they even *smell* good." The next sentence out of her mouth was, "And money seems to be showing up now for the wildlife projects, as if by magic! It's just flowing. I even found $400 cash on the street last week!" I said, "Did it occur to you that money is coming to you because you have truly appreciated it and seen into its deeper character? When you love things, they love you back."

Yes, Ellen is lucky, but it's because she's loving, courageous, and willing to commit to her own truth. Whenever we do that, life flows gladly in support, and we see the correlation of the inner and outer worlds.

I am aware of both worlds.

Pay attention today to the energy on the surfaces of things and to the energy under the surfaces. There is always a correlation between the visible and the invisible reality. When you don't see how they match, you'll experience some level of suffering.

**I choose
to participate
fully in life.**

*Notice any
sacrificial,
victimlike
thoughts today,
in yourself or
others.
How do you
hold yourself
back from being
involved, from
loving fully?*

So many people tell me they hope this will be their last lifetime. They don't feel they fit in on this planet, and they just want to go "home." But we need to commit to this physical world and merge with it entirely to achieve completion. Then we'll know that the physical world isn't solid, but a responsive field of conscious particles of light, and that *light* is our real body. Then we'll know the joy of creation, and it won't matter where we are or what dimension we inhabit. We'll be "home" everywhere.

And yet I was deeply affected by the dying words of the alchemist Paracelsus. He said, "I have traveled through this land, and was a pilgrim all my life, alone, and a stranger feeling alien. Then thou hast made grow in me thine art, under the breath of the terrible storm in me. *Da amantem et sentit quod dico:* Only another lover, with love like mine, could understand."

We all feel like aliens in a hostile world sometimes. Sometimes it seems ridiculously useless to make observations, or ask questions, or analyze our inner and outer selves. If all exists, past and future, completed already, then all is already known. What's the point of my life then, my mind whines? It's easy to dip into hopelessness and indulge in nihilism. But out of this dead-end moroseness unfailingly emerges Don Quixote and the heroic/comic fool's choice to dive once again into the waters of illusion. I'm compelled to hold my light here a little bit longer to see if I can burn off some of the fog. The choice to create, to commit, is the ultimate koan. There is no reason, and no reason not to. When we resist full participation, we never discover how free and loving we really are.

January 13

Here is a collection of free-form haikus written in my four-month Intuition and Imagination intensive:

a silent garden
the gardener on a tea break
a coiled hose waits

spider spins its web
silken threads of hope and death
reweave the morning

one drop of clear water
in a puddle under the branch
causes the sound that shatters the silence

pain, anger, grief, and hollowness
a feeling on this side
and light on the other

plank fence steams in morning sun
woman smokes in old Volvo
after the rain, wispy fog on green hill

blossoms on branches
the wheel turns once more to spring
I know my own strength

my car died safely at a stop sign
a man towed me and we laughed
life was bigger than my immobility

fat tadpoles in tire-track pools
growing ever faster as the
water dries up

a faucet dripping
its rhythm makes me restless
moments escaping

radio says beef is "lushly marbled"
the woman has a "pneumatic vest"
morning fun with words

*Write a short
haiku or poem
about something
special you
notice today.
Brief nuggets
often contain the
greatest wisdom.*

The outside world is my greater self; it provides what I need.

Notice what comes to you from outside yourself today, and make use of it. The world is trying to offer us exactly what we need but we often resist its wisdom.

Brian is an innovative entrepreneur and management consultant who lost almost everything after a hostile takeover of his successful company. He resisted filing bankruptcy, however, believing that he would build himself back up and honorably pay off his debts. In the ensuing years, instead of another immediate business success, life dealt him further manifestations of limitation and lack of self-worth. It was hard not to buy into the idea that life was against him. Every time the phone rang, it was an angry creditor. Brian became averse to answering the phone and got into the habit of letting his answering machine filter all his messages. Because he was so overwhelmed with negativity, he only picked up his messages twice a week and took even longer returning calls.

Brian had a few consulting jobs but longed to become a corporate trainer. He wanted to teach businesspeople what he was learning about the correlation of the inner spiritual and psychological worlds with business processes. He visualized the way he wanted it to work and how much money he wanted to make, but he had no experience in this, and making cold calls was getting no response. He complained to a friend that he wasn't getting what he asked for and that everything he did was taking ten times more effort than it should. She said, "Brian, why don't you start by answering your phone in person for one hour per day? Begin by being available and willing to deal with the real issues of your life." This idea was shocking in its simplicity and common sense, and he started the next day.

By talking with one creditor and being fully available, Brian worked out a deal to exchange consulting services for part of his debt. By talking to a man he had been avoiding for months, he discovered the man wanted to hire him as a corporate trainer for a new series of seminars he'd developed! Brian said that by responding to what was already coming into his world, that which he had been avoiding for so long, he saved a tremendous amount of energy. After all, the people calling him already had an interest in him and he didn't have to sell himself. The people he had defined as bothersome turned out to be the very ones who had a message or an opportunity for him. As Brian met the incoming tide head-on, his luck turned around and his talents were freed to flow into new channels.

January 15

Do you hear the message in the wind? The voice of the apple tree whispering to the plum tree as they grow side by side? When a cloud passes overhead, do you hear the words that match the sudden dimming of light? Can you hear the sound made by a lush green park or a littered, weedy vacant lot? What thoughts cycle through the mind of the person across from you on the train? What tone does a sleeping newborn baby make? What message does a burning building scream to the world? Do we listen?

What is the sound of your own soul? Or your stomach when it's stuffed after a dinner party? Or your blood circulating through the tiniest capillaries? What is the song of your life purpose or your most joyful self-expression? What does your voice sound like when you're telling a lie? When you're giving a heartfelt compliment? What is your hand saying as it cradles your head during the course of the day, or rubs your tense shoulder, or covers the center of your chest during a heated argument? Do you notice what people are really saying? What you're really saying?

Creativity teacher Michell Cassou says that being creative means responding to the moment, which we do by listening. She says that creation is about manifesting your inner voice, and the voice is always there. It is the part of us that is alive, and we love what is alive.

The real song sung by every form of life is "I love." Like whales in the deep ocean, we sing our personal song of the soul in the essence of all that we do, in answer to all the other songs being sung to us. In the *Hymn of Jesus* from the Leucian Acts of John, an ancient mystical gnostic ritual, Jesus says, "First, then, understand the Verb, then thou shalt understand the Lord. . . . As for me, if thou wouldst know what I was: in a word, I am the Word who did play and dance all things. . . ." Sound is the root of life, the first creative wave. When you hear, become aware of life's basic movements. Where was the wave before it entered the sound you're hearing? What did it animate before it entered you?

I hear the voices and songs of the world.

Be aware of sounds today and how they affect you. Listen for both the audible, physical sounds and the ones just below the surface, discernible only by the inner ear. Sound, or "the Word," is close to the origin of life.

January 16

I am generous.

Throw a handful of change onto the ground in a public place today; give a big tip; do a favor; pay a compliment; buy a gift for someone you appreciate. You may be surprised at the results that come back to you, often from a different direction.

I was visiting my sister, and together we had put on a dinner party for some mutual friends. My niece Julia was three; as each person came in, she greeted them officially at the door. When our friend Deborah arrived, Julia gravitated toward her and stayed close all evening.

The next day I was to go to Deborah's house to do a life reading for her. As I prepared to leave, Julia called me over to the table where she was coloring on a sheet of paper. "I want to send Deborah a note," she said. On the paper was a series of strange little symbols. She said, "I want you to tell her this message . . ." I interrupted and suggested that we write it on the card. "No, Penney, just remember this. Tell her Julia says, 'I like you and I love you and you can come and live at my house any time.' Then tell her what these pictures are: '*This* is a tepee. *This* is a shooting star for good luck. *This* is a bundled baby. *This* is a little piece of light. *This* is a laughing dog.'" She insisted I repeat the entire message back to her verbatim, then she folded the paper neatly in half and sent me on my way.

In Deborah's kitchen, I presented her with the paper and stood at attention, cleared my throat, and obediently delivered Julia's message. Deborah's eyes widened and a big grin spread across her face. "Well, as you can see, we've just gotten a new dog—an Australian shepherd—and she not only laughs but also now recognizes seventy vocabulary words! And the tepee—I've been studying shamanism with a Native American woman for the past six months! The 'bundled baby' is particularly appropriate because we've been trying to get pregnant for months now—and maybe the shooting star and the little piece of light mean we're about to connect with a new being. So thanks for coming over," she joked, "but I think I've just had my reading!"

January 17

David Newlin, a successful high-level corporate recruiter and management consultant in the San Francisco Bay Area, says that when he first expanded his consulting practice to head-hunting, people in the business told him how hard it would be and how he would have to make at least fifty cold calls a day. Intuitively, he had another sense of how things could work. David was actively experimenting with the power of his imagination and with a philosophy of how everything in life was interrelated and cooperative. He clearly saw that his goal in business was to achieve a true experience of abundance so he could someday offer financial assistance to worthy projects. He saw himself as a wide tube funneling abundant resources, opportunities, and money into and through his life.

So when David started his new head-hunting practice, the first thing he did was turn his desk toward the east so he could face the whole United States. Each morning he'd sit at his desk, close his eyes, and connect with the entire country. He'd then visualize thousands of points of light peppering the land all the way to the eastern seaboard. Each point of light was a person, and each was connected by a thread of light back to him at his desk in San Francisco. Next, he reviewed the job listings he needed to fill and got a sense of the kind of people he needed for each job. In his imagination he then sent requests out along the lines of light, as though he were striking a dinner bell, calling people to come. He saw certain points of light swell and grow larger. Then he let go of the image and turned his attention to the names on his to-call list. The name that jumped off the page at him first was the one he called.

Within a very short time, David was having phenomenal success. His colleagues didn't understand why he was so charmed. Instead of fifty calls per day, David made about ten—but they were the right ten! Most of the positions he filled came from people calling him out of the blue or from referrals. Clients say they enjoy his quality of effortlessness and ease and how things magically manifest around him. He gives credit to the spirit of all the people involved and to the truth of our interconnectedness.

What I picture and feel in my imagination becomes real.

Take time to visualize your intended results before you begin activities today. At the end of the day, review your day's process. How efficient were you? Did you have an increased experience of connectedness and smoothness?

When I let go of things, I make space for my soul to surprise me with new creativity and forms of support.

Today, throw out or give away some things you no longer use. As you do, be aware that you are opening yourself to receive new, more useful experiences and things. Notice what flows into the space you clear. It could even be a new sense of yourself.

When you give something away or lose something or someone, it's important to understand that space is as real, as important, and as enjoyable as form. Your soul may not be ready to manifest another concrete reality yet. Maybe you need to indulge in imagining the feeling of falling backward into a warm pool of welcoming, buoyant water. Or feel the sublime state of having your worries removed. When you feel caught in concern for outcomes, results, and stimulation, try making space and becoming spacious yourself.

I called Goodwill to come pick up an old refrigerator, washer, and dryer I'd been hanging onto for eight years. I also gave away my record collection, bags of clothes, old luggage, jewelry, and kitchen stuff. Then I went through file cabinets and threw out papers I'd been saving and sorted through photographs, discarding everything that wasn't top quality. My home, office, and garage now feel quiet and naked. I feel simple. I have enough. I don't *need*. I am free. My chest feels open as though my lungs now occupy twice as much space and are filling with twice as much oxygen.

When you surrender totally, it feels at first as though you are in a game of strip poker, giving up your clothes piece by piece. Then you must give up ownership of the parts of your body, then of your thoughts and feelings, and even of your life purpose. Every part of your identity must go, everything that makes you feel finite. What's left, ironically, when you think you have nothing, is the vastness of what you *are*—your spiritual self, spread out through all time and space. It's the same result when you receive everything instead of giving it away. There is an ego death accompanied by a spiritual birth of equal power and significance.

Do we ever let ourselves approach that total sloughing off of every identity or the supersaturation of our mind with the infinite varieties of life? I think both paths to the soul feel much the same. Just as it is difficult to distinguish between *really* hot water and *really* cold water, giving up self and receiving self produce the same release of defined boundaries, followed by a surprisingly peaceful revelation of familiarity and belonging.

January 19

Ralph Waldo Emerson said, "For everything you have missed, you have gained something else." But I wonder whether there's a positive way to view envy. When I was seven, I envied my friend Joyce because she had iron-strong fingernails that were set into graceful, naturally tapered fingers. Mine were bitten, bendy, hideously bruised with white dots, and they broke off when they grew even a millimeter beyond the end of my squarish fingers.

Later, I envied the girls in high school who made the cheerleading squad and wore trendy outfits, while I spent my time cleaning stalls in the barn and riding my horse in dirty dungarees. In college it was my sorority sisters who were so at ease with men that they were "pinned" in their second year, while I was a pensive, tortured art major, questioning reality at every turn. Later yet, it was various colleagues who got more public recognition than I.

When I spot an interesting character trait, talent, or natural attribute in another person, I want to absorb it and know it *as if it were in me.* I want to know how it feels to be everyone! I don't have time in just one life to be a jeweler, a rancher, a pop singer, a politician, or a mountain climber—*and* do what my own life purpose directs me to do. So, as a result, I must be grateful to those I envy because they are contributing things I find valuable to the world.

The people I envy embody a trait that is meaningful to me, something latent that could pop into expression and integrate into my known self at any moment. They educate me about the existence of this hitherto unhighlighted part of myself and thus make the way easier for me. Deny them or reduce their worth because they got there first and I reduce my own value.

Joyce helped me notice the power of hands. She had her own way of having beautiful hands, yet now I see the idiosyncratic beauty of mine. My colleagues pointed out paths for expansion of my work, yet if I'd tried to mimic them, my own gifts might never have ripened. My sorority sisters made me think about womanly skills, but time has brought me a deeper, more metaphysical understanding of the feminine. So don't worry too much about what you envy; it's just your soul showing you more of who you are. Once you take notice, you'll find your own way of being all you can be.

What I envy is a sign of my deeper, and future, self.

Notice when you experience envy today, then activate the quality of what you envy in yourself. What you envy may be what you're about to become.

What's worth doing is worth doing well.

Go back to a task you recently did partially or halfheartedly and redo it with full respect and attention to quality and detail. It may take you longer, but through this patience, you'll discover something new about yourself.

Novelist James Michener once said, "The master in the art of living makes little distinction between his work and his play, his labor and his leisure, his mind and his body, his information and his recreation, his love and his religion. He hardly knows which is which. He simply focuses his vision of excellence at whatever he does, leaving others to decide whether he is working or playing. To him it is always doing both." You'll always do a good and authentic job when the two halves of your consciousness—be they past and future, inside and outside, actor and audience, male and female, or head and hands—are supporting each other, flowing in a figure eight, and you are experiencing communion in the present moment.

If you begin to experience distraction or perfection-ism, you have probably hit a fear below the surface, and some self-protective part of you is refusing to let the flow move forward. If you are caught in perfectionism, before you can do anything truly well, you might consider, as creativity teacher Julia Cameron says, "Anything worth doing might even be worth doing badly!" Break the false standards of form your mind imposes and let the result take care of itself. It's the process your soul is interested in. You can return to mindfulness, or the ability to pay close and timeless attention, by unifying your mind and body once again. Be present in the moment, on the crosshairs of the here and now, and notice the one thing that wants to be done, the one idea that wants to be thought, the one feeling that wants to be felt. One thing in each moment. Remember, self-expression, work, even play are the god in you, paying attention to the god in your task, bringing forth a greater experience of the sacred for the god in all of us.

January 21

Down in the body of knowledge,
immersed beneath the waters,
buried under the soils,
dissolved into granules of air,
moving to the songs of heat and cold,
I eat the bread and am eaten.
I am the twin who isn't asleep, but is waiting
as the snake, coiled far below.

Down, down under the pen,
below the importance of the word,
I dive
into the world where all holds together in harmony
and shifts naturally without description.
I am the silent python with no eyes, ready to release power
and the jaguar of the night sky, body of stars,
leaping to the north and rising on a cold draft of light
as the white eagle, effortless on the arctic wind,
its piercing cry reaching to the heart of the Mother,
sending the sound:
"The Father Is with You."
I am the earth then, sighing her peace up into mountains,
groves of pine, baking deserts, buzzing jungles,
into birds floating over moving mists and raging waters.
I am the cocreation of soul and sun,
star rays shine each to light a cell.
I am unable to separate from this body of knowledge,
from stone, fire, water, wood, wind, west, north, south, east,
inside, outside, above, below,
animal, angel, or kin.

**I am
down inside
my body.**

*Your body is not
an object; it's a
kind of mind.
Be aware of the
consciousness
of your cells
today and how
your body's
awareness is
connected to the
awareness of
every other
physical thing.*

I can communicate nonverbally.

We're much more interconnected with others than we realize. Can you send messages to other people, either near or far, with just your mind and imagination? Today, practice radiating energy to others and communicating with your eyes, hands, and mind.

Morgan, a five-year-old boy, told me he could talk to his mother in his head. He said it was easy, but when she didn't answer him the same way and couldn't send him a message of her own, he got frustrated. He finally blurted out to his mother, "Mom, just think it to me, *LOUD!*"

We all communicate with each other nonverbally. It's been a month since I've talked to my friend Kay, and I notice she's been in my thoughts the last few days. I think I'd better call her but keep forgetting. And on my answering machine this morning, there she was. "I've been thinking about you the past few days, and thought I'd call," she said. She and I do this all the time. If you'd like to try sending a telepathic message to a friend, experiment with the following exercise:

SEND A MENTAL MESSAGE

1. Close your eyes, relax, and center yourself. Imagine stepping out of your physical body in your energy body. As you step away from your resting physical body, you are in the realm where energy and knowledge travel faster.

2. Think of a person you want to send a message to. You must feel convinced about communicating with him or her. Visualize the person in as much detail as you can and call that person's name: "Michael, I want you to become aware of me now." See him or her appear in front of you. Make eye contact.

3. Form the thought clearly in your mind. If you can see pictures connected with the thought, visualize the images clearly. Walk up to your friend and speak your message into the left ear, calmly and directly. Simultaneously send the images into the center of the person's midbrain. Then ask the person, "Did you hear, see, and understand what I said?"

4. Thank the person and imagine both of you going back to your physical bodies and reconnecting with your normal reality. Make a note later of any response you get in your waking reality or in your dreams.

January 23

In my "Writing Direct from Intuition" workshop, people pretend they're at a sidewalk café in Paris, France. They concentrate on a question or issue they'd like insight about. Then they envision that someone knowledgeable about the subject, often a celebrity, comes to sit down and chat with them. The guidance they receive through the filter of the new persona actually comes from their own, deeper self. Here are a few samples.

One woman, who wanted insight about feeling more loved and beautiful, had a vision of Princess Diana, who said to her, "Let yourself be seen by others as *they* want and need to see you. Don't try to control your role in their lives. Let your natural beauty shine in spite of some people's small view of you. God sees you as incredibly beautiful, and if you feel God's attention, you will radiate that image to others. To overcome feelings of isolation, look at what you truly want to give—not to be loved or to get something in return—but what does God want to give through you? You can have untold impact and inter-connection, and *while you still live to enjoy it*, by not hold-ing back."

Another participant, who was concerned about going public in her work, heard Oprah Winfrey offer this advice. "When you're living in harmony with your soul's destiny, opportunities, good support people, and rapid interconnections come your way. Remember that you are always able to say how available you want to be and how much you want to contribute. Keep your enthusiasm for people and for the family feeling you have with them and they will love you back. Let the heart of the audience tell you what it wants you to offer them, and serve warmly."

I wanted insights on manifesting my life's work, and in my mind's eye the Dalai Lama sat down at my table and said, "What's important in manifesting the life purpose is maintaining a quality of sweetness, a kind of innocence, that allows you to entertain any thoughts as solutions. Watch for the ideas that are lit from within and for the players with that special 'psychic weight.' Don't be afraid of losing your work or your momentum; expressing your life work, creativity, and insight is like passing the baton in a relay race—receive it when it comes to you and hand it off to whomever needs it next. The unified field will give you everything."

I can receive accurate guidance and insight from my imagination.

When solving problems, getting insights, or being innovative today, pretend you're a famous celebrity or historical figure. How might that person's wisdom assist you and stretch you into new ways of knowing?

January 24

The world sends messages to me without words.

Watch for repeating symbols, images, and omens today. What is your life process trying to make known to you? You can interpret certain real-life experiences as if they were dreams.

A Lesson from Two Insects: Several summers ago I was presenting a seminar and giving a keynote speech at a weeklong conference on the East Coast. The day before my big talk, I attended a Native American medicine wheel ceremony. As I sat in my assigned spot on the perimeter of the circle, watching people one at a time placing objects at specific points on the wheel, a butterfly flew through the medicine wheel from east to west. No one seemed to notice. When it was my turn to set a piece of the wheel, I walked to the eastern entryway, was handed a feather, and was told to put it in the place of air or wind, represented by . . . the butterfly.

The next night as I was waiting to be called onstage for my keynote speech, my stomach was seized by a severe case of the "butterflies." As an introduction to the evening's program, the master of ceremonies led the audience in a short visualization meditation to imagine putting something we didn't want anymore into a bag and throwing it out. I thought about putting my "butterflies" in the bag, but as I tried, I knew intuitively that they absolutely did *not* want to be contained. Instead I saw an image of thousands of butterflies being released through my aura and fluttering like glittering gold all around me as I gave my speech. I decided to keep them and to receive and transmit their energy, guidance, and wisdom. That night, I was funny, spontaneous, and connected with the audience more easily than ever before.

The following night, I sat as a regular member of the audience, watching a phenomenal slide show about astronomy, full of suns, supernovas, and galaxies of countless twinkling stars. As I stared raptly at the huge screen, I noticed a lone lightning bug that had somehow found its way into the auditorium. It was flying high up near the screen, twinkling like Tinkerbell. I pointed it out to my friend and whispered, "It wants to be a star!" It flew across the screen and I lost track of it. When the lights finally came on, several women sitting behind me leaned forward and excitedly told me that a lightning bug had flown into my hair and had been blinking on and off for a while now! I knew it was the little "star" who had come to remind me, just as the butterfly had, that it's OK to sparkle and shine.

January 25

I am in Japan, working. It is late spring and the economy is not good. I hear a story about three CEOs of failed Japanese corporations who checked into a hotel together and shot themselves, leaving suicide notes, not to their families, but to their employees. Someone tells me about a new book with a title something like *The Ten Best Places in Japan to Commit Suicide.*

There are two strong earthquakes. Oddly, I am alone, quiet, and alert during both of them and sense a watery quality to the energy under the concrete city. Three clients fall on the same step in the hotel lobby; my interpreter is on crutches. At a seminar I give jointly with a Japanese spiritual teacher, Juan Nakamori, Juan says that in the Chinese astrology system she studies this is called the "time when the earth becomes watery and people fall and hit their heads." She herself had fallen just the week before. All this cultural "shuddering" makes me remember the sign, new this year, in Immigration at Narita Airport: "Welcome to Japan. Have a nice stay. Please follow the rules." Toward the end of my stay, nuclear tests are set off in the Near East. I wonder if people have been sensing the precursor "event waves" of these explosions and have been thrown off balance as a result.

My first week home, I see five clients in a row who are suicidal, two of my father's friends die, and a young man I know dies. On top of that, every clock and watch I own, even the one in my computer, stops! I dream I'm on a boat in the Atlantic and far to the west I see a nuclear blast. The ocean is rocking with huge, steep waves and a voice says, "Hold on and ride it out!" When I wake, I receive an insight that the real nuclear explosions have affected the energy of the planet and we are all feeling a subliminal disturbance. Many upsetting events are still to come. When I ask what this string of related omens means, my inner voice says it is difficult now to hold secure ideas of identity; our egos are dying.

Sometimes, when the ego starts to die, we think *we* are dying. Then we're tempted to kill ourselves, like the Japanese CEOs who so thoroughly identified with their jobs that when their companies failed, they saw their own lives as over. It is important now, my voice says, to be fluid in our thought processes. If we try to move forward in old, habitual, unconscious ways, chances are we will fall.

Everything I notice and think about is meaningful.

Practice seeing the connections between events and ideas today. What themes do you notice? Your deeper awareness is always trying to get through to you with information you need, and it speaks through synchronicity and repetition.

**I choose
my worldview.**

*Notice whether
your first
thoughts are
motivated by
self-protection
and control
or by learning
and creativity.
Practice shifting
from fear
to love today.*

As we open our intuition, if there is fear lurking below the surface, it's bound to rise into the light. We've asked for clarity and more love, and our subconscious mind takes the request seriously. Anything that's in the way of our knowing truth and compassion will be tossed up for review so our request can be granted. Thus, the process of intuition development becomes the hero's journey through the underworld, as we face the subtle and not-so-subtle cover-ups for our fears. It takes courage and persistence to continually confront these monsters and penetrate them to uncover the hidden beauty in them.

Sometimes fear-based behaviors are not easy to discern. Marge is a good example. As she opened spiritually, she discovered she had a talent for healing people, which she eventually made her livelihood. She had a robust sense of humor and a warm manner. Her confidence grew and she radiated a take-charge attitude. She always seemed certain about what was causing her clients' pain and presented her assessments with great authority. "You're a mess, but I can help you!" she would cheerfully say. Though this reassured many people, her presentation was subtly geared to bring *her* attention, and it actually complicated the clients' healing process. To heal, they now had to overcome a judgment about their basic flawed nature and realize that their healing did not come from Marge but from their own soul and the divine. Marge's motivation was largely loving and she contributed much good. But how much more pure might her healing have been had she been able to cut through the subtle ego fears that laced her work? At her core, Marge didn't feel lovable, and she was helping other people to avoid being alone, making herself indispensible to avoid rejection.

If you're caught in a subtle fear behavior and want to shift to a love-based behavior, first, don't criticize yourself. Just suspend the action and take a breath. Then affirm that you trust that something bigger and wiser than you knows what it's doing and all is well. Have it be OK to *not do* whatever you were doing. Shift from feeling isolated to feeling connected—to anything. Gradually let yourself feel part of a field of loving awareness that nurtures and helps you. Then ask what wants to happen now, for the happiness and good of everyone involved. Before long, you'll feel entirely different!

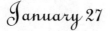

Ann has been working on healing the emotional wounds caused by early sexual and physical abuse. She has continually fallen prey to accidents and has often been incapacitated with residual physical pains that mirror her interior emotional ones. It's difficult for her to feel consistently good about herself for there is always some hurt near the surface, be it in her hip or her heart, that makes her think, "There's something wrong with me if these kinds of things keep happening."

Ann is blessed with a good marriage, however, and after years of trying to get pregnant, they finally conceived. She was elated! But within weeks her morning sickness grew extreme. She lost weight, felt dissipated, eventually miscarried, and almost died. With the loss of the baby, Ann sank into a deep depression. To her subconscious mind, here was irrefutable proof that she was inadequate. She spoke of what she should have done, what she didn't have, what she wouldn't be able to be or do. "I'll never be a mother, I'll always be unhealthy, my husband won't love me anymore, I'll be alone." Her mind was creating fictitious negative potential realities that might never happen and had nothing to do with her soul's purpose.

By living in the memory of her abuse, pain, and loss, as well as in future images of negativity, Ann's reality was completely outside her present physical experience. She sat in the empty hole in her middle, avoiding the experience of her body, which carried so much suppressed pain. By placing her mind elsewhere, she couldn't feel her own vitality and creativity, which were also in her body. She needed to reel in her mind, breathe, and come into an awareness of her body in the moment. If she could stay with the sensations long enough and let them evolve, she'd eventually see that what she defined as pain was actually vitality that had become frozen. When she could release these contractions and feel her body again, she'd find her love and creativity as well.

Ann heroically turned her situation around. By focusing on what she *was* doing, what she *did* have, what she *did* like, and the sensations she *was* experiencing many times throughout the day, she formed a new habit of staying in her body and feeling worthy. By being willing to experience the fullness of the present moment, Ann healed her old wounds. Within a year, she gave birth to a healthy baby.

There is plenty of life inside me.

Notice how you become drained today, and practice filling back up with your own essential energy. There is always energy inside you; it's just that you forget to feel it.

**I am in
the flow; I am
a process.**

*Be detached
from outcomes
today; be totally
merged with
your actions.
When you stay
in the present
moment while
you act, you can
more easily reach
your soul's
goals.*

I attended a talk by author Roger Housden because the
write-up mentioned that he had traveled to St. Catherine's Monastery in the Sinai, a spot sacred for over a thousand years. I wanted all the juicy details about the remote
sanctuary. After days of traveling across the desert, mostly
on foot because camel riding proved to be so painful,
Roger and his bedouin guides encountered a shift in the
weather. A cold head wind forced them to stop. The
bedouins informed him that they would have to turn
back. "Turn back! But we're almost there!" he protested.
"Yes," they replied, "but the camels don't like the wind
blowing into their faces. And besides, within an hour's
walk is the main road and you can make that easily."
"The main road!" Roger exclaimed ruefully. "I thought
we were far from civilization!" The bedouins just bid him
good-bye and sent him off in search of the highway.

Amazingly, Roger emerged from the desert at a small
coffee stand plunked in the middle of nowhere. Sitting
around makeshift wooden crate tables were truck drivers
sipping strong tea and coffee. The driver of a Fanta truck
was going to St. Catherine's and would gladly give him a
ride. So Roger, the noble spiritual quester, arrived at the
sacred monastery along with a shipment of Coca-Cola.
He proceeded to the massive gates, knocked loudly, and
yelled, "Is anybody here?" A tiny window opened, and the
wizened little face of an old monk peered out and said,
"Not today!" The peephole shut tightly back up. So much
for a warm welcome for weary pilgrims. Roger walked
back to town where the few hotels were crowded with
busloads of yammering tourists. Later that night, as he sat
in his tiny room that could have doubled for a monk's
cell, absorbing the buzz of voices through paper-thin
walls, he thought: *"What on earth am I doing here?"*

At this point Roger's narrative diverged into another
story, and I realized I wasn't going to get my highly anticipated juicy details about the Sinai the same way he hadn't
had the spiritually enlightening experience he had anticipated. Yet perhaps riding down the road with a load of
soda pop instead of plowing through a cold, sandy head
wind on foot is enlightenment enough. Maybe the silly
old mundane world at hand, be it his crowded tourist
hotel or my folding chair in the bookstore alcove, offers
the most relevant juicy details of all.

January 29

Colleen Mauro, editor of *Intuition* magazine, always knew she wanted to help disseminate information on health, well-being, and spirituality. She was fortunate in the formative years of her career—she got several plum jobs in her field, one of which was running the West Coast sales office of *New Age Journal*. At a certain point, however, she knew she needed to do something that was her own creation. Some years before, Colleen had met Dr. William Kautz, who was a scientist at SRI International and had started an organization called the Center for Applied Intuition. She was fascinated with the innovative work he was doing bridging science and intuition. She had a strong urge to call and ask for the literature from his center.

In the material Dr. Kautz sent was a newsletter called *Applied Psi*. "This has possibilities," she thought. They met and agreed that the Center for Applied Intuition would pay her to expand the newsletter into a magazine that she renamed *Intuition*. They printed 500 copies, which sold out to members and local bookstores. As Colleen was putting together the second issue, Dr. Kautz apologetically informed her that their funding had dried up. She then decided to buy the magazine rights. Wow! She was now the proud owner of a magazine! But what next? The bookstores were calling, saying, "Where's the next issue? We can sell any that you give us." Determined to keep up her momentum, she borrowed several thousand dollars from a friend and put out the second issue on a shoestring. All the copies sold again! But now what?

At this point, Colleen was approached by an organization, backed by a philanthropist in the Midwest, that wanted to buy her magazine. "It's not for sale," she politely replied. Soon she received an invitation to meet with the philanthropist. In person, the pressure continued. Finally he said, "Why won't you let us buy your magazine?" She said, "I guess it's just my calling." The man's eyes brightened. He too had had a calling and had made his fortune from an intuitive hunch. In a twinkling, everything turned around. "How much do you need to take your magazine to the next step?" he asked. She told him. "You've got it," he said. And thus by following her hunches, being loyal to her vision, and having faith in herself, Colleen launched *Intuition* magazine nationally. It has since grown steadily.

I am strong and capable.

Go the extra distance today; do more than you thought you could. When you experience conviction and commitment to an idea, you'll also experience your inner strength.

**I am
thankful for
being alive.**

*Write a hymn
of thanksgiving
that expresses
your heartfelt
gratitude.
Sometimes just
by putting things
in writing,
your body helps
you experience
the truth of what
you say.*

The Dead Sea Scrolls contain some of the most beautiful
songs, or psalms, I have ever read. Written by the ancient
Essenes before the time of Christ, the "Hymns of
Thanksgiving" convey the reverence the Essenes felt for
nature. Here is one of my favorites:

I will praise Thy works
with songs of Thanksgiving
continually, from period to period,
in the circuits of the day, and in its fixed order;
with the coming of light from its source
and at the turning of evening and the outgoing of light,
at the outgoing of darkness and the coming in of day,
continually,
in all the generations of time.

I wrote the following hymn of thanksgiving after
being inspired by the Essenes:

Thank you, Father-Mother God,
for bringing me to see You in these small ways.
I revel in the common, I open with Your eyes.
See me here, handing my talent to You.
I am spindly and weak but carry a love seed.
I bring You with me wherever I go,
You bring me along,
You bring me along.

I am grateful for the heart in me
through which You speak,
for the warmth of mind You cause to flow in me,
for the cosmic fire that glows all about me whenever I think of You
and the love We are . . .
You create me as a god;
I enable You to know the point of excruciating focus.
You enable me to bear this; in this we are inseparable.
Our creations are one another,
forever.

January 31

I've never been good at using intuition to pick winning lottery numbers or hit it big in Las Vegas—some unconscious belief about spirituality and gambling not mixing, no doubt. But if we're living a conscious life, why not use intuition to track the trends in the stock market, for instance? There's nothing inherently wrong with money unless we value it above our own creativity. The woman who first taught me about intuition wanted with every fiber of her being to buy a house, so she concentrated on learning about stocks and played the market with a clear goal in mind—she would make enough to buy her house, then get out. In a year, she had her house and kept her agreement with herself. Perhaps her clear goal orientation overrode any subconscious sabotage that might have otherwise interfered.

When I had some money to invest, I started to cast around for ideas. I read magazines and newspapers, thought about what trends I saw emerging in the future, and one day I read that a large software company was interested in education. This was one of the areas I felt would be growing significantly, so I threw that fact into the hopper. One morning, I woke up and my first thought of the day was that this company's stock had just split and this would be a good time to buy. I did some research and it had not split, but I invested in it anyway. Within a few short years it has split twice.

William, a client, supplements his income with options trading. In spite of the risks, he has learned to recognize a certain feeling that tells him a trade is definitely wrong. He says that when he goes to the phone or computer to place his trade, he feels the energy of the buy. He's learned the hard way that when he gets a sour, sinking feeling or a feeling like a rock in the pit of his stomach as he is about to commit himself to a trade, the investment will be bad. If he doesn't get that "pull-back feeling," he goes ahead, and he has largely been successful. Even if it's not about money, notice how your truly good decisions always come from a feeling of release into the next natural thing.

I am in synch with a greater rhythm that leads me to sound decisions.

Notice natural inclinations and timing today; let yourself release into the flow. Your mind by itself rarely knows what is best. If you trust the process of what you notice, life will help you choose correctly.

February

February 1

Kermin, a young man I knew only as a casual acquaintance, recently died. He accomplished a lot in his short life, both professionally and spiritually. Although I was not involved in his dying process, which was gradual but rapid, many of my close friends were. They told stories about how absolutely kind he was throughout the entire process of dying, which occurred at home. Though he was often in excruciating pain and losing control of his bodily functions, he never yelled at anyone. He drifted in and out, and as he would come back to his body and open his eyes, he'd tell whatever friend who sat at his bedside about the beautiful things he had seen on the other side. All the people who served him felt they had received a priceless gift.

After he died, one of my friends told me that Kermin had traveled a great deal in his business and was often a victim of the airlines' overbooking policy. And yet it never bothered him. He enthusiastically embraced the delay every time, always saying, "Great—a free upgrade!" Even his untimely death became just one more opportunity for him to inspire his friends to optimistically let go of one reality for a higher one and to turn difficulty to advantage. His friends termed this practice the "Kermin Upgrade," and they apply it to their lives as often as possible.

What I see in others and in life is what life becomes to me, and what I become.

Believe the best about people and life today. Look for the gold. For one day, give up negative thoughts and views and notice your knowledge increasing as a result.

February 2

**The first
will be last
and
the last will
be first.**

*Let other
people go ahead
of you today
and help them
on their way.
Relax and
trust natural
timing.*

Sometimes when we hurry or get ahead of ourselves,
we end up being slowed down later. I was having one of
those jam-packed days, with errands and appointments
scattered across a thirty-mile span. Traffic was heavy, and
I was hitting every red light. On the freeway, I got into a
long line of barely moving cars. I started driving more
aggressively, weaving around slower cars, passing where I
could, but I was late and getting later. By the time I finished with my first appointment and got back on the road,
I was extra-late. I tried to make up time by taking a
shortcut, but there was road work that delayed me further.
I tried to make myself calm down, but my mind was in
permanent warning mode, telling me that I would miss
one of my appointments or would have to give up doing a
necessary errand.

I was finally making headway driving down a two-lane
road in a rural town. A huge truck, stacked to the gills
with bales of hay, was ahead in the left lane. I pulled to
the right and started to pass in a cloud of dust and blowing debris. When I was halfway past him, he started
pulling over into my lane! I honked loud and long but it
had no effect. He forced me off the road, and I had a
scary moment of almost losing control on the soft shoulder. In a minute, I was back in my lane and the hay truck
was turning into the driveway of a feed store, still blithely
unaware of me. I took a few deep breaths and eased up on
the accelerator. My reality snapped back like a rubber
band, and I found myself simply taking up my own space
on the road, sharing life with what was around me in the
moment. With that softening, I also realized that treating
people as though they were hurdles in my life that I must
leap over was not the way I wanted to think about others.
I even slowed down and let someone cut in front of me.
After all, they seemed like they were in such a hurry. . . .

When I finally made it to the lunch place where I was
to meet my friend, there was a fair-sized line of hungry
folks standing around the deli counter vying for position.
Certain aggressive personalities were shouldering their
way to the front. A man behind the counter moved down
closer to where I was waiting and asked the woman next
to me, "What can I get for you?" She smiled and glanced
over at me and said sweetly, "I believe *she* was here first."

February 3

The poem came from one of the participants in my writing class after a walk around the front yard of the house where we were holding the seminar.

The world
I see is a work
of art in
progress.

HOSE   green, coiled
FLOWERS   purple
BRIARS   scratchy, gray
BASKETBALL   alone, under tree
RIVER ROCKS   round, smooth
MAILBOX   door, front

Scratchy briars, gray and graphic, poke holes in my brain.
The openings grow, letting in light. I can be trusting.
I've been quiet and simple like these round river rocks,
    polished, smooth, self-contained.
I'm a little like the basketball, too, sitting alone
    under that bush where it rolled to rest
    after whooshing through the hoop.
    But now I'm ready to reveal myself
    the way the front door of the mailbox
    folds down to show what's inside—yes,
I am the coiled garden hose, green and wet inside,
    I'm ready, READY, ready to squirt again!
    Ready to turn into the brilliant purple flowers
of the winter bush that doesn't know dormancy.

*Make a list of
symbols, images,
and scenes you
see, complete
with colorful
adjectives, then
write a poem
or dream
sequence using
all of them in
random order.
Watch the beauty
emerge.*

I am grateful for the kindness of others.

Write and send some thank-you notes today, make a special gesture to show appreciation, or give a compliment. You might actually change someone's life.

When I first started on my path as a spiritual counselor and teacher, I didn't know if I would be of much use to people. I only knew that I had to proceed; I had to offer my energy, attitude, and insights and let the interpretation of what I did fall where it may. I knew some people might not hear me at all, some might like me, some might dislike me. It didn't matter; I wanted to be of service. Now it's over twenty years later, and I have a file full of thank-you notes people have sent me. In fact, I just dragged it out and pored over the deeply felt sentiments people have shared. In no time I was crying and my heart was wide open.

Of the thousands of people I have counseled and taught, at least a hundred took time to give me meaningful feedback in writing, to speak from their heart and express gratitude. I can hardly believe it but many of them actually thanked me for being alive. I even found a note from an old boss, back when I worked as a corporate art director. "Just wanted to tell you the convention booth looked like a million dollars." I'm not sharing this so you'll think I'm a fabulous person—but because it was those people, taking the extra moment out of their busy lives to give something back, who empowered me to know I was real and connected in a meaningful way to others and that the risky decision I made to give up the security of my corporate job had proved to be valid. We can, and must, have faith and supply ourselves with the experience of love and self-respect, but isn't it a wonderful gift to have another person reinforce it?

February 5

On a recent trip to New Mexico I made a pilgrimage to the sanctuary of Chimayo, near Santa Fe. It is a lovely adobe church, famous for its healing powers. I've been going to Chimayo every few years for the past twenty years. Amid the colorful primitive frescoes, the smell of dust, candles, and incense, I sit, bow my head, get quiet, and feel the ancient energy of the place. Without fail, each time I have a vision in which Mary talks to me in my imagination, teaching me and lightening my heart. Sometimes concentrating is difficult, however, since even in this sacred place tourists pour through, snapping pictures, talking loudly, and generally ignoring the people who are there to pray.

I told this to my friend Jaye in Santa Fe, and she told me about a friend of hers who makes a yearly trip to Chimayo from Albuquerque to pray. Her friend was deep in meditation, head bowed, hands together in her lap, when she heard a woman say, "Ah—excuse me . . ." It seemed far away so she ignored it. Once again, "Ex-*cuse* me!" She thought the woman couldn't possibly be disturbing her, deeply involved in prayer as she was. But once again, the woman cleared her voice and repeated, louder this time, "AH-HEMM: *Excuse me!!*" Finally, she opened her eyes, and the woman exclaimed, "I just LOVE those earrings! Wherever did you get them?"

What is it about the power of sacred places that causes some people to become nervous or unconsciously want to destroy the field of aligned energy that exists in these special spots? I have led spiritual tours to Egypt and Peru, and on many occasions as our group has been meditating or performing a ceremony, no matter how early in the morning we begin, tourists walk directly into our circle, talking loudly and disrupting the focus. Once as I was meditating at the astounding Zen garden of Ryoanji in Kyoto, a class of Japanese high school students rushed in, and the power of the place amplified their giggling and talking to immense proportions. Do we simply not know how to recognize the quiet intensity and value of these places? Or do we not know what to do with ourselves and our minds when we feel the presence of quiet energy? What might become a sacred experience or place in your life? How could you foster your own experience of sacredness?

I experience the sacred within the ordinary.

Enter a sacred space today, or make or consecrate one of your own. Pray, meditate, or contemplate something of key importance. A sacred space makes higher knowing easy.

**I let go
of worry,
tension,
struggle, and
effort.**

*Think about
what physical,
emotional,
and mental
tensions you're
holding and
release these
contractions
100 percent.
When your body
is soft and
relaxed, it's
easier to receive
appropriate
guidance.*

A few years ago a family I know well lost their four-year-old daughter in a terrible accident. The father, who is sensitive to the energy in his body, wrote the following:

"During Malina's two-month hospital stay my body was so tense, so self-compressed, I began collapsing into myself. When she died I was overcome by how beautiful she was, even as the life force drifted out of her body. Later, though, I noticed my heart was so constricted it was beating irregularly. Breathing became an unbearable act of healing love. My expressions became highly energized; rapid-pant breathing, shrill-toned crying and screaming, shivering body gestures, aggressive language, dismissing the beautiful and despondent thoughts. I was so blocked there was only now. I wasn't interested in the future and the past didn't exist anymore. The trauma was draining me.

"I turned to friends, therapists, books, healers, and angels. I met many people with deceased loved ones. One lady, whose son had died twenty years earlier, still moped with her lower lip and tightened her chest until the pressure crushed tears out of her. She said if she quit her painful mourning there wouldn't be anything left of her son. I met a large, uncoordinated man with thick glasses. His father had died some years before. He moved with the exuberant freedom of a satisfied child. He told me, 'Your daughter will become more to you than you have ever imagined, just like my father has for me.' This man didn't look like an angel, but he felt like one. I have met many such people who have helped me let go of the clenching-trauma responses in my physical body.

"Then one day I noticed something familiar in my chest, some fundamental love connection. It was Malina. I was able to feel the part of Malina that hadn't died in the hospital. From inside my chest, from my heart, I felt a tunnel about twelve inches across extending outward, reaching into the air, disappearing high up in the multi-dimensional sky, where it connects directly to Malina's heart. This connection is so familiar; it was there before she was born, while she was alive, and is still there now after she died. I am clearly aware that it is our primary relationship. Father-daughter is only one circumstance in our infinite chain of experiences. I am constantly aware of Malina now; she is a primary participant in my life. Feeling her in the future is effortless. She is here, forever."

February 7

I've lived in my neighborhood for ten years, and there's a house down the block that is always exquisitely kept up, with a lawn like a thick golf course, flowers that match the house trim, perfectly shaped bushes, and two shiny black cars in the driveway—always clean. At Christmas, the house sports an elegant starburst of tiny white lights. I drive past the house every day, and each time its visual harmony is so palpable, I feel healed just by looking at it. And yet after all this time, I'd never met the owners. One day as I was swooping around the corner, I noticed the man, with his back to me, trimming the front hedges. Impulsively, I pulled over, rolled down my window, and shouted across my passenger seat, "Hi! I've always meant to tell you how beautiful your house is! You do such a great job!" It took a moment for my words to register, coming as they had from behind him and from out of the blue. In slow motion he stopped, turned around, and looked stunned. He thanked me quietly in a truly touching way. I waved and drove off, and for the next ten minutes, my own heart felt like I'd just fallen in love. It was bouncing like a happy puppy, as if *he* were the one who'd complimented *me*. I realized that, because I'd said this little thing out loud, I liked those people even more now, though I still don't know their names.

When I receive consciously and gratefully, it's a gift to the one giving.

Be aware of what you are given and let it in all the way. Stay connected to the giver as you receive and see how you feel; notice how the giver responds. When you pay attention, without preconceived notions, it's hard to tell who's giving and who's receiving.

February 8

My intuition tells me the truth about people immediately.

Notice and record your first impressions of each new person you meet today. Look both at the surface impressions and underneath. People's outer presentations may trigger your biases, but your heart will always know their true natures if you look deeper.

A woman in a faded gingham dress and her husband, dressed in a threadbare suit, stepped off the train in Boston. Though they had no appointment, they walked timidly into the outer office of the president of Harvard University. The president's secretary made a snap judgment—these backwoods country hicks had no business at Harvard. She frowned at them. "We'd like to see the president," the man said softly. "He'll be busy all day," the secretary replied coldly. "Then we'll wait," said the woman.

For hours, the secretary ignored the couple, hoping they would become discouraged and go away, but they didn't. Finally the secretary grew frustrated and decided to disturb the president. "Maybe if you see them for a few minutes, they'll leave," she told him. He sighed, exasperated, and nodded. He was an important man and had important things to do. He didn't particularly want gingham dresses and homespun suits cluttering his outer office. The president, stern-faced, strutted toward the couple.

The woman smiled and explained why they had come. "We had a son who attended Harvard for one year. He loved Harvard and was very happy here. But about a year ago he was killed in an accident. My husband and I would like to erect a memorial to him somewhere on the Harvard campus."

"Madam," the president said gruffly, "we can't put up a statue for every person who attended Harvard and died. If we did, this place would look like a cemetery." "Oh, no," the woman explained quickly, "we don't want to erect a statue. We would like to give a *building* to Harvard." The president rolled his eyes. He glanced at the gingham dress and the old suit, then exclaimed, "A building! Do you have any idea how much a building costs? We have over seven and a half million dollars alone in the physical plant at Harvard." For a moment the couple was silent. The president was pleased. Maybe they'd finally leave now.

The woman turned to her husband and asked quietly, "Is that all it costs to start a university? Why don't we just start our own?" Her husband nodded. The president's face wilted in bewilderment. And Mr. and Mrs. Leland Stanford walked away, traveling to Palo Alto, California, where they established the university that still bears their name—a memorial to a son that Harvard no longer cared about.

44

February 9

I recently attended the last meeting of a ten-week Intuitive Way study group in Davis, California. The group had been working with my intuitive development guidebook, reading a chapter a week, doing the exercises, and keeping a journal. Many of the participants shared how important it had been for them to learn to pay attention to their body. One woman said it had been a shocking revelation to practice doing things that made her body feel good. "I couldn't believe it! Living in my body! What a concept! It's been absolutely foreign to me all my life." Another woman, who had been dealing with her mother's slow process of dying from cancer, said, "I'm able to feel the pain of my mom's cancer and her confusion about dying without trying to deny it in my body. She and I are so deeply connected, and I see her every day in the hospital. Some days I'm just knotted with fear, but then somehow I find a way to untangle the knot and go on. I can feel it all but I don't have to hold it."

One of the men in the group talked about how interesting it had been for him to work with the exercise in which he imagined a dialogue with a part of his body that was tense. He had been practicing talking to the chronic pain in the back of his neck, asking it what it needed from him and what it wanted to say. His painful spot told him to trust the upcoming changes in his life even though they might look radically different from what he'd been doing for the last ten years. His neck pain also told him to call it "Bill." Weeks later as he was riding his bike, he got an intuitive flash that "Bill" stood for "Better Intuitive Living through Love!"

My body needs my loving attention.

Take time today to drop your attention down into a place in your body that feels painful or tense. Flood the area with love. When fear is replaced by love, you can have miraculous insights and healings.

I am the
student and
the teacher,
teaching
myself.

*Today notice the
questions you
ask youself and
the answers
that already exist
within you.
Some intelligent
force is at work
within you
prompting self-
revelation.*

Write a series of lines starting with "I want to know why
_____" and "I really want to know _____." List frivo-
lous things that capture your interest and let the syncopated
rhythm flow, open your mind, and flush out the pipes!

I want to know why fireflies blink.
I want to know why I sneeze.
I really want to know if I'm going to become rich soon.
I want to know why the stars don't show at noon.
I want to know why houses have to be square.
I really want to know that there are soul mates.
I want to know why money is green.
I want to know why sailors love the sea.
I really want to know why clouds gather.
I want to know how to fly.
I want to know how singers hit the high notes.
I really want to know if I'll be a mischievous old lady.
I want to know how to make Japanese food.
I want to know how to train horses with kindness.
I really want to know when the earth will change its
rotational spin.

Then list more serious things: "What I really need to
understand is _____." Follow each one with "What I
already know about this is _____."

What I really need to know is how it works when the
universe gives me exactly what I need for success.
What I already know about this is that I'll feel the
rightness of the energy in what comes to me as opportunities, and I'll be able to choose what's appropriate. I know
that I need to ask specifically and often for what I want.

What I really need to understand is how to lose weight.
What I already know about this is I can walk and I can
eat two-thirds of what I usually do. What I already know
about this is I can eat at more regular intervals all day long.

What I really need to understand is how to feel spacious
in a crowd.
What I already know about this is there are huge spaces
between all the atoms in my body. What I already know
about this is the universe is inside all of us. What I already
know about this is, when I think I have plenty of time, I
also feel I have plenty of space.

February 11

This morning I woke in a slightly agitated mood. I'd been dreaming that wasps were making nests in the walls of my house. In the dream I'd contemplated the best methods for getting rid of them. Should I spray them with poison? Should I sneak out at night and plaster the opening to their nests with mud? Surely they'd become enraged and fly after me before I could run to safety. But maybe they'd dig out and come hunting for me later. So my morning began with a subtly ominous tone. It didn't help when I took some empty cans to the garage and noticed a huge, glossy, black widow spider hanging next to my recycling bins.

Mrs. Spider Mother, I figured, had come in out of the summer heat, seeking a cool spot to rest and continue the life cycle of her kind. I admit to vehemently mashing her and her egg sac, but her demise sent a shiver through me, which set me to thinking. There are little poisonous creatures living in my shadow self, in the very walls of my personal space, mere feet away from my conscious, light-hearted life! They're invading and multiplying. My fear-based self wants to obliterate every teeny bit of negativity and danger from the world. But another part of me, my simple, unbiased body consciousness, has a different response. When I quiet down and drop through the adrenaline rush, I feel myself living around the little pests like people in India live with cobras. They are just different children of God, going about their business. Perhaps they believe in danger even more than I because they have adapted themselves for the swift delivery of venom to their enemies. I can afford to be generous and loving. I'm supposed to be evolved.

I see that I cannot rid my energy field of negativity. There is nowhere to place the ugly and dangerous parts of life, just as we are never rid of radioactive waste in spite of burying it deep in toxic dumps. My aura continues to infinity and includes everything—spiders, wasps, lovers, and angels alike. I have been bothered this week by disharmonious stimuli from my environment over which I have no control—early morning contruction workers, barking dogs, machines malfunctioning, rude checkout clerks. From my dream and waking omen, I see I've arrogantly defined these things as disharmonies and given them the authority to threaten my peace of mind.

My night dreams and my daytime reality are connected.

Write your dreams in a journal when you wake up; if you can't remember one, make one up. How do the themes from your dreams or first thoughts relate to what happens today? Watch for issues from your unconscious that act out in your waking world.

I am protected by my alertness.

Take responsibility today for making yourself feel safe. When you pay attention to what gives you a sense of deep comfort—and make decisions to maintain that feeling—you'll develop greater confidence.

Jeannie had just finished going through an arduous three-year court case, and she felt beaten down. Having to think about victimization, unfairness, and greed for so long had been incredibly nerve-wracking, and she'd been unable to sleep through the night since the whole ordeal started. With the case finally put to rest, she turned her attention to more rejuvenating and self-expressive activities that she'd put on the back burner. She took dance lessons and decided to improve her intuitive abilities by attending a series of intuition development classes. In the middle of the intuition classes, she had been scheduled to take a quick trip to Florida. Just before she was supposed to go, her traveling companion called to change the flight time. She had an odd reaction—suddenly her stomach got tight and she knew she didn't want to go. She didn't feel safe, and when she imagined getting on the plane, her legs felt weak. "Cancel me," she said, "I'm not going. Don't ask me why, I'm just not going."

Well, the plane didn't crash, as she'd feared. It landed, but not without a lot of difficulty. It turned out that there was water in the fuel tank. The plane had to make two emergency landings. Jeannie told the instructor of the intuition classes that she was amazed. She said she'd always been intuitive but had never had the courage to act on an intuitive impulse before. What was truly interesting was that because she trusted herself and followed through on her own inner wisdom, Jeannie lost the feeling of vulnerability, lack of safety, and the psychic exhaustion that had been plaguing her through the court case. After the incident with the plane, she suddenly regained her peace of mind and was able to sleep through the night again.

February 13

I was on vacation visiting an old and dear friend. He had cooked dinner the night before, and I decided I'd go to the store and get the fixings for the next evening's meal. We hadn't seen each other for several years, and I was looking forward to another cozy experience catching up on conversation. Maybe I was greedy for the special rapport we were able to enter into. I could almost smell the meal already; it was going to be warm, nurturing, and balanced in color, shape, texture, and flavor. Preparing the meal, even setting the table, felt like a carefully designed ceremony that would create just the right balance of every factor to allow the free flow of heart and communication. That evening, I started the preparation as my friend got cleaned up after work. We listened to relaxing music and he read aloud from some books. Then as the food was nearing completion, he left the house for a moment.

When he came back, he informed me that he'd just thought to invite his neighbor Ichiro, a sweet Japanese man who lived in a trailer next door, to join us for dinner. Suddenly, the image of the evening that I'd been envisioning and inhabiting began to melt away. I wondered if I would have enough food to stretch for three people. Ruefully, I realized I'd have to give up the idea of intimacy I'd been hoping for.

Ichiro arrived with a big smile on his face, bearing a small, beautiful appetizer of daikon and fish on a lovely Japanese plate. We shared the food, and the smaller portions seemed somehow even more filling because they were laced with generosity. The conversation was lively, took unexpected turns, and I saw my friend in an even more intimate light than if we'd been there by ourselves. New aspects of both of us reflected in the elegant, humble awareness of Ichiro, who served unaware as the bearer of new direction and light.

I'm open to new directions.

Stop your thought process midstream as often as you can today to allow new directions. Sometimes we project thoughts into the future so strongly that we don't allow life to show us where it wants to go.

**I am
responsible for
getting
what I ask for.**

*Be extra specific
in the way you
ask questions
today,
listing all the
variables and con-
ditions you'd like
met. If you speak
vaguely to your
inner self, you
may handicap
your ability to
create what you
need.*

Brenda had for years been planning to create a combination spa—health club—conference center offering nutri-
tional counseling and leading-edge bodywork therapies.
She had worked arduously on her business plan and had
many leads to real estate, investors, and talented staff
members. However, her forward movement seemed
blocked. One time it was investors pulling out, then
someone else bought the property she wanted. Another
time she had to move to a new residence. Finally, last year,
just as she was gearing up for another launch date, her sister got seriously ill with cancer. With few knowledgeable
people to care for her sister, Brenda put her own plans on
hold and went back to the East Coast to help. A month
stretched to two, then three, then four, and Brenda wondered whether her own dreams would ever come true.

Her sister's health improved and Brenda returned
home. As she contemplated her plans anew, she realized
that both her interests and her skills had been dramatically
affected by her work with her sister's breast cancer. She
had learned a tremendous amount about the medical and
legal systems and about the inner needs of women in such
trauma. All at once she knew that her spa—health club
wasn't quite the right expression of her life's work. She
wanted more than anything to work with women who
were in the midst of dramatic life changes. In a blitz of
intense work, she reformulated her business plan, wrote
grant proposals, organized a marathon to raise money for
breast cancer research, stirred up new interest from her
supporters, and started a nonprofit organization to help
women in transition.

I spoke to Brenda last week, and she told me that now
that she has gathered all the pieces of her life work puzzle
and has spoken the truth about what her soul wants
her to do, the doors are opening effortlessly. People have
appeared from nowhere offering connections to new
investors, a sympathetic attorney, and a public relations
expert. Someone has even arranged the donation of a not-
too-dated BMW. As she voiced her need for some new
clothes, one executive told her about a businesswomen's
collective that donates and swaps old designer business
suits! Now that she has found her truth, everything is
falling right into place.

February 15

Daryl and I met for our quarterly rendezvous to have dinner and catch up on each other's lives. We chose one of those trendy, bustling California restaurants filled with Stanford students and Silicon Valley executives. We perused the extensive menu, commenting how everything looked good. I quickly made up my mind about what I wanted to eat. But Daryl was slightly distracted by various conversations going on at nearby tables and was not ready to order when the perky waitress came to our table.

I told her I was going to have the salmon pasta. She cheerily replied, "Oh, that's an *excellent* choice! You're going to love it. Everyone's been enjoying that tonight. And what can I get for you, sir?"

Daryl was still mulling over the menu and mumbled, "I think I'll have the roasted chicken with garlic mashed potatoes." The waitress responded in her upbeat manner, "Oh, that's an *excellent* choice! The mashed potatoes are fantastic. You'll love the way the chef does them." And she slid her order pad back into her apron pocket and turned to go.

"No, wait a minute," Daryl said. "I think instead I'll get the Chinese chicken salad with the dressing on the side." "*Excellent* choice," chirped the waitress. "It's a huge portion and has lots of chicken in it." She changed the order on her pad, and as she prepared to depart, Daryl once more blurted out, "You're going to kill me, but can I change my mind again? I think I'd rather have something warm after all. How about the eggplant parmagiana with a caesar salad?"

"Now that's a *really excellent* choice. The sauce is loaded with basil and we use three kinds of cheese!" She gathered up our menus and finally was able to go, orders tucked securely under her belt.

I made eye contact with Daryl and looked at him seriously. "Daryl, this was a *really excellent* choice of a restaurant tonight. I think we're going to *love it*!" We laughed together for a moment, and he said, "Yes, that should be our first response to *every* option that comes our way— food, or clients, or challenges, or chores!"

My body knows exactly what it wants.

Pick the foods you eat today based on your body's sense of truth. When you pay attention, you'll notice that your body has very specific preferences.

When I stop forcing things, I see what life wants to do.

Notice any excess effort or willpower you're using today. Whenever you're pushing or pulling at life, your intuition will be blocked.

Ken was an entrepreneur who had started a successful small company, which nevertheless was fraught with an unusual number of crises he felt compelled to handle personally. The more competent Ken became at putting out fires, the more crises seemed to arise. His constant involvement with his business turned him into a workaholic. Finally, he made plans to take his girlfriend out on his boat for a rare weekend of fun. He had visions of sun, swimming, and good food. When he checked the boat that morning, however, the battery was dead, and he had to drive to his father's house to borrow a charger. Then, when they finally arrived at the lake to launch the boat, his girlfriend realized that Ken had left the cooler back at the house. Muttering under his breath, Ken drove to the nearest grocery store to buy a new supply of food. When they came out of the market, Ken discovered that he'd locked his keys inside his truck. Now he had to call a locksmith while his frustrated girlfriend waited and the potato salad got warm.

Ken's soul had probably been trying to get a message through to him for a while. If he would just slow down and stop rushing, let go of handling emergencies, and stop trying so hard to force things to work, he might be able to see what the flow of life naturally wanted to create next. But Ken's mind was deriving a kind of identity from being a rescuer and problem solver. He was due for some big changes, but he didn't want to face the prospect of change, and he wouldn't pause long enough to hear the guidance of his inner voice. As a consequence, Ken's day of fun turned into another series of blocked movements and problems to be solved. If you're encountering snags, it's probably a sign that there's a message waiting to be heard!

February 17

When I was on my book tour, I met some amazing people, many of whom took the time to come to me after I spoke and relate entertaining stories. One woman had been very pleased with what I'd said about trusting intuition as it first occurs as either a truth signal or an anxiety signal. She said her intuition had a specific method of informing her about what was appropriate for her to do. She would often see a stoplight superimposed over a situation or a person. The light would turn either green, yellow, or red, giving her the guidance she needed. She said she had come to see me because she was in a bookstore, passing a display, when suddenly all she could see was green light! It was everywhere. When she stopped to see what was happening to her, she noticed there was a book in the center of her field of vision. The green light was surrounding my book *The Intuitive Way*. So she bought it. A few weeks later, a friend happened to invite her to my lecture, not knowing she had already purchased my book. She said, "When I see that green light, I GO!"

Another woman from Florida tracked me down by phone and told me that for several weeks she had been seeing bright, shiny new pennies at her feet everywhere she went—on airplanes, in supermarkets, in restaurants. She commented about it to a man sitting next to her on the plane, and he told her she should pay attention because it was a message or maybe she was on a trail. One evening, while she was lounging at home, she got an overwhelming desire to drive to the local bookstore. She immediately threw a jacket on over her long nightshirt and went book browsing. As she walked down the self-help aisle, my book literally fell off the shelf at her feet, and in one glance she saw my first name as though in a spotlight: "Penney." She remembered the string of pennies in her path and exclaimed to herself, "Ah, so *this* is what I've been after!" And she bought the book. It ended up providing her with crucial information she needed to crystallize the next steps in her career.

**My path
is illuminated.**

*Pretend your
choices have
different amounts
of light on
them today.
Choose the
brightest options
and follow
the spotlight. It's
surprising how
well lit our next
step truly is.*

In each moment I can experience some kind of joy.

Give up a perfectionistic expectation of yourself today. Let yourself simply feel what you feel, know what you know, do what you do, and just be the way you are. The divine is in the ordinary.

When Jenna was young, she was fairly wild and lived a lifestyle of drinking, partying, and experimenting with drugs and sex. She lived with unusual men and moved all over the country. She never settled down for long and, within a few short years, lived in a converted barn in New England, a condo overlooking Lake Michigan, on a ranch in Colorado, and on a nature preserve in the hills outside San Francisco. She was a talented artist and extremely sensitive to the world around her. At a certain point in her life, all the men and the adventures gradually fell away. She spent several years as a recluse, talking only to her cats and dogs.

One day as she was sitting under her apple tree, pausing between chapters of the book she was reading, she had what can only be described as an epiphany. Something came over her suddenly, flooding her with a joy so intensely uplifting, she wasn't sure if her body was still sitting in the chair. All at once she had no more sense of personal self, no more worries, no more desires. The experience eventually released her back into her earthly life, and for days she felt as if she were glowing. She knew people's innermost thoughts, dreams, gifts, and fears, and she felt blessed. But then she said, "The experience faded and it was just sex, drugs, and rock and roll again!" What happened to her high? Why couldn't she maintain it? She beat herself up, thinking she was totally unenlightened.

If we're lucky, we have a peak experience like Jenna did. But maybe all we ever get is the warm look in a baby's eyes or unconditional love from a pet. We shouldn't expect to be superhuman. Even if we experience an epiphany, the next day we still have to clean the toilet, water our plants, and pay the bills. The trick is to find small ecstasies, and more and more of them, to string across our days like holiday lights.

February 19

Laura was driving down the main street in San Rafael, California, home of Guide Dogs for the Blind, and noticed a woman training a young golden retriever in a harness, a fairly common sight in downtown San Rafael. They were approaching an intersection and the woman was pretending to be blind. As they neared the curb, the young dog looked nervously back at the woman and haltingly stopped. Just at that moment, a large white commercial van ahead of Laura pulled toward the sidewalk and the driver laid on his horn, making a terrible racket. The poor dog, slightly nervous already, started to cross the street, then stopped, then started, then stopped again. But the driver wouldn't stop honking.

Laura was infuriated with the rudeness of the driver ahead of her. "How dare he scare that innocent dog like that!" she exclaimed to herself. In minutes she had worked herself up into a furor and decided to pull up next to the van, get the company's name, and call to report the bad manners of the driver. Righteously, she swerved alongside the van, slowed down, and looked over through her passenger window. On the side of the van, painted neatly, it said "Guide Dogs for the Blind: Test Vehicle."

I can be bothered or aggravated, or I can choose to be amused.

Be extra willing to laugh and be entertained by life today. There's always something humorous just under your nose, often where you least expect it.

February 20

**I notice
what others
really need.**

*Give people
what they need
for their peace
of mind today.
It doesn't take
much extra time
or energy to
reaffirm our
common
humanity.*

Diane was having an unusually stressful time. She was dealing with an amazing *eleven* deaths that seemed to be clustered for some strange cosmic reason within the space of two weeks. Most of the people who had died were actually in her personal circle of friends. As she grieved, she also experienced a heightened level of nervous hyperactivity. Under it all, she sensed in herself an encroaching apathy and lethargy that was frightening her. What was life all about anyway? Was she living her life purpose? Was this *it*? She said she'd finally given an ultimatum to God. "If there's no self-fulfilling purpose for me, if I can't get through my problems more easily, then just take me out of here! I don't want to be here anymore!"

The next day, Diane was driving at high speed on the freeway when the cars ahead of her started to brake and swerve wildly. Traffic became chaotic as everyone tried to avoid a large box that had fallen off a pickup truck. As Diane stepped on the brake pedal, her old car froze up and died. She fishtailed and finally came to a stop in the right-hand lane, traffic whizzing by and now trying to avoid *her*. Terrified and shocked, she just sat there, unable to get out or move. She looked in her rearview mirror and watched as a green minivan pulled up and stopped behind her, emergency blinkers flashing. A woman crawled out on the shoulder side of the road and came up to the right side of Diane's car.

"I saw you swerving from quite a ways back," she said. "Are you OK? Can I help you?" Diane told her the car wouldn't start. The woman said, "I'm going to push you off the freeway. Then I'll use my cellular phone and call the highway patrol, and I'll wait with you until someone gets here to help you." Diane was stunned. She could barely contain her tears as this angel of mercy proceeded to stay with her for *one full hour* until the highway patrol arrived. Here was the response to Diane's ultimatum. She said she still wasn't clear about the specifics of her life purpose, but this experience had validated the importance of expressing compassion, service, and unselfishness— values that had always fueled her work but that had paled lately. Knowing now that she was loved, she felt this was as good a sign as any to signal a renewed motivation in life.

February 21

One of the exercises I often use in my intuition training workshops is designed to focus the mind into the body, particularly into painful joints, tense muscles, or the organs. By doing this, information from these normally nonverbal sources of data can be made conscious and useful.

TALK TO YOUR INTERNAL ORGANS

1. Pay attention to your body, bringing your attention inside your skin, down through the muscles, scanning from brain to intestines, feeling into your organs. Which ones draw your attention? Do you feel a throbbing around your kidneys or sense that your lungs are giving off a greenish light? Is your stomach sluggish? Is your brain too electric? Whichever organ catches your attention, drop your roving point of view into the organ's territory, and surround it with an aura of your full and loving attention.

2. Notice the energy state of the organ. Is it tense, hyper, sleepy? What emotional tones can you feel? Does it seem pressured, scared, wistful, lonely, unconscious? Can you even sense the texture of the tissues, the amount of blood and oxygen the organ is getting?

3. Ask the organ, "What do you need to tell me that I haven't been hearing?" "What are you the most worried about?" "What do you know about the current situation I'm dealing with?" Let the organ talk to you. If you have a notebook nearby, write down the messages. When the communication seems complete, thank this part of you and ask it how you will know when it needs to talk to you again.

My body is a community of intelligent beings.

Practice having a conversation with various parts of your body today. You can use your intuition to understand what your body needs for optimum health.

February 22

I learn by trying.

Step forward courageously into a new activity today. You don't need to know how things will turn out; just take that first step.

Suzanne Falter-Barns, author of *How Much Joy Can You Stand?*, describes how when she finally dredged up enough courage to leave a long, torturous relationship, she felt as though she'd been stripped absolutely clean and no longer knew what to pursue. She came home every night from her job of writing toothpaste commercials for an ad agency and, to ease her pain, took out a notebook and pen and waited for something to come. Slowly, some tender, wise person inside her started making notes, and the words eventually shaped themselves into song lyrics.

Oddly, though Suzanne had sung a little, she'd never written a song before in her life. Yet she started hearing partial melodies and rhythms in her head, and the verses seemed to snap neatly into place. She says that what was driving the songs into existence was a whole new aspect of her personality that had been longing to express itself. Eventually she felt an urge to do something with the stack of lyrics piling up on her desk, but she had no idea how to find a songwriting partner. Her little voice wouldn't stop pestering her, however, and three weeks later a friend introduced her to a jazz pianist and composer who fully understood Suzanne's lyrics. She wrote achingly beautiful music that matched Suzanne's words, and when Suzanne heard it, all she could do was cry.

She says, "Carey and Falter, the act that our songs turned into, never played Carnegie Hall but did play New York's small backroom cabarets for a wonderful three-year run. . . . For two restless women in their twenties, this undertaking became an act of pure and wonderful defiance, a thousand defining moments squeezed into one forty-five-minute cabaret act. . . . Because we didn't realize how little we actually knew about creating a cabaret act, we acted with a marvelous creative certainty that came entirely from our guts. . . . There was joy to be found in even the most mundane technical rehearsals and midnight stamp-licking sessions. . . . We discovered that we had weight in the world and that the simple sharing of ourselves, our true selves, was in and of itself quite moving."

February 23

In the early years of my spiritual path, I worked with a full-trance medium, a colorful woman around whom a variety of erratic phenomena regularly occurred. Objects would dematerialize and materialize in her presence. Once, she opened a sealed cassette tape, put the tape in the recorder to begin a reading for me, and, as she entered trance, the entity who spoke through her said, "Please push the play button instead of the record button." I did, and a strange man's voice spoke to me from the tape. He identified himself as Native American, called me by name, and gave me a specific message. Over and over again during my involvement with her, I experienced dips into other realms in which I could not doubt the existence of discarnate beings and psychic phenomena.

On one occasion, I had typed out an inspirational quote from a book and sent it to a friend, who taped it onto his refrigerator. Later, I sent some questions to the medium, asking for a reading by mail. A month passed with no word. I finally got a packet from her. Clipped to the top of my page of questions was a page with the exact quote I had sent to my friend—it was, in fact, the *exact same page*, complete with fold marks!

The medium's letter explained that she had put my questions on her desk but, when she went back to start the reading the next morning, the page had disappeared. Two weeks later it reappeared with the new paper on top. Her guides told her the new page came from somewhere near me (my friend lived in a neighboring town) and that the message in the quote was really meant for me. They also wanted to remind me of the reality of spirit. I called my friend. The paper had mysteriously disappeared from his refrigerator several weeks earlier!

Invisible wise voices are speaking to me.

Today, stop often and listen for the subtle whispers in the air near your ear, the message in the vanity license plate, or the lyrics of the song you find yourself humming. There may be angels talking softly to you.

My body knows exactly when to sleep and rest.

Hesitate, rest, and go to bed today based on your body's preference, not your mind's opinion. When you stop disciplining yourself, you may find a more efficient, natural way to live and work.

Judith attended a conference at which I spoke. She was a freelance corporate coach and psychotherapist and had taken a three-month sabbatical from her day job working with account and crisis management for a large corporation. She was close to her deadline for letting the corporation know whether she would be coming back. As she described the company to me, she called it a toxic environment in which people were asked to work great amounts of overtime with no thanks and basically to sacrifice their health and happiness to keep their jobs. In fact, she said that when she finally decided to take care of herself and ask for what she needed—a restful sabbatical—the other employees became snotty and critical and began sabotaging her. How dare she ask for what she needed when *they* weren't getting what *they* needed? They all seemed to be in collusion to maintain the self-sacrificial tone of the company. As the hour grew near for Judith to make the dreaded phone call, when she would have to speak her whole truth and nothing but the truth, her body actually broke out in a severe case of hives. What could it mean? Suddenly she had a flash.

During the workshop I gave at the conference, I asked people to think of a problem in their lives and three possible solutions. I had them imagine the solutions one by one and imagine each option turning into a smell. She had used the situation of whether to return to this corporate job. When she contemplated the option of going back full-time, she got the overpowering odor of sulfur, to which she is highly allergic. Now here she was entertaining the thought of returning to a job that was murdering her soul because she was afraid to lose the steady income, and her body was having an allergic reaction!

Judith realized her body was giving her a clear message and that she needed to trust herself implicitly now. She was absolutely NOT to proceed. Though she knew she'd encounter some distress resulting from temporary uncertainty about her new career direction, she knew the alternative would be much worse. She was finally ready to make that phone call.

February 25

I was presenting an intuition training in the back room of a spiritual bookstore, and I had come early to arrange the space so it would facilitate the students' abilities to stay alert and open. I've learned from experience that the way energy flows, the way insights come, the end result, is determined in large part by harmony in the environment. Context helps shape content. To open intuition, we must feel safe, connected with our body and the field of energy around us.

It was raining heavily outside as we began the class, chairs in a semicircle, no podium between us, door closed to the bustle of the bookstore out front. Even so, I knew the room, which doubled as a catchall for overflow inventory from the store, presented a challenge. So I raised the issue. "How many of you feel totally comfortable in this room? And are you sitting where you want to sit?" A couple of people scooted around. "Get quiet and notice what parts of the environment are drawing even the smallest part of your attention."

"The ceiling is very low, and these exposed air ducts are hanging down into the room," one woman said. "They're ugly and they worry me, like I might stand up and hit my head." Another woman said, "There are no windows in here. And the lights are bluish and cold, and they're buzzing." Another person commented that the roof was leaking into some plastic dishes. She wondered when they would overflow. Someone else added that the clutter in the corner of the room, the concrete block walls, and the stains on the carpet didn't feel very cozy.

I explained that each of these environmental oddities would absorb some attention if we weren't alert and, to the extent that we ignored our body's subtle impressions, we wouldn't be fully present. About that time, to add to everything else, the heat came on, and we all laughed as I tried to talk above the din of the furnace.

There are two things you can do when the environment doesn't exactly suit your comfort level. One, physically rearrange the environment to the extent you can. And two, when you can't do anything else, name the disturbing factor aloud to yourself, include it in your personal reality, and let it be OK *exactly as it is.*

My body continually receives information from its surroundings.

Notice your first impressions of spaces and environments today. Your environment affects your ability to pay attention and receive insight, so how could you align yourself more harmoniously with what's around you?

I am a child at heart.

If you were five years old, how would you think, speak, and act? Let your innocent responses to people and to life come out unchecked today.

When I was visiting my sister and young nieces in Denver one summer, I met some of the other children who live around their short suburban cul-de-sac. Directly across from my sister's house live three children who are delightfully outgoing and upbeat. Sandwiched between two sisters, Zack was about four years old, tanned to a deep nut brown by the summer sun, with a tiny wrestler's body and short fuzzy hair that, in my opinion, needed to be rubbed. When my sister introduced me he said, "I haven't met you before. Hi!" From then on, he waved every time he saw me.

One afternoon I took a cup of coffee out to the front stoop and sat quietly watching the Colorado sky, enjoying the dramatic buildup of the charcoal gray storm clouds that would soon bring the typical afternoon downpour. Zack was playing in his front yard, and, as he stood up and noticed me, he raised his arm up high, waved enthusiastically, and proceeded to ride his tricycle at top speed over to where I sat. He plopped down next to me, and we chatted about what he'd been doing in his front yard and his favorite TV programs. Then I said, "Do ya think it's gonna rain?" We both looked up at the sky. "Yep," he said. "It sure does get quiet right before it rains, have you noticed that?" I asked him. "Yep," he said. Then he paused a long moment and said, "Those *flowers* are really quiet." I looked over at the petunias he was pointing to, and I listened. "Yes, they sure are," I said. "They're really quiet, too."

Sue grew up with physical abuse. When her father died when she was four, she became the protector and nurturer for the other children. At age twenty Sue had a dramatic near-death experience. After this, she was drawn to paramedic work, helping save lives. Sue had been living with a value system in which she unconsciously expected life to be full of violence and mayhem. If adrenaline wasn't pumping, it didn't seem real. Now she was trying to decide whether to leave her profession and had come to see me for a life reading.

The turning point had come when she was involved in a horrific ambulance accident. She was sitting near the door, and rain started leaking through the ceiling of the vehicle onto her face. Just as she scooted over to a more comfortable spot, a car plowed into the ambulance door at high speed, right where she had been sitting. She only sustained a few scratches, but the driver of the other car was killed.

She soon realized she was disillusioned by the way many of the people she helped screamed obscenities at her or tried to attack her. She felt drained and contemplated going back to school to become a physician's assistant. As she told me her plan, I sensed no life in the idea. Sue was taking the logical parts from her past and trying to force them into her future.

"You should be writing, teaching, and traveling around the world!" I said. She said she was a recluse, so what I was describing seemed alien. But I could see she was a recluse only because she was so overwhelmed with negative input from the damaged people she dealt with daily and that she needed huge amounts of privacy to recoup her energy. I saw her working with women, especially in third-world countries, teaching them about childbirth and nutrition, or training people to build houses or develop alternate sources of energy. Sue confessed that she loved to travel and had dreamed of joining the Peace Corps or working on an Indian reservation. She had always loved midwifery and had actually studied alternative forms of energy generation. As we fleshed out this potential reality, her body came alive. She realized her mind, accustomed to fear and emergency, had simply not been able to recognize a possibility that might be based on love, peace, and self-fulfillment.

I clear my mind so I can recognize new possibilities.

Wherever your thoughts are cluttered and clogged today, let your mind go blank. Ask for the simplest answer, or the beginning of the answer, that lets your body feel happy.

**This earth
and I are
mostly made
of water.**

*Be aware of
and grateful to
water in all its
forms. Water
supports our
ability to feel
and intuit and
reminds us to be
fluid.*

When I was working on my first book, I would write for much of the day, then print out what I'd done and run a bath. Across my tub lies a board I designed especially so I could read, write, and work in the tub. I'd take a cup of tea, the new manuscript pages, and a red pen and work at my bathtub desk as the waters soaked away the electrical buzz I'd picked up from the computer. I'm convinced that being in water helped soften my linear/analytical mind-set and allowed me to perceive more poetically and holistically. Water is the great equalizer, the gracious healer, the receiver and eliminator of our impurities. Being aware of the innate power of our watery nature can rejuvenate us and give us surprising new strategies for problem solving.

Lao-tzu said, "Nothing in the world is more flexible and yielding than water. Yet when it attacks the firm and the strong, none can withstand it, because they have no way to change it. So the flexible overcome the adamant, the yielding overcome the forceful. Everyone knows this, but no one can do it. This is why sages say those who can take on the disgrace of nations are leaders of lands; those who can take on the misfortune of nations are rulers of the world."

March

March 1

Driving home late one night, I was listening to a radio talk show whose guest claimed to be a time traveler sent here from the year 2063 to gather seeds from nonhybrid crops that would survive in the hotter climate of the future. In spite of my skepticism, I found myself totally engrossed in what this man said; if he was a phony, he had an incredible act. In the days that followed, I became increasingly distracted and was unable to sleep through the night. The clients who came to me that week for counsel were similarly distracted, even panic-stricken and delusional. By the end of the week I was severely drained and couldn't reclaim my energy.

Luckily, I had scheduled a massage with an intuitive friend for the end of the week. As she released the tension my body had been holding, she said, "You know, you're really not in your body. You're in the future." I told her then about the radio interview with the time traveler. She said, "You've projected right into that reality to see if it's true. You're so fascinated with the big story that you've left yourself wide open to invasion from all manner of needy people. You're not living your own life. You need to come back to yourself, get centered, and pay attention to the present moment and the short stories that exist right now."

It took a minute for the light to dawn. "Guess what the title of my new book is?" I chortled. "*The Present Moment!* And I'm writing 365 anecdotes—short stories—about what's happening in the here and now! So is this a matter of teaching what you need to learn, or *what?*"

Our minds, when displaced into another time, be it past or future—even the distant future—can separate us from our soul's wisdom. And when we are separated from this fundamental guidance and life force, we feel drained. So no matter what happens tomorrow, this is still the place to be.

This is the moment that matters.

When you project your mind into the future, you will inevitably feel drained. Practice returning to the here and now as often as possible today. Notice how your energy perks up when you do.

**I have some-
thing to do
with the way
others see me.**

*Be aware of the
qualities you
radiate today.
Does your mood
affect the way
others respond to
you?*

Has someone ever snapped a photo of you while you
were distracted or before you had time to pose in your
favorite face and stance? It's a shock to see how we look
when we're unconscious! Vacant eyes, droopy mouth,
sometimes the trace of a grimace, even a bit of hardness
or sadness sneaking through. I watch other people walking in and out of stores or sitting at intersections waiting
for the light to change; they are lost in thought and their
faces have fallen into a flatness, their posture reflecting a
sense of burden. Where is the joy? Then I see my own
reflection in the plate glass window of the department
store, walking sturdily by like a "little trouper," my image
slightly boxy, not as graceful as I would like, and I should
have fixed my hair better before I left the house . . . I
straighten up, take a deep breath, broaden my chest, raise
my chin. I pick up my pace, act perky. I've been slumping
and slack. How can I seem beautiful to anyone when I'm
not feeling my own beauty? How can I appear graceful
when I'm not enjoying the sensuality of my own fluidity?

Don Juan once told Carlos Castañeda to practice making his eyes shiny—that act would bring him a particular
kind of wisdom. I do this whenever I remember. The act
of filling my own eyes with energy and light and projecting that light out to others makes me feel more awake,
alive, and interested in what's in front of me. When I feel
"twinkly," I immediately become amused and entertained
by life and am more willing to participate and see the
good in others. Yet there are days when I pay for my pur-
chases and walk out with the bag under my arm, realizing
that I never once made eye contact with the checkout
person.

Our energy precedes us and swirls away in our wake.
We have many opportunities to touch other people, to
have an impact—even if it's just with our posture, our
gaze, or our smile. When we radiate consciously what we
want to convey, it helps others come alive and feel centered, and it helps us enjoy and love ourselves.

March 3

Lois works for an international corporation in Tokyo and is responsible for all their training programs in Japan. Recently she was overseeing the largest all-employee training program ever undertaken by her company. The first session was to be taught in English, but neither of the trainers was a native speaker; both were fairly inexperienced. Many executives would be there—in particular, two notoriously uncooperative senior officers. At the first day's presentation, Lois sat behind one of the difficult men. Mr. A complained loudly about having to be there and that he couldn't smoke in the room. He subsequently took his frustrations out on the naive trainer, arguing relentlessly about everything.

After the break, it got worse. Mr. B began using profane language and told the trainers that what they were saying was "a load of crap." His vocabulary deteriorated from there. Lois's body tightened, and she could barely maintain a neutral expression on her face. After lunch she moved to the other side of the room, away from the two men, but her tension decreased only slightly.

The trainers were so distressed that they couldn't manage their material or the time. The evaluation sheets at the end of the day summed things up—it was the worst training experience the participants had ever had. Lois suspected that if she had tried to stop the two men, they would have escalated their obnoxiousness to prove they couldn't be controlled by a woman. Now Lois's body was almost shaking. She knew she had to do something, yet dreaded the thought of a confrontation. Lois and I had spoken about the concept of maintaining deep comfort in the body so accurate intuition can make itself known. She realized she was experiencing an anxiety signal and that to think clearly she must release the tension. When she let go and felt what would make *her* comfortable, an insight flooded through.

The next morning Lois went to Mr. A and Mr. B separately and told them, in a quiet voice, that other people in the class were uncomfortable with what they had done the previous day. Her nonconfrontational communication style worked—both men were contrite and thanked her for bringing the matter to their attention. The class improved dramatically, the trainers were able to relax, and their teachings had a more positive impact on the employees.

Contraction is a natural part of my life.

Your body naturally contracts when your instincts tell you something is unsafe or inappropriate or when a subconscious fear is triggered. Each tightening contains information. See if you can read the various kinds of contractions you experience today.

My soul moves my mind.

Notice the surprising turns your mind takes today, especially when you're slightly absentminded. Watch for happy accidents and magical synchronicities. These are signs of higher guidance.

It was the kind of warm, sunny Sunday morning in spring that gives me wanderlust. I was up early and got the vague idea of driving somewhere new for a good breakfast and an hour of reading. OK! I'd drive to some different town, I'd have a mini-adventure—then come home and turn the soil in my garden.

My vagueness continued as I left the house and headed down the road. Should I go north or south? Each direction held promise, though. As I scanned the restaurants I knew, my mind rejected each of them. One was too noisy, another too expensive, another too cold. As I became conscious of driving again, I realized I'd passed the turnoff where I might have headed north. "That's OK," I said to myself, "I can still go north at the next junction if I want to." But at the next choice point, I was off somewhere in my head again and automatically got on the southbound on-ramp to the freeway. "OK. I see I'm going south." Projecting ahead to the restaurants I knew along the way, I felt paralyzed with indecision. "Wasn't there a place behind that shopping center? I'll go over and check." But as I got off the freeway, I realized I'd taken the exit before the one I wanted. Suddenly my mind flashed on a cozy little place on this road called Eddie's.

I slowed at Eddie's, and though the sign said OPEN, the place looked dead. My body kept driving the car right past Eddie's. "What am I doing?" I whined. Then, two blocks farther on, I spied a place I'd never seen before with a big sign that said BRUNCH and CAFÉ. People were chatting in amiable groups by the door, and there was one parking space directly in front, as though they'd been expecting me.

As if my life had been touched by a magic wand, the atmosphere turned out to be cozy, the waitress was happy, they had homemade bread and fresh strong coffee, and made menu substitutions without a fuss! My slightly unformed dream had come true! As I savored the subtle flavors of food and fine writing, a thought intruded. "Who took such good care of me this morning?" It certainly wasn't my usually organized and determined mind. Perhaps there *is* a higher awareness that directs us unerringly toward experiences that satisfy our true needs, even if some days it's only a need for good food and a positive atmosphere.

My father tells a story about a remarkable man, Cliff Davis, who came to work for him in the early 1950s in a large concrete-pipe-manufacturing business. My father was officially the boss, but Cliff rapidly demonstrated an effortless engineering expertise and unrivaled people skills. Soon, my father says, he became Cliff's student.

Their first big job together was to construct and operate a large production facility for a new sewer system in Miami, Florida. As part of the contract, the head office dictated that every construction worker must wear a safety hard hat, which was a novelty at the time. The macho workers rebelled in spite of my father's efforts at persuasion. But fate stepped in, in the form of Cliff Davis. Cliff was out in the field one day when a huge wooden plank fell twenty-five feet from a structure above and dealt him a glancing blow to the head. The injury was not serious, but there was a tremendous reaction from the men, who respected Cliff. They gathered around him as he lay on the ground, and he looked up and said, "I was really lucky I wasn't wearing a hard hat." Given the amount of blood, the men couldn't understand, and they questioned him on the spot. His response: "If I'd had a hard hat on, that plank would've slipped right off the hat and could've broken both legs." A week later, without any further mention, all the men were wearing hard hats, which soon became a symbol to them of team pride.

I like this story because I believe at a deep level that Cliff was motivated to teach the men some powerful principles of love and clarity even at the risk of personal injury. He put himself on the line and became a living example of someone who supported his fellow man and the tasks that needed to be done. By generously and self-deprecatingly making an example of himself, he showed others how to be more conscious and how to care more for their own and each other's safety. From then on, by putting on a hard hat, each man dedicated himself to their collaborative work. Cliff had somehow managed to introduce a sacred element to what had previously been mundane.

I create a sacred space for myself and my work.

Clean off the surfaces and prepare an area lovingly to use for creative expression today. The activity that follows is sure to occur more effectively.

March 6

I take time to understand what I say and what other people really mean.

Make certain you understand your own and others' communications today by checking: "I heard myself/you say _____; is that what I/you meant?"

If I listen between the lines, slow down, and stop second-guessing other people and finishing their sentences for them in my head, I can hear several communications happening simultaneously. There's the superficial one, which can often be overly negative or positive, while just under the surface is something much more vulnerable and real. My sister says, "That material you sent looks good; I'll try to get time to read it soon." What I hear underneath is, "Please stop sending me things that clutter my life." When I say to my friend, "I don't know why I keep attracting people who are victims," if I listen under the complaint and profession of ignorance, I hear, "I feel trapped in a way of thinking that drains my energy and frustrates my creativity." When your coworker says, "Sure, I could take on that project . . ." does his tone of voice say, "I feel so burdened that one more thing may cause me to drown"? Listen deeply and experiment with addressing and voicing the real issues.

HIDDEN COMMUNICATION AGENDAS

1. Pay attention to when you obsess, complain, doubt, or criticize. What might be causing you to want to damage other people? Are you jealous? Hurt? What can't you accept? If the other people, or your own soul, were sitting with you, hearing you speak, how might they feel? And what might they say to you if they gave you honest feedback?

2. Examine the motives behind what you say. To what extent does insecurity prompt you? Do you need attention to feel accepted or right? If you succeed in each communication, what do you gain by it? Might you be talking to maintain control? Make a practice of "If you can't say something positive, from a clear motivation, don't say anything."

March 7

Janice was in severe debt, feeling helpless, and wanted to learn to manage her money and become financially independent. She began working with a life and business coach, who first helped her with simple logistical issues—balancing her checkbook, creating budgets, talking to creditors productively. As that work progressed, they dipped into some of the deeper, more emotional issues underlying the debt. It turned out that Janice had a hard time receiving love, and she never felt she had enough love to be safe. She felt abandoned and alone and had filled the empty feeling inside by buying clothes, jewelry, and beautiful things for her house. As they brought these feelings to light, the coach suggested that she do something to counteract her habit of hoarding, which kept her in a contracted, fearful state.

Janice decided that she would volunteer a few hours a week at the local human needs center. After working there for a week, she learned of an old woman whose family was too busy to take care of her or spend time with her. The old woman's isolation touched a chord in Janice, and she said, "I'll help her out." So she spent her extra time doing the old woman's grocery shopping, cooking her an occasional meal, talking with her over tea, and helping to clean her house. She enjoyed helping the old woman so much that the time passed quickly.

One day she got a phone call from the family saying that the old woman had died suddenly during the night. They said they appreciated very much the time she had spent with their mother, and evidently their mother had, too, because she had taken the time to revise her will and had left Janice a sum of money. When she protested, they said, "No, no, the estate is very large and we want you to have this money for everything you did." Can you guess? The amount of money that came to her from the beneficence of her own heart-motivated actions and the appreciative heart of the old woman was *exactly* the amount she and her coach had determined would pay off her debts and allow her to be financially independent.

What I am given is what I need.

Simplify your life today by accepting without protest what comes. When you use what you have, you enable yourself to receive even more.

I bless the flora, the fauna, and the forces of nature.

Send energy into plants and animals today; receive energy and insights from nature. You are part of nature, and it is eager to give as much to you as you give to it.

It was the first sunny spring morning after days of rain that had swollen the local streams to roiling rivers. I took a hike around the reservoir near my home, the wind still brisk and crisp. The new, rapidly growing grasses were dripping and shiny. It was just me, a few grazing cows, and some geese. I waded through flooded paths in my rubber boots until I came to the rushing creek, making a mighty sound in the otherwise still morning.

I paused to listen, to smell the raw wetness and the sharp scent of the bay laurel trees, and to feel the mist from the charging stream blowing onto my face. I stood on the bank and faced the oncoming water, feeling its force and surrendering to its energy. The power seemed almost too much to receive. As I relaxed and let the force flow through me, it slowly turned me, as though I were a log temporarily caught in a jam, and directed me to face downstream. Then I could feel the gleeful movement, the help the creek was giving me, the ease of moving with the current instead of against it. As I let the energy push on me from behind, I could feel how much farther I might go in my life, how rapid my progress could be.

"Ah," I thought, remembering how I'd been avoiding returning an overwhelming slew of phone calls and E-mails, "facing into the phone calls is like trying to go upstream. Instead of resisting the force that potential information represents, I can just dive in, let the communications themselves propel me into a forward movement. Who knows where I'll end up if I flow with what's coming at me, if I let it turn me and move me?" I offered my appreciation to the creek and its innate truths and turned homeward, following the currents of my own river.

March 9

David, a talented healer and one of the most compassionate people I know, made some extra money one summer by hawking choppers, grinders, graters, and knives at food shows and expos across the Midwest. I had to laugh at the image of this usually quiet man getting revved up to pitch the trick of grating cheese in three seconds, but he said he actually had a great time transforming himself into a salesperson. During this adventure David worked with a man who was a chopper/grinder/expo "lifer" and made his living entirely on the road. Years of doing this had hardened him considerably, and he was often abrupt, rude, and willful.

They pulled into a home show in Kansas and began to cart their equipment into the hall to set up. David's partner, with a fully loaded dolly, proceeded toward a door that looked like the entrance. It was guarded by a woman in a uniform. As he started to enter, she told him all deliveries had to be made through another door around the corner. He gave her the cold shoulder, uttered a crude comment, and pushed through anyway. David watched from a vantage point near their van. His partner continued to unload the van and bully his way into the exposition hall, totally unconscious of the effect he was having.

David brought the last load into the building through the correct entrance, and, after they were set up, he walked back outside and approached the woman. "What do *you* want?" she asked cynically. David looked her in the eye and said, "I came back to apologize for my friend's behavior." "What do you mean?" she asked, cocking her head in suspicion. "Well," David replied, "I didn't like the way my partner acted. I don't think anyone should treat another person the way he treated you. And I know he won't apologize so I'm apologizing. I wouldn't have wanted to be in your position and receive that kind of disrespect." She just stared at him, and suddenly her face softened. "Thanks," she said. "Thanks."

I make amends.

Apologize to someone you mistreated or feel was mistreated by others. You can be a force for good in the world.

**If I can't help,
I can turn
things over to
a higher
power.**

*Notice the places
today where
your willpower,
cleverness, and
skills don't get
results, and ask
for help from the
invisible realms.
There's really
no such thing as
helplessness.*

I had a client, a long-time Buddhist in her early seventies, who claimed her mind attacked her and incapacitated her for weeks. It was obvious the woman was a scholar and had studied many philosophies and meditation techniques. Yet she spoke with her head tilted downward from behind closed eyes. She'd open them, glance at me momentarily, then shut them again, fidgeting nervously. When she arrived for her appointment, she hadn't brought a tape. "They're a waste," she declared. I explained that there would be a lot of detail, but she waved me off.

When I began telling her about the patterns in her numerological cycles, she interrupted me, panic building. "Well, this is valuable information! I should have brought a tape. Oh now what am I going to do?" I stopped and said I'd wait for her to go buy one.

When she returned from the store, we began taping the session. I noticed a pattern I often see with physical and sexual abuse and asked, "Were your parents angry or violent? Did they hit you? Did they lock you in a closet or do something that felt terrorizing or victimizing?"

"Well they did hit me, and they did lock me in a closet, but I can't remember anything else," she said. It was apparent that she had been hurt so badly that she felt totally unsafe being herself. Every time she tried to be authentic and expressive, her now-internalized punishing parents beat it down again. These were the attacks she had complained about. I could see why the detachment of Buddhism was so appealing to her.

No matter what suggestions I gave for reversing the pattern, the punishing parental part of her smashed the ideas and me. This was a no-win situation. During the two hours I'd spent with her, nothing I'd said had been allowed in. "I've tried this before!" she said, her voice full of frustration. "No one can help me." She became nearly hysterical. As I handed her the tape, she said, "See? I knew this would be a waste."

As I processed this feeling of helplessness, on my part and hers, I was tempted to complain just as she'd been complaining. Someone has to break the chain, I thought. I stopped beating myself up for not being able to make a difference and asked for a blessing for us both. I was no longer helpless.

Each of us has an archetypal wise woman and wise man who live inside us. Because of the way our parents model masculinity and femininity, we often distort these ideal images and limit the way we receive wisdom from them. Imagine meeting your inner female and male. Imagine that the inner female, the part of you connected to unlimited knowledge, energy, and love, backs out of you and stands behind you on the left. The inner male, the part of you that knows exactly how to shape energy, focus information, and produce results, backs out of you and stands behind you to the right. Before you see the images, feel them and their respective qualities. Then imagine them walking around to the front and introducing themselves. When you first see them, each appears distorted in a way that symbolizes how your subconscious views the basic relationship between men and women.

When Alice's inner female and male walked into sight, she was surprised. She thought of herself as a high-powered businesswoman, but her inner female was a wispy, fairylike creature who barely spoke above a whisper. Her inner male looked like Paul Bunyan, muscles bulging beneath a plaid flannel shirt. When she watched them relate to each other, the male strutted around like a hero. But soon he said he felt he had to do everything by himself, that he wasn't getting the information, energy, nurturing, and validation he needed from his "pathetic" partner. She didn't inspire him, and he didn't care if he pleased her. Her inner female said she felt ignored and taken for granted. Her "insensitive" partner didn't see her delicacy or beauty, never thanked her or listened to her, and acted domineering.

Alice saw from this how her mother had given up her independence and creativity to raise a family and had lived vicariously through her husband and children. Alice took on her father's pattern and became successful in the world. Yet whenever she had an intimate relationship, she reverted to her mother's subservient role, and her business failed. By working on a dialogue between her inner female and male and helping them hear each other and ask for what they needed, she was able to change a deep-seated relationship habit that had been frustrating her for years.

My inner male and female selves are knowledgeable and powerful.

Tune in to your wise feminine self and your wise masculine self today. How does each guide you in finding the answers you need, using your energy effectively, taking action, and relating positively to the world?

I listen to my heart; it is a kind of mind.

Let the knowledge in your heart guide you today. Your heart can speak, and your mind knows how to listen cooperatively. Your heart knows how to create win-win situations.

I was looking for someone new to organize my work in Japan. I had asked for references from every Japan-connected friend and followed every lead. A young man who was interested in psychology and had started a consciousness institute in Tokyo contacted me. We corresponded, and, though my mind could recite a list of the benefits of working with him, my body was distinctly uncomfortable. I sensed the young man was inexperienced and would not promote me aggressively enough. When I tried to sense his energy, he seemed to recede as I came forward. As we made plans, my anxiety deepened. I began to feel a contraction in my chest like a heart attack. When I asked what was under the heart-attack feeling, my body said it didn't feel safe. The young man was coming to San Francisco, so I'd have a chance to meet him, but if my doubts were verified, there would be no time to find someone else. I decided I was willing to cancel everything and lose the hefty plane fare if I continued to have the heart contractions.

Literally an hour after I made my decision and let go of trying to control things, I got a fax from a woman in Japan who I'd done a reading for three years earlier. "When are you coming to Japan?" she queried. I faxed her back and described my current situation. She responded immediately, saying, "Three years ago you told me I should start my own business and do public relations work, and that is what I've done. I'd be more than happy to set up a program for you. What do you need?" My jaw dropped and my heart heaved an enormous sigh of relief. Here was an enthusiastic, bilingual person with fantastic communication skills who knew my work. It was perfect! Yet I still had to play out the other scenario.

When I finally met the young man, my sense about him was confirmed. He confessed he also felt unprepared to do the job but still wanted to help. I had him call the woman when he returned to Toyko, and he ended up assisting her. Eventually we all benefited from our collaboration.

Later, when I related the whole story to the woman, she said, "I don't know why, but one afternoon I had a strong, sudden thought, "Contact Penney right now! I didn't know why I was doing it, but I guess we really are all connected!"

Lisa, who has been recovering from cancer and rebuilding her life, was reading in bed the other night. She finally turned off the light to go to sleep. As she did, she realized her body was vibrating, not with anxiety or stress or the electrical buzz that has often beset her during her healing process, but with bliss! She directed her awareness into what her body was feeling, merging with the refined, smooth, happy energy and allowing herself to just enjoy it. "What a powerful healing force this is," she thought. "How could cancer, or a sinus infection, or even a bruise exist in a reality this affirming? If my body knows how to do this, how did I ever get sick in the first place?"

It was then that Lisa realized the tyrannical nature of her mind, which had kept her a human whirlwind for most of her life so that she would avoid feeling some uncomfortable emotions. Now, since she had learned to meditate, be conscious of her diet, understand and clear her fears, and make herself rest, her body was finally getting the chance to talk to her and bring its own natural energy to her conscious mind. She discovered that night that she loved her own energy! There was something about the real Lisa that was so beautiful and nurturing. She just wanted to bask in herself, to feel her own state of being forever! That night she stayed awake for hours indulging in her body's simple bliss, its internal communion, and connection with all of life. She says the experience was so memorable, she can easily re-create it whenever she thinks of it again. This, she determined was the secret to a centered life—choose your highest state and live inside it. When you forget it, remind yourself of it again as soon as you can!

I am vibrating with life.

Be quiet and feel your pulse and the tingling in your body as often as you can today. Your body relays information to you through states of vibration.

**My back
is a source of
useful
information.**

*Be aware of
what's going on
behind you today.
Your back is
actually one of
the most sensitive
areas of your
body and picks
up an amazing
amount of
information.*

Monica grew up hitchhiking all over Europe and traveling by herself through Asia and Africa. She had always felt safe because she was perceptive to people's intent and knew how to take control of a situation that looked like it might get out of hand.

There was only one time when her early warning system gave her the red alert with a ferocious intensity. She had been walking across Central Park in New York City when she felt a wave of energy that contracted her entire body. It was coming from behind, as though someone were glaring at her or stalking her. The energy felt "black and murderous," and she turned around immediately and noticed a man some distance behind her. Without thinking, she started running at full speed toward the nearest exit from the park. She says even now her back is sometimes more sensitive to, and accurate about, other people's intent than what her eyes see happening right in front of her.

March 15

I had dinner with a friend and two of her friends. I had a passing acquaintance with the other two women but no deep rapport. The conversation began lightly, politely. They had many more stories and insider jokes as a threesome than I had with any one of them, so it wasn't long before I felt like an outsider. No matter how witty or insightful I tried to be, my comments landed with a thud. The others just smiled wanly and changed the subject.

Then one of them declared her belief that it was untrue that illness was caused by "wrong thinking" and that the New Age was just blaming people for getting sick. I replied that I felt the ideas we hold in our deep subconscious mind really do have the capacity to block the flow of energy in the body, and it's not about blame at all but rather about being unaware of the true nature of the self. They immediately labeled this kind of thinking "megalomaniacal." They thought that we aren't in control of our own lives and that it's ridiculous to think we are.

If I'd been slightly more courageous at that moment, I might have risked saying that I was uncomfortable, that something seemed to be going astray, that I was feeling misunderstood and unsafe, and it wasn't my intention to irritate everyone. Often, speaking the truth of a situation out loud immediately relieves the tension. But instead, I heightened the sense of alienation by saying I thought health was created through being intentional about our own choices and being part of a collective consciousness, or group mind, where we would "feel our brothers and sisters as ourselves." They thought the idea of a group mind negated their own individual rights, that it was impossible to feel another person's reality. I said I did it all the time when I do life readings and that I'd experienced that compassion facilitates communion. But again this only provided more fodder for their scorn. It was evident that no matter what I said there was no way to correct the "off" quality of the evening.

We walked to our cars afterward, and naturally theirs were parked together, while mine was in the opposite direction. As I walked away from them, they called my name. I turned and saw them standing in a tight cluster, giggling. One of them yelled, "Hey! Don't get lost in the group mind on your way home!"

I create comfort wherever I am.

Help yourself and others feel comfortable physically and emotionally today. When you take responsibility for relieving unnecessary tension, clarity occurs.

I notice the natural gifts of others.

Tell people today how talented they are. When you take time to look for excellence, beauty, and uniqueness in others, you create a healing quality in yourself.

Lauren was in a major life transition when she came to see me. She'd just been through a messy divorce and had moved to a new home. Now she was losing interest in her career as an engineer and mathematician. Lauren was a beautiful woman—tall, blond, and graceful yet reticent. There was distance in her eyes and a kind of angularity that overlaid her natural grace, the way teenage girls can sometimes seem gawky. She shared that, though she had a phenomenal job, she was bored and resentful about working on problems that had no emotional relevance. She was being drawn much more to designing the landscaping for her new home and taking nature photographs.

I could feel a new woman emerging from inside Lauren. Her image kept shifting like a mirage. The woman who sat before me was dressed in khakis and a work shirt with the sleeves rolled up, but I saw her draped in a silky, flowing dress, floating over water. It looked like she was drifting toward Hawaii with flowers in her hair; I smelled the tropics and saw volcanoes. I described these images to Lauren, expressing how beautiful and feminine she was. Her body wanted to absorb the deep feminine energy from the ocean, the Pacific islands, even from the goddess Pele. She was evolving away from the linear, masculine world into one that was fluid, colorful, and sensual. Then I was flooded with a joyful image. I saw all the five-year-old girls on the planet together in one huge gaggle, holding hands and laughing. She was to imagine the archetypal energy of all those girls—their sweetness, innocence, playfulness, and openness—and transfer it into her own body. A new creativity and sense of connectedness wanted to be born in her.

When I told her this, Lauren's body language changed. "I just bought an underwater camera!" she said. "I want to do underwater photography, so I've booked myself for a special cruise and dive trip in Hawaii. After that, I'm thinking of spending some time in Belize." She continued enthusiastically. "And then I thought of creating a website that would be a gallery for nature photographs!" I could see it all unfolding. All Lauren had needed was someone to give her a warm validation of the beautiful woman she really was.

March 17

There are times when we don't mind living inside the societal, tribal mind, when fitting in seems like an act of warmth and compassion, when compressing our consciousness into time and space seems like an interesting experiment. There are other days when we are all too aware of the mass hypnosis, the pain and limitation people resign themselves to. Rod McDaniel wrote the following poem, and I read it every so often to remind myself to stay awake.

> I hear the screaming.
> Go out, socialize, get a life, make friends.
> I go out,
> sink into the culture,
> listen to the insistence,
> become sluggish in the gooey ideas,
> struggle for easy air,
> latch my focus onto solidifying resignations,
> pant out a plan of acquirement,
> bind myself with the rules of maintenance,
> monitor all progress with local comparisons,
> label strong contrasts as dreams or ideals,
> share in the group's thick, wet feet,
> conclude for the necessity of labor in our attitudes,
> minister the game's minutest details.
> Chumming around with callous people,
> those who rely on conclusions,
> poets who write about things they have no personal relationship with,
> artists who have never acknowledged seeing auras,
> doctors with no children of their own,
> lovers who clench around their orgasms,
> preachers who pray with tense bodies—
> We are all here, all toiling.
> I hear the screams.

I am aware of the "tribal mind" and its effect on me.

Say no to ideas and behaviors that dampen your authenticity and vitality today. Notice that sometimes the mores and expectations of society are numbing and frustrating to your soul's deepest motives.

March 18

Part of me is old and very wise.

If you were 100 years old, how would you think, speak, and act today? Imagine the freedom and perspective that come with having lived a long time.

Last Thanksgiving I flew to Florida to visit my parents, now separated in their later years, with lives branching in new directions. I spent several days with each of them and their friends. No one was under seventy and most were closer to eighty. For a week I lunched, brunched, met for coffee, shopped the flea market, went to museums, went to the hardware store, and watched videos of Jack Lemmon and Walter Matthau with an array of funny, lively folks. My mother and I sat by the pool in the late afternoon, watching chameleons skitter across the screens, poring over photos of her travels around the world. We talked of things like recipes for Jell-O with pineapple and cottage cheese and what clothing styles best suited our figures. With my father, I walked slowly down the beach, kicking at dead jellyfish, picking up the occasional sand dollar, and enjoying long lines of low-soaring pelicans. We drove around the neighborhood to see if Bob was working in his garage woodworking shop and to check out his latest project. Then we went to the tiny marina nearby to inspect my father's little Boston Whaler and its good location under a tree.

Life was slow and easy. My body attuned to the eighty-year-old bodies, and I could feel how it was to get tired walking, how the topics of doctors, surgeries, and medication gained such relevance. I said to my father, after we'd gone to breakfast one morning and were walking again along the beach, "Do you ever feel your parents' gestures in your body? Because sometimes I suddenly feel that I'm walking just the way you walk, or I'm holding my jaw the way Mom does." Yes, he said, his father had had a certain way of holding his chest, and his mother had had short legs like he did, and he often felt them in him. I'm glad to know this.

They had their worries but they had freedom as well. The projects they were involved with—managing their money on-line, collecting bromeliads, making furniture from found objects, having theme parties, painting watercolors, breeding Yorkshire terriers—expressed their true interests. They valued their friends and neighbors. They worked in their yards. By the time I left to come home, I had a new perspective on life.

March 19

Henry has worked in the Nashville music business for years, but lately he's been getting spontaneous insights about other people's problems and what they can do to be happier. It took him a while before he felt it was OK to share this information with others. One of the first insights he had was that a man he was working with had been struggling with the lint filter on his clothes dryer! "Why I got that particular piece of mundane information I don't know," he says, "but I shared it with him anyway, and it was true. Maybe it was just to show me that we're all connected and even the most ordinary things are known in the bigger scheme of things."

Once as they were setting up for a concert, Henry looked at one of the audio technicians and got the name "Robert." So he asked if the man knew a Robert. Indeed he did, and he had just gotten off the phone with him. Then more information came through, and he said to the technician, "I just get this feeling that Robert is having a hard time right now, that he's in dire financial trouble, and emotionally he's going through a long, dark tunnel. If you and a few other friends of his could get together, and one person from the group call him each day next week to see how he's doing, that would really help him." The technician admitted that Robert's wife had just died and his father had died only a few months ago. In addition, he truly was in bad financial shape.

Henry said that the information that comes to him always involves someone known to the person he's talking to, and it usually requires that the person offer help of some sort. It seems that Henry's willingness to receive these insights, be they about lint filters, relieving emotional pain, or what herbs someone needs to cleanse their blood, starts a chain reaction of people helping others.

I care about the lives of others.

Ask blessings for strangers today. Part of what we're here to do is make life less difficult for one another.

**I notice my
true intent.**

*Pay attention to
whether you
really want to do
what you say you
do. When we
agree to things
that aren't in our
best interests
or when we
pressure ourselves
to do false things,
sometimes the
best remedy
is to do a bit of
wandering.*

I am supposed to be designing a series of training sessions
for the corporate market. Adapting spiritual and intuitive
principles to business functions is an intriguing concept,
one that hovers around me constantly. So why wasn't I
getting revved up about it? I called my management consultant and trainer friends and interviewed them, took
copious notes, and haltingly ground out some ideas. As
I'd start to conceptualize the specific course content, my
brain would go fuzzy and I'd feel like I was drowning.
This didn't make sense! The ideas were so interesting! My
mind was willing to dive into this material, but another
part of me definitely wasn't. So I got up from my desk
and walked around aimlessly.

I washed some dishes. I wandered into my bedroom
and put on some baggy sweats. As I came back to the
kitchen, I noticed I wanted to go out in the yard. There
I noticed I wanted to pick up the dead branches that had
blown down in the high winds the previous week. After
that I noticed I wanted to weed my garden. After that I
noticed I was dirty and thirsty, so I went in, washed my
hands, and had some lemonade. Then I noticed my journal lying on the table and just felt like writing something.
So I wrote a haiku:

> apple blossoms flake like ash
> speckle the grass
> trees leaf fast

I could feel the powerful push of the trees returning to
life, the anxiousness of the apple leaves to push the delicate white blossoms out of the way and get on with things.
That inexorable life force was so comforting! Computers,
words, concepts, making intuition logical—these things
didn't interest my body at all. You can only go so far with
the mind alone, I commented in my journal, and if you
ignore the body and its hungry senses, it will drag the
vital force down, out of the higher brain and back to the
animal self. That's where I wanted to be—soaking up the
green, getting dirt under my nails. In this present moment
I was a Zen gardener, a lemonade drinker. Tomorrow
maybe the corporate intuition trainer would be reborn.

A client wanted to work on communicating more clearly with her fourteen-year-old daughter who was developing a strange vagueness. I suggested we do a meditation to focus on her daughter's seven energy centers, or chakras, that run from the tailbone to the top of the head. We visualized her daughter and asked permission to work with her.

In the first center at the base of the spine, an area that helps us feel grounded, safe, and confident, we saw an amorphous, dirty brown energy. We sensed the girl might be feeling unrooted, precarious, or sexually confused. The girl's second energy center, which is below the navel and helps fuel creativity and connect us outwardly through sympathy, looked wide open like a flat plate. It appeared the girl was giving her energy to her friends and not keeping much for her own creative process. The third center relates to personal power and ability to take action in the world, and hers seemed contracted, as though she was monitoring her self-expression, judging how her actions might look to others.

The fourth center, the heart, the seat of compassion, was open yet shadowy at its core. We sensed this related to the girl's fear of being hurt. The fifth center, at the throat, which helps with self-expression, looked dark and contracted, as though her communications might be dominated by fear or skepticism or that she lacked trust in her self-expression. The sixth center, at the brow, which governs clear perception, looked bright and glowing, though occasionally we saw a window shade drawn down over this "third eye," as if she didn't want to see too much or might be pretending to not know. The seventh center, at the top of the head, which connects us to the spiritual self, felt open but hazy, as though she secretly used it but didn't allow it to be conscious. We imagined clear energy flowing up and down the spine, adjusting each center to its optimal expression.

Several days later, the girl said to her mother, "You know, sometimes I just wish someone would hold me and I could cry." They talked. She said she kept having insights about her friends but didn't know how to offer the advice without alienating the other girls. This allowed them to clear the way to talk about how she could share her ideas and stimulate her own creativity instead of paying so much attention to her friends.

Energy and life flow vertically through me, from earth to heaven, from heaven to earth.

Your spine carries an amazing amount of information. Today, notice its flexibility, its uprightness, its life force. Imagine that your spine and the seven chakras along the spine are transmitting into you the energy and wisdom from the Father in heaven as it descends and from the Mother in earth as it ascends.

**My body is a
sweet, obedient
friend;
it tries to do
whatever I ask
of it.**

*Your body is one
of your prime
sources of guid-
ance, and it
also helps create
what you need.
Take time today
to attend to
your body in
special ways.
Make it feel
attractive, lovable,
respected, and
appreciated.*

In one of my writing workshops, we wrote for a few
minutes on "I appreciate my body/I love my body
because . . . " Then we imagined we were our body and
talked back to our personality about what we needed,
liked, and were able to do. Linda was a slightly plump,
petite woman in her fifties. She wrote:

I appreciate my body because it is warm and full and very feminine. It
has smooth skin. I love the kind of energy my body contains and the
way it transmits and shapes energy into creative outlets, like my pot-
tery. It holds extra weight, but that's only because I don't let it move
as much as it wants to. I love my body because it is sensitive and very
alert. I love my breasts. They are gracious and giving. My body is
kind yet also capable of great intensity.

I am the body. I am doing the best I can with what Linda gives me to
do. I like energy. I like sensations, harmony, forcefulness, gentleness—
all kinds of stimulation. I need more oxygen and I need it to be
forced through me, into all my cells. I need new experiences of life to
rid myself of the old that is stored here. I don't want to store old
stuff. I want food that is fresher, lighter—not clogging. I can clear
away tendencies to any disease! I need fresh air, beauty, loving the
ugly, not having to protect myself from silly things that aren't dangerous, clear water, fluid movement, sunlight.

March 23

Several years ago I drove with a friend from San Francisco to Colorado. I have made the trip alone many times and know where the good gas stations and food stops are and how long to go between refuelings. But my friend had a different level of tolerance for how long she could sit or go without food and what kind of food she could eat. She is a successful entrepreneur with a sharp, analytical mind and a sense of innate authority. So I noticed myself adapting my usual travel habits to her needs.

As we left Salt Lake City the second morning, I had a strong sense that we could get on the highway we needed by going east, but she thought we should go south. I checked the map and east seemed fine. So we proceeded through town. At first the numbered blocks went from west to east, but then they veered north, then south, as the roads progressively became more residential and windy and were blocked by construction. We never found the entrance to the highway. I couldn't understand why we'd gotten so tangled up and why I was so turned around.

My friend, on the verge of exasperation, told me to go in a direction that seemed totally illogical to me. Lo and behold, within a few blocks we intersected with a road that took us straight to the highway. We laughed it off, but for miles I kept wondering, "Why did this happen?"

I realized my friend's perception works visually. Mine, on the other hand, works through my body's relationship with whatever I'm paying attention to. So, when navigating, I feel the land and sense how everything connects to where my body is. Our perceptual styles were quite different. Hers was faster, more mental and abstract; mine more tactile, emotional, and slow. My way was below the level of her normal awareness, so she didn't have faith in my ability. Since I'd been deferring to her preferences for most of the trip, I realized I'd inadvertently given away my perceptual authority as well. The result was that my way of navigating became ineffectual, and I got us lost. Had I been by myself I'd have found the route easily. The embarrassing experience helped me reconnect with my center and be more conscious of where I needed to be.

I'm just where I need to be just when I need to be there.

Pay attention today to your body's innate sense of when to begin and how to navigate so you'll be on time and in the right place effortlessly. If you trust your body and not just your brain, you'll wind up where you need to be.

The little me doesn't know, but the Big Me does.

Even if your personality and mind don't know what to do, the real you—your soul—always does. Let go of your opinions today, and see what wisdom takes their place.

There is something at work in my dreams and somewhere out in the far reaches of my aura. Something is teaching me, weaving new colored threads into my consciousness, tying beautiful knots with my loose ends. Someone is sending a new song into my cells. A tuning fork with the tone of my new name is being struck. It's a new blueprint, a new way of being organized, a new life dream. I sense the dissolution of the old as my memory fades repeatedly, as my past seems like it could belong to someone else. I am being drawn elsewhere—is it the future? Another dimension? Am I being seduced into boredom and spaciousness in preparation for the next explosion?

My daily habits, my longstanding ideas about who I am are becoming empty, meaningless. Somehow, though, I know I am heeding the call. I am turning toward the unknown that knows better than I what the next creation might be, who my new friends might be, what my new place might be. The silent call is asking me to reinvent myself in a way that is much more powerful, yet more subtle, than ever before. More faith, less ambition. More passion, less meaning. More involvement, less attachment. More color, texture, rhythm, and tone, less overstimulation. More me, more us, more one, more true, greater and smaller, dramatic and invisible, social and secluded, domestic and exotic. Someone is teaching my mind. Someone is inspiring my mind to be the servant, not the tyrant, at long last.

March 25

I pretend to be the conch shell I see lying on the table. I enter it, feel its life, feel what it knows, where it came from. I fall into it and speak as it. "I am the final outcome of a long process of preserving the sound of the universe. I started in the heavens, rolling, turning, spiraling down through the sounds of God breathing, angels humming, divas laughing; I entered the waters and knew the rocking of the waves against the shore, the heaving of the ocean toward the moon and away. I wrapped around the wave; the sounds all became one. I captured them in my curl. I said, 'I'll be the mouth, I'll do it forever.' I invite all to enter, to come down into my pink throat and know their beginnings."

Every form of life gives to me.

Receive wisdom and energy from plants, objects, and animals today. Try merging your awareness with various things then speaking about what you know as the daffodil, the candle, or the bird.

I validate my intuitions in whatever way they come.

You can validate your intuitions and make them real by sharing them, applying them, or writing them in your journal. Share or act on a hunch, an inkling, or a vision today.

A therapist I know told me she was learning how to offer insights so that they didn't interfere with her clients' processes. She told me about a woman who was fixated on finding a relationship. They'd spent several sessions focusing the woman's attention back into present time and into her body so she could feel her own joy and creativity. This allowed them to discover why she was compelled to keep leaping into fantasies of the perfect man. It turned out the woman felt that *nothing* was happening in her own center, that on her own she was nothing. As a child, her parents had never acknowledged her originality and had only validated her when she was a "helper" or when she was confused and needed straightening out. Hence she often created disturbances so she could get help from more authoritative people.

As the woman was talking one day, the therapist received an image of a campfire burning cozily; the woman came and fanned it to greater intensity with a bellows, then fed it more wood and fanned it some more until it was a raging bonfire, nearly leaping its bounds into the surrounding forest. She ventured to tell her client about the image and asked, "Does this mean anything to you?"

"Yes," the woman said thoughtfully. "That feels exactly like what I'm doing by obsessing about having a man in my life. I'm creating a potential problem out of something that could simply give me light and warmth. Maybe the campfire is my own creativity and I'm not letting myself enjoy it." The client came to her own conclusions —that by fanning the flames she was not accomplishing anything useful—just creating more potentially distracting dramas for herself. By fully experiencing her own peaceful, inner creative fire, she would become the kind of person she wanted to be and attract the right kind of partner. The therapist saw that by being willing to share her image without forcing a meaning, the client's intuition allowed her to find her own useful interpretation.

March 27

I've always thought that the state of mind we're in when we take the first step of a journey will somehow be lived out in the rest of the journey, that the way a new process begins will be symbolic of its outcome. If I'm preoccupied and start things in a hurry, without clear intentionality, the results I get are similarly haphazard, and the process itself is often fraught with indecision and various snags. For this reason, I always write in my journal on New Year's Day and my birthday every year, and I visualize the results I want to accomplish and the kind of experience I want to have before I leave on a business trip or vacation. I practice dedicating myself before I see every client and before I write each paragraph. There are an infinite number of beginnings every day.

How do you enter into a conversation? Or a new room in a house or office? How do you respond to incoming opportunities or to meeting new people? What thoughts are in your mind as you take each first step? And what was your first thought this morning as you awoke? Did you immediately start making your to-do list? Did you recall your dreams? Did you greet the dawn gratefully or were you resentful of your alarm clock? Did you smile?

Someone gave me this affirmation: "The goal is God. I start my day by taking my first thought of God within my own form." This is powerful. So are the words of St. Patrick's ancient and beautiful prayer: "I arise today through the strength of heaven: light of sun, radiance of moon, splendor of fire, speed of lightning, swiftness of wind, depth of sea, stability of earth, firmness of rock. . . . I arise today through a mighty strength, the invocation of the trinity, through belief in the threeness, through confession of the oneness, of the Creator of Creation."

I begin things consciously.

Notice the first thought of the day, and the way you enter new experiences.

The light in me sees and knows the light in you.

Make eye contact with everyone you meet today. Look for the soul inside each person; you'll find something you can relate to in everyone.

When I first studied meditation and the development of clairvoyant abilities, my teacher gave us an assignment. We were to look for the soul in each person we met and see the light in their eyes, the real essence of the person inside the personality. Silently, in our own mind, we were to say, "The light in me sees and knows the light in you." As I went about my errands and my daily life as a corporate art director, this practice began to peel away the outer layers of what insulated me from others. I sank into life having more direct contact with the one energy that seeps up and radiates out through everyone and everything. Instead of being upset when an executive at the office changed his mind in the middle of a project, I looked in his eyes and found the light. OK, I thought, there must be a good reason for his new request—why don't I just support him? This helped me enjoy my work more than I ever had before.

It's easy to look into a baby's eyes and maintain eye contact joyfully, indefinitely, without the slightest bit of discomfort. But as we become adults, eye contact takes on more serious consequences. The intimacy it engenders seems to require a response—we think someone wants something from us when we are addressed so directly. Either we protect our personal space and shoo the intruder out, or we shift a simple intimate connection to a sexual one, or we feel compelled to avert our eyes, break the connection, retreat, or start talking. How does eye contact make you respond?

You might try this. Soften the muscles around your eyes and in your brows and cheeks. Allow your face to settle into a pleasant, open, rounded, neutral composure, like a curious baby's. Then make eye contact with someone. Don't act ingratiating or engaging. Don't try to penetrate into their eyes, just let their light slowly flow into you through your own open windows. Let yourself receive impressions about who they are. Let your light flow out. Don't worry about what they're seeing, just notice what you're feeling. Let the souls say hello. How do you like this person now?

March 29

Jonathan Driscoll, who lives in New Mexico, wrote this song of praise.

I.
To the East
dark, graceful mesa shoulders
just beginning to show from a blanket of starry blue
slowly brighten into soft oranges and yellows
shadow patterns of rimrock and piñon
interlaced with light
shift and slip away like an opening kimono
soft red brown Jurassic land body
turning, awakening, revealing

II.
Low and to the South
morning star watches
whispering
this love
this gift
this mystery

III.
High and to the North
Truces Peak, proud standing protector of all
breathing in the big empty morning
sits silently
a single cloud dragon
sky dancing, circles above
with mantra, prayers, and respect
greet the great awakening!
praise to the diamond body of light
that burns away all darkness
in the heart!

IV.
And Out West
out here on the old western plateau
of eternal enlightenment
filled with cholla, tumbleweed, and sage
the horse Cheyenne takes to singin' too
when he sees me comin'

I give thanks to the four directions today.

In many cultures, the four directions represent archetypal, foundational qualities of life. Take time today to face the east, south, west, and north, and receive the particular energy and message from each source.

I don't need to be so loud and busy.

Simplify your life today by being quieter than usual.

I love the way my friends have their own quirky interests and share their discoveries with me. This way I get to digest many incisive and artistic observations about topics I wouldn't think to be interested in but that I warm to instantly because of my friends' contagious passions. It's like one soul with a network of interconnected brains, relaying perceptions not only vertically, but horizontally as well. One of my friends writes to me of his love of Abraham Lincoln. And yes, I'd been drawn to something in Honest Abe, some deep quality that inspires profound respect—but I'd never thought to read extensively about his life.

My friend sends this quote from Carl Sandburg's *Abraham Lincoln*."Often Abe worked alone in the timbers, daylong with only the sound of his own ax, or his own voice speaking to himself, or the cracking and swaying of branches in the wind, or the cries and whirrs of animals, of brown and silver-gray squirrels, of partridges, hawks, crows, turkeys, grouse, sparrows, and the occasional wildcat. In the wilderness he companioned loneliness with trees, with the faces of the open sky and weather in changing seasons, with that individual one-man instrument, the ax. Silence found him for her own. In the making of him, the element of silence was immense."

On occasions I have hired clients to transcribe my lectures. One woman I worked with seemed especially enthusiastic about the material. However, though there was no deadline to meet, she kept stalling. I'd call to see how the project was progressing and she'd apologize profusely for neglecting it. I'd ask if she really wanted to do it and she'd say, "Yes, yes." Finally, when my patience wore out, I confronted her. I told her I didn't understand what the problem was—why was it taking so long? If she made an agreement with me, I wanted her to keep it or be honest about not wanting to do the work so I could find someone else. She told me then that she felt a bit afraid of me, that she thought I was strong and might criticize her or make her feel like a failure, and that she had been scared to be honest with me. I was surprised because responding to people harshly is not natural to me. As we talked, it became evident that she had misinterpreted my morality and penchant for clear definition as dominance. Our work arrangement was really so she could reexperience wounds from her dominating mother in a safe context so she could heal them.

In another situation, a woman house-sat for me for several months. She damaged my home and didn't pay me the rent she owed. After months of asking her to make amends and getting only sob stories and the cold shoulder, I took her to small-claims court. She didn't show up and I won. But even that didn't convince her to pay me. She was intimidated and ashamed that I had confronted her. The situation became draining, and I wondered why I kept banging my head on this brick wall of a person. When I asked what to do, my inner voice said, "Keep on!" So I told her that I had made a commitment to her to not give up on this, and I would keep calling until my last day on earth if that's what it took. I realized after those words popped out of my mouth that I was embodying commitment for her, something she was afraid to do herself.

None of us likes being cast as the bad guy, but if we can play our role with patience, integrity, and kindness, the other person often has a chance to heal.

By doing what comes naturally, I trust that I provide guidance to others from a higher source.

Sometimes we unknowingly act as teachers to others. What opportunities or insights is the collective consciousness trying to give to others through you today?

April

April 1

Two men, both seriously ill, shared a hospital room. One was allowed to sit up for an hour each afternoon to help drain the fluid from his lungs. The other had to spend all his time flat on his back. The men talked endlessly about their wives and families, their homes, jobs, involvement in the military, and where they'd been on vacation. Every afternoon when the man next to the wall could sit up, he'd describe the things he saw outside the window. The other man lived for those one-hour periods when his life would be broadened by the activity and color of the world outside. He could visualize just how their room overlooked a park with a lovely lake and how ducks and swans played on the water while children sailed their model boats. He could almost see the young lovers walking arm-in-arm amid flowers, while grand old trees provided shade. In the distance he could imagine the fine view of the city skyline. One warm afternoon the man by the window described a parade passing by. Although the other man couldn't hear the band, he could see it in his mind's eye.

Weeks passed. One morning the nurse arrived to find that the man by the wall had died peacefully in his sleep. She called the hospital attendants to take the body away. The other man soon asked if he could be moved to the other bed. The nurse was happy to make the switch and, after making sure he was comfortable, left him alone. Slowly, painfully, he propped himself up on one elbow to take his first look at the world outside. Finally, he would have the joy of seeing it for himself. He strained to turn and look out the window. But all he saw was a blank wall.

The man asked the nurse what could have compelled his roommate to describe such wonderful things outside an imaginary window. She told him that, in fact, the man had been blind and couldn't even see the wall. She said, "Maybe he wanted to encourage you. Maybe he just loved beauty."

I walk in beauty, I see beauty, I become beauty.

Notice beauty all day today.

April 2

I notice what's just below the surface of reality.

Today, pay attention to subliminal messages. What are your houseplants saying? What is the underlying tone of the day? What's behind the look on a friend's face or beneath her words? When you sense a discrepancy between the superficial and the deep, your intuition is telling you to pay close attention.

A friend recently told me of a popular metaphysical teacher whose seminars were always full. One day a minister came to him and said, "I wish I knew how you get so many people to come to you and pay your prices. People come to my church, but when it's time to pass the collection plate, they all seem to go to sleep and hardly anyone donates."

"Well, maybe I shouldn't tell you this, but here's what you do. You get yourself a big hall, and you fill it full of chairs and big plants. You rent some giant speakers and put them on either side of the audience, and you run an ultra-low rumbling tone alternatingly back and forth between the speakers. It has to be so low that people can hardly hear it. Then you dim the lights, and you speak very softly through the microphone so the people have to strain a bit to hear you. You'll get your donations."

Some months later, the seminar leader received a paper asking if he would cosign for a set of huge audio speakers for the minister. He politely declined. In a year, he ran into the reverend, who exclaimed, "You were absolutely right. I have you to thank! What you told me to do really worked—and now I have *three* churches and plenty of money flowing in!" The moral of this story: Be aware of what you can just barely hear, of what's implied, and of what lulls you into complacency. There may be an ulterior motive.

April 3

Marcus has had an adventurous life. He listened to his "little voice" at key times and always had the courage to act on what it told him. Each time his inner voice piped up, it was to give him direction about where to go and what interests to pursue. His inner voice first made itself known to him as a teenager during World War II when it told him to leave his family, ride his bicycle across the East German border at night, and make his way to Canada! He worked as a scenic carpenter in Canada until his little voice told him to carve sculptures out of wood and showed him what shapes to make. Then it told him to open an art gallery, which became quite successful. He was then directed to travel throughout Asia and to live in Japan for a while, where he became acquainted with Buddhism and other Eastern spiritual philosophies. Next, his inner voice told him to return to Canada and study psychology. And as he completed his university studies and developed a thriving practice, his voice once again chimed in, commanding him, "Go to California!"

Today, Marcus uses his intuition actively in his work as a therapist and spiritual counselor. As he looks back over the often-radical things he chose to do, he can see a logical development. Though his intuitions didn't always make sense and often involved dramatic change, Marcus was willing to trust his inner self. He says, "Actually, it wasn't that hard—I felt that I couldn't NOT do these things— they were the most obvious, most imperative actions to take. The next thing always seemed like the right thing, and it would have been more uncomfortable to stay in the old reality I'd been living."

My inner voice guides me.

Listen carefully to your little voice today. It speaks to you of the right moves, of your soul's passion, and it never uses the word should.

April 4

**The power is
in the present
moment.**

*How do you fill
your moments
and use your
time? You can
either maintain a
positive attitude
and be fully
involved or com-
plain and be dis-
tracted. Don't
judge yourself
today; just watch
your natural
tendencies.*

Serena had a childhood that she suspects was full of sexual abuse and events she would prefer not to remember. She does remember vaguely that she "clouded over" at age nine and became very shy, in fear of attracting the wrong kind of attention. As an adult, she has a memory block and has been unable to gain access to the experiences, positive or negative, from her first nine years.

Last year she began an inner journey with the help of a spiritually oriented counselor. She meditated each day and met with the counselor to report the images that surfaced during her weekly inner explorations. Together they delved into deeper meanings and processed the insights. During one meditation, Serena went into a library. As she looked around, she noticed some books lying underneath the tables. She brought them into the light. There were nine of them, one for each of her missing years. As she contemplated opening them, she was afraid of what she might find. Instead she turned to a man who seemed to be a guide or companion to her in the vision, and she asked him to read the books and tell her what he found.

He read through them, then looked at her. "These are beautiful," he said. Serena couldn't believe it—surely they must be filled with horrendous events to have made her suppress the memories so strongly. "No," he said, "the records here don't show the events but rather *what you made out of the events.* These books describe how you put your own life together, and what is beautiful is how your spirit intended your life to be and the choices you actually made. You made something good from something fearful. There is nothing ugly in your past."

This was a major turning point for Serena. It helped her understand that her life was not a collection of events in the outside world but rather a collection of attitudes, choices, and actions coming from within her. This released her from her obsession with the past and allowed her to live more fully in the present moment.

April 5

Is there anyone in your life to whom you owe an explanation, an apology, or a heartfelt thank-you? Or is there perhaps someone you have had trouble understanding in the past? Might you open a discussion with that person to discover how you might communicate more successfully in the future? The most difficult communications are the ones you anticipate as being confrontational or negative. You don't want to hurt the other person, and you don't want to create a situation where *you* might be criticized or rejected. Yet, if you are courageous, keep your heart open, and communicate without blame, these tricky conversations can release pent-up energy and free both of you to move on to happier, more productive exchanges.

Shirley had a friend for fifteen years whom she loved dearly yet who never made time for them to do things together. If Shirley wanted to see her friend, she would have to drive an hour to her friend's house, or meet her at her workplace for lunch, or run around town and do errands with her. Whenever she got fed up and stopped calling, her friend immediately phoned and was warm and charming. She started to resent the one-sided nature of their friendship. Finally, Shirley wrote her friend a letter expressing her concerns and asking that they try to improve the situation.

Shirley's friend was upset but acknowledged many of the points in the letter and made more of an effort to see Shirley. Their relationship improved.

However, the friend was unable to maintain her new behavior, and things deteriorated to their previous state. Shirley was disappointed, but, because she had released her resentment in her first communication, she was now able to see her friend clearly and realistically. This was a workaholic with poor time-management skills who was incapable of any greater commitment. She realized that her friend's behavior was not a personal affront but simply her way of life. This allowed Shirley to make the decision to end the friendship. When she delivered the last difficult communication and told her friend that it just wouldn't work for her anymore, Shirley was surprised to find that what she'd thought would be depressing and sad actually brought an increase in her own energy and enthusiasm.

I gain energy from complete communication.

Deliver an undelivered communication today.

April 6

I notice when I hide and what I avoid.

When you pull back, close down, get irritable, or head for your favorite addiction, there's a useful insight lurking nearby. Pay attention to what triggers automatic reactions today, and see what vulnerability lies beneath.

I was happily typing away at the computer when the phone rang. When I answered, a woman's voice said, "You did a life reading for me about ten years ago and it was excellent. Then I had another reading with you, and it wasn't as good as the first one. I just wondered, do you still think you're any good? Do you think maybe now that you've written a book and travel more in your work that maybe you just say the same thing to everybody? I went to a lecture you did last week, and a lot of what you said were things you told me in my reading ten years ago. Do you think you've evolved at all over the years?"

I just stood there with my mouth open then gathered my wits and tried to politely answer her rude comments. Afterward, I felt overwhelmed and shaky. I couldn't concentrate on my work. I tried taking a hot bath and reading a favorite book, but I was still agitated. I thought, "This woman had to have thought specifically of me out of the blue, formulated these negative comments, then found my number and called me expressly to rag on me for five solid minutes. Why?" I really didn't want to feel that people might think I was incompetent, insensitive, or stagnant!

I called a therapist friend and told him the story. He used his intuition to tune in and said, "She was voicing thoughts that you hold unconsciously. You feel that you must provide everyone with a high-quality experience, yet that is not entirely up to you. People find their own value in life. Also, you believe that you must take care of people who are wounded, and if you don't do it effectively and if they aren't happy, you will be rejected. You must be ready to get rid of these limiting ideas once and for all now since this came in such a punctuated way. Some higher part of you probably invited that woman to call and push all your fear buttons!"

I decided that having someone spew out my worst possible self-image to my face was unpleasant but it wasn't worth suppressing the fears any longer. So I booked a therapy session with my friend to start clearing the old beliefs. After that I was much more able to offer my truth freely, without fear of judgment and allow others to make of it what they would.

April 7

A man studied in a seminary for seven years to become a priest. During that time he was sexually harassed by several of his superiors within the priesthood. He finally filed a sexual harassment suit against the church but lost. His boyhood dream and plans for his life had been ruined. Instead of becoming bitter and feeling like a victim of both the church and the legal system, he thought about why he had been the one to experience this and how he could turn it into something positive. He realized he might be able to help prevent other men and women from suffering similar ordeals, and he made the difficult decision to make his case public. It got a fair amount of media attention because sexual harassment against men had previously not been publicized.

Because of this odd turn of events and the seeming misfortune he suffered, the man found his true calling. He dedicated himself to creating a new model of the ministry, one based on honesty, true respect for others, and lack of victimization and self-sacrifice. Sometimes the very thing that seems like a wall or a heavy burden proves to hold the knowledge and new perspective you need for your next steps in life.

I learn from my opponents.

Notice what you disagree with today. What could you learn from that point of view? When you understand both sides of an issue, you'll gain the perspective that lets you choose a higher path.

April 8

**I look beyond
the obvious.**

*There's often a
parallel stream of
activity happen-
ing under
ordinary reality.
Today, look for
this parallel flow,
its inner mean-
ing, and the gifts
staring you right
in the face.*

On a visit to the Arizona desert, I came face-to-face with
the legendary Coyote trickster energy. My friend and I
were working with Native American practices at the time,
and we decided we'd go for a hike in a canyon where a
"doorway between worlds" was supposed to exist.

The trickster began by disorienting us. Though we
knew we needed to refuel the Jeep, a little voice kept
saying, "No, not yet" and "No, not here" as we passed
gas station after gas station. After we drove fifteen miles
down a dirt road, we realized we probably wouldn't make
it back out. So we detoured to a remote, dusty camp-
ground and filled up with ultra-expensive fuel. The whole
gas junket had us going in circles and took us a good
forty miles out of our way.

Then we needed to determine which wash was the
one that had been described to us: "about ten miles to the
right after the big wash, and you'll find the little wash
that leads to the canyon." Using intuition, we stopped
where it seemed right and began our hike. This area of
the desert was marked by petroglyphs and giant geoglyphs
and was known to have caves, sacred springs, and sacred
mountains. As we walked, we chatted about women's
wisdom traditions and how caves and kivas were places
of feminine wisdom. We'd been walking a long time and
hadn't felt anything like a "doorway." It was now very hot
so reluctantly we turned back. We came blithely around
a bend and stopped in our tracks. There ahead was a
humongous hole gaping at us from the side of the canyon
wall. "Would you say that was a cave?" I commented
dryly. "I'd say so," my friend responded. "How did we
pass this on the way in and not see it? It's big enough to
hold a seminar in!" We made our way up into the cave,
which was marvelously echoey and cool and littered with
animal bones. We sat and meditated a good long while
and had another laugh at Coyote's lesson on observation.
"I guess what is revealed to us has its own timetable," my
friend mused. "Yes," I added, "Coyote had to flatten our
minds before we could realize the value and dimension of
these special places."

April 9

When my niece Julia was three, we went for a nature walk along a nearby creek, equipped with Baggies to hold all the goodies we might find and want to bring home. As we trundled along slowly, I pointed out interesting plants and leaves, and she noticed things closer to the ground like anthills, rocks, and animal tracks. We picked up odd pieces of wood, red pebbles, dead beetles, and chunks of broken glass. Then we decided that her mom might like a bouquet of wildflowers and set about to find all the different varieties.

There were big white ones, little daisylike ones, yellow sticky ones, and weeds with purple flowers and lots of leaves. As we stooped down to pick a low-growing dandelion, I said, "Thank you, Mr. Plant." Julia didn't miss a beat. She reached for the next stem and, as she broke it off, she said, "Thank you, Mr. Plant. We love you for letting us have part of yourself."

All forms of life exist to support each other.

Notice how "things" contribute to you, as though they were consciously choosing to help. When you feel the desire to get, have, or take something today, pause and allow the object of your attention to give to you instead. Now, what will you give in return?

April 10

I listen.

When you use your intuition, you can hear through your inner ears. Make decisions today based on your sense of hearing. Does a situation seem screechy, melodious, clangy, whispery, or too loud?

A man called who was interested in working with me by phone. He said that as a musician he wanted to hear the sound of my voice before he decided whether I was the right one. After we spoke for a while, he told me he trusted me from the way I laughed and how long I paused, and from the timbre of my voice, which told him I was centered. I realized then that I, too, make decisions about people and get insights based on their voices. Some people sound as though they're walking on their tiptoes holding their breath; others like they've just run five blocks to catch a bus. Others have a monotone feel, as if their world is flat instead of wavy. Still others are seductive and honeyed with resonant tones, and, though the sound is pleasing, I don't trust them. Some people have little hitches and jerks in their voice like their synapses are misfiring, while some don't pause at all for normal punctuation and crash their sentences together, leaping from point to point with no normal transitions. Others sound like they're talking through a megaphone from a faraway place. In my old lecture tapes, I can hear the times I was inspired and the times I wasn't quite trusting enough in the flow of information. The sound of my own lack of faith is almost painful for me to hear.

If we use our intuition, we can "hear" someone's personality or an event. A woman whose outer personality seems charming and smooth actually sounds like objects crashing out of an overstuffed closet when the door is opened. Underneath, the neighbor whose husband died recently sounds like fingernails screeching across a chalkboard. The powerful entrepreneur actually sounds like a chanted heart sutra. The chance to travel to Dallas sounds like a child giggling; the party Friday night sounds like a train whistle; the opportunity to give a workshop for a group of businessmen sounds like an off-key concert. Sounds are all around in every thought, every color, every form, every act.

April 11

A client today is my teacher. When we first spoke by phone, she tried to convince me to reduce my rate. I said I didn't do that but I could arrange a payment plan. She said no but then called back to book a session. Sitting with me now, I notice her doelike brown eyes full of saintly kindness. She radiates old Catholicism, the path of renunciation, of selfless service. I hear echoes of vows of poverty and silence. I smell dust and incense and am transported to another time, taken in by the spell of her devotion. She says, however, that she wants to break through the limitations of her religion, to update her spirituality for today's world. She says she believes she is a manifestation of God but can't say she *is* God. I tell her she is not an object but a continuous process of "God manifesting," as are all forms, and how could any part of life not be God?

There is a subtle feeling of entrapment here. Her mind glories in being devout yet her heart has induced her to question her reality. She speaks of the power of prayer and faith, yet I hear myself talking about the power of blessing and being in communion instead, because these come from the experience of connectedness, not separation. As the session progresses, it becomes evident that her religion is not integrated into the fiber of her being. She is in her head and wears her piousness, at least in part, as a way to be both accepted and unique. Her religious form lies between her and her experience of the divine instead of connecting her seamlessly to it. These things feel old: sacrificial service, original sin, mindless ceremonies done by rote, renunciation of the flesh, intermediaries between self and God.

As we finish the session, my saintly client informs me that she has come today without any money in faith that I will give her the reading. I say, "This was not what we discussed and agreed to over the phone. I clearly spelled out the terms of our exchange." She says, "I will send you the payment." She leaves and I know it is the last I will hear from her.

There are several valuable lessons here: distinguishing clever control games of the mind, weeding out true spiritual motives and actions from false, understanding the sacred nature of money, forgiving myself and others for our blind spots.

I deserve to be supported.

Say no to what doesn't support your well-being today. When you are clear about your standards, boundaries, and the exchanges you make with others, your vitality will increase.

April 12

I am original.

*Today, let
yourself bend
the rules, take
a chance, rebel,
be inconsistent,
stand out.
Give yourself
to be new-in-
the-now.*

What is so attractive about being a misfit? We Americans glorify our James Deans, Marilyn Monroes, Janis Joplins, Neal Cassadys, our Thelma and Louise outlaws, our rebel geniuses. The American mystique reveres those who burn bright and die young, those who are talented yet wounded or deeply confused. Maybe we all feel like misfits. In a sense, our country is a land of misfits who left their various cultures to make new lives. We champion not fitting in and being stand-out individuals. Fitting in often feels like sacrifice, as though the culture has all the power. Once I acquiesce totally to the tribal mind, it will tell me who I can be and I'll slowly suffocate.

I want to make sure I'm not buying into a myth that keeps me limited, though. I like what medical intuitive Carolyn Myss says about pulling out all the power cords we have plugged into the tribal mind and sourcing ourselves directly from our own divine nature instead of from the culture. She says when we dare to *not* feed the culture in the manner to which it's become accustomed by not automatically buying into society's traditions, it rejects and betrays us. This frees us, but it takes continuing courage to buck the system and not do what's expected.

We misfits have to be careful about getting caught in a mystique based on victimization. Sure, it's challenging at first to express a different vision, an unusual creative turn. We can get so used to rejection and criticism that we begin to glory in it and miss the next phase of the process where suffering is transformed into love. Instead of being victim misfits, we can take the roles of teacher, inspirer, leader, healer. When one person expresses a new view, the tribe reacts to suppress the disruptive force. But when that person speaks inclusively and encouragingly to the others, they get interested. "Do you mean I could do something like this, too? Do you mean I can be free to express and create from my own inner vision?" This is how misfits become shamans and holy people, artists, and builders, modeling a new way for society to evolve in alignment with inner truth and universal laws.

April 13

In his book *Timeshifting*, Dr. Stephan Rechtschaffen says, "Stress stops when you've arrived 'there.' Being present means giving up the low buzz of anxiety about the future we keep anticipating all the time. Being present means taking time to feel feelings like pain, sorrow, and joy, which take longer to experience than does the whiz of our thoughts. When these feelings crop up (and anger and anxiety have a faster rhythm than pain or sadness), we think we need to hurry faster, to catch up, to solve problems more quickly. Actually, the solution is counterintuitive. You need to slow down so you can feel what is going on. This allows you to expand the moment. Even with a deadline, it will feel like you have more time. When are you going to get there? Expand the moment by using your senses, and small events will become awesome."

To expand your sense of the present moment, simply drop your attention out of your to-do list into one of your senses. Try your sense of smell or touch today. Pretend you're an animal, knowing the world directly through your nose, or through the nerve endings on your skin, or through hearing as far into the distance as you can. Your senses connect you directly with your body, which is always in the moment. As you attend to what one of your senses is receiving, your mind will slow down automatically and your intuition will open. Then you can get the truly important and inspired messages.

My body is trying to tell me something important.

What are your body's key concerns and questions today? Take time to attend to your physical and emotional needs so your mind can operate clearly.

The parts of me I criticize contain valuable lessons.

Everything that happens to you contains a lesson, provides an opportunity. Pay attention to the things you criticize yourself for. If you loved each one instead, what gift or insight would it give you?

Wishing to encourage her young son's progress on the piano, a mother took her boy to an Ignacy Paderewski concert. After they were seated, the mother spotted a friend in the audience and walked down the aisle to greet her. Taking the opportunity to explore, the boy wandered through a door marked "No Admittance." The house lights dimmed as the concert was about to begin, and the mother returned to her seat only to discover that her child was missing! Suddenly the curtains parted and spotlights focused on the impressive Steinway on stage. In horror, the mother saw her little boy sitting at the keyboard innocently picking out "Twinkle, Twinkle, Little Star."

At that moment the great piano master strode onstage. He moved quickly to the piano and whispered in the boy's ear, "Don't quit. Please keep playing." Then, leaning forward, Paderewski reached down with his left hand and began filling in a bass part. Soon his right arm reached around to the other side of the child and he added a running obbligato. The audience sat mesmerized as the old master and the young novice together transformed a potentially awkward and frightening situation into an experience of sweetness, wonder, and beauty.

April 15

Marlane Miller, author of *BrainStyles: Change Your Life Without Changing Who You Are,* tells of an artist she knows who is at last fulfilling her dream to have her work featured in a major art gallery in Dallas. She would have been happy to be part of a group exhibition, but her dream came true in a bigger-than-life way when the gallery gave her a one-woman show, complete with a full-color brochure and a banner outside. She is now exhibiting twenty-seven luminous oil paintings of great intensity, skill, and extraordinary depth. Nearly all of them have sold.

Last fall, the artist discovered she had cancer, so horrific and widespread that, when she called to tell Marlane, she didn't know if she would live through the surgery scheduled for the end of that week. She not only survived the surgery, she continued painting through the strongest form of chemotherapy the doctors could administer.

Now she sits smiling and radiant in her wig at her long-awaited show. She cheerfully explains her work, entertains people, graciously offers refreshments, and never once flags in energy or attention. Marlane says, "She has the gift of life and spirit strengthened by seeing the face of Death. She laughs at herself for how 'upside down' it all is—achieving success and terminal illness at the same time. I think she has it just right. She let go of any restraints in being herself, her own artist, and got everything she ever wanted. She can stare head-on into life because of her clear purpose for being here: the expression of her talent. You see her inner character not only in her paintings but also in the way she chooses to live. She inspires everyone to live fully by expressing their own gifts, no matter the circumstances."

The world sees the good in me.

Feel good about yourself today no matter what you do. Live undefended and assume people will like you. When you come from a state of cheerful relaxation, you'll optimize everything you do.

**I notice when
I shut down.**

*What makes
your mind turn
off? What makes
you leave your
body temporarily?
List the times
you close the flow
of consciousness
today and what
triggers each
response.*

It worries me that so many of our young people seem so disassociated from each other, their families, their bodies, their deep feelings, and their inner, spiritual selves. Dr. Margaret Paul, who wrote *Do I Have to Give Up Me to Be Loved by You?* and *Do I Have to Give Up Me to Be Loved by God?*, wrote this about the troubling increase in violence by children today.

"Many child development experts state that people who disconnect from empathy and compassion generally do so between the ages of two and four. If our parents lacked empathy and compassion for our feelings and needs, we might choose to be caretakers and take care of other people's needs, or we might choose to become like them and not care about others at all. If our parents shut themselves down to our pain and their own, we may have learned to shut down to our own and others' vulnerable feelings. If, in addition, we were physically, sexually, emotionally, or verbally abused, we may have shut down just to survive.

"Some children manage to stay connected with their core self through contact with animals such as dogs or horses, or through contact with relatives or friends with whom they identify. But many young children just disconnect to survive. When in this disconnected state, if they watch violence on TV or practice violence through video games, they may further train themselves to numb out against compassion, empathy, and the pain of harming others. Likewise, if children grow up with no personal connection to their spiritual guidance, they may not know that we are all one, and without connection with their core Self and their spiritual guidance, they are left with only their wounded selves. If they happen to be operating from an enraged wounded self, this self can certainly act out in violent ways. This violence will not stop until we no longer need to learn, as very young children, to barricade our hearts. The change in our society must come from within each of us."

April 17

Everywhere we look there is someone or something that could use some attention and help. The plants in the office would love to be repotted into bigger containers; Karen, who is moving, could use some help packing; another friend would like me to read and comment on an essay he's written. Perhaps you're so busy you think you hardly have enough time to meet your own needs and those of your children, let alone feed your neighbor's dog while she's out of town. But somehow when we're helping others, more gets done naturally.

This true story came from a woman who worked many years ago as a volunteer at Stanford Hospital. She got to know a little girl there who was suffering from a serious disease. Her only chance of recovery appeared to be a blood transfusion from her five-year-old brother who had miraculously survived the same disease and had developed the antibodies needed to combat the illness. The doctor explained the situation to her little brother and asked the boy if he would be willing to give his blood to his sister. The little boy hesitated for only a moment before taking a deep breath and saying, "Yes, I'll do it if it will save her." As the transfusion progressed, he lay in the bed next to his sister. He looked up at the doctor and asked with a trembling voice, "Will I start to die right away?" Being so young, the boy had misunderstood; he thought he was going to give his sister all his blood.

I remember hearing a man on a radio talk show tell about how when he was a boy the old man who lived next door had a stroke and was taken to the hospital for an extended stay. During that time, his mother insisted they cut the man's lawn, tend his garden, and keep his birdbath and feeders full, in addition to doing their own work. It seemed there was extra work to do over there every afternoon, and he didn't see why they had to. But his mother was adamant, and the two of them kept at it, doing it well and lovingly. The boy began to feel good about himself, and his enthusiasm for life grew. When the old man came home, the joy on his face was palpable, and the boy learned one of the most powerful lessons of his life—that helping others actually produces more energy.

I contribute positively to others.

Take the lead today. Let yourself be a good influence in other people's lives. Notice how you feel when you choose to keep your heart open.

April 18

The heart of the Mother nurtures me.

Our bodies draw energy from the earth—up through our feet and tailbone— to help us survive physically. Today, be aware of the sustenance generated in the center of the earth as it flows into you.

Barbara Hand Clow, astrologer, author, and publisher, gave a talk on opening the heart. After the lecture, Barbara guided the audience in a meditation. The purpose of the meditation was to align our hearts with the heart of the planet. The imagery that came to me was so vivid and powerful that I still remember it. We began by imagining that we were descending slowly through the outer layers of the earth—down through the crust, through the magma, and into the iron crystal core of the planet. As we settled our awareness inside this crystal center, our vision cleared and we found ourselves standing inside a primeval forest full of all the trees, vines, plants, flowers, and animals that have existed throughout history. She suggested that this was the archetypal garden of Eden.

I stood in a clearing in my garden of Eden surrounded by the massive trunks of towering trees, feasting my eyes on the multitude of spearlike, or frilly, or heart-shaped tropical leaves, the colors radiant and glistening. Animals peeked from behind enormous bushes with bulbous hanging fruits, and birds sat close. Dangerous animals such as prehistoric tigers, wild boars, and bears came up to nuzzle me, and all the flora and fauna were much larger than in real life, like giant versions of themselves that might be found in an imaginative children's book.

I felt I was "home" and became happier and happier until I couldn't contain the energy. I could feel how each form of life supported the others in existing, and, as my appreciation grew, I began hugging the animals and talking with the plants. Lush, raucous, sensual, and shy flowers actually made music. The smells were a sublime mix that was the very essence of love. Here, every creature received energy and love perfectly and became the truest manifestation of itself. There was no fear, only life expressing itself abundantly. After my interactions, I looked at myself and I, too, had changed. I was giving off light and a clean high scent, and I was smoother with big relaxed eyes. Since that meditation, I have often dropped down into this imaginary garden of Eden in the heart of the earth to re-center into my ideal form and reconnect with my kinship with all life.

April 19

The founders of Starbucks live in the Seattle area and love sailing. When it came time to name their new coffee company, they researched classic literature to locate a suitable nautical name. The prime candidate after reading Herman Melville's *Moby Dick* was the "Pequod Coffee Shops" in honor of the whaling ship *Pequod* from which Captain Ahab hunted the white whale. When they announced the new name to their startled advertising agency, the agency tactfully offered to make a study of Northwest Indian tribes and find a name that might be a little more comfortable to the American consumer. After thorough research of over 250 tribes, the big day came in the corporate boardroom, and the agency unveiled their chosen tribal name: "Starbo." With that the coffee entrepreneurs turned to one another and said: "Yes! *Starbucks!*"—the first mate on the ship *Pequod*.

When you become aware of a real question inside you, assume that the answer wants to make itself known. One of the laws of intuition is that *the question and answer always exist together and arise in the same moment*. For each question, there is one answer that is perfect for your present circumstances. Relax and know that the answer is trying to find you—that's why it planted the question in your awareness! When listening for the answer, listen deeply; each creature, each sound aims you in the right direction, reveals the answer symbolically in its own way. Let the voices build until your own inner voice proclaims the truth. You know! Everything knows what wants to happen next.

Life delivers one message at a time with many different voices.

Listen to the sounds of animals, birds, wind, and people today. What singular message do you hear?

The tiniest things in life are often the most powerful.

Pay attention today to little things. Take time to notice the behavior of an insect or each detail of a task you're performing. Even a pinhole in a piece of paper can reveal a broad view.

Carl is a computer software designer who told me the story of a cockroach that crawled into one of the first big computers and wreaked havoc with its functioning, hence the common computer term "bug." When Carl is designing a piece of software, he pays special attention to bugs—the kind that can freeze up his program and the physical kind.

"Sometimes," he says, "I'll be typing away and look down and see an ant crawling on my hand. Or I'll notice when a fly lands on my monitor. I don't discount it; I take it as a sign that I may be making a mistake in what I'm doing. I immediately stop and go back over everything to double-check for internal bugs. So far, every time an insect has shown up unexpectedly, I've found something I missed."

This reminds me of how Don Juan told Carlos Castañeda that the common gnat was really an ally, a being that existed in a higher dimension that could help mankind when called on. In this reality it looked helpless and tiny, but in the higher dimension it was a gigantic, monstrous-looking creature. I used to smash gnats when they flew around my eyes but now I hesitate. Instead, I remember that the little gnat expands through the dimensions, leading me to a huge ally, as though its pinprick-like body were a tiny doorway. Now I ask gnats for help.

April 21

Often we have a tendency to judge things by how long
they last. Relationships, furniture, clothing—even
people—as if time were the measurement standard of
beauty and goodness.

Erika was in Wisconsin visiting her best friend, and
while they were driving through the rural countryside,
where cows outnumbered people, they came upon a small
town in which there was a tiny Buddhist temple. Struck
by the anomaly, they stopped. They quietly explored the
grounds and poked their heads inside the temple door.
There, in a ray of filtered afternoon light, sat a Tibetan
monk chanting over an exquisite, finely detailed, brightly
colored sand mandala he had spent the past four months
constructing.

Erika says, "He welcomed us warmly and told us we
were just in time—he was about to disassemble the precious mandala. My friend and I looked at him in horror.
'What do you mean, *disassemble*?!' we nearly screeched.
'After building it one grain at a time for the past four
months? You're going to *ruin* it!' He patiently explained to
us the spiritual significance behind the mandala and how
we must understand the temporary nature of all things so
we might truly recognize the beauty of each moment.

"It was still difficult to watch him sweep the colored
grains together into a pile of dirty-looking sand. We
almost wept. But then we went outside with him and
watched in awe as he poured the sand into the river, sending positive energy back to the world. I felt like he taught
us a precious lesson that day, and I vowed to take that
timeless quality and the awareness of the value and beauty
of each fleeting moment with me back to my chaotic
world in New York City."

**There is
beauty in the
temporary.**

*Let yourself
experience awe
and wonder
today, in each
fleeting moment.*

**I welcome the
unknown.**

*Notice what
surprises you,
what you're
forced to let go of,
or what causes
you to stretch
out for a new
understanding.
The unknown
is really just
the bigger you
beckoning.*

I have left my wallet at a pay phone and now it is gone along with my official identity. Two weeks ago I went through an airport security scanner and erased the data on an important floppy disk in my purse. Why do I trip myself up like this? I become quiet and feel down deeply into what is going on inside me. There is an "I" in here who knows what she's doing, who is trying to wake up the semihypnotized daily me to educate me, shift my purpose or direction, give me a reward perhaps. As I fall into this deeper self, I realize how much I've been skimming across the surface of life, what a tiny percentage of my perception I've been using—and how bored I actually am. How important was my official identity? Who am I when I'm not being *her*? How important was that data anyway? Information comes and goes and comes and goes. I'm more than my information. What's truly important? What do I long for?

My longing is for a kind of forgetfulness and memory that occurs at the same time, that I release myself into fully and faithfully, like falling into a cloud. It is a desire for unity, the "home" experience, total connection, that warm pool that saturates into me as I sink into it, until there's no more me, or everything is me, and there's no contrast left. It's right here; I don't have to go anywhere to get it. I can always fall into this pool. So my longing is for the fullest experience of falling into what I have right now. It's not to achieve a future goal but for a loss of separation.

These small, so-called losses lead me into the unknown, and the unknown is only the first glimpse of a new known.

April 23

Fran, a successful businesswoman who meditates and exercises regularly, recently had a bout with irritable bowel syndrome. Since she takes such good care of herself, she was surprised that her body would contract in such an unruly and painful manner. Obviously she needed to pay attention to something she was overlooking. She saw her illness as her body's attempt to get a message through to her conscious mind. But what was the message?

She meditated one morning and brought her attention into the area of her colon. As she merged with that part of her body, she could feel a subtle turbulence and got the image of a sourdough starter fermenting and producing its leavening gases. She addressed her colon directly. "What are you trying to tell me?" she asked. "What is causing you such distress?"

Her colon, in spite of its disturbed condition, said, "First, you are giving too much of your energy away to your clients and friends. When you try to save them, your energy drains from my area of this body. I feel weakened. Also, you are taking on other people's emotional problems, and the energy from those problems is also stored and processed in this part of your body. I have too many energies to sort out and I feel overwhelmed. I'm having trouble doing my job." Then, as she paid closer attention, she became aware of the taste of sugar and fat. She recalled that she had eaten a danish pastry and coffee for breakfast every single workday for the past fourteen years! She asked, "What would you like to eat?" Immediately, two words came strongly into her mind: pineapple and papaya.

So, armed with this information, Fran worked on her codependent behaviors and changed her diet. She started to eat fresh fruit and bran in the morning and learned to let her friends and clients solve their own problems. Within weeks, her health improved dramatically. In fact, she never had the problem again.

My body knows what and how much fuel it needs.

Let your body decide what, when, and how much to eat today. The voice of your body is the voice of your intuition.

April 24

I am aware of what's before me, behind me, above me, and below me.

As you walk, stand, and sit today, keep your attention focused throughout the space around you. Be attuned to the sensations of the bird above your head, the person passing on the sidewalk, the objects behind you. Practice using your body's 360-degree awareness.

Pretend you are a great samurai or a deer in the forest, alert to every noise and movement. Every part of your body is aware. Your feet are a kind of brain, your back is a nerve center. What do you know about what goes on around you?

THE WARRIOR'S WALK

You can begin anywhere—inside or outside. Stand and become alert yet relaxed. Don't fix your attention on anything. Notice everything around you in a full circle. When you feel the current flow into you, let yourself begin to move. Let your body experience the natural shape of the surroundings using all your senses. Do not describe your experience to yourself. As you pass by the protruding corner of a hallway and change directions, notice the different impressions the old and new spaces make on you. Feel the impact of the sharp line of the corner coming toward you.

As you walk notice what your back is aware of. Can you feel an object behind you when it's ten feet away, five feet away, one foot away? Can you feel when someone is looking at you? Let yourself feel simultaneous attraction toward and repulsion from objects and directions. Where does the movement itself want to go? If you're walking down a busy street, notice how your body responds to people passing by, to mailboxes, lampposts, storefronts. What is the top of your head aware of? Can you feel the pressure or temperature of the light? What is down in the earth under your feet?

April 25

One of the laws of intuition is *you know just what you need to know, just when you need to know it*. The universe doesn't waste energy. From many years of working with intuition, I have learned to let go of planning too far ahead, or hoarding information, or trying to memorize data. I assume that if I need a piece of information, it's stored somewhere in my inner library and will be taken off the shelf, brought forward to be shared, then put back on the shelf again by my mysterious inner librarian.

I also realize how much energy and time we waste asking unnecessary questions that don't provide useful answers, to which we don't really want a truthful answer, or that we forgot the purpose of asking. "Oh, what's wrong with me?" "How are you today?" "Are you serious?" "What do *you* think?" Try committing to act on every answer you get or to use each answer to consciously propel you to another thought or question. What is the purpose of each question?

Remember, too, that your body always speaks the truth and will give you reliable answers. One of Marilyn Mackey's students in Dallas was worried about a multiple-choice test for which he hadn't studied enough. She told him that when he had doubts to simply read the question carefully and feel it, then put his thumb over each potential answer—a, b, c, d, e—and place his other hand over his navel. Over one of those options his body would give him a signal, and he should choose that answer. So, when test time came, he placed his thumb carefully over each choice and went systematically down the page, circling the answers that his body responded to. Occasionally he knew the answer on his own. When the test results came back, he was astounded. He had gotten an A-minus. When he shared this with Marilyn later, she asked how many he had missed. "Four," he answered, "and they were the ones I thought I knew."

I know just what I need to know.

Ask only the questions you need answers for today— and only the ones you intend to take action on.

April 26

I am collected.

Keep your energy field, or aura, drawn close to you today.

When you first meet someone, do they seem "up front," "laid back," oblique, straightforward, "beside themselves," or "above you"? It's not your imagination—you're actually perceiving the other person's energy field. You can tell quite a bit about other people by learning to sense where they carry their energy and awareness. Some people send their energy out ahead of them as an early warning system to protect themselves or gather subtle data about upcoming interactions. Others keep most of their energy behind them, protecting their back, hesitating to enter new situations, and often come across as shy. Some people occupy the top part of their body and can seem heady, excited, verbal, and electric, while others occupy the bottom part of their body and seem seductive, sexual, silent, earthy, and magnetic. How do you fill out your aura?

In my workshops, participants practice rounding out their energy fields by placing equal attention in front and back, to the left and right sides, above the waist and below. Then we practice expanding and contracting the energy fields until we find the most comfortable radius for operating in everyday life. Most people find a distance of five to ten feet around their body to be normal and comfortable.

Try this experiment. Even out your energy field as described above. Then contract the field in toward your body, slowly, in increments: from ten feet to six feet, to four feet, down to three, then to two, and finally to one foot out around your skin. You'll probably notice that as you pull in your energy field, you'll feel more focused and able to concentrate. You'll feel your physical energy more clearly and have a stronger sense of your personal self. In fact, you may feel more selfish or cut off from others. Know that anything you are feeling is valid.

The closer you hold your energy to your body, the clearer your personal boundaries and uniqueness will be. You may also feel slightly more quiet and invisible. It might seem that if you walked down the street this way, no one would notice you. As you practice this today, make a note of how it works and how you feel in different situations.

April 27

Just as you experimented with holding your energy field close to you yesterday, try the opposite today. First, even and round out your energy by placing equal attention in the front and back of your body, to the left and right sides, above the waist and below. Next, feel your normal radius of energy—how big you are typically comfortable being. Then expand the field slowly in increments: from five feet to seven feet, to ten, then outward to twelve and fifteen feet. Keep including more inside your sphere of awareness. Twenty feet. Twenty-five feet. Thirty? Fifty? Where does it get too difficult to maintain your focus?

As you feel this great expansion of energy, imagine filling the entire field with sparkling light; everything within your aura is alive, alert, and aware. You may notice that as you become used to taking up more space and feeling larger, you also have an increased sensation of openness and generosity. You can share easily, are more ready to laugh, and are more aware of your interconnectedness with things. You may lose some sense of your personal boundaries and not be as aware of your individual identity and the mechanics of your physical body.

The larger you allow your energy field to be, the more impersonal and universal you will feel. Let other people walk right through your aura; let them be affected by you. You are a healing space. Your energy is a force for good in the world. As you walk down the street in this expanded state, more people may notice you, feel comfortable with you, and make overtures toward you, or you toward them. As you experiment with this today, make a note of what works better for you and how you feel in different situations.

I am expansive.

Keep your energy field, or aura, expanded widely and evenly around you today.

I let go of my controlling actions.

When we enter the present moment, we learn that it's far more pleasurable to interrelate with the spontaneous process of life than to waste energy trying to control it. Today, practice surrendering; try creating a ritual to release a controlling thought pattern.

Ron from Tennessee writes, "Several weeks ago, I found myself unable to enjoy the passage of time. I had a substantial break in my schedule, and there were many projects I wanted to finish. As I set out to accomplish my tasks, I found that I became fixated on the duration of my break, which seemed shorter and shorter every time I thought about it because I had so many things to do. I was totally concerned about the passing of time. I felt like time was simply flying by without allowing me to imbibe in life. During these weeks, my young son told me that I was frequently too stern with him. It dawned on me that I was upset with him because I was trying to be in control.

"When I quieted my mind, I saw this was the same problem I was having with my frustrating perception of time. I was struggling because I was attempting to be in control of time instead of being part of the flow of time. The first was a combative approach and the latter was an acknowledgment of the partnership we have with time. Once I recognized my subconscious, covert efforts to control life, I immediately relaxed. I saw a remarkable improvement in both my relationship with my son and with my day. Then I noticed how I slowed down when I was watering the flowers. I heard my inner voice say, 'Flowers will never bloom if we don't take the time to water them. Flowers aren't in a hurry to bloom; they don't comprehend the idea of speed and results.' I could feel that I was blooming, and my life was blooming in a way, too. Control is the antithesis of flow. Inner peace and personal accomplishments only exist in the natural flow of life."

April 29

I heard that the chairman of the board of Sony Corporation had an unusual, highly intuitive way of making important decisions. He pretended the potential solution to a problem was a piece of food and tried to eat it. If it had a pleasant taste or left him feeling satisfied, he took it as a sign of truth. But if the solution stuck in his throat, was hard to swallow, left a bad taste in his mouth, sat like a rock in his stomach, or gave him a feeling of indigestion, it was definitely not the answer. Your body can gauge any idea in terms of the senses, and you have your own internal value system concerning each sense. For you, watermelon might rate a ten, while I might rate steamed spinach right off the scale.

Some people are more taste oriented than others. Have you ever said, "How sweet it is!" "I want that so much I can taste it!" or "I just can't swallow that . . ."? I have a friend who loves to eat and passionately refers to certain people and new ideas as "yummy" and "delicious." Try imagining things you want as kinds of food or as having certain flavors. If your dream house were a piece of food, what would it taste like? What flavor would new job possibility number one be as opposed to new job possibility number two?

A man in one of my lectures got an orange for the first possible solution to his problem and a medium-rare steak for the second. Since he liked both foods, I asked him to describe the subtle feelings the orange and steak aroused in him. The orange felt fresh and perky, and the steak felt robust and earthy. Concerning his problem, he realized he'd rather take a fresh approach, so he went with the first solution.

I know the world though my sense of taste.

You can use any of the five senses to receive useful information about people and situations. Make decisions today by applying your sense of taste. Do situations seem sweet, sour, bitter, tangy, rancid, or spicy?

I am full, then empty, then full again.

It's natural to experience an oscillation between the action and gestation phases of the creative process. Be aware of these shifts today: when you are prompted to focus and when you need to soften that focus so you can access the next thing.

As I write this book, each day I pay attention to the feeling of what I want to do, how I want to do it, and the tone I want to convey. I look through my awareness for stories, ideas, the thought that floats near the front of my mind or the one that is just emerging from below. My concentration builds and one idea flows into the next, the serendipity of sequences entertaining me, the sound of words and the rhythm of sentences resonating like music. I write with no background noise most days. Time slides by quickly. I hear the hourly chiming of my clock and think only twenty minutes have passed between chimes. And then, for no apparent reason, sometimes midsentence, my body stands up! My mind has gone completely blank and has refilled with the image of watering the tomato plants outside, or the sensation of standing in the sun and a brisk afternoon breeze, or the craving for an English muffin and peanut butter. My body is already on the way there as the thought registers. Sometimes, I just find myself walking into my library with a sense that there is a book somewhere that has a quote or poem I want, and I spend half an hour browsing.

I let myself have these sudden turns. I let myself mop the floor between April 10th's story and April 11th's and the warm water and lemon scent of soap invigorate me. I give myself a cup of Earl Grey tea between April 28th and April 29th because the taste of bergamot makes me happy. Then, when I am drawn back to the computer and the magic of watching characters appear on the monitor, I am innocent again. The newness of any arising desire focuses and motivates me, makes me experience aliveness. When I honor the arisings, I see that the One inside me who plants these desires is creative, productive, and joyful. Given her way, this One inside is never lazy nor a procrastinator but is always in tune with the nuances of the creative cycle. I like how she moves me.

May

May 1

I am distracted, running errands, waiting in lines, having too little time, then too much. I've stopped at a bookstore to have a cup of coffee while I waste an hour before my next appointment. As I write in my journal, it occurs to me to notice the vibration of my body. Usually my body's natural tone is warm, steady, and smooth. But today it feels gritty and revved up like a buzz saw. "What is it?" I ask my inner self. "Is this too much willpower? Is it fear?" My inner voice explains, "No. It's an energy wave of a higher-than-normal frequency and a new activating quality passing through." I feel like a helicopter rotor winding up as though I might soon lift out of my normal reality. This is not comfortable. In fact it's so disturbing at a cellular level that I've been trying to avoid it, yearning to be home taking a bath or nap. Yet I've been riding its jagged edge, having a raggedy rhythm to my day.

Can I let it have more space? If I imagine letting it out, not holding the wave in my body, maybe it will dissipate and soften. I close my eyes here in the bookstore café and try it but nothing changes. It refuses to budge; its attention is on my body's particles. This gritty wave of energy is relentlessly working on me seeking my surrender. It's jack-hammering loose my blockages. "Actually," my inner voice tells me, "the wave isn't going anywhere, it just wants you to match it." It likes pooling, then dissolving, and its intensity or height determines what I become. As the wave dissolves and these identities are released, the wave turns to diamond light or a diamond spaciousness, and I experience the clear essence of self, of life.

So this is what I've been noticing as I look at my morning face in the mirror lately, not quite recognizing myself, thinking, "Am I aging or what?" My body, eyes, cheeks, skin are oscillating in and out of moist and dry realities. Full and prescient, empty and vaguely worried. The buzz of this destructive/creative wave eating away at my solidity and habits like maggots cleaning a skeleton in time-lapse photography feels a lot like irritation. But nothing will rid me of it. I must just let it work, be with it, be patient, and trust it. It's not easy to remain dense anymore.

I allow.

If you pay close attention to the subtle vibrations in your body, you may notice your frequency varying as you allow the waves of the planet's energy to pass through you. Today, let your body adjust to the sea of energy that exists within.

Helping others helps me love them and myself more.

The more conscious and enlightened we become, the more we know that nonsacrificial service is what we truly want to do. Offer your services or a helping hand to someone who needs it today.

I was working in Tokyo for three weeks, doing lectures and workshops in the evenings and private consultations during the day. On a normal day, I would see four clients for ninety minutes to two hours each, counseling them about their lives and careers, and I worked every day with no time off. For the private appointments, I worked with an interpreter. The process was painstaking but intimate, loving, and uplifting. Even so, after weeks of delving into the hidden emotional and subconscious mental realities of that many people, keeping my energy up got to be a problem. When my mind became restless or rebellious, I could feel tired and impatient.

On one of these days, my interpreter, Masako, and I were taking a coffee break between sessions and were stopped at a crosswalk. Ahead of us were two women and a tiny little boy wearing bright red shorts and a yellow beanie cap. They'd obviously been on a shopping spree because each of the women carried a huge shopping bag, and the little boy, who stood between them, was loaded down with four or five smaller bags, which he was gleefully hugging to himself, heroically trying to keep them from dragging on the ground. He looked lovingly up at one of the women and enthusiastically made a loud pronouncement.

I turned to Masako and asked what he had just said. She smiled and told me that it translated as something like, *"I live to serve ANYBODY!"* With those words of wisdom, something in me snapped back into alignment. I remembered the real reason I do what I do. I stared at his beaming face and felt his generosity flooding off his little body in happy waves. And without even knowing it, in his innocent joy, he had just served me.

May 3

One of my colleagues, Larry Leigon, is good at helping people get to the heart of what's important to them. He does it by asking a series of questions that directs them into what's real. He worked with a friend of ours over brunch one Sunday. She had lost an important relationship recently and was not doing well on her own. She wanted to know what to do to make herself feel better. Larry began by asking her an odd question: "What is the worst possible job you could imagine doing?"

She thought for a moment and responded, "Working in a sweatshop, sewing or doing menial tasks for virtually no money and no thanks. That would be awful! You'd have no freedom! And it would go on and on like that forever. It's so unfair and abusive!" He listened carefully then asked, "What would it take for you to be able to do that job in a really excellent way?" "I could NEVER do that job!" she exclaimed. "But if you *were* doing that job, what would you have to do to be the best at it?" It took a while for her to even imagine being in that situation let alone imagine doing it well. Larry kept acknowledging each comment she made and repeating the same question to her, phrased slightly differently, until finally she had a new thought. "Well I would probably enjoy talking with the other women and that would help me be in a good mood. And then I wouldn't mind doing a repetitive task so much, and I wouldn't mind that I didn't have any freedom because I guess I'd feel more free because of my attitude." Larry repeated these points back to her then asked the same basic question again.

"So if I had this attitude," she answered, "maybe I'd want to be good at what I was doing, and I'd be interested in how much I could do and how I did every little thing. I'd pay closer attention and compete against myself just for a game. That's how I'd be excellent." Larry said these were the very skills she needed to solve the problem concerning her loneliness: develop a cheerful, positive attitude then do what's right in front of her. No matter how mundane her task may be, by paying close attention to the subtle refinements of her performance and action and by competing against her own last result, she will be in the present moment without protest and without mourning.

When I hear people out, they surprise me.

Listen deeply and fully to others today. It's amazing how much information people reveal about themselves and about life in ordinary conversation.

I am exchanging energy with everything around me.

Your body is intimately interconnected with all other bodies through the unified field of matter. It's natural for us to know what's happening elsewhere, especially with the people we know and love. Let yourself feel porous and connected to what's around you today, both near and far.

Jaye tells how one night, after sitting in her chair and reading, she experienced that quiet moment of transition when what she had read was settling into her body and she anticipated her ritual of going to bed. Suddenly she felt a wave of something so intangible, yet so definite, that she didn't know how to describe it to herself. Was it dread? Fear? Was an earthquake or catastrophe coming? Or was it a message from her soul? A strange resoluteness came over her. "Maybe I'm going to die soon," she thought to herself. "Yes. That's it. I know I'm going to die. Odd—I should be scared, but it feels OK." She determined that tomorrow she would make sure her will was in good order and start tidying up her business, family communications, and inner spiritual life.

The next afternoon, out of the blue, a friend called to tell her that Jim, a man she had worked with on a variety of projects several years back, had just died. "Jim had been sick a long time," her friend said, "and he finally just slipped away about eleven P.M. last night." Jaye was stunned. That was almost exactly when she'd felt the unexplainable wave of energy. Not knowing about Jim's illness, Jaye had correctly felt the impression of death in her body but had incorrectly assumed it was related to herself.

What happened? Bodies don't by themselves have a strong sense of distinctness from other bodies; they don't distinguish between the sensations in themselves versus sensations in another body. Your body is likely to stay attuned to anyone's body you've been close to in your life. Just as the pain or joy of a loved one can be experienced as your own, be they near or far away, a friend's death might also register on your body, in your own tissues. With intuitive awareness, you can learn to sense the subtle differences between what's happening in your body and sensations that emanate from somewhere else.

May 5

In a speech I gave at a large conference, I asked people to turn to the person sitting next to them and tune in to them quietly. Then I asked them to spontaneously tell the other person three positive qualities that were obvious and radiated effortlessly from them. Then I asked them to describe three hidden talents that were not so obvious. Third, I asked them to give their partner one piece of advice that would make their life happier and more successful. Within minutes the banquet hall was abuzz with animated conversation. Afterward, when I asked for someone to share what they learned, one woman raised her hand. She said her partner had told her such valuable things about herself that she was moved to tears. Her partner had seen her as having a talent for public speaking and for motivating people to be who they really are. This had been one of her secret dreams, though she'd been afraid to try it. The advice her partner gave was to always offer her insight to others and not judge the situation in any way, but to believe in others and trust them to use the information as they saw fit.

Other people raised their hands. They were astounded that someone they'd never met before could see them so clearly, and that the other person could be so wise and kind. Later, after the talk, more people stopped to tell me what had been said to them. One man who was a skeptic said his partner had seen him as detailed, analytical, and good with money—all true. His hidden talents, however, were that he would be a good hands-on healer, he could cook, and he was patient and listened well to people in trouble. He was surprised by this. The advice his partner offered was for him to not be too critical of the people he encountered but to see what was beautiful and vulnerable about them and to use his sense of hearing to tune in to their deepest requests and help them. He said he'd been thinking about this all day and it was making him feel different, as though a new part of him had pecked a big hole in the shell of his identity and was slowly going to emerge. Letting someone give to him in this way, he said, had shown him that he wasn't as isolated and invisible as he'd always believed.

Other people can see me accurately.

Contrary to popular belief, we are much easier to know than we think. Ask people to give you a piece of useful advice today. Make it safe for them to answer honestly.

May 6

The empty space around me is really full of life.

Be aware of and grateful to the air today. The air teaches us that what seems invisible is actually real; since air is real, other invisible worlds must be as well.

It is because the air is transparent that our minds jump to the conclusion that we are separate beings, that there is empty space around us and chasms between us. We forget that the air exerts an influence, a pressure; that it fills our lungs and keeps us from collapsing; that it helps hold us up as we walk. We breathe it without realizing its continuous gift of life, how it exchanges the fresh with the used and makes the old new again. The particles of the air dance with the particles of our skin, perhaps exchanging places, blurring the boundary between body and field, or self and essence. The molecules of my body talk to the molecules of the air, and they speak to the tree's particles, and those particles send the message on, in a wave, to the air again, and on to the bird, and so on and so on to a person on the other side of the world. We are connected. The air shows us we are kin. Breathe in and you inhale particles that have known the inner life of the whale, the worm, and the eagle. Your air has flowed through the blood of kings, babies, prisoners, gifted artists, astronauts, lovers, and the insane. Our shared air brings us the full life.

May 7

The personal field of energy radiating out around us is alive with a subtle sensitivity. It gives others an early warning of our mood and reveals our level of internal harmony. This aura (from the Greek word for air, or atmosphere) also filters incoming emotional and energetic data. Think of it as a kind of extremely refined brain tissue. Since we are all telepathic, it's actually normal for people to read the pictures carried within the auras of others. Are you holding a vivid memory of being beaten as a child? Others may unconsciously read this and act similarly toward you by physically, emotionally, or verbally abusing you. The same is true for positive images. Try holding an image of yourself as a warm radiant sun or a happy animated performer. Try the following technique for conveying subtle messages to yourself and others via your aura.

YOUR AURA TOTEMS

1. Sit quietly, eyes closed, and center yourself in your body and the moment. Sense the energy radiating out around you. Let it expand to a ball at least five feet in diameter. Now pay attention to the space at the very top and bottom of your aura. Two animal helpers will appear to you in these spots. The top one helps you receive wisdom and energy from your soul; the bottom one helps transmit the wisdom and energy of the earth.

2. Now pay attention to the space at the very front and back of your aura. Two animal helpers will appear in these spots. The front one will greet people, help them understand you accurately, and protect you. The one in back will back you up, give you knowledge from the unconscious, and protect you.

3. Next place attention in the left and right sides of your aura. Two animal helpers will appear in these spots. The animal to the left brings you energy and knowledge from the world. The one on your right helps you express yourself optimally in the world. If you're left-handed, reverse the functions.

Trust what you receive and make friends with the animals; watch how they look when they're doing their jobs. What characteristics does each offer you? Establish these totem animals in your aura and carry them with you. Allow them to be perceived telepathically by others. Remember to interact with them.

I am aware of my personal boundaries.

Pay attention today to your personal energy field, or aura. Notice how it helps you receive and give, greet and complete with people.

May 8

**I receive
fully what
I have been
given.**

*Notice how what
you have today
is what you
set into motion a
little while ago
and use it,
appreciate it.*

One idea that lurks in our collective unconscious is that
if we let ourselves be happy with what we have in the
moment, we'll become lazy and nondirected and our creativity and motivation will dry up. We harbor a secret
belief that we must keep ourselves slightly hungry and
dissatisfied to keep growing in life, that we must live
from yearning and a sense of incompletion to progress.
And yet when children feel unsafe, unloved, unfed,
unconnected, and unhappy, they simply wail—they don't
suddenly become more motivated and creative! On the
other hand, when children get what they need to survive,
their playful spirits emerge with full-blown imagination
and enthusiasm. They are full of themselves in the best
way, unself-consciously confident, open to experimenta-
tion and relationship, and overflowing with endless creative expressions.

When I read back through my journals, I see that I
would routinely go through a process of first noticing a
problem then complaining about a related situation and
analyzing why it was happening. This might go on for
weeks or months. Then I'd finally pull myself together,
summarize the insight I was learning about, and make a
crisp, confident list of what I wanted. In the next journal
I'd be on a whole new round of restlessness and wanting
things to be different, but what I was now protesting
about was what I had put on my list of goals six months
or a year earlier! I hadn't even noticed that I had received
what I wanted!

So what I have today is the result of what I was thinking about and drawing to myself, consciously or unconsciously, yesterday. I realize I'm so used to the phase in the
creative process when I contemplate the new concept and
ask for the new experience that I forget to notice the part
when I actually have the experience and am living in it.
My body never gets a chance to enjoy the full feeling
of creating, attaining, and basking inside the experience
of a thought that's been realized. And because of that,
it's difficult to create something new since the old cycle
of manifestation was never consciously completed. By
protesting about what I have in the present moment, I
don't acknowledge my creative power.

May 9

As I begin to write something substantial such as an article or a book, I must gather myself. First, I cut down on the components of my work; I stop promoting, giving lectures and seminars, traveling; I cut down on the number of clients. Then I make myself not answer the phone during certain hours, run errands less often, and I stop fussing around the house finding that one last little chore that needs to be done.

But the hardest transition of all is to take a break from reading novels, listening to radio, and watching television. When I'm constantly filling myself up with other people's words, I have the illusion that I'm being creative because I can merge with an author's fluid dialogue style, or a journalist's insightful mind, or a filmmaker's whimsy and colorful imagination. And then nothing comes *out* of me. So I taper off. I drive in the car without the accompaniment from music and talk shows. I write in my journal instead of reading the latest Patricia Cornwell mystery.

Something inside me changes from being a tweeting baby bird waiting for the next feeding to the fledgling standing on the edge of its nest, anxious to spread its wings and fly. Here is where I rediscover inner silence and my own creative, quirky mind and voice. Julia Cameron, in *The Artist's Way,* says, "Without distractions, we are once again thrust into the sensory world. With no newspaper to shield us, a train becomes a viewing gallery. With no novel to sink into . . . an evening becomes a vast savannah in which furniture—and other assumptions—get rearranged." What's inside *you* waiting to sneak out?

I am aware of my wellspring of creativity.

Abstain from television, radio, and reading today. Instead, allow something original to rise from your own creative depths. Deprivation can act as a catalyst for your ingenuity.

I am always home, no matter where I am.

When you allow yourself to experience belonging, you'll participate more fully in life. Love the spot of earth under your feet today.

Wherever you are, look down. Squarely beneath your feet are the invisible crosshairs of the here and now, and you're always standing smack dab in the center. Move ten feet to the left, or a hundred miles to the south, and look down. There are those crosshairs again! Directly below this X, imagine a long column of energy descending straight into the center of the earth. This is the conduit for life force from the planet that continually feeds your physical body and connects it to all other forms of life. Even in an airplane, this strand of elastic energy stretches through the sky, keeping you oriented, feeding you its special kind of vitality. Wherever you go, you are connected directly to the center of the planet like a balloon tied to a string, tied to a big crystal ball down below.

Feel downward with your imagination, through your feet into the ground, through the layers of the earth under you. What is the character of your spot? When I do this in different parts of the world, I sense varying flavors and images in the land as I pass down my column of energy. In California, I feel as if I'm sitting in the center of a flower, looking down through pistils and stamen through the stem. In Japan, I feel a group of ancient women directly below, under the concrete jungle of Tokyo, and I hear them singing sublime harmonies. At Machu Picchu I could fall down through the earth like Alice in Wonderland. There is no resistance, no density, just an open chute. And in the deserts of the Southwest, under me I have felt a lake of fire purifying all the ignorance that dared to touch it.

Wherever you are, you are in the crosshairs, you are aligned, you are home. Send your love down the column, thank the earth for its constant support, and receive what you need this day.

May 11

I went for a therapy session because I'd become tense and worried, brittle and blocked creatively. As the session progressed, the therapist got up and put three chairs facing me in a row. "Sit in the left one," he instructed, "and close your eyes. Imagine you are your Primal self. Describe what you feel." I got an image of a dirty olive-green pond. As I went into the pond, I felt alive and warm, earthy and creative. Messy as it was, I loved being that pond. Then he had me come out of my reverie and move to the right-hand chair. "Now be your Enterpriser self and describe what you feel." In this role, I became the organized list maker, the ambitious goal setter and achiever, never doing enough to be satisfied. Next, he had me take the middle seat. "Bring the Primal self and Enterpriser self into you so there's a 50/50 balance. How comfortable are the parts with each other?" From my Primal self's view, the Enterpriser was not listening, was ignorant of the big picture and cut off from the creative flow, which the Primal self accessed effortlessly. The Enterpriser felt the Primal self was ugly, lazy, and stupid. Next, the therapist asked me to let them come into the right mix that would produce happiness. It quickly shifted to 98 percent Primal, 2 percent Enterpriser. I could see that I'd been exhausted because I'd been living with the exact opposite percents. After the session, I felt renewed and back in touch with my source of supply. This poem was a result.

> I'm a deep green pond on a hot summer day,
> covered by clouds of gnats, ringed in cattails.
> Particles of olive and teal algae shimmer
> in the slanting rays of sun angling down
> through my murky brown;
> mosquito larvae and tadpoles teem and wiggle,
> dragonflies, gleaming turquoise, rise and land.
> Water beetles and surface skimmers,
> minnows and bullfrogs,
> reeds and lilies,
> bitterns and kingfishers,
> come and go, dive and dart;
> they know the silent richness here,
> a generosity camouflaged by slime and scum,
> this perfect fertile opportunity.

**I am
kinesthetic.**

Pick what to wear today based solely on textures. Touch people and know about them from their skin. Feel the smooth fluidity of your motions. When you are aware of touch, your body will feel intensely alive.

May 12

**I am
responsible
for who I think
I am.**

*We usually
think of ourselves
as flawed and
unevolved, and
our souls as being
high above or
in the future.
How would you
act if you
assumed that you
are your soul
right now.
Whenever you
say "I" today,
pretend your soul
is speaking.*

Last year Nicole had a seizure, the first ever in her life, and she was unconscious for thirty-five minutes. The doctors could find nothing wrong. But afterward she felt different, not interested in her normal activities. She asked herself, "Where did I go while I was unconscious?" A clear voice answered from within her own mind. "It's not about where, it's about being *aware*." She didn't understand but she allowed herself to not know and went on with her life. Over the next few months, she began to hear the voices of people she knew had died. They were talking to her as easily as you or I might. Then small items started disappearing from her house. At first she thought she was having memory lapses and doubted herself—but she *knew* she wasn't making it up. These subtle psychic phenomena around her were a bit scary. But, as if to validate her experience, she had another episode, which her mother witnessed firsthand.

Nicole had been chopping vegetables, preparing a salad for dinner. She spaced out for a few moments, and when she came to, literally one-third of the salad was gone along with one of the salad tongs that had been sitting in the bowl. She and her mother searched everywhere, but to no avail. Later, when she asked herself what happened, the same clear voice said, "It all went into the black void." Scared now, and more confused than ever, she called me.

Nicole had almost died at birth. Her whole life she had never really wanted to be here. At the slightest hint of trouble, she'd always been ready to run, even to die. It seemed that Nicole was finally committing to be here all the way and to bring her awareness of the higher realms, into which she'd always escaped, into this reality. The seizure was her soul blasting through the rigidity of her old mind-set. Subsequently, she began to experience the omnipresence of all beings, dimensions, and knowledge and her own ability to manifest (or demanifest) anything she wanted. Her soul was taking up residence in her body consciously and educating her mind about what the new rules of her life were—basically, that *anything is possible!* Realizing that her own soul was engineering her experience helped Nicole move into a new world where she could have her higher dimensions while still being present in this one.

May 13

I'm looking for a mood: loose, cozy, affectionate, sophisticated, artistic, refined—a romantic way of being. Certain foods, books, and the thought of exotic lands give me a hint of this mood. Actually, by being drawn to these externals, I am trying to feel a quality of the soul. This mood is really a state where love and abundance are the norm. I want the intimacy, the constant connection, the attention and love of soul. I want enlightenment!

I asked a colleague whether he wanted to be enlightened in this lifetime. To my surprise, he danced noncommitally around the idea. He seemed to see the concept of enlightenment as being presumptuous and final. When I ask myself the same question, I leap up and shout "Yes! I'm enlightened every other minute!" Maybe we *are* enlightened but just don't know how to hold it very long. Maybe every time we notice something and think we don't have it enlightenment fades.

I asked another colleague what enlightenment meant to him and what would it be like to live *after* he was enlightened? He joked that it probably wouldn't be much like *his* life. We don't have many models for this because people who are enlightened are supposed to live in caves holding the world together so we never see them in action, or they don't let us know they're enlightened and pass us right by on the street. We decided that many people think enlightenment is a peak experience, something in which we are engulfed in white light, hear angel choruses, receive the entire collective wisdom of the universe in one blast, and become a saint or ascended master forever thereafter. But what happens the day after enlightenment?

My friend thought about this and said, "I'd probably make many of the same choices I make now, but I wouldn't worry. I wouldn't doubt my abilities or my guidance or my creative urges. I'd naturally gravitate to the loving view and the win-win solution instead of choosing punishment or sacrifice. I wouldn't feel the world is unfair; I'd understand the hidden meaning and benefit of events, and I'd live a simple life. Everything would be simpler." Probably true. Not so different, but very different. A client today said: "My son is always happy—he just glows through life!" Perhaps that is an enlightened state of being.

There is awareness in everything all the time.

Feel the presence of divine awareness all around you, and in you, today. Would it be OK for you to be enlightened in this lifetime?

May 14

I give myself permission to do or have whatever I think I can't.

What frustrates you today? Release the pent-up energy each time you notice yourself holding back or holding on. When your body is free of tension, it's easier to receive clear insights.

Connie was recently laid off from a large corporation where she had worked for twenty years. The company was downsizing and she had hinted strongly that she wouldn't mind being laid off and getting the substantial bonus package. Even though she received what she asked for and was now in what should have been a restful free period, she was having panic attacks. When we spoke, I told her that she was getting ready to take everything she had learned in the corporation and apply it to a socially relevant cause that was close to her heart, perhaps as a director of a nonprofit organization. She lit up. In fact she *had* been dreaming along those lines, but her mind was only showing her images of herself working as a receptionist at a veterinarian's office. She said she wouldn't know how to get a job as a director of a nonprofit even though she was qualified as a high-level manager.

Now that Connie was on the verge of stepping into her dream, her mind was freezing up and backtracking. "Maybe I won't have enough money. I should just go back to my old job. They'd take me back, I know." "How will I ever be convincing in a job interview?" "Maybe I should just settle for being a receptionist—then I wouldn't have to sell myself." Connie's body was very tense. When I had her visualize how it might be to go through a typical day working with people who shared her vision, who were open-hearted and cocreative and who liked her, she softened noticeably and became more aware of her true qualifications and expertise.

Connie had unconsciously been visualizing herself as the kind of leader she'd just left the big corporation to get away from! She wasn't going to let herself be in a leadership position if that's the way she had to be. When she re-created the tense feeling of being a dictatorial leader, then released the entire pattern from her body, her true leadership images began to emerge. In these pictures, she saw herself inspiring by example, drawing excellence out of others through dialogue, and facilitating a group awareness by simply focusing the flow. By learning to drop the feelings of contraction as soon as she felt them, Connie found her own wisdom and motives, and moving forward in a new direction seemed attainable.

May 15

I finally read Edward Abbey's *Desert Solitaire*, which I'd
had for years. The pages in my ancient paperback were
brittle and yellowed, but his words were still wonder producing. As Abbey stares out at Arches National Monu-
ment he says, "I feel a ridiculous greed and possessiveness
come over me. I want to know it all, possess it all,
embrace this entire scene intimately. He reminds me that
"I am here . . . to confront, immediately and directly if
possible, the bare bones of existence, the bedrock that sus-
tains us." Another passage takes me into that eternal quality of quiet centeredness and clarity that one achieves so
easily in the desert: "We greet each other, the sun and
I, across the black void of ninety-three million miles. . . .
Three ravens are wheeling near the balanced rock,
squawking at each other and at the dawn. I'd sooner
exchange ideas with the birds on earth than learn to carry
on intergalactic communications with some obscure race
of humanoids on a satellite planet from the world of
Betelgeuse."

I'm very glad Mr. Abbey took the time to pause and
reflect on ravens, rocks, and sunrise. And that he had the
unsuppressable urge to write it down and then the gall to
share it publicly, so I could look out through his eyes and
be transported to a reality where I can expand so effortlessly. I would be poorer for not having read this, and the
world would be poorer if he hadn't spoken his truth.

**I share my
observations
for the
enjoyment
of all.**

*How entitled do
you feel to share
your ideas and
opinions with
others? If you let
yourself talk
more freely, you
may find that
you actually help
people. Enthusi-
astically describe
what you notice
today.*

Animals help me.

When solving problems or getting insights today, pretend you're an animal. Animals represent archetypal patterns and each has a specific kind of wisdom.

My question for today: How might I become a better writer? An image comes to mind. I descend into the center of the earth in a glass elevator. I step out onto a broad, open prairie with mountains in the far distance and not a tree or bush in sight. I am surrounded by a sea of short yellow-green grass. I know I'm here to meet an animal who will be my messenger and teacher. I look up; I think I see an eagle. No, the teacher is not an eagle. I am supposed to lie down flat on my back, arms outstretched. I open to the sky and let it in. Then I hear it—a scratching in the earth near my right ear, then a high-pitched squeaking. Out of a tiny hole emerges the tiniest of creatures, a mole only two inches long. He slowly crawls toward me and, with his strong front claws, climbs my Mt. Everest of a body. He makes his way to my waist and burrows under my blouse, squiggling up toward my chest, then finally settles in the hollow of my throat, just beneath my shirt collar. Here he seems content, and he starts radiating a fantastically warm energy into my throat, loosening and broadening my vocal cords, almost causing them to sing.

I ask him my question. Inside my mind I hear him clearly, and my body simultaneously feels what he means. He says, "You must follow your deeper senses. There is always a path through life, though at times it looks like a wall of solid earth blocking your way. But the path is there and you must sense it. Sometimes you can smell the path because scent carries even through dirt. Smell the water, smell the fresh roots that will make a good meal, smell the unoccupied versus occupied territory. Feel your way. Feel the coolness or the warmth, the depth and the shallowness. Sense the places of density, like rock and clay, versus the more porous way where the dirt will crumble easily in front of you as you proceed. Listen for the subtle sounds carried through your world that are received by your entire body; there are clicks and taps, moans and long grinding sounds, creakings and ticks. Sometimes you hear your name called by a faraway voice you think you recognize. Go toward it. When you write, let your body put the words together. Let one sense bleed through into the next until you don't know how you know. I trust my claws to dig in the right direction. You trust your fingers to type letters."

May 17

Don't you sometimes wish you could recapture the uncensored flow of perceptions we had as children? I spent Christmas at my sister's house a few years ago and stayed in my four-year-old niece Julia's room with her. As we made up the beds, Julia candidly told me she needed two pillows because she had bumps on the back of her head. Then she asked me, "Do you make any noise at night?" She politely let me know that she might stay up late and read, because "I have trouble sleeping when I don't get enough attention." The next morning, I felt a little tap on my shoulder and, as I blinked awake, I saw Julia close up, staring into my face. She started right in. "Do you believe in heaven and hell?" she asked. I said I did, but why did she ask?

"Well people who steal things go to hell and burn," she explained. "And in heaven your eyes are open, you're awake, and you're magical. And what you can do with your magic is reach your hand down through the sky and sprinkle some fairy dust on your family. If you use it up, God gives you some more. And when you die of a heart attack, your heart gets littler and littler 'til it's about the size of a pea, and then everything inside you disappears but your skin and nails still stay and you just lay there. God slides you out into heaven. In heaven you're a baby. You start out as a seed and grow into a baby and then you get a new mother. The angels watch over the bad people and take them to hell. The angels in hell are boys and the ones in heaven are girls. God makes the girl angels and the people in hell make their own angels."

"Wow," I said.

"Yes, and when I grow up I'm *not* getting married and I'm *not* going to have any kids. I don't want a job, I just want to shop."

"But what about travel? Or teaching people things?" I asked.

"No, Penney!!! That's a job! But I might be a judge. I would call the cops because the cops are my friends. And the lawyers all work for me. If somebody beats up a dog, I'd make them take boxing lessons so they'd know what it feels like to be hit." And with that, she marched out of the room to start her day.

I'm amazed by what comes to me and through me.

Be alert to mystery today as it emerges word by word in your conversations, makes you start a new action, gives you sudden insight, or stops you in your tracks. Life is about self-entertainment!

May 18

**I speak
from my heart.**

*Align your
words with your
intentions today.
When the mind
and heart become
one, your life will
flow smoothly
and others will
respond to you
favorably.*

One way to speak from your soul is to imagine that your mind is in your heart. Ask your heart what it thinks about any given situation. Ask your heart to speak. In Paolo Coelho's wonderful book *The Alchemist*, he describes the magic that happens when you are truly trying to live your destiny—that when you ask for something with this intention, "all the universe conspires to help you achieve it." And when you ask for something with all your heart, that's when you're closest to "the Soul of the World."

In the book, a little boy talks to his mentor as they travel across the desert. He asks how he can listen to the desert. "Listen to your heart. It knows all things because it came from the Soul of the World and it will one day return there." So the little boy begins to understand his heart. "He asked it, please, never to stop speaking to him. He asked that when he wandered far from his dreams, his heart press him and sound the alarm. The boy swore that every time he heard the alarm he would heed its message."

Contrary to popular belief, the heart is not the center of our emotions. The heart is the place of compassionate understanding, of perfect balanced perception, a place where the masculine and feminine, the spiritual and earthy, and the past and future parts of our awareness come together in an equal, mutually supportive way. It is in our hearts that we have fairness and wisdom, kindness and neutrality. The heart knows an integrated, whole world.

May 19

I remember the first time I told a lie as a young child. I was playing with a friend, and we had been exploring a bureau in which my mother kept her personal keepsakes. I knew I shouldn't touch her things but curiosity won out. We looked at all the photos, handled her old jewelry, and contemplated her dead father's mementos. Later she asked me if I'd been in that bureau. I remember the strange sensation of time slowing down and a bubble of amber light closing in all around me. As if in a scientific experiment, I tried the word *no*. Time stood still. And then *she believed me!* Something connected in my brain— I could *pretend*— pretend to be another person—be one way on the inside and another way on the outside. Thinking back on it now, I see it was one more crack leading to the fundamental split between soul and personality that we all experience in life.

I have been taken in by people who were good at telling lies. Perhaps they also lied to themselves regularly and didn't know they were doing anything out of the ordinary. They didn't send off any warning signals; I couldn't pick up the usual clues with my body. And yet each had a superficial quality, what some people describe as shifty energy. If we could see that energy field clearly, it might look like shimmering heat waves. That kind of energy is not found in responsible, grounded, honest people who speak clearly from their hearts. But I glossed over it and tricked myself into learning some hard lessons.

People who lie and even betray us often tell us who they are in an unconscious way right up front. A man who eventually became my boyfriend said as he came through my front door for the first time, "Don't get too close to me, I have a cold." As our relationship progressed to the romantic stage, he seemed to be enjoying it yet I could always feel the underlying "Don't get too close to me" warning. After several years of acting as if he were happily committed to me, he suddenly started seeing other women with no explanation. I ended the relationship and though I felt betrayed, I realized that he had told me who he was all along. I had chosen to ignore the subtle clues.

Listen for the discrepancies between people's unspoken and spoken words today, and ask your intuition why they're being deceptive.

What I procrastinate about is just what I need to move ahead in life.

Make a list of your incomplete projects. Then write about how you could find them interesting, educational, or amusing. When your interest flows into something, action is sure to follow.

Feng shui, the Chinese art of placement, teaches the correlations between the shapes of the spaces we live in, the arrangement of our furniture, and the ways our personal energy functions. One of the principles is that energy in a space should not become stagnant, blocked, or dissipated. Any area of your home that attracts clutter, for instance, is indicative of an area in your life or personality that you are avoiding. Does your mail, E-mail, or voicemail pile up? Maybe you need to practice clearer communication or listen more attentively to others. Does your laundry collect on the floor of your bedroom or on the dresser after it's been folded? Maybe it's garbage cans overflowing or dishes stacked in the sink. You might need to experience the satisfaction of completing a full cycle of activity instead of always feeling that you are catching up. If it's piling up, it's calling for your attention because you activated that area of your life and haven't yet experienced it fully. Why did you activate it?

Part of me sends off for new information, buys books on intriguing topics, signs me up to do lectures, volunteers me for participation in events, and fires me up to write a book. Another part of me must then read, digest, file, remember where I filed, and apply the information. This part must also outline the talks, perform well in front of groups, and show up every day at the keyboard to craft words into some meaningful form. Often this worker part feels separate from the enthusiast part, as though she must trail along with a broom, sweeping up. It is this gap between the two roles that blocks my creative expression. I am the self who likes wearing new clothes, *and* the self who feels good washing clothes and folding laundry neatly, *and* the self who likes organizing the closet and dresser drawers. The self who thought up the book idea and outlined it and whose enthusiasm convinced others to publish it is the same self who can't wait to turn on the computer each morning and open the spigot.

The things I procrastinate about show me where I need to bring the separated parts of myself back into oneness. I have one purpose in life: to be creative, mindful, and merged lovingly with the flow of all action. Everything is a creative act. Everything is an act of love. If I start it, I engage fully with the doing of it, and I finish it. Otherwise I never truly know the full process of creation or appreciate the beauty of a finished product.

May 21

There are times in our lives when we must smoothly disengage ourselves and shift effortlessly to a new direction.
These pauses might be likened to little deaths; enter the
pauses and they immediately transform into little births.

Lydia is a psychotherapist and has trained for many
years with Native American shamans and healers from
other cultures. She tells me that in the past month she has
experienced nearly a dozen animal deaths. First her
beloved dog got sick and became almost paralyzed. She left
home to do a quick errand, and, while she was gone, he
died in the middle of her living room, his body twisted
oddly as though he had spiraled out of it. Then a hummingbird got caught in her skylight and exhausted itself.
It fell to the floor and died in her hands. Next she saw a
young doe bound out in front of a speeding truck just
ahead of her on a winding road. The impact was so hard
that the doe was thrown high above the vehicles, landed
with her legs up in the air, and dropped out of sight down
a grassy embankment. Lydia prayed and prayed for miles
after that. If the truck hadn't been there, she might have
been the one to hit the deer. Next, she found a very large
reddish moth with mouse-brown edges to its wings; it too
died peacefully in her cupped hands. As the deaths continued, she asked herself what the meaning of this string of
surrealistic experiences was. Was she about to die? Was she
too attached to form?

She said her inner voice told her that animals teach us
about the true experience of dying, which is simply shifting the focus of energy from one frequency to another.
Animals do not resist the process when it comes but move
fluidly from one focus to another. Her inner voice said she
was soon to be in a process of dying out of an old way of
being into a new focus, a new chapter of her life; and for
her to integrate it easily and fully, she needed to surrender
the same way the animals had.

**I am aware
when it's time
to stop and
replenish
myself.**

*There is a
natural point at
the end of every
creative cycle
when the mind
needs to reenter
the state of being
so it can be
recharged.
Be aware
when you tire
of moving and
doing today.
What triggers
the change?
What do your
body and soul
want?*

May 22

I notice the story line in my life.

Do you ever notice how certain life experiences take on a quality of heightened drama and symbolism? Interpret the dramas you see today; they offer powerful insights.

It is the late 1970s and I am attending a consciousness-raising seminar in a large hotel in downtown San Francisco. The theme of the seminar is "Breaking Through Barriers." I sit rather uncomfortably in a huge ballroom with hundreds of other seekers. We have paired up and are staring into each other's eyes. Maintaining eye contact, staying open, staying with the energy, giving no feedback, no smiling, one person at a time just saying what we see in the other. I'm getting hot, I'm dizzy, it feels like I'm under water, the space feels like a steaming jungle teeming with howler monkeys. We're breaking through barriers, and I've gone as far as I want to go. I'm done! Let me out of here! I want to be in the quiet cocoon of my car cockpit, want to reorient my swirling vapors.

Afterward, I'm in a long line of cars idling and waiting, snaking slowly toward the exit of the downtown garage. Everyone, ahead and behind, has looked into eyes and broken through barriers and, now in the traffic, are barriers themselves. I approach the ticket man at last but can't find my parking ticket. I see it on the floor. Getting closer to the man, I roll down my window, and I reach down and pick up the ticket. I'm saying, "It fell . . ." The man suddenly yells, "Lady watch out!" I realize my car is rolling, but I can't find the brake. Suddenly I'm crashing through the bright red barrier! The broken wooden guard gate is now poking through my open window right by my eyes. I'm mortified. A hundred seminar attendees are witnessing my colossal act of clarity and I'm shaking and blushing. The man just laughs. "Hey lady—far out!" He's looking in my eyes and saying, "I was hoping somebody would do that!"

May 23

When we create we are not alone. We have partners in the nonphysical world, other creative beings who enjoy helping us shape the flow of energy and ideas. We and those beings can have fun together. We can share the experience of writing, painting, cooking, or dancing with them through our body, and they feed us a continual stream of new material.

I wrote in my journal, "Even now as I write, I forget to write with Spirit. I think I'm alone. My spiritual writing partners don't care if my handwriting sticks inside the lines, in fact they would like to make BIG LETTERS AND SEE WHAT IT FEELS LIKE TO CHANGE THE SHAPES. My inner writing partners like to make up free-form writing, to describe images the moment they appear. IMAGE: a dog with jowls shaking his head and that sound they make: flubber flubber flubber flub. IMAGE: a blast of heat and light from a shotgun muzzle in slow motion, the light streams and arcs through space. IMAGE: roller skating feet; the fluidity, the strokes, the gliding, the weaving, the alternating S-curves, the sound of wheels on smooth asphalt, no pebbles to break the silky ride. Purposeless creative fun!

I see I'm not going anywhere with my creativity; it stays with me in the now. The releasing of the flow is the point of the game. Form follows centeredness, compassion, and communion. Writing teacher Brenda Ueland says, "Think of yourself as an incandescent power, illumined and perhaps forever talked to by God and his messengers."

I create in partnership with the unseen.

Watch and feel your creative process today in all areas of your life. Contemplate its origin.

I surrender to the process of becoming and dissolving.

There are moments when you release awareness of self and moments where the self emerges again. Today, remember to feel that you are continually being created and dissolved, moment by moment, by a force much greater and wiser than you.

It is late and I'm bored in the living room. My body starts turning out lights and walking down the hall. My body is heading home to the bed, like my car heads home of its own accord from a late-night party. Here I am again in the bedroom looking at the bed where I will sacrifice my consciousness once more, as on an altar. I make a ritual, pushing around the objects on my nightstand, touching eyeglasses, water bottle, earrings I've taken off, hand cream, TV remote, travel alarm. I'm puffing up pillows, smoothing sheets. It's another night after another day in the life of this person I am. She has had thoughts all day, has watched images, heard sounds, felt the world's texture, comprehended meanings—and now she prepares to leave.

How many nights are left, how many times shall I lay this body down, turn out these lights, say these prayers, close these eyes? Is this the way old people feel a day before they die? At night the circle closes again and again and again. And what happened during the day that I thought was so special and important? I can hardly make it real now.

I sometimes think my bed is a raft being pulled out to sea by dolphins as I leave the shores of the known world. They take me far beyond the land of my people to a place where I must speak the old language to be known. In speaking it, I remember myself. I love the easy conversations I have in sleep, far out in the ocean in the dark of night with these telepathic friends. Tomorrow I will reconstruct my image for credibility's sake and take up my continuing concerns, but the memory of the deep conversations will still be there, and they will surface silently to fuel me.

May 25

The Japanese believe that to be healthy we must eat something like thirty-five different foods per day. They don't have to be the same foods every day and not in huge quantities, but one should try to sample many. That is partly why dinner is served in so many tiny bowls and plates.

In my intuition development seminars, I encourage participants to find three different ways they might do a routine task. What are your unconscious rules and habits? Try mixing them up a bit and see what new thought patterns emerge. Do you always brush your teeth before you wash your face and fix your hair? Try it the other way around. What if you used cold water instead of hot? Used a different toothpaste? Used your left hand instead of your right? If you always put your right sock on and put your right leg into your pants first, try reversing it. If you always have coffee, try black tea or cranberry juice. Do you always take the same route to work? Could you turn onto the frontage road or go the back way?

Varying your routine, rearranging the furniture in your living room, or doing the habitual in a nonhabitual way injects new life and creativity into your world. Habits blind us to the glorious detail in the world close at hand. We speed by the snowy egret in the cattails in the ditch. We don't notice the spider snoozing in the corner above the sink. Some of our brain tracks get rigid from overuse; others atrophy and feel neglected. It's important to use both sides of your brain and both sides of your body. Let your nondominant hand, foot, leg, eye, ear, and hemisphere have a little more fun! Let your dominant side rest a bit and feel supported instead of working so hard.

A Canadian man in my seminar in Tokyo did this exercise for a week and reported back that his feelings of being cynical, blocked, and bored with his job teaching English had miraculously dissolved and his sense of humor had returned. And all because he put his right shoe on before his left and washed his dinner dishes at night instead of in the morning!

I am flexible and open-minded.

Open a few more tracks in your brain today! Vary the way you do routine tasks and look for alternate solutions to problems.

**I conserve
my vitality.**

*Hold your energy
in and build
up power today;
don't let your
energy leak.
A fruit doesn't
fall off the tree
until it is entirely
ripe; let your
vitality ripen.*

Don Juan told Carlos Castañeda that his reason for choosing Carlos as a student was "Power pointed you out to me." When a life experience is highlighted, power is at work. When we build up personal power, we become visible.

Several years ago, as I was trying to get the early drafts of my first book, *The Intuitive Way*, recognized by agents and editors, I often felt frustrated. I knew I had some good material, but why couldn't anyone else see that? I did an intuitive direct-writing process to get insights on this issue. I began by writing my question in my journal: WHY IS MY WORK NOT BEING RECOGNIZED? My inner voice responded:

When you put yourself out into the world and don't get the results you think you deserve, it's not necessarily because your work is substandard or because you're doing something wrong. You must keep going, keep walking, taking the steps that come from the deepest, truest impulses. What makes people notice you and your work is *power*, and you have not built up enough of it yet. Power accumulates by consistently using the talents you were given, from doing what you love repeatedly in the world. So be creative every day. *Be* the artist and *do* the artwork. Don't siphon off energy into other activities and people. Be convincing. Your energy field must be fully saturated with who and what you are.

I realized then that I was using up the energy from my magnetic center by getting involved in my friends' life dramas. I was constantly trying to help them when I should really have been focusing more on myself. I lost vital energy and momentum by reading other people's good writing instead of making some myself, by comparing myself to successful friends who were successful in a different way than I would be, or by telling people about the details of my plans before they'd gelled enough to hold up on their own.

May 27

During a trip to Baltimore, my mood suddenly changed and I became unreasonably upset simply because a client was late. As I sat with the woman and dropped into a deep intuitive state to do her reading, I heard people talking in the hallway of my friend's house where I was working. I thought my friend must have come home early from work. My client pointed out that we were alone, but I didn't believe her. My impressions were so real that I came back to normal awareness and went to look. Sure enough, there was no one there. After the client left, I felt like a stone, fell onto the sofa, and went into a heavy, jerking sleep.

I woke when my friend came home. I was still unable to focus and had to teach in a few hours. She took me to dinner, talked animatedly at me, and plied me with coffee, but I remained a zombie. "Do you mind if I sleep on the way to the seminar?" I asked. At the seminar, I described what had been happening. Amazingly, six of the participants had had similar distraction and agitation, though none had gone unconscious over it. At around 8:30 P.M., we all felt much better and were rolling along in good humor and mental clarity. Whatever had been bothering us had cleared. It wasn't until the next morning that I heard that TWA flight 800 had exploded near New York, close to 8:30 P.M., only a few hundred miles away.

What had happened? Did my body actually feel the coming event waves of the explosion and respond, like animals do to upcoming earthquakes? Was my consciousness drawn into higher realms to help counsel the people who died? Were the voices I heard related in some way to the accident victims? Did the event begin in the higher dimensions long before the physical explosion occurred in real time? This odd experience demonstrated to me that we all may deal with the future and other dimensions of awareness in our present reality.

This example was so dramatic that it broke through and disrupted my daily consciousness. But perhaps part of us is in the future all the time; perhaps working back and forth between present and future is totally normal. What if we could become more alert to this kind of perceptual activity? We might experience a new kind of empowerment and know our creativity is sublimely coordinated.

My future is in my present.

Be aware when your mind projects into the future today, then come back to the present moment consciously and see if you can tell where you went and why. There may actually be an event that is drawing your attention.

**I take
responsibility
for my moods.**

*We all react emo-
tionally to certain
situations, but
if the negative
emotion lasts,
we're probably
indulging in it to
get some sort of
payoff. Today,
notice when you
indulge in anger,
sadness, helpless-
ness, or morose-
ness—and choose
to drop the mood.
If you can shift
to neutrality, you
can see what the
real issues are.*

Tom and Gina had been together five years, and though
Gina loved Tom, she was thinking of ending the relationship because of his chronic bad temper. She said driving
with him was terrifying because he flew into rages and
made loud, obscene comments. Though she knew he
would never hurt her, he became unreasonably angry over
minor things. She didn't think her body could take it
much longer; even when the anger wasn't aimed at her,
her body cringed when Tom vented.

Tom and Gina had had similar childhoods with physically abusive, crazy-making parents who never positively
acknowledged their children. Both had left home very
early. Their late teens and early twenties had been wild
and unsettled. In their late twenties, both had taken
secure jobs in which they learned discipline and responsibility. Gina understood Tom's anger because she had been
the same way but had gotten over it.

Tom had some character traits that were difficult to
integrate. First, he was a nurturer who needed harmony.
He liked helping people. He was upset that he was hurting Gina and didn't want to ruin their relationship. At the
same time, he was impulsive and expressive and wanted
recognition for excellence. Tom had a hard time feeling
who he was because of the early programming he had
received from his parents, who actually punished him for
expressing himself and insisted that he be alert to make
sure *their* needs were met. Tom never knew where he
stood. This had created a huge backlog of unconscious
resentment and frustration. So now, every time some little
thing got in the way of his free expression, Tom's frustration grew to gigantic proportions and he blasted the
world for blocking him. When he understood how the
frustration had been created, he was able to see that he
actually did have a choice and he wasn't a bad person.

Tom was able to learn some techniques for keeping
his awareness inside his body and finding his true self-
expression. In addition, he practiced the idea that there is
plenty of space for all people to live and express their
truth whether it agreed with his or not. Tom realized that
he was not the effect of his anger, but that his anger was
the result of frustration he didn't need to feel.

May 29

Can you tell when a friend needs help or is thinking about you? One indication of this is that you may become preoccupied with thoughts of them or even dream about them. This happened to me once in a startling way. I was scheduled to lead a retreat in Arizona at a ranch that was leased from the local Native American tribes. The ranch sat at the foot of a sacred mountain.

My friend had become close with the local shaman, who often stopped by early in the morning to chat about things that seemed meaningless on the surface but which always carried deeper significance. I had heard stories of this man for years, but he never stopped by when I was there. On one occasion, I gave my friend a beautiful crystal to give to the shaman as a gift. When she handed it to him, he said, "What's this for?" and stuffed it in his pocket.

Two weeks before the retreat, early in the morning, I had a strange dream. I was in a cabin in the desert, hovering in the air looking through an open door. I began to fly through the door but encountered a Native American man blocking my path. He was watching a team of men with wheelbarrows dig old bones out of the walls of a canyon. The man would not let me leave the cabin and finally turned and attacked me in the air. I became disoriented and woke up. Almost immediately the phone rang. It was my friend in Arizona, and she was upset.

The shaman had just stopped by and had nonchalantly pulled the crystal I had given him out of his pocket. "Do you know what this is?" he asked her. "We use these to locate buried treasure. Some of the shamans from the other tribes dreamed that a bunch of white people were coming into the valley to practice witchcraft. So last night we did a ceremony in the canyon and dug up some of our old records."

It was obvious that we were being warned not to interfere with the sacred order of things. What surprised me was that I was visible to the shamans at a time when I still felt like a novice. Had I literally been in that canyon watching? Had the crystal connected us somehow? Had we been perceived as such a threat that they felt a need to protect some buried "treasure"? Whatever the explanation, the synchronicity of my dream in California and my friend's reality in Arizona had a sobering effect on us, and we proceeded with a much greater respect for all involved.

I can sense when other people's attentions are directed toward me.

Try to notice when other people's energies or attentions enter your personal space and make an impression on you today. Who's there?

I live in a technicolor world.

Let color be the influencing factor in what you wear today and how you make decisions. How do the colors you encounter make you feel, physically and emotionally?

Color is a major force in our world. Each color has a function and contains certain information. Pay attention to the colors that appear throughout your day in the clothes you wear, the food you eat, and the environment that surrounds you. Let color move you and heal you.

Days when I dress in neutral colors—black, gray, oatmeal, taupe, khaki, or ivory—I want to feel quiet and collected. Black absorbs, and though intellectually I don't resonate with the trendy idea of artists swathed head to toe in black, I can see that it can keep a person centered. Lighter neutrals let me blend in anywhere and field the wildest creative process calmly. Wine red, blood red, and cranberry bring out a feeling of power; purple and lavender soothe and uplift; golds and lemon yellows brighten the mind. On a dreary day I often choose turquoise, aqua, or teal, which seem humorous and promote openness and easy flow.

Have you ever judged someone based on the color of their car? What color dishes do you have? How does food taste when eaten from black plates, or from terra-cotta bowls, or from brightly colored ceramics? When you write in your journal, do you write in purple some days, brown on others, and green after that? Do you notice that words flow more easily when the color is right and that the color attracts a certain kind of writing? Have you ever bought a book because the colors on the cover spoke to you? What colors are the walls in your house? Is there any reason you chose bright yellow for the kitchen and adobe brown for the living room? How do you feel when you enter those spaces? Have you ever dyed your hair and felt how the color changed your mood and personality? I have even heard of diets that recommended eating only purple and red foods one day and yellow foods the next.

May 31

Lloyd's three-year-old son, Brian, had a terrible accident; he was trapped beneath their automatic garage door and, when his mother found him, he appeared to be dead. A neighbor performed CPR, and the paramedics continued treatment on the way to the hospital. Brian was revived, but he'd been severely crushed. Miraculously, the doctors found no brain or heart damage. Brian recovered quickly.

A month later, Brian woke from a nap and said to his mother, "Do you remember when I got stuck under the garage door? It was so heavy and it hurt really bad. I called to you, but you couldn't hear me. I started to cry, but then it hurt too bad. And then the 'birdies' came." "The birdies?" his mother asked puzzled. "Yes, the birdies made a whooshing sound and flew into the garage. They took care of me. One of the birdies came and got you." "What did the birdies look like?" she asked. Brian answered, "They were dressed in white, some of them had green and white. They told me the baby would be all right." "The baby?" his mother asked. Brian answered, "The baby lying on the garage floor. You came out and opened the garage door and ran to the baby. You told the baby to stay and not leave." Lloyd's wife had indeed knelt beside Brian's body and whispered, "Don't leave us, Brian; please stay if you can."

"Then what happened?" she asked. "We went on a trip far, far away. We flew so fast up in the air. There is lots and lots of birdies." Brian told her they brought him back and a big fire truck and ambulance were there. A man was bringing the baby out on a white bed. He tried to tell the man the baby would be OK but the man couldn't hear him. Then the bright light came. He said the light was so warm and he loved the light so much. Someone was in the bright light and put their arms around him and told him, "I love you but you have to go back. You have to play baseball and tell everyone about the birdies."

Lloyd said that Brian taught them that the birdies were always with us but the only way we could see them was with our hearts, not with our eyes and ears. Brian explained, "I have a plan, Mommy. You have a plan. Daddy has a plan. Everyone has a plan. We must all live our plan and keep our promises. The birdies help us to do that. They whisper the things to help us do what is right because they love us so much."

Anything is possible; I have help I cannot see.

Today, notice when you feel alone, helpless, scared, blocked, or confused. Remember: you are not alone. Open yourself to receive help from higher levels.

June

June 1

Donna is lush and unabashed in her femininity and sensuality. She radiates huggability and is ready on a moment's notice to go dancing, jump into a hot tub, take a weekend seminar on tantric sex, or go to a full-moon meditation on a mountaintop. She speaks as though everyone in the world swims with dolphins, hikes through the forests of Mt. Shasta, and meets in a goddess group to rediscover the sacred feminine. I have only to think of Donna to experience a greater connection with the Divine Mother.

Donna's boyfriend tells many "Donna stories," which all feature the contagious nature of her enthusiasm—like the time he overheard her on the phone explaining to the people at a credit card company that the reason she couldn't pay her bill this month was because Mercury was retrograde and Pluto was in her second house. And odd as it sounded, apparently the person on the other end of the line was in total sympathy with the stars' sometimes deleterious effect on personal finances. Donna will often host a dinner party, and, when the guests leave, she'll put on her coat and head out to catch the last remnants of a birthday party or meet friends who have gone dancing. Her capacity for pleasure amazes me. I often wonder if she experiences the same sensations I do. What does music sound like to her? Is it richer, fuller? What does a hug feel like? Does it penetrate deeper into her tissues? What do walking, swimming, climbing, and yoga do to her brain synapses?

I remember riding with her and her boyfriend to an outing. Donna was so hungry she couldn't wait until we got to the party so she gathered an array of foods from her refrigerator and ate as we drove. "Mmmmmm. Ahhhhhh. Mmmmm," she cooed, savoring every bite. Smack of lips. Slurp of beverage. Little grunts. Long sigh. Chomp chomp crunch crunch. "Oooooooh. Oh. Ahhhh." Her boyfriend and I looked at each other as the sound effects continued. Then we both burst into laughter. I don't know that food has ever tasted that good to me. I'd like to be able to enjoy the senses the way Donna does—just once!

My body is ready for pleasure.

Concentrate on experiencing pleasure today. What does pleasure mean to you? Notice that pleasure is strongly connected with sensual awareness, the desire to be entertained by life, and an ability to maintain sustained attention.

June 2

Whatever I do deserves my full attention.

Do a thorough job on everything today. You may find that a surprising break-through awaits when you commit to doing things completely.

I took a creativity seminar, "The Painting Experience," with artist Michell Cassou, coauthor of *Life, Paint, and Passion*. Michell's creativity is fresh and childlike, and by having us paint on big pieces of paper with tempera paint, she encouraged us to not be too precious, stiff, or formal. She helped us pay attention to what wanted to be painted, to what color wanted to go onto the paper next, instead of what our minds said made the most sense. As I began the process, the images I made came more from my mind than my heart. Each was properly balanced according to the graphic design principles I had learned in art school. They were interesting, abstract, and colorful but lacked a sense of life. Michell let me go on for several paintings that way.

Finally, she stopped at what I thought was my finished painting and said simply, "Could you please put one more thing on that painting?" I looked at her dumbfounded. "But I'm finished," I protested. "Well just put a black dot on the painting somewhere," she insisted. And she dipped my paintbrush into a big glob of black paint, handed it to me, and waited. I sheepishly took it, hesitatingly aimed it at my perfectly balanced creation, and blobbed a thick black dot just off center. The shock of seeing it there elicited an immediate and thunderous response from my body. I broke down sobbing.

"The hand is connected to the soul," Michell gently reassured me. "Now paint something real from deep within yourself. And paint it until it is complete." And she walked away. I put up a fresh piece of paper and stood staring at it. Something real? Then all at once I was flooded with an impression of a powerful dream I'd had the week before. A dolphin from a UFO swam up a river to find me. He rose out of the water with glowing eyes and a golden crown on his head. I painted him with such absorption I could barely stop at the end of class. From then on, my paintings came from my core imagination.

Even mundane chores can be like those paintings. I can clean up my living room and "add one more black dot" by putting out a vase of fresh flowers or dusting underneath my stereo. When we take the extra time to go the rest of the way, we gain a profound sense of reality and a feeling of true authenticity.

June 3

When I first started working with intuition, I received information primarily through my visual sense. I had been a graphic designer and was used to communicating in symbols and imagery. When I started doing life readings, I saw odd symbols superimposed over parts of the client's body—a ballerina, an olive, a flashlight, a sofa. Sometimes I'd see answers spelled out in different typefaces: bold, italic, capitals if the message was important, lowercase if it was familiar or personal. Gradually I started to hear a voice whispering in my ear. It would begin with something like, "Tell them their father dominated them when they were growing up but now they're learning to be authentic by . . . " As I related the message, the voice would drop off and words would keep pouring out of me.

I then began to feel textures of energy in and around my clients' bodies—sandpapery, pockmarked textures for people who had abused stimulant drugs; a yellow sticky texture that corresponded to marijuana abuse; ashen gray dishwater energy for people who were emotionally exhausted; prickly, electrical energy in people who were anxious or self-critical. Some people had a silky, satiny texture that seemed to denote emotional sensitivity and refinement. Others felt hot inside, which correlated to a passionate creativity and strong life force. Still other people had a foggy, misty quality that made me feel forgetful and distracted. I learned that if my body felt cold and contracted, their body was feeling the same thing emotionally. If I became unusually fluid and eloquent, I knew their body ran energy fluidly through all its conduits. Sometimes you can tell what people are like by the shape of their chests and shoulders, or the way their flesh plumps up beneath their skin, or by the shine on their face and eyes. If you are visual or auditory, try perceiving through your sense of touch and movement.

I can feel intangible textures.

Your kinesthetic sense does more than help you know through physical touch; it can help you discern subtle insights about the world around you. Notice the texture of people's energy today.

June 4

When I breathe
in, I receive
the gifts of the
world; when
I breathe out,
I share my
gifts with the
world.

*Pay attention to
your breath today.
By remembering
what you're
receiving freely
when you inhale
and giving
freely when you
exhale, you'll
easily maintain
an attitude of
gratitude and
generosity.*

In the days when an ice cream sundae cost much less than it does now, a ten-year-old boy entered a hotel coffee shop and sat at a table. The waitress put a glass of water in front of him. "How much is an ice cream sundae?" he asked. "Fifty cents," replied the waitress. The little boy pulled his hand out of his pocket and studied the coins in it. "How much is a dish of plain ice cream?" he inquired. Some people were now waiting for a table and the waitress became a bit impatient. "Thirty-five cents," she said brusquely. The little boy again counted the coins. "I'll have the plain ice cream," he decided. The waitress brought the ice cream, put the bill on the table, and walked away. The boy finished his ice cream, paid the cashier, and departed. When the waitress came back, she began wiping down the table and was surprised to find, placed neatly beside the empty dish, two nickels and five pennies—her tip.

June 5

Talking personally to a higher power is the true form of prayer. Alfred Tennyson wrote, "More things are wrought by prayer than the world dreams of. Wherefore let thy voice rise like a fountain for me night and day. For what are men better than sheep or goats, that nourish a blind life within the brain, if knowing God, they lift not hands of prayer both for themselves, (and) those that call them friend?"

One of my all-time favorite books is *Mr. God, This Is Anna*, by Fynn. In it a precocious little street urchin delves into the mysteries of life, metaphysical truths, and her personal relationship with "Mr. God." Anna believed that churchgoing was "so you could get the message when you were very little." Once you had gotten it, you were supposed to "go out and do something with it." Plus, the idea of collective worship went against her idea of having private conversations with "Mr. God." One time a parson questioned her. Did she believe in God? Yes. Did she know what God was? Yes. What was God then? "He's God!" Did she go to church? No. Why not? "Because I know it all!" What did she know? " 'I know to love Mr. God and to love people and cats and dogs and spiders and flowers and trees'—and the catalog went on—'with all of me.' " Anna reduced her religious philosophy to one sentence: "And God said love me, love them, love it, and don't forget to love yourself."

The divine is my friend.

Write a prayer today.

**Unspoken
undercurrents
affect
outcomes.**

*Listen and feel
for people's
hidden agendas
today, and name
them to yourself
so you can act
more consciously.
When hidden
agendas are made
conscious, they
cease to interfere
with the
natural flow.*

One of my clients, a management consultant, invited me to come with him to talk to one of his clients, a box manufacturing company. The company was owned by two brothers, both with Harvard MBAs, one of whom was just opening to an understanding of the influence of invisible factors on his health and business success. We listened as Jim described his frustrations with his head of production and management team. No one was taking responsibility, no one was thinking creatively, there was poor goal setting and a low level of ambition. Jim felt he had to micromanage everything and ride people constantly.

Jim's energy was intense. He was distracted easily. In fact, I wondered if he had adult attention deficit disorder. I mentioned that part of the reason he might not be connecting with his staff was that he processed information very quickly and with the upper part of his brain. When he communicated, he spoke rapidly and used terms that other people couldn't understand. It was as if he were talking at the pitch of a dog whistle when his staff could only comprehend a bullhorn. This was partly because he was not connected with his body. He could learn, however, to drop to a pitch where he'd be more comprehensible.

The numerological cycles for the management team revealed that the production manager had a pattern, as would be expected, that was heavy in structural elements, making him methodical, reliable, and thorough but not necessarily speedy and innovative. Jim and his brother both had patterns that were weighted toward communication, networking, agile mental activity, and personal self-expression—not what I would expect of people producing square, practical containers.

As I mentioned this Jim said, "I've been doing a little acting. I was an extra in a Bruce Willis movie." I said, "Well that's a great direction for you!" He needed to get his ideas out into the world, be in front of people, and be involved with imagination and creative works. "Have you and your brother thought of switching businesses and getting involved with cable television, satellites, education, a media or production company?" His face lit up and gears began turning. Jim realized he was out of alignment with what his soul wanted to do. He'd stuck with the box company because it was the responsible thing but it wasn't fulfilling. He saw that he needed to be in his own element.

June 7

In a university commencement address, Brian Dyson, CEO of Coca-Cola Enterprises, said, "Imagine life as a game in which you are juggling five balls in the air. These balls are work, family, health, friends, and spirit. You will soon understand that work is a rubber ball. If you drop it, it will bounce back. But the other four balls—family, health, friends, and spirit—are made of glass. If you drop one of these, it will be irrevocably scuffed, marked, nicked, damaged, or even shattered. You must understand that and strive for balance in your life."

Dyson also suggested that a certain philosophy of life could promote balance:

1. Value the differences among people.
2. Set goals by being loyal to your own way, not by what others deem important.
3. Value the things closest to your heart and don't take them for granted.
4. Live in the present, one day at a time.
5. Don't give up when you still have something to give.
6. Taking chances helps us learn how to be brave and confident.
7. The quickest way to receive love is to give it; the quickest way to lose love is to hold it too tightly.
8. A person's greatest emotional need is to feel appreciated.
9. Knowledge is a weightless treasure you can always carry easily.
10. Don't use time or words carelessly. Neither can be retrieved.

How do we find this balance? Look at your habits. Listen to your complaints. What is your conscience nagging you about? Do you need to get a little more exercise? Cut down on coffee or sugar? Do you need quality time with your children? Some frivolity with friends? Is your work lacking creativity and heart? Maybe you need to go on a meditation retreat or take a pilgrimage to the Yucatan. Which areas need adjustment? What can you do to massage each area into greater functionality and joy?

I balance the important components of my life.

Notice the parts of yourself that have been neglected lately, and give time to your whole self today. Have you been too mental, domestic, aggressive, or extroverted? Have you spent enough time on personal hygiene, chatting with friends, organizing your office, or meditating?

**I vary my
stance,
my rhythm,
my breath.**

*Notice your
subtle inner pos-
tures today, and
break them up
or change them as
much as possible.
By shifting the
way you hold
yourself, you
increase your
potential for
inspired insight
and creativity.*

Direct your attention to your own inner postures and
notice when you take a position about something. Where
do you hold energy? Do you twist or angle your body
toward or away from the situation? Do you lead with
your chin? Or with the top of your head, as though you
were a charging ram? When someone says something that
frustrates or scares you, where does your body contract?
Do you frown, squint, or close your eyes to focus your
attention? When do you stop breathing? When do you
cross your arms or legs? What parts of your body do you
protect by covering them with your hands? When you
notice yourself holding energy, stretch, twist, move,
breathe, sigh, laugh, stand up, walk around, and vary your
physical position so the energy can move on.

A friend who does deep tissue bodywork tells me that
he often encounters people's *inner postures*, a term he uses
to describe various subtle holding patterns in the body.
He says that some people, for instance, tilt their head and
angle one ear slightly forward when they listen. Others
don't breathe when they listen, holding tension near the
sternum. When we are trying to understand something,
we will run through a series of extremely subtle maneuvers, holding the focus of energy in certain places then
releasing it, squeezing it, or fluttering it. When processing
a new insight, some people give the impression of energy
zipping around in their head like a ball in a pinball
machine, almost making their eyes blink. As he spoke to a
woman over lunch one day, he inadvertently said something that made her feel vulnerable. She responded with a
subtle jutting of her chin that appeared belligerent. He
had the feeling she might bite him. She said she had once
been sexually attacked by a man she'd gotten a ride from,
and she could trace the feeling in her jaw to the moment
right before she fought off her molester.

June 9

Christine Wicker, a freelance columnist for the *Dallas Morning News*, wrote about her experience as part of a group of 5,000 people who came together in Indiana to receive the Kalachakra initiation and empowerment from the Dalai Lama. This sacred ceremony is dedicated to world peace and the development of compassion. She tells how she was hungry, cold, bored, and squirmy through much of the day's spiritual practice. She explained, "I didn't have the Buddha nature, and the lack of it was making me miserable."

On her way out, she encountered a beatific woman who was certain the ceremony would change her life. When Christine expressed her own mixed feelings, the woman sweetly said, "Don't worry. You'll get a blessing anyway."

After the Kalachakra, the Dalai Lama gave a news conference. Christine was in the front row. As journalists from around the world began to ask questions, the Dalai Lama took time to shake hands with each one. People squealed and shouted and pushed forward. Christine was only three people away from touching the holy man when she heard a woman's wail from behind her. "I want to shake hands with the Dalai Lama!" a young journalist cried. The look on her face was so desperate that Christine thought, "How could I reach toward a god with the cries of the dispossessed ringing in my ears?" And she gave up her place. By the time the young woman stepped away, the Dalai Lama had moved on.

"What a dope you are," Christine chided herself. "You tossed away your big chance and all for a woman you don't even know." Then the Dalai Lama stopped, turned around, and looked at her. "I want to shake this woman's hand," he said. He leaned far over the table and laughingly said, "It's hard to reach!" Christine says that the warmth of his palm lingered a long time. She realized his action fit perfectly with the meaning of the day's ceremony. For her it was an affirmation. "Those who give up for others don't get left behind."

I'm rewarded when I act on my soul's urges.

Notice the difference today between your mind's pettiness and your soul's integrity. Feel your deepest motivations today, and act on them. You may be surprised how often people acknowledge you for it.

**I am
upbeat and
contributory.**

*Share positive
observations with
others today,
and see what
happens to your
energy level.
When you stop
complaining and
look for the
small, interesting
details of life,
you will often
experience
endurance and
clarity.*

I have worked in Japan every year since 1985 giving private intuitive counseling and seminars. In the beginning, I felt pressured by the sheer number of people in Tokyo. Working with an interpreter and learning new language rhythms, social mores, and an entirely new perceptual orientation were challenging. The stress level was so great that I often got sick. When I arrived, I'd copy my appointments into my calendar; there would be lists of names filling every day, the days marching off toward the horizon. Each morning, I'd get up and go to McDonald's for breakfast. Then I'd see clients, take a break, see more clients, take a break, see more clients; and in the evening I'd curl up in a tiny bathtub and try to relax with my knees folded to my chest. Then the same thing would happen the next day, and the next, and the next. Some days I'd suddenly realize I was in a tiny hotel room in a foreign country with an interpreter and a client and I had no idea what day it was or how far along in the schedule I was. I'd admonish myself to combat the boredom by saying, "Get in your body! Stay present! Say the next real thing!" And so, though I love my work, I would plow through the seemingly endless days.

I've since come to see my Japan time as a meditation. It is devoid of normal distractions and is a powerful opportunity to focus on the consciousness of my body. I've learned that it's important to keep my energy level up and to receive as much as I give. If I cast one day ahead in my mind, my energy drops. If I complain, even slightly, my energy drops. But if I stay simple, cheerful, appreciative, and willing to be entertained, my energy and attitude remain high. I can easily deal with the full range of human suffering and joy.

I have come to see cheerfulness as an extremely high spiritual state. It keeps my body healthy and my mind adaptable and focused in a compassionate way. Cheerfulness teaches me that the small, interesting details are as powerful as dramatic events. Perceived through cheerfulness, each client is fascinating and each day's clients often share themes. Finding these patterns rejuvenates and entertains me.

June 11

I tuned in a metaphysically oriented radio talk show late the other night and heard a caller named Erik telling the following story. His mother had just died and he was contemplating getting married to a woman he'd been dating for several years. He was confused about what to do, and as he was driving home after work, he was talking to his mother in his imagination. "Mom, I wish you were here. I know you'd know how to advise me on this. So, Mom, if you are really here with me, show me a sign. If it's right for me to marry Jenny, let me see a deer in the wooded section of the road ahead." He drove on around the bend and there, carefully crossing the road, was not just one deer but a whole family. He took the omen as reassurance that his mother was indeed with him, went ahead and married his girlfriend, and has been quite happy with the decision. But how do these things happen?

Did Erik's mother actually create deer for him, or was Erik telepathically tuned in to the animals' presence long before he approached that bend in the road? Did Erik's higher mind use that opportunity to give him an experience of mystery, something that would help him open spiritually into a greater understanding of how life works? Was his mother flying along next to the car, cheering from on high at Erik's wonderful ability to get through to himself? Perhaps creating this synchronicity experience was a way Erik could allow himself to feel a more profound connection between his inner mind and outer reality, with the unseen dimensions and his mother's soul, with the wiser part of the Big Self, and with unconditional love—which makes it all possible.

I look for the meanings in coincidence.

Notice synchronicities today. Your soul influences your perception by highlighting certain scenes and ideas, causing you to interpret your experience in particular ways. What are you trying to tell yourself?

I love fluidity.

Be aware of your body's joy in movement today. Fluidity promotes intuition.

Energy waves continually move through you, bringing you information and lifting you and carrying you down the long curl of a wave. The more you let these waves flow, the more your movement in the world will become fluid, adaptable, and effortlessly natural. To improve your fluidity, try the following exercise:

WORKING WITH ENERGY WAVES

1. Imagine your skin is porous and your tissues are transparent. Let every cell, molecule, and atom in your body feel cooperative with the rest. Visualize millions of tiny wavelike threads of light coming from every direction, entering your body, each running on a particular pathway from particle to particle, then going out the other side and back into space again. Relax and let yourself feel suspended in this wondrous, safe, loving web of oscillating light.

2. Sit for a while, simply tracing these waves of energy, light, and information through different parts of your body. Notice any tendency to stop a wave and hold it. Are there places in your body where you've stopped waves and jammed up your circuits? Let those waves pass through now and clear any spots that may seem flooded, chaotic, or dead. Hint: You won't know what wisdom the wave has for you until you let it pass all the way through.

3. After you've practiced relaying the tiny waves of energy, stand up and tune in to a bigger wave of motion or action. What direction does your body want to go? With what speed and intensity does it want to move? What kind of rhythm feels natural? Let yourself step into a current; go with the flow. As you do, let it move and direct you without your mind having to know ahead of time.

June 13

How magnificent might we be if we could respond
entirely to life's shifting currents with everything we've
got? If I had to start fresh right now and relearn who I am
and how to live, I'd want lots of curiosity, innocence,
fresh perceptions, and fullness. I'd be fluid, adaptable, and
playful. How much fixed identity do we really need? How
continuous must we be? Do I need to build credibility by
leaving a trail of recognizable accomplishments?

Maybe what we are is some mathematical formula that
continually recombines to produce different results. If I let
myself be the evolving result and serve the formula, my
ways could change easily. I could stay up at night and go
to sleep at dawn. I could know people who might normally upset me. I could learn a new language in which the
modifiers come after the nouns. I could rewire my brain.
I could be a rancher, volunteer at a hospice, learn about
television production, and facilitate international good
works. I wouldn't know what I couldn't do. What seems
important is an open mind and a loose, responsive body,
an attitude of amazement and amusement, joy in finding
the incredible connections between things, feeling the
wondrous accentuating power of contrast.

Sometimes I shift entirely out of caring and interest,
away from meaningfulness. The world pales and becomes
the clear, pure mathematical expression of universal laws.
Then I don't feel connected because connection isn't even
a reality in the oneness. I can hardly remember what it is
to be human. Maybe this happens when the formula is
pulling me out of the form I've been occupying as it begins
its recombination. Maybe it's not bad. Maybe I shouldn't
label it boredom or depression but a phase of reinvention.

Next thing I know, I am fascinated again by a new
possibility, my attention totally captured by the design of
a brochure or the way a sparrow comically splatters water
out of the birdbath. Creative projects seem totally worth-
while—and there aren't going to be nearly enough years
in my lifetime to translate my inner blueprints into art!
Maybe this is not *good*, not really passion, but the moment
when the formula settles into its next new pattern and I
am reinvented.

**I reinvent
myself.**

*Let yourself
be new today,
free of past
habits and con-
cepts of identity.
When you let
go of old ideas,
the unknown
will surprise you
with something
even better.
We don't have
to be so tightly
defined.*

June 14

**I admire
what I want to
become.**

*Who are your
heroes and
heroines? What
do they embody
that you feel
is lacking in
yourself?*

In my classes I often have people list their heroes and heroines and then have conversations with them about situations in their lives. In one group the list included Princess Diana, Shirley MacLaine, Vanessa Redgrave, Albert Einstein, Jesus Christ, Oprah Winfrey, Carl Jung, Moses, Jimmy Carter, Roseanne, Harry Truman, Anne Frank, Abraham Lincoln, Joan of Arc, Jackie Kennedy, Helen Keller, Frank Lloyd Wright, Robert Redford, Madame Blavatsky, the Dalai Lama, and "my grand-mother." Who are your heroes and heroines?

Each role model symbolizes a particular character trait that you feel needs development in your personality. Each is an archetype for you; you notice your heroes and heroines because this trait is trying to make itself known to you so it can become an integrated part of your life. If you didn't have the trait in you already, you couldn't notice it. So what are you attracting to yourself as a new personality trait?

Here's what the group participants said their heroes meant to them. Princess Diana was beautiful, gracious, and loving in spite of hardship. Shirley MacLaine was a creative risk taker who spoke her truth. Vanessa Redgrave stood up for her unpopular beliefs. Einstein was in touch with inspiration. Jesus had faith and courage. Oprah was compassionate and made something of herself. Carl Jung was wise and a leading-edge thinker. Moses was faithful to his mission even when it was hard. Jimmy Carter was a gentle, nonegotistical humanitarian leader. Roseanne revealed herself and was vulnerable but positive. Harry Truman was real and honest. Anne Frank was hopeful and loving. Lincoln was a catalyst for humanitarian change. Joan of Arc was loyal, faithful, courageous. Jackie Kennedy endured hardships with class. Helen Keller was life affirming. Frank Lloyd Wright was a practical vision-ary. Robert Redford had integrity and vision and gave back to the land and his community. Madame Blavatsky was inspired and lived her mission. The Dalai Lama was compassionate and patient. Our various grandmothers were nurturing and inspiring.

June 15

Certain creations have a will to be born, a life of their own, and an ability to reach the people who need them. I did some intensive alpha brain-wave training years ago during which the participants sat in darkened individual cubicles with carpeting on the floor and walls, staring at a video screen, tracking the level of alpha waves we were able to produce and maintain. Experimenting with combinations of visualization and tactile imagination worked well for me in creating this state of engaged indifference. Spontaneously, a vision came to me in the midst of a session.

I saw myself climbing up a cedar tree that grew next to the house I lived in when I was three years old. I went up farther than I ever had in real life, emerging through the top branches to find a huge bird's nest. A monstrous white eagle descended from the heavens and landed on the edge of the nest. He introduced himself and said that he was God's messenger. If I wanted he'd take me to see God. What ensued was a shamanic journey through the three levels of heaven to meet God, who, of course, sat on a throne. But God was just a big bright light and had no shape. As I watched the light, it changed into recognizable shapes, and after quite a kaleidoscopic array, the light turned into the exact shape of my three-year-old self and came off the throne and stepped inside me, becoming me. With that, there was a series of powerful revelations and a descent through the heavens back to earth. What did it mean? A voice said, "This is to be a children's book."

Six months later the vision came back into my awareness with an insistence so great that I was compelled to write it out. The result was a story called "White Eagle and the Girl with the Hole in Her Middle." A client saw it on my desk and exclaimed, "I've *got* to read this!" She had been severely abused as a girl and had felt all her life that she had a hole in her middle. I lent her a copy, and in several weeks she called back. "I've been reading this story again and again and every time I cry. It's helping me feel myself. I *love* this story!" Months later I got a letter from the woman's psychotherapist. "I hope you don't mind, but my client shared your story with me. I found it so moving that I've been reading it to other clients who have suffered abuse, and we are all getting great value from it."

The flow moves me in surprising ways.

Notice happy accidents today, and follow them. When things don't go your way, it may mean that you don't really know the way! Perhaps you're being drawn to a new person or idea that could change your life.

June 16

I gain energy by completing challenging actions.

Make a list of actions you've intended to take but have postponed. What's the real reason you've avoided doing each thing? Can you complete one today? Each incompleted goal drains you a bit and weakens your integrity.

Karen wanted to challenge herself by making a parachute jump. She'd been experiencing many birth metaphors and felt she was on the verge of something new happening in her life. Acting out a birth symbolically seemed like a good idea, and stepping into nothingness was a great metaphor. After three reschedulings, the skydive finally happened, but not before her daughter told her, "Don't die, Mom," and her five-year-old grandaughter advised, "Be careful, Grammy, and land softly."

Karen writes, "It was a tandem jump and as we were suiting up, my instructor said, 'Don't worry, I'll take care of everything.' Kind of like the message that God tries to get through to all of us, but we refuse to listen. I wasn't prepared for the force of the wind when I followed my guide into the emptiness of space. I found myself struggling to breathe, just like I did in the early stages of labor. I also found myself doing what I do in real life—trying to stay in control. I realize now that I may have missed the magic because I was so intent on doing it right. How many moments of magic on the ground have I missed for the same reason?

"When the chute opened, there was a powerful jerk upward as the air rushed into the pockets of fabric. And then everything got silent, just like the world sounds after a carpeting of fresh snow. It was there in the silence, in space, that I really felt God. I would have liked to remain there forever, suspended and floating in time, gazing around in wonder. Landing was uneventful and anticlimactic, like coming down from a mountain. I have yet to experience the adrenaline rush my instructor talked about; I find an evening of wild Zydeco dancing to be more of a high than skydiving, but then, I didn't jump for the high— I jumped to find my feet. Driving home, I couldn't hold back the tears of awe and gratitude; it was as if I were seeing life on the ground for the first time. Everything was at once more peaceful and vibrant yet subdued. How strange it is that falling down affects how one looks up.

"I also learned something about fear up there, 10,000 feet above my everyday life. It is the *fear* of the unknown, not the unknown, that causes pain in life. It reminds me of one of my favorite quotes by the dancer Gabrielle Roth: 'After you jump and before you land, there is God.'"

June 17

What are the important things in your life? Time with your loved ones? Your faith, your education, your dreams? A worthy cause? Teaching or mentoring others? Do you devote enough time to each of them?

A time-management expert was speaking to a group of high-powered business students and said, "Ok time for a quiz." He pulled out a one-gallon mason jar and set it on the table in front of him. Then he produced a dozen fist-sized rocks and carefully placed them one at a time into the jar. When no more rocks would fit inside, he asked, "Is this jar full?" Everyone in the class said yes. "Really?" he asked. He reached under the table, pulled out a bucket of gravel, dumped some in, and shook the jar, causing the pebbles to work themselves down into the spaces between the big rocks. He asked the group once more, "Is the jar full?" This time the class was onto him. "Probably not," one of them ventured.

"Good!" he replied. He reached under the table and brought out a bucket of sand. He dumped the sand in the jar, and it settled into all of the spaces left between the rocks and the gravel. Once more he asked, "Is this jar full?" "No!" the class shouted. Once again he said, "Good!" Then he grabbed a pitcher of water and poured it into the jar until it was filled to the brim. He looked at the class and asked, "What is the point of this illustration?" One eager beaver raised his hand and said, "The point is, no matter how full your schedule is, if you try hard, you can always fit some more things in." "No," the speaker replied, "that's not the point. The truth this illustration teaches us is this. *If you don't put the big rocks in first, you'll never get them in at all.*"

Take some time to define your priorities—the big rocks, the gravel, the sand, the water. As you choose experiences and activities for each category, notice how your body feels as you realize the truth of each choice. What are your certainty signals? How do you make your decisions?

Pay attention to your left brain today, to your way of defining, describing, and drawing conclusions.

**I see you;
I know you;
I like you.**

*Look for and
talk to the soul
in the people
you meet today.
Support the
expression of
their dreams.*

Inside everyone is a dream wanting to come true. Look for it, lend it an ear, love it, and bring your own and others' dreams to life. Winston Churchill said, "We make a living by what we get, but we make a life by what we give."

Stacy Brice is a colleague who trains and coaches virtual assistants. She once wrote about one of her friends who had profoundly thanked Stacy for her faith in her personal and professional vision. Stacy said, "She and her work are one of those things in life that shine so brilliantly there's no way they can be ignored. They light me up inside. That's why my friend and her work are a huge part of my life. I just know I am supposed to contribute to her in a sizable way, so I do my best to do that." She said she realized that at certain points in our lives we are introduced to people, places, and things that light us up inside. And those are the people, places, and things that we absolutely must pay attention to, make time for, and give energy to. "The universe is giving us, in those moments, clear and brilliant access to our individual 'big pictures,'" Stacy says. "And for all the seemingly trite words of wisdom we've read, these opportunities are rare. It's up to all of us to follow our intuition in these situations, whether it seems logical or not, and lend our support to 'the Dream.'"

Stacy emphasizes the importance of never letting go of what lights us up inside. "Be tenacious!" she says. "Don't let the loveless ones sell you a world wrapped in gray. Everything you want is just around the next corner. If you have trouble finding it, consider the possibility that just when you've decided to give up, someone else may be sensing the rightness of your vision and feeling how perfect it is to assist you."

June 19

Cameron Hogan from Baltimore tells the story of how when he was in college he became interested in martial arts and Zen Buddhism. He gave himself a challenge. He would do a Zen meditative practice for at least twenty minutes every day. If he didn't do it, he vowed, he'd have to be dead! He kept his word, and after practicing this simple meditation for a year, he noticed he was performing at a much higher level intellectually than he ever had before. His capacity for remembering what he heard and read was immense and effortless. In fact, he says if he did forget anything, all he'd have to do was visualize his professor walking into the room and telling him the answer and his memory would snap right back.

Just a few months ago, Cam came across an old book, *The Relaxation Response*, by Herbert Benson. He was surprised to find that the technique recommended in the book was almost identical to what he had instinctively done in college. Benson recommended meditating for fifteen to twenty minutes daily, silently witnessing what was happening in the mind, body, and environment. In that short time, the "relaxation response" would occur, when the right and left brain come into synchronization. The left brain maintains the structures of our lives and doesn't like change, whereas the right brain is creative and adaptable and thrives on change. When the relaxation response occurs, the two parts of the brain can cooperate and feed information to each other, and it is then that we realize our truth and genius. Cam wasn't too surprised, then, to read Benson's documentation of memory enhancement and mental clarity as a result of this simple meditative practice.

When I fully relax, I know clearly.

Notice what insights come to you when you're calm today. When your body is free of tension, your mind will be, too, and then your inner knowing can beam through without interference.

**I protect
myself.**

*Your hands often
act out mini-
dramas that
reveal the deeper
relationship
between your
masculine and
feminine natures.
Let your
dominant-side
hand take
care of your
nondominant-side
hand today.
Imagine your
strong, masculine
self is protecting
your vulnerable,
feminine self.*

I was chopping broccoli absentmindedly one night when
the knife went too far and sliced deeply into my left
forefinger. The cut bled profusely and took a long time
to staunch with a towel. As I stood at the cutting board,
I tried to calm myself. I looked at my hands, and they
seemed to be involved in a drama of their own, separate
from me. My right hand cradled my left one, holding the
towel in place and squeezing just the right amount to
close the wound. My mind went into the cut area. I could
feel it was in shock and that the cells were scared because
they'd been suddenly separated from each other. There
was chaos in there. I knew the tissues needed loving
attention. My left finger felt like an overwhelmed little
child.

Then I put my attention in my right hand. Immediately I sensed a conversation going on. My right hand was
saying to the left, "I want to apologize to you. I was
going too fast and not thinking of your safety. I feel terrible that through my haste and unconsciousness I have
wounded you. I'm going to hold you and send love into
you. I'll hold you for as long as you want until you calm
down and can feel your own life again." My right thumb
pressed quietly on the cut, and I could feel energy flowing
steadily into it. I sensed the separated cells beginning to
have a conversation with each other. "Where are you?"
one side called out to the other. "I'm right here," the
other side answered. They started to recognize each other
and connect their lines of energy, reassured by the right
thumb and forefinger, which continued supporting them.
I let my left and right sides keep talking to each other to
reestablish harmony.

My left hand said, "I feel safe when you give me this
kind of attention." My right hand said, "I realize you
were trying to serve and help me, and I appreciate that. I
couldn't have done my part unless you were doing yours."
When the bleeding stopped, I let my right hand stroke my
left one. This made my left hand very happy and content.
Within a few days, the cut had healed entirely without a
trace of a scar.

June 21

My left hand was as active as my right when I was a child. It took the initiative in finger painting; it reached for the little bunches of green grapes my mother snipped apart into child-sized servings. Even today my left hand scrubs my teeth, blows my hair dry, and claps on top when I applaud. I remember my mother teaching me to use my right hand intentionally, correcting me when I forgot and started forward with the left.

Barry Lopez in *About This Life* has a wonderful chapter called "The Passage of Hands." Like me, he says, "I do not remember the ascendency of the right hand. It was the one I was forced to write with. . . . I remember a furious nun grabbing my six-year-old hands in prayer and wrenching the right thumb from under the left. Right over left, she insisted. *Right over left.* Right over left in praying to God."

Some days I am aware that my right side and right hand have tired of being so responsible. They feel martyred by having to do everything, taking care of the bulk of my daily business. If I pay attention at times like these, I can feel my left hand waiting in the wings like an anxious understudy hoping for a chance to go on. My left hand loves to put food in my mouth, care for my body, type words on the keyboard, and hold the telephone. When I'm absentminded and look down and see my left hand lying flat across my sternum, or cradling the back of my neck, or squeezing that acupressure point between the thumb and palm of my right hand, I realize it is healing me, nurturing a weary part by sending in new energy. I love the sweetness and generosity of my left hand, and I try to remember to give it equal time.

Lopez says, "I will ask my hands to undress me. Before I turn out the light, I will fold and set my reading glasses aside. Then I will cup my hands, the left in the right, and slide them under the pillow, beneath my head, where they will speculate, as I will, about what we shall handle the next day. . . ."

I nurture myself.

Notice what your hands tell you about how you provide love. Let your non-dominant-side hand take care of your dominant-side hand today. Imagine your receptive, feminine self is nurturing your dynamic, masculine self.

**My basic
nature is light.**

*Be aware of
how light and
lack of light
affect you today,
physically and
emotionally.
Light is a
powerful force
that can facilitate
extroversion or
introversion,
positive moods or
depressive ones.*

Just north of San Francisco, the mornings and late afternoons are characterized by a dense fog. Seen with time-lapse photography, maps of the Bay Area show white tendrils streaking inward, then dancing out toward the ocean again; the whole place seems to be throbbing. Just beyond the chilly, damp boundaries of the San Francisco Bay and the city itself, where the fog blankets the land day and night, lie warmer, drier, balmier zones with only partial fog. I live in one of these.

I've never become comfortable with the dark mornings. I blink awake, sensing the slight change in light, but never quite fill with the joy of a new day. The light is not butter yellow, shining through my blinds casting golden lines across the wall. Nor do I have subtle streaks of lavender dawn glowing rosily over my face. My bedroom is a cave and rising can seem unnatural. It feels as though I should be hibernating. The shadowy quality of morning in the North Bay makes me feel cold. I layer on extra clothes, knowing that later I will need to peel. Sometime around ten o'clock the sun gets high and hot enough to burn through the mist, and the perfect, cloudless, robin's egg–colored sky takes its rightful place above me again. Heat builds and birds sing.

The quality of midday summer light here is often crystalline, accenting the crisp edges of leaves and outlining each flower petal. It reveals intense apple and emerald greens, lovingly sculpts the rolling hills covered with golden grasses, and highlights the deep blues of the bay. My heart is happy; my body wants to soak up that light like the vegetables in my garden.

Then the afternoon breeze begins blowing in from the sea, sometimes roughly. Shadows from the big leafy trees stipple the lawn with wildly moving splotches. My energy rises. Creativity breaks loose in new ways. The temperature drops sharply. The light becomes more muted, refracted through the growing moisture content. Soon the fog will swoop through for the night, and I will draw in once again to the inner realms.

June 23

If you see a world full of disparate, unrelated objects or if you can't see the effect of your actions, you'll feel cut off and your intuition will hibernate. It's only when we see how one thing is like another that information and creativity flow effortlessly and abundantly. The grass is like a carpet; Bill's bald head is a beacon; her thighs are like cucumbers; my new boyfriend is like my last one; his voice sounds like he's under water; she smells like pumpkin pie; I feel golden; my boss is like my mother; there is a mountain of work; his eyes were like little black BBs; she has creamy skin.

What meanings do symbols suggest to you? Look at corporate logos and think consciously about what qualities they mean to convey. What emotions are elicited by photos in today's newspaper or scenes on the television news? Look at the clothing styles people choose—what message are they sending? Anne Lamott in *Bird by Bird* lets her mind make wonderful, wild connections. She says about writing, "It is only when I go ahead and decide to shoot my literary, creative wad on a daily basis that I get any sense of full presence, of being Zorba the Greek at the keyboard. Otherwise I am a wired little rodent squirreling things away, hoarding and worrying about supply." And, "Writers are like vacuum cleaners, sucking up all that we can see and hear and read and think and feel and articulate. . . ." And, "Try looking at your mind as a wayward puppy that you are trying to paper train. You don't drop-kick a puppy into the neighbor's yard every time it piddles on the floor. You just keep bringing it back to the newspaper."

Fill your conversations with colorful comparisons and interesting connections today, and see how much fun you can have.

Everything is like something else.

Practice thinking and speaking in similes and metaphors today. One of the keys in intuition development is the ability to see similarities and make connections.

I am exact.

*Eliminate
extraneous
language today.*

To practice saying what you mean, try eliminating throw-away phrases and words such as "to make a long story short," " 'ya know?," "let me tell you," "I mean," "frankly," and "I could be wrong but." Try not prefacing what you're going to say. Just say it. Take an extra long time to consider what you need to say. Let the other person be comfortable or uncomfortable with the pause. Say what you mean the first time and only one way. Don't explain too much or justify your perception. Let that thought plop right out there and sit in the limelight. Enjoy the open space at the end of your sentence as you wait for a response. As you reduce the number of words, your inner sense of telepathy may emerge and show you how good you are at instinctual and intuitive communication.

Try this: write out directions to your house for people coming from the north, south, east, and west, imagining that you are going to give these instructions to someone over the phone. Be succinct. Use good sensory descriptive words such as "hairpin turn" instead of "U-turn" so people don't get confused by misleading images.

You might also write some haikus today to practice boiling an observation down to its key words. Here are some examples.

my face was wrinkled
in the dream
an older me was smiling

> coffee and Sting at Dr. Insomnia's
> a sunny Sunday morning moment
> one of my life jewels

great blue heron wading
toward me purposefully, pausing
cocks his head, stops time

June 25

Did you think you only had a physical life in time and space? There is so much more to us than the daily round! At night you fly high and reconnect with great amounts of your innate knowledge, but by the time you shrink back to your earthly personality again each morning, your expanded experiences may translate into strange images or may even be reduced to simple geometric patterns. If you can reenter the dream and feel it again, then extend it, you can get insights about what your dreaming self knows. Here's a dream I explored in meditation: *I'm on a scientific mission to pick up a researcher who's made a discovery about a new layer of history by finding a peculiar fossil. The fossil is a small snail-like spiral three inches in diameter and pure white. As we start our return journey, I realize we're on Pluto!*

I decided to go back into the dream and focus on the fossil. This is what I wrote: *As I concentrate on the fossil, I am drawn closer and closer, and soon the spiral turns from rock into a living, vibrating vortex of white energy. It is the core entry/exit point into and out of matter; I dive in and come out the other side into blue sky; I don't fall because there's no ground to fall onto. I am the sky, cheerful and light. Now I can feel the sky suddenly wants to turn itself inside out and become a particle. I'm imploding impossibly into one tiny point. Now I am tumbling over and over in a forward somersault, down down darker darker denser denser until I can barely stand it. When I can go no further, I explode and become the sky again.*

From this spontaneous dream extension, I could sense that we enact this cycle of transformation continually day and night, deep within ourselves in the particles of our bodies and in our thoughts. When we try to stop the process or identify with either sky or particle, we inadvertently repress the natural flow of the process of life blinking in and out.

My dreams hold meaning.

Your dreams can provide glimpses into your higher-dimensional activities. Pick a nighttime dream and explore it today by reentering and extending it.

*Tell people what
you love and
are excited about
today. How else
will they know
how to help you
succeed?*

Larry has discovered it is crucial to know what truly pleases you. He had a conversation with a woman who was feeling bored and unsuccessful with her public speaking career. She complained that she had to do so much herself, and, just when she thought she'd made progress, she'd backslide due to a lack of support from others. He asked her, "What would happen if you were really successful as a public speaker?" She answered, "I wouldn't have any time to myself, and I might have to talk about subjects repeatedly that had become boring to me."

He said, "So if you achieved your goal of becoming a successful public speaker, you'd feel like you were sacrificing yourself by having to work too much, and you'd feel trapped by an obligation to continue presenting material that had no relevance to your truth?" "Yes, that's about it," she replied. Larry said, "So what makes you think anyone is going to help you achieve your goal of becoming a successful public speaker when underneath they know it's going to make you unhappy?"

Larry told the woman that he himself had only recently realized that other people actually *want* to help us. He said that our true inner motive is to promote the flow of creativity, happiness, and life. When people are unhappy and self-sacrificing, the flow of life is blocked and no one is served. It's important to give other people clear messages about what we love, about our true desires and curiosities, so they can align with us and provide whatever help they're capable of giving. When we unconsciously ask for something that will produce misery, the world and other people won't cooperate. In this case, what this woman loved was to talk to people about what was real in their lives and how they could fulfill their life purpose. She didn't want to give canned talks that held no passion for her. She wanted to tell people that what gave her joy was relating spontaneously with audiences who were interested in finding their ideal livelihood. After that, she could easily recommit to her public speaking career.

June 27

Many years ago, I made a vision-quest journey to the Southwest. I was studying shamanism, working with a man who was close to the Hopi elders. He asked me to go to Hopiland to deliver a gift of tobacco to Grandfather David, who was then nearly a hundred years old. My friend said, "Listen carefully to what he says to you—he may talk about your shoes, but he will give you a message."

I arrived at Grandfather David's adobe house and, once inside, a woman who was cooking yelled over her shoulder, "Grandfather! This is Penney."

"Come over and sit next to me," Grandfather David said. He sat propped against a wall, wearing a red shirt, thick glasses, and a headband. I sat next to him, and he put his hand on my knee. I gave him the gift, which he tucked inside his shirt. I noticed that he had lost an eye and the empty socket was tearing considerably. I remembered someone had given me some special ionized water, and I said, "Grandfather, I have some healing water that might be good for your eye." "Go get it!" he commanded me.

I returned and gave him the bottle. "Go get a spoon and put some in my eye," he ordered. "Oh, my God," I thought. "I'm not a nurse." He'd taken his glasses off and tilted his head back, waiting for me. I gingerly poured some water into the spoon and nervously inched toward his missing eye. As I dropped a little into the socket, he let out a loud "EEEEOOUUWA, EEEEOHWAOHH" that seemed to go on for thirty seconds. "Oh, great," I thought, "I've wounded him!" But he dropped his head, blinked, put his glasses back on, and said, "Mmmm. That *is* good water."

He stared at me for a long time. Then he said, "The kachinas are here today." Another long pause, then, *"Are you a medicine woman?"* I knew that if I said no, I wouldn't ever be one, and if I said yes, I'd *have* to be one. I started to laugh and squeaked out, "Maybe." He laughed, too, at the underlying complex of meaning. After a while, I said I had to go because I had a long drive ahead. "Why are you in such a hurry?" he asked. "You have all the time in the world."

Now of course, I realize he was talking directly to my soul, reminding me to see the unseen, asking me if I was going to commit to a life as a healer, and teaching me about the power of the present moment.

Normal conversations contain great wisdom.

Listen for the real messages in what people say today. In spite of our normal levels of mental distraction, the soul is present in much of what we exchange with each other.

I do what is right, for my own sake.

Take that one extra little action today that betters the world, even if no one else knows. Everything we do is really for our own benefit, especially when we begin to realize our oneness with the world. We learn that we are other people and serving others is serving ourselves.

I was visiting my friend John Charles on a ranch north of Santa Barbara. One morning we drove into town in his old pickup truck. As we rounded one of the numerous bends along the road, we came upon several bags of trash that someone had dumped and that had started to scatter across the landscape. John Charles pulled over and spent a good ten minutes cleaning up the side of the road, putting the garbage in the back of his own truck. "People!" he muttered under his breath as he climbed back in. "No sense of beauty anymore." And we drove on. This reminded me of a fable.

In ancient times, a king had a boulder placed in the middle of a road. Then he carefully hid himself and watched to see if anyone would remove the huge rock. Many of the king's wealthiest merchants and courtiers came by but simply walked around it. They loudly blamed the king for not keeping the roads clear, but none did anything about getting the big stone out of the way. Finally, a peasant came along carrying a heavy load of vegetables. On approaching the boulder, the peasant laid down his burden and tried to move the stone to the side of the road. After much pushing and straining, he finally succeeded. As the peasant bent to pick up his load of vegetables again, he noticed a purse lying in the road where the boulder had been. The purse contained many gold coins and a note from the king indicating that the gold was for the person who removed the boulder from the road. The peasant learned what many others would never understand. *Every obstacle presents an opportunity to improve one's condition.*

June 29

Glenda, in spite of amazing success as a travel writer, was focusing on the fact that she didn't like where she was living, didn't have a relationship, didn't have any children, and felt old at forty-two. If she moved, she would lose a part-time job where she lived. Though she didn't like the job anymore, at least it was easy. However, if she stayed where she was, she'd never meet any men because she lived too far from the stimulating urban environment where interesting men were. With her second book just released and poised to be a success, her publisher had made a proposal to her for a third book that would offer exciting travel and research opportunities. She was worried about having to write the book, though, because she felt that when she was on the road, she couldn't center herself and become magnetic enough to attract a man. But she didn't like her home, so she couldn't really center herself there either. To top it all off, she had been a lifelong athlete but had recently suffered an automobile accident in which she had torn the tendons in her right side. She was having trouble healing, and the lack of her normal physical prowess was frustrating her.

Glenda was looking for her happiness to come exclusively from outside sources. She saw this happiness as something she had to obtain and maintain with constant effort. What she really needed was to be quiet and look within. She needed to feel the connection she already had internally to the experience of love and fulfillment, independent of external forms. Instead, she was subjecting herself to a barrage of negative thinking, telling herself repeatedly what she didn't like, what she didn't have, and why she couldn't do and have what she said she wanted. The more she declared these things to be true, the more her reality obeyed and shaped itself accordingly. No wonder her body was acting out these feelings of paralysis and being torn apart. By complaining and protesting, she was not allowing her true health, creativity, and destiny to unfold.

My reality mimics my words.

You can speak the negative or the positive into being. When you notice yourself complaining today, either externally or internally, suspend your words and start over again with positive intent.

I know through symbols and imagery.

Get insights and make decisions today based on your visual sense—color, radiance, style, shape, contrast, size. Visual data bridges intuitive knowing to your logical mind. If you notice the immediate impressions that imagery elicits from you, you'll know more.

In my intuition and imagination workshop, participants do an exercise with a partner. On a large sheet of newsprint, two people draw together with colored pencils, crayons, and markers. It's interesting to watch how they work out the collaborative process. At first they take turns drawing or draw in separate corners of the paper, respecting each other's space. As the process continues and they learn to sense each other's intensity and rhythm, they take more chances, drawing around their partner's shapes, embroidering the edges, even crossing through and layering over what the other has done. Some people merge their styles; others accentuate their contrasts. The results are fascinating. In the second part of the process, I ask each person to make a list of six pairs of images from their drawings, then compose a poem that integrates those six phrases and that will be a message to them from their inner self. Here's what one of the women wrote:

star eyes	apex light
mountain morning	igloo mind
wheel wind	beam clouds

In the mountain morning
I stood on the cliff
staring with my star eyes into the pink.
I came from my old igloo mind, breaking loose
and feeling the wheel of wind
spiraling me up and out—
I let myself be lifted,
I let myself travel the beam to the clouds;
there I climbed the sky pyramid
and soon was the apex light,
and I was free.

July

July 1

Even if you don't leave your house, you're sure to travel today. As you get your child ready for school, you'll probably visualize the route she'll walk, see her in the school cafeteria eating lunch, and playing at a friend's house after school. Perhaps you'll watch the news and as you see the footage of some disaster in another country, you'll go there in your imagination. Maybe you'll work at your desk writing letters and as you address the envelopes, your mind will project to the final destination. Or it could be that you'll daydream for five minutes about a time when you lived in a different house, or went on vacation to Italy, or had that fabulous dinner at the little French restaurant downtown. With each thought of a different location, part of your vital force actually leaves and inhabits that place temporarily. It's important to bring that attention back to your present moment or you'll feel drained.

There are, of course, intuition-related benefits to mind traveling. If you visit a friend who lives a thousand miles away, you may pick up impressions about him and sense that he's not happy. Follow up on the intuition and give him a call. A mother mentally tracking her daughter's path to school may sense an obstacle and decide to call the teacher to make sure her daughter got there. If you're engaged in a creative process, traveling back to a fulfilling vacation might give you the ambiance you need to write the perfect nuances of your short story or get the colors just right on your painting. But usually these projections into other locations are temporary distractions that move awareness away from the now and the here, preventing us from accessing the guidance and inspiration we need for the task at hand. If you are literally spaced out, it's difficult to be clear, confident, creative, and effective.

See if you can be aware when your mind visits other places, and think about why you're going there. Are you reaching back for a scene that will help inspire something you're currently working on? Or for an insight that will be applicable to a process you're in the middle of now? Are you being drawn to check on another person who might need help? Or are you just avoiding something? Each time you project somewhere, remember to retract your attention and energy back into your body and use the information for what you're doing *right now, right here.* Don't wander too far for too long, but do notice where you go.

I am conscious of my mental travels.

Be aware when you project into other locations today, then come back to your body consciously. There may be a good reason for visits elsewhere.

I know why people do what they do.

Pay attention to other people's superficial motives and underlying intents today. There is no need to feign ignorance about others' actions; your intuition always gives accurate feedback.

People's behavior can be confusing. With words they say one thing, then they do something else, and underneath it all their intention may be aimed in yet another direction. A woman told me about her boyfriend who was always pleasant and acted like he wanted to see her. If she said, "I've got Saturday totally free—shall I come over and we can go for a hike in the hills?" he'd agree enthusiastically. Yet when she arrived at the appointed time, he'd be gone and there'd be a note on the door: "I had an emergency and had to run over to the office—come on in and I'll be back in an hour." Two or three hours would pass as she read magazines and paced the floor. By the time he returned, it would be too late to go where they'd planned. This scene repeated many times until she finally ended the relationship. She said she realized his deepest motivation was to please others so he wouldn't be rejected but also to maintain his independence so he wouldn't be controlled. He acted friendly and affectionate without ever being intimate. He couldn't say no or set clear boundaries with her, his clients, his employees, his friends, or his parents.

I have some friends from Japan with whom I have often been confused because, for the sake of being honorable and polite, they avoid speaking the truth, saying what they mean, or asking for what they need. It's easy, then, for a Westerner to think something is deliberately being withheld or that there is a lack of trust. They may say yes when they mean no, or nothing when they mean yes, figuring the communication process will go on much longer and be much more subtle than we Americans are accustomed to and that eventually everyone will get what they need. I have often thought I was being rejected when they thought they were doing me a favor. On the other hand, they have felt offended when I was too fast, honest, or direct. In these cases both sides had to look below the surface for the deepest intent. Knowing in our hearts that we were trying to serve each other gave us all the patience to keep going for the best mutually supportive outcome.

July 3

In almost every spiritual tradition, there is a reason why people place their left and right hands together, palm to palm, when they are ready to talk to the higher power. If you pay attention to your awareness when you hold this posture, you'll notice your body coming into natural harmony.

BALANCING YOUR BODY WITH PRAYER HANDS

1. Sit upright, feet on the floor. Close your eyes. Bring your palms together in front of your body, fingertips touching and facing upward. Adjust the pressure from both hands so it is exactly equal. Move your prayer hands back and forth, up and down, tilt them side to side, until they come to rest at the exact center of your body.

2. Adjust your feet so they're parallel, with the same amount of weight on both. Then adjust your knees so they feel parallel. Wiggle your buttocks and hips until you feel that each side carries equal weight and the pelvis is straight. Adjust your elbows and shoulders so both sides are symmetrical. Nod your head forward and back, tip it side to side; arrange it so it feels perfectly level.

3. Notice your hearing. Which ear seems more sensitive? Balance your ears so they are equally alert and functional. Then pay attention to your eyes. Which eye seems bigger, more tense, more swollen? Higher, or farther forward? Make any adjustments necessary. Now pay attention to the muscles in your face. Which side seems tighter? Smile. Adjust the muscles so both sides of your face feel equal.

4. Now visualize your left and right brain. Which side is bigger? Lighter? Darker? Are they two different colors? Does one side seem tense? Imagine removing an imaginary partition between the two sides and allowing energy to flow back and forth until it equalizes.

5. Finally, notice your breath. Follow the air in through your right nostril into your right lung then back out again. Then do the same thing with the left nostril and left lung. Which side of your lungs seems bigger, lighter, more open? Does the air penetrate to the same depth in both? Make adjustments to equalize the size and efficiency of both lungs. Breathe equally: left side to left lung; right side to right lung.

6. Feel the balance and harmony in your entire body and mind.

My left and right sides contribute equally to my life.

Balance the left and right sides of your body and brain today, then use the resulting equilibrium for increased enjoyment, creativity, or insight.

July 4

**I am free
to be my
whole self.**

*Say yes to
what supports
your well-being
today. Rotate
among your
various facets
and let yourself
be fully involved
with each.*

Paula's life is unbelievably busy, her time and attention stretched among many components. She runs a home-based company, consults and does public speaking, is president of a state professional association, and is in a good marriage raising two children. Every day, she looks at her options. Spend time with the kids? Do something fun with her husband? Exercise? Organize her office? Write a grant proposal? Figure out her new computer program? Vacuum? Go to the market? Read her professional journals? Make some cold calls and develop new business? She can't do it all. So she asks herself, "How do I stay in touch with my values today? Which things do I choose *not* to do? And how do I experience the most satisfaction?"

Her time-management advice: Some time alone each day is vital, whether it be twenty minutes on the treadmill or a hot bath at the end of the day with an escapist book. Next, focus fully on doing each task while you're doing it. Splitting your attention by thinking ahead to the next thing you "should" do creates pressure and dissatisfaction and makes you feel you don't have enough time. Staying focused in the moment produces the experience of having more time.

When problems arise, Paula says she reminds herself constantly that "The world isn't doing this to me!" She also maintains a level head by asking herself, "Is there anything I can do about this now?" If not, she lets it go until later. Finally, she says, remember that a list of any one day's accomplishments usually covers only a handful of topics. Don't expect an inhuman amount from yourself.

It's tricky getting all of ourselves into a single day as we become more well-rounded and complex human beings. In fact, given the broad nature of who we really are, it takes a string of days to touch all the aspects in our makeup. We must learn to rotate our facets to the fore, allowing our personality to change like a kaleidoscope. Yes, we have a greater number of personal components than ever before, but what's important is that we maintain the quality and depth of our experience. Each moment, each task can bring pleasure and satisfaction, and, if we have an experience of satisfaction all day, we'll feel more whole than we would if we'd rushed to complete double the amount in a shallower way.

July 5

To write every day, I must eliminate much of the distraction of daily life. With this narrower, intense focus, it's easy to become too electrical, too mental and be thrown for a loop by even the smallest bit of negativity. I was working cheerily one day when I received a call from a colleague. "Did you hear that so-and-so came out with a new cassette series? And so-and-so's new book has already sold X number of copies?" She continued telling me what everyone in my field was doing to further their careers. I hung up and immediately felt a sinking sensation around my solar plexus. My happy mood was flattened. My creativity went down the drain. Now I was thinking, "Here I am being productive, but the world is passing me by! You can't rest for a second—even spirituality has become competitive!"

For the next few days, which included the July 4th holiday, I lost my center and motivation. Would this draggy state ever end? Instead of writing, I found myself driving to a plant nursery one morning to get flowers for my garden. As I walked through the aisles of greenery, the moist air and loamy smell began to revive me. The woman who waited on me said, "Did you go to the parade this weekend?" I said no. "Well," she said, "they had a hundred bassett hounds there! There were bassett hound puppies and big fat ones riding in little red wagons—every shape and size! It was a sight!" As I imagined the gaggle of waddling dogs with droopy hound faces and wagging tails, I couldn't help but laugh. The image woke me up a little more. Imagination was stirring.

Instead of going straight home, I detoured to a nearby college located in the hills under some gorgeous oak trees. The campus was closed, so I ambled around smelling the dryness of the California summer—bay laurel, rattlesnake grass, musty oak leaves. The insects were buzzing around lazily as I lay down on a bench to stare up into layers of leaves filtering the sun. Instead of resisting the direction my mind was taking me, I completely let go and received the gifts of nature like a soothing balm. I didn't know if I'd ever write again or if I'd have a future. It was just fine to be alive right now. Then, mysteriously, my body had had enough; it sat up, drove home, and enthusiastically turned on the computer to start writing again.

My energy responds to thoughts, emotions, and events.

Notice when the frequency of your energy rises or falls today. As you become conscious of what triggers the shifts, you'll be able to stabilize your moods and not be debilitated by sudden dips.

My body knows which options are best.

Project yourself fully into future scenarios today and see how your body responds to each. You can solve problems intuitively by letting your body decide which options provide the greatest experience of deep comfort.

Your body never lies. Ask it about any situation, person, or place, and it will give you an honest response. Would it be better to take a vacation driving through Italy or diving in Hawaii? Would it be better to pay off your credit cards and feel secure financially or take a one-time opportunity to visit Egypt's pyramids? Should you take an expensive seminar that would give you new credentials or spend the money on a new car? You have three job offers! One would provide a prestigious title and look good on the resume; one would let you travel in your work; one would pay for schooling. How do you know which one to choose?

You can solve problems intuitively by letting your body decide which options provide the greatest experience of comfort. Be quiet, calm your mind, and bring your awareness inside your skin. Pay attention to your body's energy and happiness level. Then close your eyes and imagine driving through Italy in as much detail as possible. How does your body respond? Maybe it feels excited, stimulated by the sights, food, language, and ambiance. You get the feeling it won't be relaxing, but it will charge your emotions. Clear that response. Visualize yourself swimming in Hawaii, diving off coral reefs. How does your body respond? This feels peaceful, quiet, nurturing. Your body enjoys the smooth, cool waters and the beach smells. As you weigh the two options, you realize that Hawaii is almost too relaxing—the longer you stay in that visualization the sleepier you get. But when you imagine Italy, everything about it wakes you up. Suddenly there's no comparison! Your body wants stimulation and energy, color and passion. You know now what to do!

Try the same thing with the job possibilities. The first option gives you a prestigious title for the resume, but your body feels like it's in prison. Your throat tightens and you feel like you can't talk. Option two lets you travel, and you feel yourself meeting new people, learning better communication skills, and creating a large network of contacts. Your body is excited. Just the thought of moving around the country makes you feel expansive. The third option, in which continuing education is emphasized, sounds great, but your body is restless, like it just doesn't want to sit in a classroom. You realize the second job is perfect for what you need now—to get out in the world, develop more confidence, and feel independent.

July 7

Beth is a mystic who makes a point of watching both the visible and invisible currents of events to sense what is happening with the inner process of the earth and of human beings. She tells of observing two separate incidents, in close succession, involving a dog and a bird. In both situations, the dog chased the bird and the bird flew just out of the way, then stopped and looked back at the dog, then flew up just enough to make the dog run and jump some more. As Beth watched, she realized they were actually playing with each other, that there was a total lack of the normal species aggression and fear responses. The dog was not trying to catch the bird, and the bird was not dive-bombing the dog. What did this mean? To see such a thing once was interesting, but twice in a matter of weeks? Beth's intuition told her that this was a sign of a shift occurring in the world—that the barriers that have kept us separate and attached to our identities might now be dissolving. Perhaps a new understanding of duality was coming, one that encouraged play instead of war. Were the animals feeling it and acting it out first?

I, too, have noticed an odd behavior shift with the blue jay who dominates my backyard. Previously a loner, he now has a mate, and they have nested just outside my bedroom window. At this point they are constantly hunting for food to feed their squawking babies. I put out bread and leftovers to help. Each day as I sit at the computer, they come and stand outside the plate-glass windows and stare directly in at me for several minutes at a time. Lately, one or the other of them flies straight at the window, lightly bumps into it, bounces off, and flies away. My intuition tells me they're trying to get me to come outside and expand my mind. "What are you doing writing a book on this lovely day?" they seem to say. "Your mind will grow dull. You'll lose your direct connection! Wake up at the crack of dawn with us! Get some air! Come out and play!"

My imagination brings me information in unusual ways.

Pay attention to animals today, and see how they're acting and what they're paying attention to at a subtle level. Animals can be messengers, bringing information from higher levels.

July 8

**I am ready
for the
miraculous.**

*Today,
contemplate the
possibility that
what we consider
impossible might
be normal.
Perhaps you can
materialize and
dematerialize
objects or teleport
yourself across
time and space.
What would
your life be like if
the supernatural
were natural?*

For most of us, teleportation only exists on "Star Trek" episodes and in science fiction. But for indigenous peoples the world over, it has been a more common phenomenon. Dan Moonhawk Alford, a professor of English and linguistics at California State University at Hayward, tells a story related to him thirty years ago by a Cheyenne Indian.

A young man just coming of age felt he needed to go on a pony raid against the Crows to prove his skill and bravery. The elders agreed, but they sent a medicine person along in case of trouble. Near dusk the boy approached a group of the Crow's ponies. He was soon spotted by a Crow scout who raised an alarm. The Cheyenne boy and the medicine person took off, with four Crows pursuing on foot. The medicine person pointed to a large, thorny thicket; they hesitated, then jumped in. Soon the Crow scouts caught up and, as the last light was fading, took positions around the thicket to make sure the Cheyennes didn't escape during the night.

Inside the thicket, the medicine person told the young man he thought he could get them out of there as long as the boy did exactly what he was told. "Close your eyes and keep them tightly closed until I tell you to open them." So the boy closed his eyes while the medicine person began to pray. Suddenly the boy began feeling very weird and opened his eyes in alarm. They tried a second and third time during the long dark hours; each time the boy opened his eyes, stopping the experience. Dawn was now approaching and the medicine person told the young man that they could only do this one more time before the Crow scouts came charging in. He *must* keep his eyes closed. This time felt the weirdest of all for the young man, but he bravely kept his eyes shut. Soon he was calm, and at that point the old man told him to open his eyes.

They were both sitting cross-legged, as they had been in the thicket, but now they were perched on a hill overlooking the thicket. As they watched quietly, first light came, and they saw the Crow scouts get up, stretch, check with one another that no one had escaped, and then plunge into the thicket after their prey. The two Cheyennes laughed quietly, got up, stretched, and headed for home.

July 9

When Becky Blanton was a child, she talked to bugs and held her hands over her little brother's head, sending him energy. From there she graduated to doing real healings and becoming an animal communicator. She says, "I experienced a horse 'talking' to me at a horse show in Lexington, Kentucky, last October. He told me his shoulder hurt from his saddle and he wanted me to fix it. I said, 'Fix what?' and he said there were rags in the saddle padding that were poking the leather into his shoulder. I mentioned this to the horse's owner, and we went into the tack room to have a look at the saddle. She reached under the flap and pulled out two dishrags she'd forgotten she had stuffed into the padding to make the saddle ride higher on his shoulders. She was shocked. The horse was happy! I'd always 'known' what animals wanted, but it took a while before I realized they were actually communicating in a direct way like this. I've talked with animals who told me when they were going to die, and they did."

I, too, have had intuitive experiences with animals. I was once asked to do a reading on a temperamental horse. I went out to watch his owner work him in a corral. Sure enough, as she saddled him and tried to mount, he turned and tried to bite her, evaded her, wouldn't move forward when asked, and was generally obstreperous. I could sense immediately that he wanted to run full out in the field across the road, which he could see from the corral and which contained cattle and other horses. He was bored stiff walking and trotting around inside the fence. He was lonely as well. In addition, he was frustrated by the woman's tentative nature. He needed some intensity. When I told her this, she said, "Yes, my husband, who is very strong willed, is the only one who can ride him, but I'm afraid to take him out of the corral." I said, "Well he'd be very happy if you'd take the chance and take him somewhere and gallop with him." I could sense the trust would build between them then, and he'd look forward to being ridden.

I can understand what animals and plants need.

Today, ask animals and plants what's important to them and what you can do to help. By validating that nonhuman forms of life are conscious and responsive, it will be easier for you to experience a state of oneness.

207

July 10

I sink into what I perceive.

Notice when you're noticing something today, then notice it longer. Are more of your senses activated? What wants to communicate to you? What do you most want to absorb from the perceived scene?

I was channel surfing and came across a riveting perform-ance on MTV by superstar Whitney Houston. She was dressed strikingly in a long, supple, black leather dress and a shiny black futuristic necklace, and her makeup was dra-matic. I was fascinated. What was that slitlike detail on the necklace? How did her dress move so fluidly even though it was leather? What were those eye-shadow col-ors—olive green and gold? How had they cut her hair— was it always covering one eye? I tried to focus on the eye shadow but the piece was edited with so many cuts that I couldn't see enough before I was thrown into another view. As I readjusted my focus on the necklace and got a vague idea of how it was constructed, I was shifted radi-cally into another view of her lifting a wing on the dress, and, as I tried to see more about the dress, I was thrown yet again into a close-up of her face. She was moving in a beautiful, languid way, and I wanted to be able to feel her body's joy in the movement but I was subjected to a dizzying series of split-second edits. As much as I wanted to stay with her, I realized her beauty was being ruined by the strobelike fragmentation of the presentation, and I was experiencing a painful disorientation. I gave up and flipped the channel to something more integrous.

What are the effects of these rapid-fire visuals on our health? Some movie trailers are so loud and chaotic I find myself literally covering my solar plexus, eyes, and third-eye area so I won't receive too much perceptual violence. When I consciously experience shock-based music and film, I feel forced to remain at an abstract level of percep-tion, in visual mode, and am unable to drop into the deeper senses where my body can process the data. No absorption is permitted, and my body gets the erroneous idea that living on adrenaline, responding to fear, is nor-mal. My sense of time is also distorted—I don't feel like I have any. My body wants to feel continuity and con-nectedness and to experience life evolving. It wants a slower pace.

Today's media seems bent on disconnecting us and keeping our nervous systems overstimulated. Without the body's earthy perception, intuition diminishes and our access to ourselves as spiritual beings is almost nil. Try watching MTV for ten minutes, then walk outside and pay attention to a tree for ten minutes. What's different?

July 11

At times ordinary life can turn dreamlike. When this subtle quality appears, something magical and important is at hand, seeking to be known. On one such day, I was to see a new client, a young Czech woman referred by a colleague in Prague. Before our appointment I went to the nearby coffeeshop for a quick breakfast. (In case my client arrived before I returned, I left a note on my door saying she could go inside.) Walking into the coffeeshop, I noticed a striking young woman with long, flaming red hair bent over a notebook, writing intently. "Ah," I thought, "a woman after my own heart." I sat at another table and wrote my dreams in my own journal. Checking my watch, I left and made my way back to the car. On the way, the young woman literally skipped past me, her red hair flying, on the way to her car. Her natural joy almost knocked me over as she bounced by in the parking lot. "Here is a lesson," I commented to myself. "Be joyful for no reason!" I sat in my car a minute and wrote this observation in my journal. When I walked in my front door moments later, I felt the dream build momentum. There on my sofa, surrounded by a warm pool of light from the lamp, sat my joyful, skipping, journal-writing, red-haired Czech client!

But the dream had only just begun. When we finished the counseling session, we continued talking enthusiastically. Though twenty years apart in age, with entirely different body types, we felt oddly identical. Had we been sisters in a past life? Had I been her mother? Or she mine? On impulse I invited her to a movie, something I never do with clients. After the movie, I invited her to a lecture; then she invited me to dinner and introduced me to a Japanese man she'd met while traveling, who eventually helped me in my work in Japan. One thing kept leading to another, and we have now known each other for several years. The dream has not stopped unfolding because we have both continued to relish its surprising, symbolic character.

Life is but a dream.

Pretend your life is a dream today, then actively influence its outcome by participating creatively and spontaneously.

The "Us" talks to me all day long.

Listen to what the collective consciousness is trying to tell you today. There is great wisdom in the soul of the world and in the pool of human knowledge that has been growing since time began. Sometimes when you're absent-minded, it can talk directly to you.

I was watching television when I became vaguely aware of a short phrase from a song lyric. It was insistent, distracting me from my media-induced reverie. I paid closer attention and thought I heard, "Meet me tonight." Then I heard something about graduation being near. I remembered a song like this by George Maharis from the 1960s. Try as I might, I couldn't remember the rest of the song. How could I find it? The next day I E-mailed a client in the music business and asked if he knew the song. He reported back, "There are lots of songs called 'Meet Me Tonight' but George Maharis didn't sing any of them." I felt driven to find the lyrics because I often receive important guidance from songs—I'll notice myself singing something, then notice that the lyrics are answering a question I've been chewing on. Was there a message here?

The very next night my friend Karen stopped by. We chatted over tea, and just before we finished I remembered she was a singer. "Hey! Have you heard of a song called 'Meet Me Tonight'?" I described what I could to her. She laughed and said, "Sure! But it's not called 'Meet Me Tonight,' it's '*Teach* Me Tonight' and it's a classic—in fact, I used to do it!" And she hummed a few bars. I was ecstatic! Later she called back; she'd found her sheet music and read me the lyrics. It's a love song punctuated with phrases that could easily have come from a spiritual teacher trying to get me to wake up—phrases such as "this is the perfect spot to learn," "help me solve the mystery," "should the teacher stand so near?" "graduation's almost here." I had a distinct feeling that someone was trying to talk to me. In the space of two days, the entire message had been delivered.

For months I'd had the feeling that I was reaching the end of a long developmental phase. I'd been living with a subtle sensation of walking through a wall of super-electrified energy, as though all my molecules were being rearranged. I sensed I'd eventually come out the other side an entirely new person though nothing would look very different on the surface. Spiritually, it *did* feel like a graduation was at hand. The song helped me recognize this consciously and know that I was now stepping over that invisible line.

July 13

As you think of something new to try, the idea might come with a worried "what if?" attached. To that you might add a "so what?" and do it anyway, keeping in mind the miracle of being alive and having so many marvelous options to explore. This is an Inuit song from the Pacific Northwest, an ode to experiencing life in all its rich adventure and depth.

> And I thought over again
> My small adventures
> As with a shore-wind I drifted out
> In my kayak
> And I thought I was in danger,
>
> My fears,
> Those small ones
> That I thought so big
> For all the vital things
> I had to get and reach
>
> And yet, there is only
> One great thing.
> The only thing:
> To live to see in huts and on journeys
> The great day that dawns,
> And the light that fills the world.

I am an explorer, an adventurer, a student of life.

Try something new today.

I am aware of my self-defeating worldview.

Write out your internal script today for why your world doesn't work, can't succeed, isn't good, isn't happy, or won't cooperate. Find and feel the fallacies.

Pam had just gone through the arduous process of starting her own identity consulting business. She produced two amazing pieces of calligraphic artwork based on the idea of worldviews discussed in my book *The Intuitive Way*. Here are some of the phrases she used. Do you find yourself plagued with similar voices?

I DON'T CARE! Nobody needs what I have to offer. *I can't trust anybody.* **I don't know how to love.** You owe me. JUST GIVE UP, NOBODY REALLY WANTS TO LEARN ABOUT LOVE. I can't live my dream and make money too. *Leave me alone.* Stay locked up in your house. You're making too much noise. *They want too much from me.* I'M ALL ALONE. I'll never have enough money; I'm just greedy. **I can't make a difference.** *Don't be so selfish—GROW UP!* What makes you think you're so special? WATCH YOUR BACK. It's my fault. They're all out to get me. **I'm spiraling down.** *You're irresponsible.* WHY BOTHER. No no no no no no no no. **I have to do everything myself.** *Who am I kidding? Why don't I just get a job?* The planet is dying and nobody cares. WHO AM I TO THINK I CAN FIND ENLIGHTENMENT? **If I follow my heart I'll lose everything I've built.** You don't clean up after yourself. MY BODY WILL ALWAYS HURT. *My heart is frozen.* What's wrong with you? Why don't you just do something normal? **I'll never get enough time for me.** *I feel small and cold.* OF COURSE I'M SCARED, THIS IS A VERY SCARY PLACE! Have you watched the news lately? **You live in a fantasy world.**

July 15

When Pam flipped her worldview over to one based on love instead of fear, her thinking changed and she was able to take the steps that led to her new business becoming a reality. Here are some of her self-empowering phrases. Can you relate?

LIFE IS A GIFT. I am an artist! Creativity is my essence. *All that is fear is illusion. All that is love is real. I AM LOVE.* I embrace all that you are. **I believe in you.** PASSION! I am you and you are me and we are all together. *My heart speaks to me of JOY! Shine brightly.* Love is all there is. **I am all Possibilities and Pure Potential.** BLISS! Heaven is within you. I am my own white canvas. SURRENDER! *I am in exactly the right place doing exactly the right thing.* **There is no past; there is no future; all is NOW.** GRACE! *I reach up, I reach down.* Light is the essence on which all form is built. YOU CANNOT BE ALONE. **I awake each day in gratitude and God just keeps on giving.** I trust in the universe. I am open to receive. Abundance flows to me and through me. *All I see is beauty. I believe in magic!* You are divine. IMAGINE YOURSELF BIGGER. You are my blessing. **Light emerges everywhere. We are all waking up together.** My body is the sacred vehicle for this journey. Take my hand. Let us walk together. MY PATH IS THE VERTICAL PATH OF THE SOUL. I am serving on God's task force. *My cup runneth over.* **Each person I meet along the way is a guide, a teacher.** When I look at you, I see only love. EVERYTHING I NEED, I HAVE RIGHT HERE RIGHT NOW.

I am aware of my self-empowering worldview.

Write out your internal script today for why your world works, what you know to be true about yourself, what's good about you, how you are loved. Feel and live this reality.

July 16

I live in a world of sacred geometry and mathematical patterns.

Notice the influence of numbers in your life today. Perhaps you'll see the number eight repeatedly or find instances of things occuring in threes. Our lives have order because we measure time and space mathematically.

Julie just discovered that her parents deceived her about her true date of birth. She thought she was born on the same day as her older sister, the 16th, but two years later. Only weeks ago, her parents "fessed up." She had actually been born on the 15th, but they thought it would be cute to have two daughters with the same birthday, so they registered it as the 16th. Julie and I had discussed the numerology cycles that derived from her birthday in a previous counseling session, and everything seemed to fit well with the way her life had gone.

It was interesting, then, to do a new numerology chart based on her new birthday and compare the two patterns. In cases like this, the registered date is associated with the outer personality, and the real date pertains to the inner self. The mere fact that two birth dates exist makes the person aware that two sides of his or her personality also exist and need to be integrated.

In Julie's case, the official date showed a pattern marked by dynamism, goal orientation, and a strong intellect. When she shifted into her second life cycle, dominated by scientific and intellectual numbers, she added a Ph.D. to her degrees in psychology and began doing research in a medical environment. The real birth date showed the pattern of a dreamer, humanitarian, and artist, with high levels of imagination. In addition, it heavily emphasized family and home, healing and nutrition. Her secret, private life had always been as a painter! And when she shifted into this birth date's second life cycle, dominated by family and healing numbers, she married and had children, then had a health crisis resulting in a hysterectomy that catapulted her into learning about alternative healing.

At the time when her parents revealed the truth, Julie was contemplating which direction to go with her life work. As we talked, ideas from her two different life patterns wove together. She could create the nonprofit residential healing center for women that she had envisioned *and* have her private practice be part of it *and* sponsor art programs as part of the curriculum *and* do a formal research project that would open traditional doctors to new forms of healing. It didn't have to be either-or as she had been thinking. Knowing all her numbers helped Julie integrate a greater diversity into her entirety.

July 17

Rebecca was working on opening her intuition and expanding her spiritual awareness. Almost immediately after she began paying attention to what was going on under the surface, her life intensified and started to rapidly change. Rebecca became aware of an old pattern of taking care of everyone in her family. She realized she didn't want to do this anymore. She wanted more freedom and to trust her family and give them opportunities to succeed or fail on their own terms. Still, breaking old habits can be difficult. She'd make some progress, then backslide. Finally her physical reality gave her a wake-up call she couldn't ignore.

It was the day before Christmas and all through Rebecca's house her appliances started to backfire and break down. The food processor jammed and broke a blade. Her vacuum burned up. The light in her stove went out, and it was the last straw when her dishwasher broke and spewed gallons of dirty water all over the kitchen. She was inundated with emotion and felt overwhelmed with helplessness. All her support systems were failing her at a time when she felt a crucial need to have her family's holidays be perfect. She picked herself up from her emotional breakdown and realized there was a message. It was time to let *herself* be assisted; she couldn't control life anymore.

Immediately after the holidays, Rebecca came down with a severe case of the flu. She was incapacitated for the next nine weeks. Her doctor assigned her to strict bed rest and forbade her to do housework or drive. When she did get up to try to participate in her normal life, she had to be taken to the emergency room. Again, the message was adamant. "*Stop* the old behaviors! Allow others to care for you and serve you." As she recovered, her husband took her for a restful vacation to Hawaii. She was still so exhausted that a friend came over and packed her suitcase for her. Rebecca says the hardest part of her recovery was the guilt she felt about other people waiting on her. But what she came away with, after she integrated the lessons and healed her body, was that she's not the coach of a team—she's *on the team*, participating equally with everyone.

I'm good just because I exist.

Simplify your life today by doing less than usual. Do you feel lazy or unworthy when you don't accomplish a lot? Remember you're not just what you do.

I contemplate the true meaning of love.

Pay attention today to what love feels like when it expresses itself through your body, your emotions, and your thoughts. How does it change the way you respond to situations?

A few years ago, I participated in a hypnosis session with a friend. She led me into a deep altered state where we hoped I would receive some insights about an upsetting rejection I had experienced. It felt wonderful to relax so profoundly and let her soothing voice drop me further and further into my inner worlds. As I released tension, I saw that what I had thought was a rejection was actually a mutual act. I had been finished with the relationship, was looking for a way to disengage, but didn't want to be disloyal. So the other person simply acted out my unconscious desire and did it for me. All was well. After that insight, I dropped further in and saw the early causes of the emotional wounds I had carried in my body, simultaneously understanding how I had made the mistake in perception that caused me to feel pain instead of love. As that happened, I went into an even deeper understanding about the perfection of the pain and how it brought consciousness to an idea that I had misunderstood. I saw that, as I healed the misunderstanding, it also healed to some degree in everyone else. All this happened in the space of a few minutes, and silently—so my friend had no idea what was happening in me.

"Go into your heart," my friend was saying, "and feel your love." I could tell from the tone in her voice that since she was still functioning from her daily personality, love meant a kind of warm fuzziness. From my more impersonal view, love meant something entirely different. I said, "From where I am now, love means 'the perfect fit.'" I could feel how love was the coordinating force of the cosmos, how love created every event and fitted all forms together in a mutually empowering way. I knew it was love that makes us, teaches us, grows us, brings life experiences, and removes life experiences. What comes from within and without is always "a perfect fit."

I saw then that love is defined differently when we view it from different vantage points. From high levels, it looks like the glue of the universe; from emotional levels, it feels warm and fuzzy. From the physical level, it looks like sex, procreation, and the balance of nature. No matter the viewpoint, perception generated within love grants us balance, beauty, dignity, grace, and perfect understanding.

July 19

When an image in your reality takes on that extra notice-ability and becomes an omen, you can be sure your soul is about to speak to you. Author Carol Adrienne was writing at her desk one day when she glanced out her window and saw a strange image. The reflected image of the book-shelves behind her desk was superimposed on the huge redwood tree on the slope outside. Suddenly she thought, "This is a sign! As a writer, I should be more conscious and responsible about the fact that the books I publish use a tremendous amount of paper, and I am contributing to the destruction of trees. I should look into this to see if there's anything I can do."

The next day, she and another writer friend were riding the shuttle bus to the airport to go to a conference, and they were talking about this very idea when, at the next stop, a woman got on and sat down near them. Carol had a strong intuition that she wanted to talk to the woman, so she began to draw her out by asking friendly questions. The woman turned out to be a therapist who wrote about ecological issues. "I have an electric car," she volunteered. This gave Carol the idea to share her concerns about authors and paper, and the woman just happened to have written extensively on the subject. She gave Carol a full rundown on a paper substitute called kenaf, made from vegetable pulp!

Every image contains information and an experience.

Interpret the symbols you see today. What message is trying to get through to you?

July 20

**I can express
myself
passionately.**

*Notice how you
respond physi-
cally to your core
passions today
as they arise.
Do you let them
pass through you
or stop them
because they're
"inappropriate"?
Can you allow
yourself to feel
like an enthusias-
tic king or queen
of the world?*

My niece Valerie is a strong, extroverted teenager now and she has always had an intensity I enjoy. When she was a toddler, I would occasionally see waves of energy rise through her body, making her shake and act hyper. She'd scrunch up her nose, grit her teeth, make a growling noise, and bounce her head up and down really fast like a horse champing at the bit. Then the wave would dissipate out the top of her head and she'd return to her sweet self.

Last New Year's Eve, Valerie and her friends stayed up until midnight to toast the new year with sparkling cider. I, the "babysitter," brought out the glasses on a tray and we all made our toasts. "To a great year!" one of her friends said. "To more fun!" another chimed in. "To family and friends!" I offered. Then it was Valerie's turn. "To WORLD DOMINATION!" she shouted gleefully. And we all clinked. Some months later, I received a copy of a message Val had written to my father, who had been asking her what activities she was involved with in school. Her answer was, "I'm playing lacrosse and doing mogul skiing, and I'm *defiantly* going out for field hockey this year." My father had drawn a tiny red arrow up toward this Freudian slip, which I'm guessing was meant to be *definitely*.

I admire Valerie's spirit and directness, her honesty. Maybe it's when we get the message that our more intense forms of self-expression are too much for the world that we shut down, lose confidence, and get negative and depressed. Though at times Valerie can seem self-absorbed, the allowing of her intense style of expression seems to foster her soul's deeper tendency toward compassion and service as a natural by-product. Intensity and exuberance can be the first signs of excellence when we feel accepted, trusted, and loved.

July 21

Charlene's cozy apartment is tucked away behind a larger building and faces onto a concrete parking area. When she moved in twelve years ago, she got permission from her landlady to use some of the empty space to make a garden with potted plants. Today the space looks like an exotic Italian patio. Shaded by colorful umbrellas and enclosed by trellises covered with jasmine and flowering vines, one has only to step into the garden to feel instantly nurtured and peaceful. Charlene is a massage therapist, and her patio garden has been her refuge helping her recover her energy and equilibrium.

But Charlene's life is changing. She senses she is about to expand into a new level of creativity. She has an idea for a romance novel and recently heard herself tell her sister that she would be coming to Washington state this summer to rent a small cabin and write. Now, as she prepares to temporarily pull away from her work helping others, the world seems to be testing her. People who have been dependent on her healing hands and generosity are suddenly having emergencies and need her desperately. Just as she is about to live for herself, no one wants her to. New neighbors in the front building have decided that they should have half the space she is using for her patio garden and have made a case to the landlady, who can't quite remember giving Charlene her word that the useless concrete was hers to improve.

Charlene said, "No one is supporting me! I have permission to use this space and it's MY space! I've done all the improvements. I'm afraid to leave for the summer now because when I'm gone, they'll take over. I don't feel safe." On the surface, it looks like she could be forced to give up her creative dream just to defend her territory. The message under the surface is, "*I have a right to have my reality be the way I want it, not the way other people want it to be. I don't have to fight to be myself, I only have to BE myself. No one else can occupy my space if I'm occupying it.*" Charlene realized that her reality was reflecting her unconscious fears: that she could only be happy if other people were happy; and that it was her responsibility to make sure others were happy so she could feel safe and loved. The way the outside world is treating her is the same way Charlene's mind had been treating her inner self.

I'm addressing myself in every conversation I have.

Notice how what you say to others is also a message to yourself today.

July 22

**My mind
is fresh,
curious, and
impressionable.**

*See the world
in a new way
today, as though
you're an
extraterrestrial or
a child visiting
a foreign country.
What ordinary
things become
totally fascinat-
ing? To keep
your perception
vital, it's impor-
tant to return
often to a
beginner's mind.*

I was visiting my sister just before my first book, *The Intuitive Way*, was due to be released. While there I had to do a final proofread of the manuscript. My sister told my five-year-old niece Julia not to bother me. As I worked, I heard a little knock at the door and Julia tip-toed in, came over to the desk, and stood next to me quietly. I kept working, and Julia said, "Is anyone drawing on this yellow pad?" "No," I answered, "but *you* can." So she drew and I edited. As I read through the exercises, I thought it would be interesting to see how Julia might respond to a few. "So Julia," I began. "Let me ask you something. How do you know when something is true for you?" She thought a minute then brightened. "I feel HAPPY!" she said. "Wow that's a great answer," I told her. "Let me ask you something else. Have you ever thought that you could look out through someone else's eyes and see what they see?" She looked at me quizzically. I said, "Just pretend to be someone you know. Pretend to step inside their body and look through their eyes. What do you see?" She closed her eyes, stood up straight with her arms at her sides, focusing intently. Then she said, "Well I'm looking through Grandma Skip's eyes, and she's looking at a lake!" This was amazing because her grand-mother was on a motor-home trip and was no doubt camped by a lake. "Fantastic, Julia! Do you want to try another one?" She nodded enthusiastically.

"Did you know you could send a message right into another person's mind? All you have to do is picture the person and think about what you want to say. Then think it really loud and send it right into the center of their head. Then let go." She wanted to send a message to her father at work. I had her picture him. "Can you see him clearly?" I asked. She nodded calmly, eyes closed. "Now what's the message you want to send to him?" I prompted. "I want to tell him 'I love you,'" she said. "OK. Think it loud and send it! Did he get it?" "Yes!" she said happily, opening her eyes. This intuition business was really FUN!

And then we went back to our respective jobs—me proofing, she drawing. It got quiet and I could feel her getting restless, wanting to talk but not wanting to bother me. Nonchalantly, while still drawing and looking at her paper, she said offhandedly, "You could ask me another question—if you *want* to . . ."

July 23

Clutter, piles, dust balls, weeds, and raggedy gardens are bothering me this week. I want to rearrange the furniture, even in other people's houses! As if, when I can get my house and gardens into pristine condition, time will stop, the air will glitter, and I will finally relax and spread out through the clean, clear space. But, I remind myself, the sparkling clear space I crave is inside the clutter and chaos as well. It's that my eyes fall on the external shapes and get stuck there, especially when there is no harmonious pattern or flow. What I look at, my body models. I feel the stain on the carpet as a shadow in my chest, the dishes in the sink scramble my brain, and the long grass in need of mowing makes my focus go fuzzy.

I took a big wall hanging down from a place it had hung for years. Later, when I went into that room to read a book, I was distracted by the naked impact of the white wall. I noticed I wanted an image there—the space made me feel uncomfortable in its emptiness and quietude. But I experimented with letting myself continue to feel the invasiveness of that big white expanse stretching up to the big white ceiling. I could sense how the arrangement of objects in my personal environment keeps me defined energetically. The white wall challenges my old patterns of self and makes me nervous. What if I took all the pictures off the walls for a few weeks? What if I gave up the Internet, television, and videos? What does the blank space offer to the me who is addicted to imagery and sensation?

My mind reflects its environment.

Clean up clutter today, and notice how you feel. What new ideas come to you? External clutter is often a sign of internal avoidance or paralysis. Once it builds up physically, it then perpetuates the experience of being overwhelmed and confused. Is it easier to be peaceful and clear? Let yourself experience spaciousness.

What other people say comes from a greater collective wisdom that knows exactly what I need to hear.

Listen deeply and fully to others today and find the hidden wisdom. How are other people teachers to you?

Several years ago, I was feeling stuck on a couple of issues that seemed complex and sophisticated, and I didn't think I could talk to most people and get useful insights. Other people found gurus and guides who helped initiate them into higher levels of knowledge, but I had never found any one person or discipline that held my interest for long. In fact, even though I worked in altered states with the spiritual realms, I never even saw entities or spirit guides around me. I was always alone with the impersonal energies and universal laws. I asked the universe to send me a teacher, if there was one for me, because I was sick of doing it all myself.

Meanwhile, a client arrived for a life reading and we sat down and started chatting. She was an ethereal, spacey kind of girl who spoke in a breathy voice about things that didn't seem connected. I wanted to reel her in and get started when out of her mouth popped a sentence that was the exquisitely phrased answer to one of the major problems I'd been chewing on. I was stunned. My next client came several hours later. Similarly, out of his mouth innocently poured the answer to another burning issue.

"Ok, I get it. I asked for a teacher right now, and you sent the Teacher to me through your messengers. The Teacher is in all things, at all times, always available whenever you become aware of a need. I can be the vehicle for the Teacher to speak to others, and other people can be the vehicle for the Teacher to reach me. There are no special teachers, just people who make themselves available as conduits." I realized I was learning trust and allowing universal teachings to connect to me directly from the Teacher—straight through my cells, in some cases, and through every conceivable vehicle in the most accelerated, streamlined way possible.

July 25

Rose's young husband had died recently of a lingering illness, and subsequently she'd been on a healing journey to recover her energy. As part of her quest to rediscover her life and passion, she traveled to Peru, exploring ancient sacred sites and enjoying the warmheartedness of the Peruvian people. In Cuzco, she met a man who had lost his wife not long ago. They had an immediate rapport based on respect for each other's loss and their need to talk about what had happened with someone who would understand. Miguel had three young daughters, and Rose took a liking to the girls, who were still in shock and not talking much. As they became better friends, Miguel suggested they drive down to the coast, where he needed to close up their winter home and pack up his wife's belongings.

Rose spoke a little Spanish, enough to get by but not enough to have any meaningful conversation with the girls. She wanted to be able to console them somehow, but couldn't find a way. Yet, as they drove toward the beach, she remembered a cassette in her purse. It was the theme from the popular movie *Titanic* sung by Celine Dion. She put it in the car's cassette player, and they were instantly transported into the haunting power of the song. When the music stopped, the youngest girl said simply, "Again?" And Rose rewound the tape and played the song again. Then again. And again. And again. For five hours, as they drove across miles and miles of desert, she played nothing but the love song whose mood addressed the loss that everyone in the car was feeling. Words were unnecessary. Something powerful was at work.

They arrived at the beach house. The next day the girls started sorting through their mother's things as Rose watched. By evening, as if by some tacit agreement, the girls each picked one favorite item and carried it gingerly to the beach. There, Rose saw them quietly and carefully bury the objects in the sand. Afterward, they waded into the surf, washed their hands and faces with sea water, and raised their arms to the sky, where they had been told their mother now lived. Then, finished with their impromptu ceremony and farewell, they returned to the house. Rose, too, feeling emotionally cleansed, walked to the water, washed herself, and gave the last remnants of her grief to the setting sun.

I value ceremony and sacred action in my life.

Our bodies respond positively to ceremonies, no matter how simple. Create and perform a ritual to integrate a positive thought pattern into your life today. You might write an affirmation on a slip of paper, fold it into a strip, and tie it onto a tree branch to release its message into the wind.

There's an underlying sanity in the process of my life.

Find the good reasons for events that happen today. When you see daily ups and downs as part of a longer process, can you sense the larger purpose in things?

Betty and her husband had lived in a beautiful home for twenty years, but they became restless and wanted to expand into new levels of success and self-expression. They decided to build a new home. As construction began, they saw that the contractor had designed a steel foundation. Betty had a negative reaction to the coldness of the material. To her it felt as if the core of her new home would have no heart. "They're giving us more structure than we want or need!" Arguments ensued. But the plans had been approved by the city and could not be changed without undue headaches. Betty said she didn't want anger to be built into the foundation of their new life so she tried to put her feelings on the back burner.

As construction progressed, Betty got the overwhelming feeling that they should put their current home on the market immediately. Even though the new place wouldn't be ready for nine months, she trusted her intuition. Amazingly, the house sold within days for more than they were asking. So, almost overnight, Betty realized that she actually *would* be leaving her home of twenty years. For many days after the sale she was plagued with waves of grief. In the midst of her turmoil, two huge branches fell from the oak tree in the backyard. To Betty, it was an externalization of her sadness.

Then Betty's uncle had a heart attack and went into the hospital. She prayed, "Please, God, don't let him die without me knowing about it." The next day, early in the morning, she woke with her hands folded over her heart. As she calmly returned to consciousness, she felt a softness and warmth spreading across her chest. Her heart was melting. She knew her uncle had died. The feeling was like a teaching, and she realized she had to let her heart feel this way concerning everything in her life.

Betty's new life in her new house promised to be much more powerful than the phase she'd just finished. The steel foundations of this new life were a gift to help her be stronger and more defined. The fact that she would need to find an interim place to live gave her the opportunity to gradually translate herself into the new space so the change wouldn't be too much of a shock. Betty realized everything was showing her that she could relax and trust the process of the unfoldment.

July 27

I write directly, role-playing my future self. My future self says, "Trust your destiny—it is absolutely compassionate. I am drawing you toward me, teaching you, planting desires in you, offering you my wisdom so you can become me. I need you to be awake! Surrender into your most authentic personality-of-the-moment and send energy through it, and you will ring with truth and beauty and I will hear that music and be soothed. Your talents are my joy. Your body radiates my message. The way you live your life is what helps me become destiny's dream. If you trust this sourcing, you will join me on the mountaintop at the final meeting place.

"Let yourself feel intimately connected to the flow so you can remain in amazement at how what you need is exactly what others want to give and what you feel impelled to create and share is exactly what they need. This movement is always happening and you're part of it and are needed. Eventually you'll see that you don't want to take time away from direct, continuous participation because conscious involvement is the best thanks you can give. Participate fully! I am in you now—an enlightened self working with you at all times to bring you home. It is only a process of remembering.

"Trust. Trust every motion, every motivation, every warning. Trust your need for realignment. Trust how your process unfolds. Trust the connections, the shifting world of meanings, the rhythm of forming and dissolving. It is I who helps coordinate these things for you. No one else is using the pathways established for you. Only you fit the circuitry. Only you can activate the piece of the whole given to you. There will never be another you. I am waiting, expecting the best."

**My future
is shaping me.**

*Whenever
you say "I"
today, pretend
your future self
is speaking.
Your future self
has wisdom
gained from
experience that
you can benefit
from to ease
your present
journey.*

**I know
when I know.**

*Pay attention
to how you
become certain
of things today.
What signals
do you get in
your body?
How do you feel
emotionally?*

Tonight you may make dinner for yourself. What will you eat? Instead of having what you usually have, you might question your body. "Body, what's your feeling about Waldorf salad? Split pea soup? Pasta with Italian sausage? Broccoli quiche?" Let your body give you a signal about the foods that would best suit its needs. Maybe your body would prefer half a grapefruit to those cheese enchiladas. You can tell when something is true for you, or when a choice is safe and purposeful, because your energy will expand in some way. You might sense energy rising, becoming active or bouncy; you might warm to an idea, get light-headed, or feel flushed with enthusiasm. You might feel magnetically drawn toward tofu tonight. Have you ever said, "I'm leaning toward having a hamburger"?

When I ask people how they know something is true for them and exactly where they experience the feeling in their body, many describe a warm, spreading sensation across their chest. Others feel energy percolating up from the lower part of their body giving them butterflies, or moving from their chest into their throat. Sometimes it flows out through the eyes as tears of joy. Some people blush. Still others describe a variety of "clicks and clunks" as if something out of alignment has snapped or dropped back into place. These feelings often occur along the vertical centerline of the body. Another sensation of something ringing true is when the body silently "whangs" like a huge reverberating bell. Another common truth signal is the movement of energy up the spine and out the shoulders and arms, giving the sensation of chills.

Today, slow down your decision making. As you settle into each choice, ask yourself, "Is this action 100 percent comfortable at the deepest level? How do I know this is appropriate for me?" Remember that your body never lies. Look for and trust your sense of deep comfort.

July 29

Margo was in her early forties and at the height of a high-powered career in New York. She worked long hours under stressful conditions, didn't exercise, and ate unconsciously, skipping meals and loading up on stimulants. She was running on pure adrenaline, she was increasingly tired, had terrible PMS, and got frequent headaches. "I'm basically healthy," she told herself, and kept up the pace. Then she met a man, fell in love, and got married. The only glitch was that he lived in Dallas and she in Manhattan. So she started commuting weekly to Texas.

Soon the pace caught up with her. Margo's back spasmed so that she couldn't stand up, lift anything, or get into a cab. She saw a chiropractor and after several sessions felt some relief. But the spasms returned. She had never known such pain. Lying in bed, she took stock. Something was obviously wrong in her life. When she tuned in, Margo became aware of the pace of her thinking, which hummed inside like a swarm of bees. She felt what the frenetic pace of her life was doing to her, how she was being drained by the commute, how she wasn't letting herself receive the full benefit of her loving marriage. She felt old.

It become clear that she needed to simplify, unify, rest. Margo committed to heal herself inside and out. To that end, she sought answers in books, seminars, and in a renewed spiritual path. She continued working with her chiropractor but also consulted with a nutritionist and a spiritual counselor. She learned about the workings of her body, emotions, and intuition and how to recognize her own inner wisdom—something she'd always been too materialistic and goal oriented to notice. Reluctantly, Margo went part-time, then left the firm in New York entirely to move to Dallas to be with her husband. She took time off, which was difficult for a stimulation junkie like herself, but it gave her the chance to quiet down, develop her intuition further, and sense which direction to take next. Eventually she started her own consulting firm, which is now prospering. She says that had it not been for her painful healing crisis, she would have continued to live a shallow life based on externals, valuing quantity over quality.

Less can be more.

Be simple today in all things— action, speech, dress, perception. Feel the power of having extra space and extra time. When your life gets too complex, there's sure to be some sort of correction that returns you to simplicity. Why not practice simplicity voluntarily?

I dedicate myself to my highest expression.

Contemplate what the higher power wants to express through you today. Write a letter to God, making your deepest requests and stating your deepest motives.

Dear God,

Please teach me how to love better. I'm sorry I've been unable to love all your creations the way you do and that I have sometimes touched my loved ones, and my own self, with fear—and made blank spots in your love. I'm sorry that I'm lazy and that I forget you so often. I know you never forget me, and I'm very grateful for your attention on me, that you keep creating me here. I want to relax and feel you creating me and not even worry about what you are doing with me in your Great Big Plan. Please pull me back in quickly when I get lost. Teach me to be simple and to do things the easy way. I ask that all the people in my life *win* and learn of you by the way you teach me to be. Please bring me the opportunities I need to be creative, productive, and expansive—and help me recognize them. I don't want to be afraid of knowing you more and more, as much as I can. I love with your love, know with your mind, and function as and within your laws. Thank you. I am yours.

July 31

You may have to wait in traffic, or on line at the bank or deli, or on hold during a phone call, or at the dentist's office. Maybe you'll wait to get into a movie, then to get popcorn, and then to use the rest room afterward. Does the line *you* get in always take the longest? Does just the fact that you're in it make the line change from a speedy one to a slow-as-molasses one? "What's the lesson here?" I continually ask myself as I enviously watch the line of cars next to me move through the toll booth faster than mine. My inner voice says, "Don't compare. Stay in your own reality. Choose your own reality. Life is not better over there. Make a commitment to believe in the spot you stand on and love it above all other spots!" I think if I choose my own spot and invest in it, maybe my line will go faster. No, it will go exactly the speed it's going. I'll just be enjoying it more.

With the increasing speediness and future orientation of our culture, it makes sense that, to balance, waiting must increase proportionately. We're being forced to get back into our bodies all the way and drop into the present moment. So waiting is life's way of rejuvenating us, of giving us opportunities to meditate during the day. You don't have time to meditate in the morning before work? Too much to do at night? You've now got the chance while you're waiting for the computer service technician on the help line.

Close your eyes, take some calming, centering breaths, feel your body, notice the air, the temperature, the light coming through your eyelids, the smells, the sounds in the distance. Are you feeling annoyed? Bored? Just drop the attitude and go blank. Feel your heart beating and the blood circulating through all your capillaries. Feel your lungs fill with fresh oxygen, then dispel the old carbon dioxide. Life is working. All is well. Open your eyes. Notice details. Entertain yourself with your point of view. Look for connections, similarities. Write a haiku in your head. Appreciate being alive and having this one moment in which you are free to perceive any way you want. Will your moment be filled with appreciation or irritation? Paul Cezanne said, "Right now a moment of time is passing by! We must become that moment."

Waiting is being.

Whenever you wait today, be fully present to what's at hand. Waiting is an opportunity to meditate and become centered.

August

August 1

The couple next door got a third dog, and she had a litter of puppies. Now there were a total of ten dogs in their yard, all hyperactive, barking most of the day and night. I finally called them one night at 2:30 A.M. "Could you please quiet your dogs down?" I asked. The wife snapped, "Well I can't help it if they bark at every little thing. What do you expect me to do?" I suggested bringing them inside and she said, "Well I just got new carpet and I'm *not* doing that!" Then she hung up on me.

I tried earplugs, running a fan, and covering my head with pillows, but nothing worked. I called several more times, and each time my neighbors responded rudely. Finally, I called the police, who came and woke them up. Now they were mad at *me*. How dare I disturb their lives like this? After calling the police two more times, the barking at night finally stopped. But during the day it continued unabated. So I got myself in a good mood, took a deep breath, and called again. As I identified myself, the wife cursed at me and slammed down the phone.

The violence of her response hit me like a gunshot. My body started to shake. I couldn't concentrate. My self-righteous fantasies were boiling. Then I caught myself. "Listen to yourself. You're supposed to know better!" I realized I had stopped her violence in my body and was now thinking her thoughts. Her energy was actually in me animating me. As long as I continued to hold it, she would feel legitimized in her abusiveness. If I let it go, her energy would fall through me, and she'd have to experience herself instead of having the distraction of an enemy. I realized that part of me liked being a victim and milking the situation, enjoyed the adrenaline that vengeance generated. My inner voice said, "Give the wave over to the beings who live beyond you in the next higher vibration. They can use the energy and move it on. Don't hold the energy."

I let go. I let myself not know how the problem would ever be solved and turned my attention to what was near at hand. The next day my doorbell rang. It was the husband, who had come to confront me about the situation. I heard him out then told him my side of it. He had not known how his wife had treated me and he apologized. We shook hands. Within a day the barking subsided.

I choose to end violence in myself.

Be aware of when you accuse or criticize someone today, even in thought. How do you feel after you express something ugly or vindictive? Reactive, self-protective behavior immediately shuts down your internal guidance system.

August 2

I am in awe of the generosity in people.

Compliment others today, do a favor, express thanks. An open heart leads to a clear mind.

I like this anonymous quote. "You can easily judge the character of a man by how he treats those who can do nothing for him." It reminds me of the time I was on my way into San Francisco for a morning meeting, driving over the Golden Gate Bridge with a thick stream of rush-hour traffic. As we crawled slowly toward the tollbooths, I dug through my purse to find the right change. Rush hour had put me in a slightly irritable mood; they'd just raised the bridge toll; it was foggy and cold outside; the news on the radio was depressing. Finally it was my turn to pay. I pulled up and rolled down my window. The toll taker smiled mischievously down at me, indicated my forward direction with a quick left jerk of his head, and said, "Go on through, ma'am. Those guys ahead of you just paid your toll!" I glanced over in time to see three construction workers jammed into the front seat of a battered red pickup truck, zooming off ahead of me, waving crazily out the windows.

I blinked a few times and the sun came out from behind the clouds in my brain. I smiled, put the car in gear, and hollered, "Have a great day!" to the toll taker as I accelerated away from my brand-new starting point.

August 3

I had lunch with Caitlin last week and asked how she was doing. "I'm falling apart," she moaned. She had taken an unpopular stand at the healing center where she had worked for ten years and had put her job at risk. It looked likely that, because she had not agreed with a new policy, she would lose her clients and need to find a new source of income. Right after that, she fell and twisted her ankle. The same week, her 100-year-old grandmother, who Caitlin cares for every few days, fell and broke her wrist. Now Caitlin was being pressured by the other members of her family to go over even more often to wait on her grandmother, when they could just as easily make time in their schedules to do it. What she really wanted was to go off for a two-week Buddhist meditation retreat in peaceful northern California. She needed some perspective. Not only were people falling in her reality, but cups, dishes, pictures on the wall, and fragile art objects were falling from their resting places and breaking into bits on the floor. She couldn't stop it no matter how careful she was.

Caitlin was feeling antsy. She was beginning to see that everyone expected her to be sweet and compliant, and when she expressed her own views they rejected her. Her boss was ready to dump her after years of loyal work just because she disagreed with a minor policy. Her family was telling her she was selfish to abandon her grandmother for something as silly as a meditation retreat. Caitlin decided it was time to be loyal to herself for a change, and she made plans to go away anyway, knowing that she'd probably displease her clients, lose her job, and upset her family. She knew she needed contact with her deepest self in a sustained way, in a quiet private place. Caitlin said she felt she was about to write a new chapter in her life. Perhaps things were falling and breaking apart around her because her life was too small for her upcoming self. Maybe she needed to break out. In a secretive way, she confided, "And you know, as I stood there and watched all my precious objects crash and explode, I just let them go and said, 'Oh, well . . .' "

I am an original.

Notice when you compare yourself to others today, then return to your own body and soul and be your true self. When people say "Get a life!" they really mean "Get fascinated with your own unique creativity and follow it!"

What needs to be said is often different from my first impulse.

Pause a long moment before you speak today and notice what words come. Let your words reflect the love of your heart and not an impatient, partial view. Sometimes you may omit certain words because of love's dictates.

I had a client who was a fashion designer. She had recently designed a line of gorgeous natural-fiber clothing that was selling well. Everything she touched became successful, and her attitude was upbeat and positive. She always looked like a million dollars. And yet, under the surface I sensed that she was running on willpower; her unflagging positive attitude seemed slightly inhuman. Nobody could be *that* happy *all* the time, could they? In spite of the subtle underlying discrepancies I sensed, I liked her very much.

When she came to me for a reading, I found myself in a slight quandary. She was high on enthusiasm as usual, and what was foremost on her mind was expanding her business and opening a retail store. She didn't ask if that was the right move. Instead she asked, "Would the real estate on Main Street be better or worse than the property on the frontage road?" I could feel that neither of the two locations would work in the long run because she wasn't supposed to expand her business. But I could also feel that she didn't want to hear about it, that she was going to steamroll her way forward so she wouldn't have to face a darker underlying reality. There was no way for me to introduce the subject of her dealing with her subconscious fears because she had an edict emblazoned in capital letters across the front of her energy body. "NOTHING NEGATIVE!" it said. So I told her which property seemed better and tried to slip in a few side comments such as, "It would be a good idea for you to take some time off or meditate more right now." And, "Are you clear that you're on the right path? Why not do a little journal writing and see what you get?"

My client proceeded to rent the new property, created a gorgeous, expensive store, and within a year closed it due to lack of sales. Subsequently she became sick with cancer. She went into a period of retreat as she embarked on an extensive healing journey from which she eventually emerged, healthy but cautious. Today, she is the same warm, creative, endearing person, but the willpower has softened, leaving true positiveness in its place. I remember this episode vividly and the helplessness I felt because it was one of the few times I was forbidden by my inner voice to interfere with the painful process I knew she would have to live through.

August 5

I was in Tokyo working with clients. On my breaks I'd go for walks. I'd stand at a crosswalk, fifty people waiting with me, with a similar group on the opposite side. The light would turn green and the two groups would head for each other, miraculously passing through each other like two schools of fish. I, being the only blond in the crowd, drew a subtle kind of attention. No one touched me or looked directly at me, but I could feel their mental and emotional energy pass through my body, as though the space inside me was open for examination. After weeks of this kind of energy invasion, coupled with a deep daily contact with the Japanese subconscious mind, I was wearing down.

I felt feverish and overwhelmed, as though I couldn't maintain my own personal space and reality. One night, I sat down and all at once was flooded with images of the crowds on the streets and all the stories of all the clients I'd seen. I felt like I was drowning. In a powerful vision that lasted only a few seconds, I felt myself drown in a sea of watery energy. I left my old reality and was reborn in a new one. Now I was swimming in an ocean of fluid awareness where everything and everyone was interconnected. I could dip up out of it like a cresting wave and take different shapes—I could be myself, or a client, or a person on the street, or a tree. When I rose up as other people, I knew them from the inside. Then I could relax back into the ocean again.

From that day on, I no longer felt crowded. My temperature went back to normal, and I felt incredibly connected and happy about everyone I saw. They all felt like family, and I could see that in this inner reality everyone knew each other and took care of each other. That was why the Japanese placed such a high priority on "saving face." My American individualism had not allowed me to experience the energy reality of Japan since I'd been programmed to hold myself separate. It had taken a consistent wearing down of my cultural behavior and mind-set until I finally surrendered how I thought reality was supposed to be. Then and only then was I given the great gift of expanded perception.

I surrender to the unknown.

Let yourself enter the void today. Allow yourself to not be in control. When you can become comfortable stretching beyond what you know, you'll discover the greater reality waiting for you.

I am home.

*Pay special
attention as
you arrive
home today.
Use it as an
excuse to
center yourself.*

What does being at home mean to you? Home should be a sacred sanctuary where you can drop the chaos of the roadways, the marketplace, and the strain of dealing with angry and unconscious people. Home is meant to make you warm and safe, to provide a reliable context for love and nurturing. There has to be one place in the world where you can recenter and drop your guard, one place where you can consistently reconnect with your inner self and with the earth beneath your feet. Home is where you can explore the dimensions of belonging and of being still. At home you can watch the trees grow taller and fuller over the years; you can see the progress of children maturing to adulthood.

We leave home and move around in the world, and, though it's possible to be mindful the entire time we're journeying, somehow the idea of coming home focuses us naturally into the idea of self-awareness. Our home is symbolic of our body and tells us much about our percep-tual habits. Where clutter builds in your home, you'll find a matching area of unconsciousness inside your mind. The room where you spend the most time, the kitchen, for example, might represent your most active inner compo-nent—a need for nurturing. So when you return to your home, stop a moment before you enter it and anticipate the welcome you will receive. Your home is loyal to you, waits for you, likes you to come back to it. Walk up to the front door and greet your own domain. Touch the doorknob consciously, turn the key consciously, step inside. Smell your home, feel the energy. Say, "Hello, house!" out loud if you feel like it. You've completed a circuit of going out and coming back. Do you remember when you left before? Now you've come full circle. Take a breath and feel the blessings of home, hearth, belonging, and once again having a chance to reunite with your private self.

August 7

Some years ago, just as I was scheduled to do a considerable amount of public speaking and teaching, I began to have disturbing dreams about being persecuted by a religious movement in which I'd unfailingly be captured and executed. Some nights I'd have to quote long memorized passages, and if I missed anything I'd draw the attention of spies who were on the lookout for people who said the wrong thing. Finally, realizing that this had to do with appearing in public, I went to a therapist to look into the root causes of the anxiety and heal them.

The therapist led me into a relaxed state, and I imagined myself drawn up into a group of nonphysical beings. When I faced them, I could sense many souls and hear them talking. But to enter the group I had to turn around and merge into them backward. I became part of a huge sphere of consciousness then. As I was drawn into the center of the sphere, the soul group downloaded into me. I remembered how much we all really do know and how omnipresent knowledge is. "Wisdom is like oxygen to us," I said. The scene shifted, and I saw myself speaking to audiences, but this time I wasn't alone or a victim; the wisdom, the sphere, the soul group was with me. I heard a voice simultaneously talking in me, through me, and in the minds of the audience, saying the same thing. There was total rapport. As long as I stayed in the "Us" state, there was perfect understanding between me and the audience. When I drifted into worry, I could feel the audience become judgmental. To reverse that, I only had to return to the "Us" feeling.

The feeling of being the "Us" is the same feeling as being in the heart. It's the same way we feel when we talk to a three-year-old and fall back into our original innocence. When we're in that divine child state, other people match it and there is safety. Perceiving from the innocent, wise heart dissolves contentiousness, irritation, superstition, and fear. Here was the key I needed to feel comfortable and excited about embracing the upcoming public work.

I facilitate perfect understanding when I come from innocence.

Practice being a divine child when you communicate today. See others as divine children also, and watch how the innocence easily promotes clarity.

August 8

I give equal attention to all things.

Hold your focus on your thoughts longer than normal today, especially when you feel rushed or jumpy. Concentrate on evening out your attention so you don't miss crucial information and enjoyment.

Stacy Brice, a colleague in Baltimore, has coined the term BWYFA, which means "Be where your feet are." She lives relatively close to the Amish country and visits there regularly. She says, "There has always been one thing about the Amish that has touched me most. It's that in their lives, every act or action is equal. No matter what they do, they are fully present in the moment. Whether they're baking a cake, or scrubbing the floor, or canning vegetables, or feeding the animals, no one thing is done with more attention or intent or is more sacred or special than any other. Everything is a ritual. There is no rushing to get to important things since all things are important. By making everything equally important, they bring excellence to each thing they do." She says she learned from the Amish example that when faced with doing something difficult or something she doesn't want to do, she finds it easier when she brings excellence into it. Approaching everything from a place of quality transforms the mundane. Contentment comes to us from giving up wishing we were somewhere else, doing something else, and focusing our attention right here, right now.

August 9

I experienced one of the most powerful healings of my
life in a dream. In the dream, I had coughed up my heart
and was holding it, still beating, in my cupped hands. It
wouldn't go back in! I screamed for help but no one came.
The longer I held it outside my body, the weaker it
became, until it broke in two. I called for help again.
Then a magnificent man materialized in front of me. He
was tall, majestic, full of power, and had a quiet dignity
and wisdom. His skin was the bluish black of the clear
night sky, and he radiated indigo-black light, cool and
penetrating, which went straight into me. His presence
was infinitely calming. His eyes glowed with the black
fire of outer space. His long·black shiny hair reached to
below his waist. "I am the angel of healing," he told me
inside my mind. He looked into my eyes and I was reassured about who I really am. He wrapped his large, long
hands around mine, gently reuniting the halves of my
broken heart.

As my heart knit itself back together, he spoke to my
frightened mind. "This is not really your heart. Did you
know this? It belongs to God and has been given to you
on loan. It is God's force that makes this heart beat and
God's truest impulse that makes this heart love. Give your
heart back to God now, and it will once again be whole
and happy and light as a feather. And God will give you
the gift of a full life, and you will give God the gift of
living as You. Relax your throat, open your mouth, make
the long sound of the universe: Ahhhhhh." And he slipped
the now-perfect heart back to its rightful place. With one
hand on my chest, he slowly passed the other up across
my forehead and over my head. The dark, absorbing
indigo-black light penetrated my skin, bones, brain, and
beliefs. "Here, now. Let me help you forget what you
know," he whispered. And I sighed and fell back against
him, released from my prison of memories, free from perceptions that were no longer appropriate for that day. I
floated in the dark peace of the cosmic mind, fresh and
clean like a baby waiting to be born and grateful for the
chance to know, and to love, anew.

**I can heal
myself by visu-
alizing healing
imagery.**

*Spend some time
meditating today
on images that
let you feel
loved, helped,
more integrated,
whole, and
peaceful. Bring
the living experi-
ences to these
images into your
body so they feel
absolutely real.*

I choose to be cheerful.

Let go of your negative moods today, as soon as you notice them. Choose to feel contentment, then notice how your body changes. Cheerfulness is a natural condition of the soul, and it promotes vitality.

Kevin is by nature upbeat and warmhearted, and even the worst troubles hardly ever get him down. He tells this story from his childhood.

He was about four years old and it was Christmas. His parents had taken him on a family outing to select the perfect Christmas tree. They picked through many kinds of trees, long-needled and short, and dragged a good-looking one out so they could see it better. "How do you like *this* one, Kevin?" his mother cooed. Kevin took one look at it and burst into tears. He was inconsolable. So they took him over to another section of the giant Christmas tree lot and looked at the flocked trees. "Look at this one, Kevin. Isn't this beautiful?" his mother asked. Again, Kevin responded with a burst of sobbing. Finally, they just picked the long-needled tree they liked, paid for it, and tied it to the car. Kevin was still crying. His mother took him by the hand and squatted down in front of him. "Now, Kevin, don't cry—it's Christmas. This is a time when everyone is supposed to be *happy* and have a good time."

"*I WANNA be happy!*" Kevin moaned, sputtering in between sobs. And he cried the whole way home.

Christmas morning, his parents got him up, and he and his sister hurried down the stairs into the living room. As he came through the door and saw the Christmas tree twinkling brightly with colored lights and shiny ornaments, his face lit up like a starburst. "I like THAT Christmas tree!" he exclaimed. "That's the kind of tree we had *last* year!"

I remember this story often because we all have some vague thought or memory of the way life is supposed to look. When things don't turn out as I had hoped, when I think the first phases of an unfolding project are the whole thing, when I think I'm going to have to live with the plain green Christmas tree, I often find Kevin's innocent wail popping up from my inner mind. Perhaps it is the voice of the soul expressing its true intent as it confronts the shallowness of our often linear, mental reality. "*I WANNA be happy!*"

August 11

In Buddhism, Bodhisattvas are enlightened beings, or saints, who have freed themselves from the cycle of reincarnation and karma yet have chosen to continue to live physical lives again and again, teaching and healing, until all sentient beings achieve enlightenment together.

The experience of fellowship, which is a natural by-product of Bodhisattva consciousness, shows us there is an incredible cooperation among souls. We use our relatedness to accelerate mutual evolution by tying ourselves together via mirrored beliefs and lessons and overlapping areas of wisdom and cocreativity. Though our spiritual work is our own to do, when we allow ourselves to be part of a mutually inclusive flow, other people's growth toward enlightenment makes conditions that much easier for us, and our clarity similarly helps them.

The Bodhisattva says, "I would be a protector for those without protection, a leader for those who would journey, and a boat, a bridge, a passage for those desiring the further shore. For all creatures, I would be a lantern for those desiring a lantern, I would be a bed for those desiring a bed, I would be a slave for those desiring a slave. I would be for creatures a magic jewel, an inexhaustible jar, a powerful spell, a universal remedy, a wishing tree, a cow of plenty. As the earth and other elements are, in various ways, for the enjoyment of innumerable beings dwelling in all of space, so may I be, in various ways, the means of sustenance for the living beings occupying space, for as long a time as all are not satisfied."

**I see the
god in you.**

*Practice truly
respecting every-
one you meet
today. Raise your
own consciousness
by giving freely
to others and by
seeing them
with the eyes of
the divine.*

August 12

**I have the
right to take
up space.**

*Let yourself
feel that you have
plenty of space
today physically,
emotionally,
and mentally.
Notice when you
experience being
invaded or
intimidated and
who you have
inadvertently let
dictate your right
to be yourself.*

Someone dumped an old wreck of a car in front of my
house two weeks ago. Not only was it hideous to look at,
but it took up the parking spaces I like to have available
for friends, clients, and the gardener. I called the police,
who eventually came out and tagged it. I'd have to wait
another week before they could legitimately tow it away.
The next day I found the red violation notice crumpled
into a ball and thrown onto my front porch. I uncrum-
pled it and carefully placed in back on the car's wind-
shield. The following day, it was gone.

In the past few years, several young families have
moved in around me. The men often schmooze with each
other on the street corner. I asked one of them in a polite
tone of voice, "Do you know whose car this is?" He
gruffly answered, "It's not mine, and I don't give a ____.
Leave it alone, lady." Were he and the other men connected to the car in some way? Was I the only person on
the block who had clear boundaries? I sensed I was being
interpreted as a troublemaker, and they were enjoying the
fact that the car was interfering with my life.

During the two weeks that the car sat there, I began to
feel irrationally unsafe. I had dreams about being ganged
up on by groups of men. Perhaps there are memory patterns of victimization in the feminine DNA; it had to be
coming from *somewhere* because I had no basis in my past
for the fears. Writing about the present moment was a
godsend. By redirecting my thoughts to ideas like "allow
things to be as they are—there's wisdom in the process"
or "look for the god in the other person," I was able to
move to a higher ground where the antics of my neighbors were just another movement of life. I saw that I was
doubting my right to be myself and have preferences, as
if as soon as I showed up and became definite, bullies
would try to take over my territory. The moment I truly
returned to my center, I looked out the window and the
car was gone.

August 13

Here are some thoughts straight from the hearts of our children. These are actual prayers from a wonderful little book called *Thank You God: The Prayers of Children* compiled by Fiona Corbridge.

Dear God, Please make public transportation from here to the moon. Because I want to go there. Charlotte, age 7. *Dear God, Teach us to be good to other people. Teach us to be quiet. Danny, age 8.* Sorry, God, that when I'm playing a game and Mommy says to get washed, I say, Oh Mom! Amen. Elizabeth, age 6. PLEASE GOD, MAKE PEOPLE SHARE. Araba, age 5. **Dear God, Thank you for giving us what we need. Thank you for giving the world animals. I really appreciate both. Hailey, age 7.** *Dear God, Thank you for the Dinosaurs but why did you send a Meteroyd down? Amen. Matthew, age 6.* **Please God, help Scruffy to stop biting his paws. Mitchell, age 4.** DEAR GOD, PLEASE FORGIVE ME FOR ALL THE BAD THINGS I HAVE DONE. HELP ME BE AN ENTERMOLOGIST WHEN I AM BIGGER. AMEN. Jonathan, age 7. *Thank you God for answering my prayer and sending me my two furry kittens, Pixey and Dixey. Danielle, age 6.* **Dear God, Thank you for my family. I love you. I wish you could come down here with me because people don't believe in you and they would if they could see you. Thank you for the animals and birds. Thank you for the world we live in. Amen. Rebecca, age 7.** PLEASE GOD, HELP US TO LOOK AFTER EVERYTHING IN YOUR WONDERFUL WORLD. Sophie, age 7.

I express deep gratitude and ask for forgiveness.

Align your mind with what is good in your life today. Anywhere you feel out of integrity, ask that you be able to return to a grace-filled flow by changing your thoughts and behaviors. Alignment is the first step to accurate intuition.

August 14

**The element
of fire
contributes to
my life.**

*Be aware of
and grateful to
fire in all its
forms today.
Be more firey.*

Ancient sun, eternally young,
giver of life and source of energy,
In coal and oil, in plant and wind and tide,
in spiritual light and human embrace,
You kindle the heavens,
you shine within us
(For we are suns with hearts afire—
we light the world as you light the sky . . .)
Your cosmic light penetrates our depths,
In your majesty we are bound to one another . . .
—CONGREGATION OF ABRAXAS

Fire is the bringer of light, insight, enlightenment, the giver of warmth and sustenance. Fire is the element of purification, releasing the old, eating away the forms, transmuting them to gas and ash, making space. How many times today will you benefit from fire? The lights by which you put your makeup on, the hot water you bathe in, the stove that bakes your lasagna, the spark plugs that make your car go, the match you light the candle with, the daylight that reveals life, the colors of sunrise and sunset.

You might write a prayer on a piece of paper or write down something you want to release from your life. Crunch up or twist the paper tightly, then burn it with intention and presence of mind, letting the fire carry the message to the heavens.

August 15

Part of what keeps us from experiencing union with life, with our deeper self, and with the divine is the constant yakking in our minds. From the moment we wake up, we're telling ourselves to do things, chiding ourselves when we don't do things, criticizing others, envying others, and indulging in fantasies. When other people talk to us, we jump ahead and finish their sentences for them, inserting thoughts into their minds and never receiving their true intent. We can't tolerate blank space, and, when someone stops talking, we immediately fill the pauses with chatter, a new question, a giggle, a sigh. Try the following practice periodically all day for as long as you can maintain it. When the chatter stops, your essential presence, and that of others, will be easier to sense.

I take time to listen neutrally to other people.

Don't second-guess others today. Hear them through to their true intent.

STOP YOUR INTERNAL DIALOGUE

1. Whether you're alone or with people, notice your internal conversation. Stop midsentence and simply go blank. Listen with total receptivity. Whatever you were discussing with yourself, it's not that important. Within a few seconds your internal commentator will make more comments, living out another scene. When you catch it happening, simply go blank again. Exhale. Isn't it a relief to feel the open space?

2. Once you can repeatedly enter the spaciousness (even if you can't hold it long), intentionally listen for the silence. At first you may hear a buzzing or be aware of a subtle vibration caused by your physical organism. Listen past that and find the quiet place of origin. When you first touch it, you may bounce off. Find it and enter it again. Learn to merge with it.

3. When you are able to spend time in the silent place, you will be able to trust wholeheartedly the ideas and desires occurring to you immediately after you've been there. These perceptions come from your direct knowing, from your intuitive voice. Take note. When you're listening to another person from a place of space and silence, you'll hear their soul talking, and you'll know their true intent.

August 16

I'm upset by some other reason than what I think.

Notice what bothers you today. There may be one explanation on the surface, but what's the real cause when you look deeper? Can you find the underlying emotions and ideas that are at the root of your upsets and start clearing them?

Lynne had just ended a relationship—it had taken her a while to realize it wasn't going anywhere and that she'd been hanging on because she didn't want to be alone. Only weeks after the breakup, she got word that her father had been diagnosed with Alzheimer's. A week after that, her sister called because she had just found out she had cancer. Lynne, alone and now suffering a triple shock, developed severe stress and insomnia. Life was speeding by extra fast, and ordinary snags were tripping her up more than usual. If she was late for an appointment, she'd practically beat herself up. "But Lynne, you were only five minutes late! It's nothing," her chiropractor would say. If someone asked her to squeeze just one more thing into her overloaded schedule, or if her plan for the day went awry, she'd blow up. Lynne's tolerance was at an all-time low. She was indulging in fits of anger and even violence, kicking the furniture, throwing household objects, hitting her head against the wall, scratching herself.

When she got some help and looked more into the cause of her outbursts, she traced it to a terrifying helplessness about being slowly abandoned by everyone she loved and losing her security. She was irrationally mad at her ex-boyfriend, sister, and father for having problems and there was nothing she could do to change things; she had no control of her life's circumstances. She was in emotional pain and couldn't let it out. Hitting her head externalized the pain a bit, but she didn't really want to hurt herself. Lynne realized that all the deep emotions that had been freed by these shocks had collected in her solar plexus. Because she had never been allowed to express herself, especially negatively or loudly, she was holding the energy in and expressing her frustration *toward herself.* She needed to yell, stomp, shake, run helter-skelter like a wild horse across a huge field, take an art class, breathe intensely, and take up more space. It helped Lynne to reconnect with her higher power, which she affirmed had a compassionate wisdom that would bring her what she needed. She also let herself feel empty. By taking off the false pressures, she was able to enter her deep feelings and gradually heal her shock and pain.

August 17

Marcus True does a specialized kind of therapy. He calls it "dowsing therapy" and has remarkable success clearing psychological blockages in the subconscious mind. He does this using a device called a recording wire that works on the same principle as dowsing rods or pendulums to measure subtle levels of energy. Marcus measures things much more subtle than I imagined were possible to measure. The first time I visited him, he took a reading on the energy field around my body. "Well, your psychic weight measures 210 and a normal woman's energy field is usually about 133. This means you have other people's energy in your aura today. Before I can get an accurate reading about you, we'll have to clear the other energies." I had terrible thoughts that I was being possessed, but Marcus explained that we connect with people constantly in our daily life and often forget to disconnect. He did some more measuring and determined that I had three people in my energy field. "Who have you been around lately?" I named off a list: Peggy, Mary, Cheryl, Margaret, June . . .

"June!" he repeated in a definite tone of voice. His recording wire was swinging around rapidly. "What does June want?" Marcus asked his wire. "Does she want approval? To show appreciation? Attention? Is she angry? Hurt? Jealous? *She wants attention!* June is a victim? *Yes.* June wants you to feel sympathy and pity for her. So say to June, 'June, this is my time and my space, so please leave right now. You have your own source of attention.' " I said it out loud and Marcus's wire spun crazily as he yawned again and again, which is his way of releasing energy. We did the same thing with the other two people—one wanted to show appreciation, the other wanted some knowledge I had. I was amazed that, within minutes of clearing these people from my energy field, I perked up and gained mental focus.

When we try to get something from someone else, or provide others with our own resources, we end up feeling drained. We each have our own resources and are meant to be supplied from within.

I can feel other people's personal auras of energy.

Notice when you enter other people's personal space today, or when other people enter yours. You may feel your energy rise or drop or sense a mild level of anxiety or vigilance. You may even notice that you start expressing opinions that really aren't yours.

My body feels connected and alive when I touch and am touched by the world.

Be aware of touch, texture, and vibrations today and how they affect you. By activating your sense of touch, your body's "reptile brain" will wake up and give you a renewed sense of motivation.

I went for a walk a few weeks ago around a lake near my home. The morning light was lemony and the air carried the scents of the ocean, the pungent bay laurels, and the odd must of the large flocks of wild birds. I was having a ball finding feathers, flowers, tiny lizards, and tree frogs. Ahead on the trail was a rise topped by a craggy outcropping of granite, out of which grew a circle of laurels. I couldn't resist climbing up and entering this tree temple. I stood there soaking up the peace of the place, turning slowly all around, making contact with every tree. The last tree I focused on was actually two trunks branching out from the same base. They grew in a wavy way, making space for each other's branches as though they were snakes in a mating dance. I was mesmerized by their grace and balance. I thought, "These trees are in love, they're like soul mates—two seemingly separate lives arising from a unified base. And when I'm home drying dishes or driving on the highway amid thousands of commuters, these trees will still be here, holding the reality of cooperating lovers, adding their peace into the tree temple." This gave me comfort.

I moved on and found a small pond I'd never seen before. A great blue heron waded majestically in the shallow water, and some wood ducks swam together in formation. At the far end of the pond was a brand-new bench. I was drawn to it. I sat and watched the birds, and I felt glad to be alive. The weeks can get so hectic without remembering nature's easy rhythms. Then I looked behind me and noticed a shiny little brass plaque mounted on the back of the bench. "For Mary White, 1918–1998. Our Mother Loved Being Here." I knew immediately that Mary loved being here at this pond, but she also loved being alive, being real, being Here. I said to her in my mind, "You can look at the pond and the birds through my eyes. I'll look with you and maybe I'll see what you saw. Thanks for reminding me how great life is."

August 19

I did a research reading recently with a friend, looking into a phenomenon she'd been encountering in her spiritually oriented psychotherapy practice. She had an increasing number of clients who called themselves *walk-ins*, a metaphysical term describing a soul that supposedly changes places with another soul and uses the existing body and personality—usually precipitated by an accident or trauma. In these cases, the personality is said to change radically, and new gifts develop that hadn't been present before.

Here are a few insights from the reading. "People are evolving rapidly today, and that means the traditional boundaries of identity are softening. We're stretching out, having experiences of greater interconnection with all the other beings in the physical world, but also with the non-physical beings in other dimensions. As this happens we have less ability to distinguish between ourselves and others. We are merging further out and up, and at some point we'll all merge into one being, which we call 'God.' But now we are experimenting with concepts like being part of a soul mate relationship, or part of a soul group family, which lets our identity expand slightly.

"In the phenomenon called walk-in, the original soul doesn't give up the body it has created, but its conscious mind expands to become aware of the next levels of the soul's vibration, which include a broader knowledge base shared by many souls. This is the collective consciousness, which is the ultimate brain center or coordinating force for all individuals. The new gifts that appear have always been present, just latent.

"People who are drawn to take an identity as a different soul don't really want to be in the physical world. They think higher beings have better answers, and by identifying with them they'll shortcut the work they have to do on themselves. But each of us has the responsibility to clear our own physical body of blocks and fear. To the extent that people avoid their personal self, they will be drawn by life to later deal only with that. This could even manifest physically, taking the form of paralysis, quadriplegia, or learning disabilities."

I see life from a higher perspective.

When solving problems or getting insights today, pretend you're an angel or a spaceship commander. Patterning your awareness around an entity with a greater collective consciousness can help you understand the big picture.

August 20

*Do one
thing for your
body today
that you don't
usually do.
Ask your body
what it really
wants.*

. . . Be strong then, and enter into your own body;
there you have a solid place for your feet.
Think about it carefully!
Don't go off somewhere else!
Kabir says this: just throw away all thoughts of imaginary things,
and stand firm in that which you are.
—Kabir

I am the foot, I am the hand, I am the eyelid and lash, the
hairs, the pores, the nails. I am the ready mouth, the
waiting ears, the pumping heart and lungs, the flowing
blood and lymph carrying, transporting, transferring,
cleansing. I am a new cell and an old cell, I am fat stored
for a lean day and muscle waiting to leap and lunge. Here
I am, a collection of memories and a spontaneous surprise.
I work, I play, I am wounded and I heal, I create form
and create space, I move through, around, and with my
creations. I can be still and I can be wild! Quiet, loud,
vertical, flat. Give me a walk, a run, a swoop, a hop; let
me drive and write and draw and dig and wave hello/
good-bye and hug a child and pet a dog and touch a
smooth tomato. Take me to the ocean, the hilltop, the
canyon, the cave, the pasture and let me smell cow dung,
pine pitch, wet soil, dry dust, whale breath, salt, and my
own hot skin. Let me bake a chocolate cake, taste a ripe
cherry, pick a bouquet of flowers, glue a broken dish, put
line-dried sheets on the bed, inhale the scent of fresh
mint. Use me, move me, stretch me, ski me, swim me,
dance me around, swirl me, pat me, lay me down gently.

August 21

Famed dancer Martha Graham once said, "There is a vitality, a life force, an energy, a quickening, that is translated through you into action, and because there is only one of you in all time, this expression is unique." Rachel is a writer, musician, artist, dancer, hiker, and teacher. She is also a single woman who has never been married and has no children. She got an idea for a book on childless women who chose art and creativity, or a spiritual path, over having a family. She began to interview women whose lives were incredibly inspiring—women who had come from nothing and achieved unique success; women who had tenacity and vision; women whose dedication to their craft, to detail, and to excellence was immense. The women were sensitive, confident, and above all courageous.

Rachel looked at her own life and wondered if she might be hiding. Had she been lulled into doing too much editing of other people's work? Could she create something that paralleled the accomplishments of these new role models? About this time, she met a new man, an artist who embodied the dynamic characteristics she was looking for in herself. She left her old relationship and started a passionate new one. He catalyzed many new creative outlets for her, but she couldn't seem to write the book. She went to a conference on childless women hoping to stimulate herself. It turned out to be a depressing experience dominated by a dry feminism to which she couldn't relate. She returned home to get further involved in doing upbeat art performances with her boyfriend. She shelved her book idea but it wouldn't go away. "Do your own work!" the women whispered silently to her.

Soon Rachel's new relationship ended. She could then feel a part of herself she'd been unable to perceive while she was focused on relationship. Now the book rose to awareness again. "What's the real message?" her inner voice asked. She realized she no longer wanted to emphasize the childless angle. These were not women *without* but women *with*. This was a book about how women create, about what motivates women to be authentic. So Rachel started again, preparing to discover the process known to the women who were destined to be in her book, and to become one herself.

I trust my deep-seated feelings and rising urges.

Pay attention today to the urges and insights that arise spontaneously from the center of your body. These are truthful.

**I notice my
internal
conflicts.**

*Notice the
times today when
you say "yes,
but . . ."
Examine the
topics you feel
split about, and
look at what
the underlying
issues might be.*

Every internal conflict boils down to something that's
vitally important to you. What do you really want and
need? Kathryn was looking for a house to buy. She is such
a positive person that she could easily find things about
every house that appealed to her. She could project inside
a house and imagine living there and how she'd fix the
place up. Yet she noticed when she was enthusiastically
describing the houses to her daughter, she was focusing
only on the high points, saying things like, "Once you
get inside, it really feels good . . ." Or, "The bedroom
does have a good view . . ." Or, "The living room has a
great fireplace . . ." At the end of every sentence was a
pause where the word *but* was implied. When she finished the thoughts honestly she heard, ". . . *but* there are
power lines too close to the yard." ". . . *but* there's no
closet space." ". . . *but* there are hardly any windows and
it's dark." She realized she had almost been willing to live
in a space that didn't fully support her health and self-
expression. Seeing underneath her "yes, buts" allowed her
to stop and get clear about what kind of nurturing and
creativity she wanted for the next phase of her life.

What things have you had a conditionally positive
response to in the last few days? Did you only partly agree
with someone in a discussion? Did you only partly like a
new restaurant, movie, or acquaintance? Are you only
allowing yourself to partly commit to a new action? Are
you only letting yourself be partly happy? Or partly
angry? See if you can write out the positive side of your
statement, then complete the second half of the thought:
"*but* . . ." What comes after the *but* is a key idea. Ask
yourself then, "Why is having good natural light so
important to me?" Maybe you'll answer, "Because natural
light makes me feel happy and expansive." "Why do I
want to be clear of power lines?" "Because I want my
personal space to feel perfectly safe." "What's so important
about having closet space?" "I want to feel there will be
enough space for me to be all of who I am."

August 23

Martin Luther King Jr. said, "We are challenged on every hand to work untiringly to achieve excellence in our life work. Not all men are called to specialized or professional jobs; even fewer rise to the heights of genius in the arts and sciences; many are called to be laborers in factories, fields, and streets. But no work is insignificant. All labor that uplifts humanity has dignity and importance and should be undertaken with painstaking excellence. If a man is called to be a street sweeper, he should sweep even as Michelangelo painted, or Beethoven composed music, or Shakespeare wrote poetry. He should sweep streets so well that all the host of heaven and earth will pause to say, 'Here lived a great street sweeper who did his job well.'"

There truly is a difference between getting the job done and doing it well. I can dust my living room, and as I do, I can zip over the surfaces with a dry cloth or I can move across them more deliberately with a special primed cloth that smells good and leaves the surfaces shiny. As I move my rag I think, "Where did this dust originate? Was it once part of the beach? Did it spew up from the earth's core when Mt. St. Helens erupted? Has it flown here on the back of a mockingbird?" I grant even the dust particles their unique stories, their own dignity. And I look lovingly on the surfaces as they reappear, clean—the wood grain, glass, and textured plaster are having the chance to be themselves, uncluttered. I move the large houseplant and clean under it instead of just around it. I touch everything carefully, intentionally. I thank each thing for existing. As I dust, a divine voice says to me, "As you clean the world I have given you, so I keep you fresh and new. As you pay loving attention to detail, so I attend to you with microscopic vision, without distraction of any kind. It is only by attending well to your work that you will see the piece of work you truly are."

I do an excellent job.

Pay close attention to improving the quality of at least one thing you do today.

I hit the mark with my communications.

Notice how precisely you communicate today—your aim, your pacing, the amount of force you use, the music in your voice, the look in your eyes.

We so often fling our words, or drop them uneventfully, or act like we're the only ones participating in the communication process.

Barbara Garro, M.A., C.P.C.U., and author of *Grow Yourself a Life You'll Love*, tells this story about her acting teacher, Joe Balfior. She says, "His weekly lessons were half acting lessons and half life lessons. When he wanted me to correct something, he would pull off the mask I was wearing and show me what was behind it." On one occasion when Barbara was saying some lines, he interrupted her abruptly and yelled, "Who are you talking to? Who? I'm two feet away from you and you're speaking to somebody out in my garage! I'll tell you—I'm not sure you're speaking to anybody. You don't need another person for what you're doing."

Then he said, "If you want people to listen to you, you have to make them feel that you are speaking personally to them. You can't make what you're saying more important than who you say it to. Communicating is like electricity—you need enough power to complete the circuit. If you don't, you get no juice." Barbara, who now makes her living as a public speaker, coach, and writer, says Joe taught her to be conscious during the communication process. It's so easy to talk without thinking or knowing what impact we want to have. Communicating is like tossing someone a ball. Can you lob it so it lands easily in their hands, or does it fall short or fly high over their head and out of the ballpark?

August 25

I consulted recently with a successful health club owner, a progressive, spiritually oriented man interested in improving the quality of his employee's lives and of the club's services. I had counseled him privately for years, and now he was interested in bringing intuitive awareness to his operations team.

At first, the group wasn't sure how a professional intuitive might help them. I explained that I would simply sit in on meetings, listening for and bringing to light the hidden agendas that might be blocking forward movement, feeling for insights that might give them a new angle on solving complex problems, or sensing when things were drifting too far from the central vision. The owner had created quite a stir by suggesting they increase their profits in the new year by 50 percent.

"How can we increase revenues that much? We already increased them significantly last year. We're working as hard as we can! Where will we find the extra time? It's impossible!" It became apparent that several underlying factors were influencing their attitudes. First, some people were doing jobs that didn't suit them; they needed to shift roles to make better use of their talents. Others were acting like victims because of problems at home. I said, "What if increasing profits by 50 percent weren't a matter of sacrifice and increased struggle? What if it could be achieved simply by eliminating waste and getting out of your own way by removing the psychological and emotional sabotages that exist below the surface in your attitudes and interactions? Let's allow this to be natural and graceful. What would your life and job be like if you were expressing 50 percent more of your real self?

They shared ideas. "If I were being 50 percent more of my true self, I'd teach classes on nutrition," Emily said. "And if I could be more of myself," said Joan, "I'd be totally positive in my attitude. I can see how I'd influence others to pitch in and cooperate more; they'd want to volunteeer because it'd be so much fun." "I'd want to do more outreach to the community," Jose said. Wayne said he'd been interested in video and would love to help make some promotional spots for local cable TV. The ideas continued to flow. Simply by freeing the group's natural creative enthusiasm and removing old habits of resistance and withholding, the club's performance soared.

I can be more of myself.

What would you do differently today if you were being 50 percent more of your real self? Would it be easier to be more inspired? More creative? Would you be better at letting other people help you? Would you feel more satisfied?

August 26

There's no end to what I can know.

Today, notice that whatever you place your attention on will reveal knowledge to you about itself. The longer you pay attention the more you'll learn.

Marilyn Mackey wrote recently to report that in one of her intuition development classes in Texas, she had placed a photograph in an envelope and sealed it. The photo depicted a man eating a hamburger at a lunch counter. She then asked the class to describe what the photo was about and to give her any impressions they received. One man put up his hand and said, "I'm getting that it's a hamburger." When she opened the envelope to reveal the contents, the fellow sitting beside him said, "Well, then, can you tell whether that hamburger is medium or well done?"

After I finished laughing, I thought, well, which was it? And after we determine that, can we tell what the man was thinking about as he ate? What kind of morning had he had? Who cooked his burger, and what kind of conversation did he have with the waitress? Where was he going after he ate? What was his name, height, weight, and Social Security number? Did he have a wife? A pickup truck or a Mercedes? How far could we take this?

We actually know everything about everything, but to keep ourselves sane, we pretend not to know. Then we thrill ourselves by letting a little psychic synchronicity pop into our awareness.

August 27

Patty is part owner of an office building that the group of owners want to sell. The last remaining tenant owes a great deal of back rent but is trying to sell his business, which would allow him to pay his debt. Should they evict him and lose the money and possibly the advantage of the building already having a tenant? Or is he an interference to a clean sale? Having to deal with this snag is bringing out the other owners' impatience, nastiness, and self-centeredness. Patty is acting as arbitrator, trying to calm the others down so they can find the best solution and get the best deal. Several of the other owners want to take a low price and get out, but Patty has done some research and has found that the property might be worth twice the amount they're willing to take.

To clarify her thinking, I had her imagine the building as a living energy field and to merge into it as if it were her own body. "How does the energy inside you feel in your current condition?" I asked. "The air smells stale, as if the energy needs to move," she replied. "Ok. How do you feel with the tenant occupying space in you? Could you, as the building, sell easily with him there?" "No, he's slowing me down; I want him out." So she imagined the tenant was gone. Next Patty imagined opening all the windows and cleaning the stale energy from every nook and cranny until the building shone like a crystal. She imagined putting a lemon scent in the building and saw the clean energy radiating outward, attracting the right agent and buyer. "Much better!" she sighed.

Next I asked Patty to visualize a large thermometer running up the side of the building. On it were markings denoting possible prices: two million, three million, etc. I asked her how high the markings went. "Up to six million," she said. The low offer they'd received was just under three. I asked her to imagine the red liquid in the thermometer and let it rise to the correct price. "Five and a half," she immediately responded. "Try three," I suggested. "I can't get it to stay down there; it wants to pop up!" "Try six," I suggested. "I can't get it to go beyond five-point-five," she responded. "I guess that's it!" She opened her eyes, stretched, and smiled widely. "I can feel that we're going to get a good price," she said enthusiastically. "I know what we need to do now to help it happen —and I know it in my body!"

Pay attention to your home and office today. What is the quality of energy inside them? What do the spaces want to provide for you and what would they like you to do for them? Clearing and cleaning your spaces can remove blockages in your life.

**My heart
shows me
what's real and
what's next.**

*Let your heart be
your barometer
today, showing
you who to
talk to, what to
participate in,
and when to rest
and be silent.*

Don was a high-powered marketing director for a large bank who decided to give it all up to explore a spiritual path, and he moved to the hills. Occasionally he helped friends with marketing problems, but mainly he rested, read, and hiked. He began to sense that he had healing abilities and could communicate with spiritual beings in his meditations. He experimented in these new arenas and had some good results.

A year ago, Don went on a pilgrimage through Europe, traveling wherever spirit directed him, striking up conversations with strangers, not knowing where he'd stay from night to night. In France, he found a special place where he was directed by his inner guidance to build a community. For the first time in a long time, he felt enthusiasm about work. But only days later, Don experienced a mild heart attack. A traveling companion made arrangements to get him back home, where he was treated and forced to rest. From then on, every time he even thought about work, be it marketing or building a spiritual community, his heart would act up. He realized he was shifting from a lifetime habit of willing things to happen (working from his solar plexus) to a new habit of allowing things to happen naturally (operating from his heart). The sudden shift of energy upward in his body had caused the heart to be overwhelmed and go into shock.

Now Don's heart was his barometer. If he activated old, ambitious, will-based thoughts, his heart contracted. With new, faith-based thoughts, it relaxed. His inner self was teaching him to be present in a very physical way.

August 29

Our life purpose and life work are in us all along, right from childhood. If you think back and recall the ways you spent your time as a child, it will give you hints about what you might want to do now. The natural creative and expressive urges of the child unfailingly become lifelong interests. One of my sister's favorite early endeavors was to start her own business so she could make enough money to buy a helicopter. She created a food product called cornballs, which were marshmallows with kernels of hard field corn stuck in all around like a pomander ball. These delicious treats were packaged handsomely in egg cartons and marketed energetically to all the neighbors and my father's business associates when they came for dinner—as a dessert item for sheep, goats, and horses. She didn't get her helicopter, but today she is a nutritionist, running her own company that deals with food.

When I was young, I put on magic shows for my parents and told fortunes with a towel tied around my head, using various fortune telling devices of my own construction. I also set up an assembly line in my bedroom to design and construct ornaments for a big dead branch I had set up in the corner. I had a far-reaching vision—I'd have ornaments for Christmas, Easter, Valentine's Day, my birthday, Halloween, and Thanksgiving. I'd change them regularly. In my assembly line I had various workstations. At the first one, I drew the pictures. At the second, I colored them. At the third, I cut them out. At the fourth, I punched holes and attached string. In my twenties, I became a graphic designer and corporate art director, and later evolved from art to working with intuition and clairvoyance.

Try making a list of the things you did spontaneously as a child. What did you enjoy doing then that you've neglected and might take up again and reinvent for your life today?

I determine my behavior by what's on purpose for me.

Go back to activities today that have always held your interest.

I am willing to laugh.

Make a list of what amuses you today. Then make a list of what could amuse you.

There is a note on my refrigerator that says, "I can be irritated or I can choose to be amused." I've thought considerably about enlightenment, and it seems to me that the enlightened people are the ones I don't feel judged by—I feel naturally attractive and humorous around them. Enlightened people, I'm guessing, would not tell us how enlightened they are but would instead have a high level of ability to entertain themselves and be amused and a ready willingness to laugh. The Dalai Lama once advised, "Choose to be optimistic, it feels better."

What amused me today: a dog rolling on her back outside the coffee shop this morning, the blue jay that hopped up to my window and stared in as I was writing, the fact that my father wrote out some ideas for anecdotes for *The Present Moment*, longhand, because he wanted to help me. What else amused me: the way my hair flipped up comically as I tried to style it this morning, and the piece of scrap paper the wind keeps lifting and playing with in my backyard. What could have amused me: the fact that my water pressure was gone when I woke up and I couldn't wash until the water district men found the debris in the filter out by the street; how my new multimedia computer monitor with built-in speakers is transmitting the CB radio broadcasts of truckers plying the northern California highways.

The mere fact that life keeps materializing, and in so many surprising varieties, is endlessly entertaining. We have the opportunity to regale ourselves with infinite surprise. What could be better?

August 31

Does your life alternate between busy extroversion and relatively quiet introversion? Sometimes when life quiets down, we think nothing is going on. Then it's time to pay attention to the tiny cycles, the delicate beauty of the small things. Gwendolyn Brooks wrote, "Exhaust the little moment. Soon it dies. And be it gash or gold it will not come again in this identical disguise." My soul seems to want me to stay in my house this month and water plants, organize closets, do laundry, and watch videos by candlelight. My focus zooms in on the quiet way dust gathers on the nightstand, the spiders hanging in high corners, the plants turning toward the window light. I look forward to the lavender streaks in the western sky at the end of every day. When I make apple crisp from fruit that fell during the windy night, I feel circuits connect in me because I'm respecting God and honoring the earth by using the bounty that springs forth and overflows. I'm thrilled by how the beefsteak tomatoes are so blatant, brightly red and fat and juice-filled. At night they hang on the vines together while I sleep, and they preserve the archetype of fullness and pleasure in the sun. They just soak it up and grow unabashedly huge with life. There is so much, truly, in so little.

I value life's tiny cycles.

Notice the beauty of the ordinary cycles in your routine, in a single day.

September

September 1

Lynn is a young woman with an impressive job in the finance industry. When she called for an appointment, however, I would never have guessed what she did for a living. Her voice was soft and hesitant, almost wistful. When she arrived at my front door she was close to tears, as if something suppressed for a long time wanted out. We settled down with some tea, and I started looking at her life patterns. As I talked, her eyes welled up several times. "I don't normally do this!" she apologized. Each time she cried, I noticed she had started talking about her inner self. Lynn's problem was that her job as a liaison in her company subjected her to enormous pressures from which she had virtually no relief—she was always being pulled by one side or another. Even with meditation, she couldn't stop worrying about work and was having difficulty feeling who she was. As she talked about work, her pitch rose, and I could easily feel the pace she was used to keeping.

After describing ways she could "fill up" from within with her own authentic self-expression, she said, "I know this is terrible, but I guess it all boils down to the money. I love nice things, and I've created a perfect home with a beautiful garden. It's my sanctuary. I'm afraid if I do what I want, I'll lose my job, and that would mean I'd lose my house." As we continued talking, the pitch of her words started to sound like fingernails scraping across a black-board. I said, "Part of the tension you're carrying is because your world is split in two. The only place you can be yourself is in your home, which you need to control carefully. At work you experience sacrificing yourself and no control at all. How about introducing more of your true self at work? Speak up, ask to shift your job responsibilities so you can work at a human pace and get more deeply into things, do each task with more presence. Then, let a little more chaos—the element of surprise—into your home. When you can be real everywhere, you'll relax and let life be more spontaneous everywhere. Then you might even get a new job that's based entirely on your true self. And without losing your home!" As she imagined this she cried again, yet when she spoke, her voice had dropped squarely into her chest. Then she gave a little belly laugh, and I could feel the insight sink the rest of the way down and become totally real.

I can "hear" people's emotional states.

Notice the frequency or pitch of the people you meet today. Let your intuition bring you insights based on your subtle, inner sense of hearing.

What I take into my body turns itself into me.

Be actively grateful to the food you eat today. See the light in it.

The art of blessing is ancient. It goes beyond prayer and is more sophisticated than prayer. It comes from experiencing oneness. In the past, people used blessing to treat food before they ate it. Because there was no refrigeration and food was often tainted, people learned to meditate on their food, to look within it beyond the outer form and see the food's energy. A talented practitioner of the art of blessing could commune with the ideal blueprint or pure essence of the food and talk to it. As she spoke to it, she'd say, "I see who you are, oh peach, oh bullock, oh potato. You embody the quality of sweetness, of power, of earth. You are beautiful and radiant. I see you as the Creator intended you to be. I love you for your true self. I ask that we become one, that you give yourself to me to nurture me. And I will appreciate you. As I eat you, I will take your essence into myself and let it flow through me. I will let you live through me. We will know each other's true selves." In this way, people could derive benefit from less-than-fresh food. And blessing became a very high form of healing human beings as well. "I bless you" meant that you had been seen by a wise and loving person, all the way to your core. Your beauty and truth had been witnessed and thus made real.

September 3

I went to a bakery the other morning and struck up a casual conversation with a woman at the next table. She was reading a romance novel, and I was writing in my journal about intuition and relationships. I noticed she was married. I politely cleared my throat and asked what she thought made a successful marriage. She was only too glad to take a break from her book and give me advice from her twenty-plus years of experience. "My husband and I agree to disagree. I don't care what they say, you have to like each other and want harmony in your lives right from the start. Oh, we get irritated with each other, all right! We've decided that we'll just always have our different points of view on some things. When one of us gets mad, eventually the other will come back and suggest doing something we both enjoy to take our minds off it. Maybe we go to a movie, or drive out and watch the birds by the lake, or go to a new place for dinner, and, before we know it, we're back to liking each other again!"

Everyone knows.

Ask people a philosophical question about life today, and see how wise they are. It's important to remember that clarity abounds everywhere if you look for it.

**My intuition is
accurate.**

*Notice your first
thoughts and
urges today and
validate them.
Intuition usually
arises first, before
logic. If you
make a practice
of trusting it,
it will grow
stronger.*

Elaine is a successful entrepreneur who has started and sold several companies. She has the magic touch. She credits much of her success to her intuition, which brings her clear visions of important scenarios, showing her how various processes will unfold and who the main players need to be. She has learned to trust her inner visual sense in doing business. When she finishes with one project and turns it over to others, she lets herself have some down time to allow new ideas to percolate and come to the surface and, gradually, a new venture takes shape. But when she sold her last software company, no new images for businesses came to mind. All she saw herself doing was staying home and being a mother to her teenage son and daughter. Eventually she realized this *was* her next job! She had been so busy during their early years that she now wanted to be there, dedicated fully to them. So she jumped back into cooking their meals, driving them to soccer games, and helping them with homework. She got to know all their friends, chatted with them over snacks after school, and encouraged them through their difficult episodes. This instinct for family continued for several years, until her children went to college.

Recently Elaine had new visions of a lifelong learning center and a company that would offer visionary training and mentoring to businesses. She was back in action again, but, because the idea was based on more holistic and spiritual principles, her usual masculine entrepreneurial mode wasn't quite enough to bring the project to life. This was a situation where the feminine way of working was as important as the traditional masculine way. Family, trust, and consensual decision making must be established simultaneously with the business plan. She realized quickly that she couldn't do everything herself and that her old methods of leadership needed modification.

Elaine noted that her intuition had once again provided her with what she needed; the years she'd spent dedicated to her family had taught her about trust, service, empowering people indirectly, facilitating group action, and coming from her heart in all she did. She was primed now to take on organizing a new kind of company, one based on an equal balance of the personal and impersonal, the head and the heart, and the feminine and masculine ways of perceiving and acting.

September 5

Try this experiment. Have a friend sit in front of a light-colored wall in a room with subdued light. Focus on her forehead, let your eyes be soft, and look simultaneously at the edges of her body and at her forehead. This engages your peripheral vision. You'll probably be aware of a thin band of light surrounding her. It may appear yellow-green, white, or even a pale blue. This is the beginning of what metaphysicians call the aura, or the energy body, and it can be captured on film with Kirlian photography. Everyone knows there is light inside matter; we talk about it all the time. "She was so happy she glowed." "The light in him died when his son died." "She was beaming." We speak commonly of people's intellectual brilliance.

As you see people and even plants and animals today, look for their light. How much light comes out of their eyes or from their skin? If you're stopped at a gas station or waiting in line at the bank, scan the various bodies you see and notice which ones seem lightest, which ones dark and dull. You might play a game with yourself: see if you can intentionally increase your light and the light in others. Light increases with love. Light increases with interest, attention, and enthusiasm. Light increases with the experience of similarity and unity. Light increases with understanding and insight. Try giving other people love, appreciation, interest, understanding, a feeling of connectedness, and see how they light up. Try being enthusiastic about something you're normally bored by. Does your love and understanding mysteriously increase as well? Is light thrown on the subject?

With my eyes focused softly, I can be aware of the light emanating from all forms of life.

Look for and sense the light in and around people, animals, and plants today. The brighter the light, the healthier or more loving the life force is.

September 6

My world can
be new right
now.

*Notice your
worldview and
the habits and
beliefs that keep
your reality
consistent today.
Then let
yourself be new,
unknown, or
even shocking to
your ordinary
mind.*

When we wake up each morning, our story wakes up
with us. Our mind recites our story as the physical world
reappears after sleep, then repeats it over and over all day,
every day. We remember our name, our sex, our age. We
remember what we looked like yesterday. We remember
our preferences and the components of our identity.
Divorced, one child, live in an apartment, like to read the
morning paper, drive a gold sedan, work downtown. "I
like this." "I don't want that to happen." "Life is unfair to
me." "I'm a hard worker." "I'm good because I please the
opposite sex." "I'm in my last lifetime." "I always lose
what I love." "I can dance but I can't sing." We believe
we are the sum of our personal past, a series of experiences that built on each other to make us what we are
today. We think we can't find a good relationship, or
make enough money, or be fully creative because we had
a bad childhood. We believe we inherited our parents'
foibles, fears, and latent talents, and that we were shaped
by our environment and by the tribal mind of our culture.
But what if you stopped your story and didn't remind
yourself who you were? What if you didn't relate everything back to one of your stored preferences? Could you
live with just a little bit less identity? And might you then
be free to create an identity based on what you are today
instead of from the past alone? What might be possible
when you're not limiting the story?

September 7

I received a call from a frustrated friend on the East Coast today. His new consulting company had bid on an unusual job in Africa. He had been fair in devising his estimate, but when the company responded to his bid, they said they didn't see why he had to have two people working on the job; the job should take five days not twenty; and could he cut his fee by two-thirds. He was shocked. What could he do? He could tell them to take it or leave it, that he'd already carved his profits down to rock bottom, or he could try to please them but take a loss. Either way, he wasn't winning.

I asked why this job was so important to him. "If I can turn them around, I'll gain credibility in my field," he said. "So you want recognition and you think it's going to be easier to get over there than here?" "Yes," he confided, "I thought I might be able to stand out there." "So, what experience does standing out give you?" I asked. "I guess, if I feel acknowledged by an outside authority, I'll be able to be myself," he said. I asked what was preventing him from being himself now? Why was he waiting for approval? My friend said he couldn't be too sensitive or talk about unbusinesslike things such as feelings and hidden agendas, which he considered important in business because he wouldn't be respected. He needed to prove his competence first.

"You're already competent, so why don't you just act like it and do things with your own flair?" I said. "What you're talking about is a leading edge in business, and, if you'll assume that God has already handed you the baton, you'll create enough centeredness and magnetism to convince people to listen to you and pay what you ask, instead of feeling you have to fight to be yourself. If you have fun being yourself, they'll beat a path to your door."

My friend realized he was sabotaging his own success because he believed that big money = acknowledgment by important others = sense of self. He immediately revised his thoughts to: feeling connected to the divine = sense of self = confident self-expression = fun with people = money = more fun with people = more self-expression = more money = more connection with the divine. He stood his ground on his bid, with a positive, open-hearted attitude, and the next week he got the contract, with no revisions.

Eliminate your sabotaging thoughts and behaviors today, toward both yourself and others. As soon as you do, a successful path forward will materialize.

September 8

**I notice omens
and find their
meaning.**

*Watch for the
subtle messages
coming to you
from the
"signs of life"
today.*

For the longest time now, since the advent of digital
clocks, some behind-the-scenes consciousness jerks me to
attention when the numbers denoting the time match my
birthday. Uncannily, I glance at the clock in the car, on
my microwave, or on the VCR when the hour and minute
reflect my month and day of birth. Is this a sign? Is some
higher force saying "Time to be centered! Time to be
yourself; time to be new again!" How can I do this so
many times a week, year after year?

There are certain items and creatures I have also
imbued with meaning. When I find a heart-shaped rock,
for example, I take it as a touch from a loved one or a
spiritual friend, and I listen for the message. When I see a
hummingbird or a dragonfly, especially when they come
very close, I feel that an angel or nature spirit is communicating. When I see snakes and lizards, I feel a message is
trying to come to me from the earth mother. A salaman-
der crawls up under my front door stoop and I feel protected and blessed.

There are also messages that come from the supposedly
inanimate objects in my life. My car's right front tire
blows out, and I take it as a sign to look at why I feel paralyzed about forward movement. The water supply to my
house is cut off, and I interpret it as a reminder to make
sure I'm in touch with my emotions. I wash the plate-
glass windows across the back of the house and read it as
a sign that my inner vision will now improve. My phone
starts picking up other conversations, and I realize how
thin the veil is between dimensions and realities. The
world is alive and it's talking to us. Finding meanings in
the signs of life can keep us alert and connected.

September 9

In 1975 Henry had just finished college and had taken a job at a church as a musical director. He didn't quite feel complete, however, and thought repeatedly about beginning a graduate program. One day it would feel right, the next day he would doubt his talents. While Henry was substitute teaching at the local high school, a teacher stopped him in the hall and handed him an announcement about a music scholarship audition at a nearby university. She said, "Henry, I feel strongly that you should look into this."

The audition would consist of conducting a section from a large choral work that Henry had performed several times. He says his body suddenly felt more alive as he was "nudged by spirit and destiny." He decided to call and set up an audition. When the date arrived and he walked into the music building, he saw eleven other candidates preparing for the audition. "For one brief moment, I got cold feet. I turned and left the building and stood on the sidewalk," Henry confessed. "But the longer I stayed out there, the more uncomfortable I became. I knew my body wanted to go back inside. After all, I had diligently prepared and taken the time to drive to the audition, so why not go through with it?"

When all the performances were complete, the professor in charge of the audition asked if he could wait just a few minutes longer while the panel discussed the candidates. Ten minutes later, the professor returned to announce that it was unanimous. Henry had won the scholarship! "That day," Henry says, "I learned the difference between listening to ego and fear and listening to spirit and destiny. Doubt is born of the ego—that which limits. Success is born of spirit—that which is limitless."

**My body helps
me decide.**

*Let your
body make
decisions today
from a feeling of
deep comfort.
Deep comfort
is not laziness
or avoidance;
it's a sense of
doing what's
really right and
most natural.
Deep comfort is
your soul talking.*

Everything contains everything else.

Practice seeing yourself in others today, and how every other form of life exists in some way inside you. An incredible clarity comes from an awareness of mirroring and mutual inclusion.

No matter what you like or don't like about someone, you are looking into a mirror when you gaze into another's face. For example, if you are upset by the way someone avoids taking responsibility for being on time, it's only because you don't want to be reminded of the way you procrastinate about something. Though the forms of your behavior are different, you're really alike. Perhaps neither of you likes to feel controlled.

Once we understand how we reflect each other and share characteristics, we move into the next phase of this relationship-oriented spiritual practice, in which we gain a greater understanding of our interrelatedness. We can use our intuition to sense how we mutually include each other in our individual realities. Everyone's awareness includes everyone else. If you're inside me, I must know about you, and if I'm inside you, you must know me, too. And if we're in others and they're in us, we're experiencing the beginning of a grand family, a spiritual kinship.

By experiencing our interrelatedness, we leap to the next revelation—that we are interdependent. If I live inside you, anything I do must affect you. Since you exist inside me, anything you do will surely have an impact on me. If I hurt you, I'm simultaneously hurting myself. Soon we learn to stop creating pain and focus entirely on pleasing and serving, because it is ultimately ourselves experiencing the pleasure and service.

At last we discover that we are not only interdependent but *cocreative*. To contemplate that cocreativity is to get the tiniest glimpse of the compassion and beauty of the divine. As I create my life, I determine conditions that affect who you will become. You, by living, shape me as well, just as trees in a crowded forest grow tall and thin to reach the light, or the chameleon that changes color when he jumps from a rock to a leaf.

So, how are you like your heroes? How is your enemy like you? How do you fuel the sun or feed the wind? How is a gnat symbolic of God? How do Democrats, Republicans, Communists, Pacifists, and Revolutionaries cocreate a better world?

September 11

One of my favorite meditations is to let my attention drop way down into the cells and even the atomic and sub-atomic particles of my body. I concentrate on imagining myself as a field of floating particles, hovering together in space like galaxies. Then I shift my viewpoint a hair to the left or right, and the whole scene shifts from particles of matter to points of light, and I'm sitting in a sea of sparkles. When I did this meditation spontaneously the first time, simply following my awareness as it revealed the different images, I was floating in this field of light when suddenly the scene shifted dramatically outward. I saw the stars floating in the universe, and they were the cells of an even greater body, which I couldn't begin to comprehend but that was a much grander form of me. I could feel how each point in my little body was connected to and fed by a star in the big body. I was a continuum of light particles.

It seems I'm not the only one to have this experience. A few years ago I was riding along in the car with my four-year-old niece Julia. She was looking out the window and said, "Penney, do you know how to make a tree?" "No, how?" "Well, you reach down inside yourself and you get a handful of fairy dust and you throw it in the air and then you pull out the branches and the leaves and the roots and everything." "Where do you get this fairy dust?" I asked. "*Inside you!*" she explained impatiently. "What's it made out of?" I probed. "*I don't know,* but you just make things out of it. And you can't run out because God always gives you some more."

The stars shine, each to light a cell in my body.

Receive energy from the stars today, even when you can't see them.

September 12

**I choose to
heal my past
wounds.**

*Notice the
choices you make
today and how
they relate
to your past.
You can use
recent difficult or
traumatic experi-
ences to change
your body's
fear response to
one of safety.*

Charlotte lost her father under tragic circumstances, and later her husband died in an auto accident. When her daughter wanted to get a motorcycle, Charlotte decided to get one too and ride with her. She realized her motivation was partially based on fear; she was going to protect her daughter—no other member of her family was going to die suddenly and leave her! So the two of them took a grueling motorcycle safety course and practiced their driving skills.

One day her daughter asked if Charlotte would follow her in the car and keep an eye out while she practiced stops and turns. They set off on a route that kept them on quiet back roads except for a half-mile stretch of one busy road. Her daughter reached the stop sign at the big road, stopped, looked, and then turned. Charlotte pulled out behind her and immediately saw a red car barreling down on her from behind. Suddenly, Charlotte's stomach turned over—she knew something out of control was about to happen and she felt powerless to stop it. She put on her hazard lights and waved crazily out her window. *Slow down!* Traffic was coming from the other direction now as well, and the red car was riding her bumper. Up ahead, Charlotte's daughter prepared to make a left turn, not seeing the red car hiding so close behind her mother. The red car whipped out just then and roared past Charlotte, just missing her daughter.

They pulled off on the side of the road, shaken. Charlotte was sobbing. She had just witnessed in her mind a nightmarish scenario, her precious daughter lying mangled and bloody, she pursuing the reckless driver and stomping him to death, being at the funeral home. They went home and put the bike away. "What was this all about?" they both asked. The inner guidance they received was that it was not a good time to ask—Charlotte's body was still in terror, and, before she could understand, she needed to be calm and not in a victim frame of mind. She was advised to stop repeating the scene in her head, to give her body time, keep patting it and reassuring it that they were totally safe now. That way she wouldn't sear fear into her body. Later she saw that she had experienced this for the express purpose of healing her past traumas about sudden loss.

September 13

We can use ordinary objects in our environment as focusing devices or excuses to center ourselves in the present moment. With the number of times we project ahead into thoughts of the future each day, we need to remind ourselves just as constantly to come back and pay attention. You can make an agreement with yourself that every time you hang up the telephone you'll ask yourself, "How do I feel now after that conversation? What was valuable about what we said?" Or each time you place your hands on the steering wheel of your car, before you turn the ignition key, you can agree that the circle will remind you that you are whole and complete, fully present in your experience.

Doorways are another powerful device that can remind you to be new and neutral about what is to come. Doors are opportunities for conscious transitions. Consciously leave and complete the old experience; consciously be in between and calmly expectant; consciously enter the new world without preconceptions.

DOORWAY MEDITATION

When you approach a door today, use it as an opportunity to set your intention. Every door is a passage between experiences, between dimensions of awareness. As you enter the arch of a doorway, pause a moment. Let yourself feel the subtle difference between the space you are leaving and the new space you are about to enter. Is there a difference in height? Spaciousness? Color? Temperature? Comfort? Smell? What was your consciousness like while you were in the space you are now leaving? Feel into the new space. Prepare to enter the new state of awareness, to welcome whatever it holds for you. When the moment is right, step through. Surprise!

I am alert to the forward movement of my mind.

Notice when your mind projects ahead today; what triggers the shift? Try not to get ahead of yourself, but gently return to the beginning of each new step. Beginnings are loaded with power and knowledge.

I honor the harmony of my body and emotions.

Practice living within a state of deep comfort today. When you pay attention to the core motives in your body, you may notice excitement and a desire for action. Or you may feel enormous quietude or a buzzing anxiety. Take your cues from these states.

Hannah had an opportunity for a great new job at a state university. It paid well, and she could move from a hot, flat, dry location she'd grown bored with to a new location with moisture, trees, hills, and more creative stimulation. She had an interview and it seemed that she was well qualified. The people were friendly, but she couldn't tell if she'd said the right things to clinch the job, and now her doubts were setting in.

I asked, "How does your body feel when you imagine living and working in the new place?" "It gets excited," she said. "I can just smell the air and the trees. It feels invigorating." "Ok. And how does your body feel when you imagine staying where you are?" "I feel like I'm going to sleep! My body is not alert and everything seems slower and duller." Hannah's body was giving her a clear message. It felt more alive and creative in the new situation. What our bodies love, our bodies create for us.

I suggested she meditate and visualize the land under her new office and under the house where she might live, then to send love into the earth there and tell it how much she'd appreciate receiving from it, being with it, and giving energy back to it. Then I asked her to visualize the land under her present office and home, send love down into these places, thank the land and buildings for having supported her, and ask if there was anything else these places wanted from her. As she lovingly connected to the new location and completed with the old one, the land itself would draw her body there if there was a good fit.

I had her imagine that her new coworkers wanted her as well, and that their bodies would help draw her there, too. Hannah did all these meditations. Then it was time to let go, trust, and wait for the outcome. I was sure she would get the new position because my body felt comfortable with her body's comfort. It was easy to tell which reality was stronger. The only interference had been a little doubt Hannah carried about possibly not being able to have what brought her joy and increased creativity. By eliminating the doubt and letting her body experience a deep physical connection with the new opportunity, Hannah was sure to get the job.

September 15

I wrote this for Malina, age 4, who died September 15, 1994, of burns after a heroic fight for life.

*Pay attention
today to
the invisible
signals that tell
you what to
do and say.*

you lie there
wandering far from your tiny body
talking to spirit friends and spirit family
the hospital monitors are beeping and ticking
and your eyes are sealed with vaseline
you're probably having spirit dinner at a big, round table
but you look so opaque
a blocky thing wrapped neck to toe
a mummy with tubes
your blood is leaving your body and coming back
just like your soul

tonight at your bedside I said a few timid words
"Hello."
"I am here."
I said your name with love
I drove an hour to say these few stumbling words
couldn't touch you
felt embarrassed at my ineffectualness
in the face of the dedicated nurses focused on tending you
I was in their way
I was swallowed by the Void
maybe a little like you

I drove home wondering
if a love unexpressed is known
if the *desire* to give is itself a good enough gift
Spirit said, "Heal her within yourself,
She lives inside you."

so I entered my inner world
where there is no time or separation
and connected with you in the way I know
I held you in my vision an hour or more
and I talked and said the words Spirit wanted me to say
about your path
and as you heard,
I was you and you were me
and I heard
I knew that what made me want to do this with you
was making someone else, somewhere
care enough to hold me too, and to say the words
we all need to hear

**I merge with
my now.**

*There is always
provision and
loving perspective
waiting for you
at the bottom
of each experi-
ence. Let your
awareness
penetrate today
and receive
what wants to
be given.*

Something is always provided, from within each moment itself, when there is a need. But it is difficult to trust this every day. I find that writing 365 short stories, each distinct, against a tight deadline has a different quality than writing in a more leisurely way from a full, well-defined outline. Writing a chapter is like making soup. I blend the important points, the examples, the rhythm, the tone, and the illustrations like ingredients, aiming for a subtle flavor. Writing a series of anecdotes is more like ticking items off a to-do list: "I got eight done today!" "I only got two done today." "Did I mention this point before?" Within each piece, I can putter and polish and make it into a shiny pearl. But what will those pearls look like when strung together? Where is the fluidity? I am forced to have faith that the higher order has something surprising and beautiful in mind, because I'm in the short view.

It seems that the reservoir of stories is getting low, but there is always one more flash of insight that comes in response to the need of the next empty page. I see how addicted one part of my mind is to reciting the dramas of what might go wrong, what I might not have, and how much effort things take. In truth, there is no effort—writing can be as fluid as reading what's already been written. Maintaining the discipline to write every day is not difficult. It is a respite from other, more strenuous tasks, and I relish the silent, informal, and private quality of my days.

I am distracted by life's busy nature. The phone conversations, social gatherings, errands, delivery men, meetings for new projects, housework, cooking, gardens, clients. I crave an immersion with this process, a quality of sustained, uninterrupted attention. If I can hold my focus and fall in, be drawn into the rhythm of the sentences, farther in, letting the words come from my chest instead of my brain or from a place in space around my entire body or from my womb, if I can fall in, let the moment swallow me, I will know writing as something transcendent. What I write about is what I need to experience, and the *way* I write—and *could* write—is what I need to experience, too. Then there's the magic of the way somebody who I think at first is a distraction actually provides content. "See?" the inner voice says. "You *can't* do this alone—this is a social process as well as a private one. See how you are given what you need just when you need it?"

September 17

Matt runs a management consulting and training business that is growing at a rapid rate. There are days he has so many tasks that he finds he cannot meet his commitments using his old methods; they're just too slow. We often have talked about how trying to push through a pile of work with sheer willpower isn't effective because there is not enough energy available with the method. He admits he ends up feeling exhausted every time he tries it. Instead Matt is now experimenting with ways to harness the power of his higher mind and his subtle energy body to help him get the job done.

One weekend Matt was down with the flu, and when he showed up for work Monday, he was still sick. In spite of his weakened state, he had to update six months' worth of training notes and distribute them to his training facilitators. He said his usual method would have been to write a first draft, edit it, then work up a final version. In addition he had to finalize a formal presentation for a big new client, which also involved a tremendous amount of writing. Getting this done in one day felt like "slogging uphill."

So Matt tried a new technique. He left his office and walked up and down the hallways. He asked himself, "Who am I really? What is my true nature?" As he walked, he opened to the light by visualizing that his physical body was occupied entirely with his subtle energy body. Then he imagined light all around him, glowing brightly like a diamond filled with knowledge and vitality. He connected himself to the field of light and invited it in. He said he felt like he was melting, but he didn't lose himself at all.

As Matt continued to walk, he asked the bright light to feed him the insights, feelings, logic, and words that he would need to complete his work effortlessly. "Instead of having to do three drafts on each project, let me do just one draft with the content 95 percent correct!" he said. "Let it all flow through me and roll out of me when I sit down at the keyboard." When he felt complete, he went back to his office and sat down, and the writing poured out of him. He said to me later, "When I get these days now that used to seem so impossible, I just say to myself, 'This is going to be easy because I don't really have to do it all!'"

I can accomplish more with less effort.

When you work toward a goal today, let your energy body and the field of light around you assist you. Using willpower alone will leave you drained.

I can nurture or disturb my machines.

Be friends with machines and objects today. They respond well to caring thoughts and often seem to serve as extensions of our emotional states.

Someone told me long ago, as I was just opening my intuition, that psychics' machines, clocks, and cars always break down. The comment made me think. Why would that be? Was it because psychics had a reputation for being spacey and didn't change their oil or service their fax machines? Maybe it was because psychics were wired differently, ran a higher voltage, or more nervous energy, through their bodies. Perhaps this would have a disturbing effect on machines. Maybe psychics were afraid of machines, thinking them to be alien to their own spiritual nature. I decided right then that I would have a good relationship with all my machines.

I started by learning to program my VCR, then figured out where all the cables went in my interconnected television/VCR/stereo system. When I got my first computer, I quickly discovered that I couldn't leap ahead of the computer's process. The computer reminded me that there is a set hierarchy of steps that perception must flow through to achieve a desired result. I went around for weeks feeling that computer windows were opening and closing inside *me*, that items in my own awareness were being selected, cut, copied, and pasted. I saw that if something jammed up, it was not the computer's fault—I was missing a crucial step in its logical functioning. I learned to summon the patience to think like the computer. When I began honoring my machines, caring for them, putting loving energy into them, even talking to them, they didn't break, crash, freeze, or explode.

Whenever I get too worried or too distracted and vacuous, though, my machines let me know by mirroring my exact energy state. When I was unable to concentrate on writing a few weeks ago, my monitor began blinking off and slowly coming back on again. When I was projecting too much into fictitious realities, my VCR stopped being able to rewind or fast forward, as though to say, "Stay with the present scene in your movie and go along at a normal pace." Earlier in the year, the batteries in ten of my watches and clocks died simultaneously. "Hey!" they seemed to be yelling. "Time out! Be in the moment without measuring the minutes." Machines are extensions of us and can be our loyal friends. I choose to believe they have their own kind of consciousness.

September 19

I went for a long hike along the beach on a brisk, cool Sunday with a friend who was a Buddhist priest. My friend and I walked along the beach for miles in the way he had been taught when he studied Buddhist mountain practices. Moving slowly, feeling down into the earth with each step, we entered into communion with the spirit of the beach and the ocean. It was idyllic and even more gorgeous as the sun began to set.

Suddenly I snapped out of my reverie and realized it would be dark soon, and we were miles from the car. The air was getting colder, and a strong wind was cutting through our light jackets. "Let's head back," I said. My friend insisted that we return by way of a road he "knew" was back there somewhere. So we tramped off over the sand dunes and through the reedy sawgrass, the fading sun at our backs.

I was soon shivering and downright tired of cutting a path through the brush. I was about to turn back when my friend spied the road. With relief we walked onto the asphalt and wove our way among the hills. "I know this road takes us where we want to go," my friend said. But the next curve dead-ended into a hillside, and I felt like we were walking through a hell-like wasteland that we would never get out of. We seemed to be going in circles and I was at the end of my rope. It seemed like we'd been wandering around for forty days and forty nights. So much for the subtle, spiritual communion we'd gained on the beach! To my friend's credit, he maintained his equilibrium, though I sensed he was just as lost as I. Then as I was about to spit nails, we stumbled down an incline and found ourselves on the road *to the parking lot!* And there it was—just one hill away—the car!

As we walked that last bit, my friend said quietly, "You know what Gary Snyder says, don't you?" "I give up," I said, still somewhat peeved. "He says, 'Off the trail, but on the Path.'" And he gave me a sly, Zenlike grin. I burst into laughter and it all came into perspective—the perfect balance between the obvious, well-worn way and the nonobvious, untrodden way.

The way is not always well trodden.

As you move through your day today, pay attention to your path. What routes do you take? Where are your feet directed? How does one location connect to the next? Look for the forks in the road that you feel impelled to take.

I take a break from having a position about everything.

Be detached from opinions and justifications today. You don't have to care so much how you appear to others or whether you're right or wrong. Notice what happens when you let go of all that.

My sister recently called me on a behavior of mine that had upset her. I responded by defensively justifying myself. It wasn't until the next day, after our exchange had gnawed on me for a while, that I realized how dominating I'd been, how my need to justify my own behavior was really a way of manipulating her. Who was I trying to convince? I realized I hadn't wanted to own up to any negative behavior, that I was spinning out a story line with me as the perpetual heroine.

It's amazing how tightly I can hold onto my ideal picture of who I want to be and how I want others to see me—even though I've worked diligently for years to clear myself of fear. If others will only see me as Ms. Wonderful, in spite of the ways I act, then I'll feel validated. If they see me as flawed, I'll have to admit I'm not perfect and not in control. So when they don't agree with my ideal projected self-image, I must immediately convince them of my rightness and their obvious mistake in perception. If I don't feel validated, I stop expressing myself. And that unconsciously feels like death.

What's the alternative? If I could allow myself to live without projecting an ideal self-image, *I'd have more energy to be creative and original.* If I could receive and benefit from other people's positive criticism, *I'd become a better person and they'd feel heard and respected, which would increase the love all around.* If I didn't have to maintain the positive self-image I hold, and if I let more variables into the mix, *I'd be a more complete human being with a greater range, maybe more talented, and I could learn about the secrets buried on my dark side.* Ultimately, if I give up positions and justifications, *I'd learn to come from my true self, which needs no defense or fortification, no outside validation.*

Try completing the above sentences yourself. How does your self-image limit you?

September 21

Will called an air-conditioning repairman to find and fix a problem with his home unit. Will was out when the repairman arrived, and his wife paid for the work with a check for $233. Will then discovered that the problem had neither been found nor repaired; the repairman had pointed out numerous other things he said needed fixing to create some easy money for his forty-minute visit. Will said, "It was obvious that we'd been hustled by a guy who had a very low level of professional and personal integrity."

He continued, "I could have written a torrid letter about the incident, but instead I calmed myself, picked up the phone, and left my pager number for the company's secretary to call me in the morning to discuss my service call. When she called back the next day, I greeted her as if she were my closest friend. I simply told her that when I spend $233 for repair work I normally get the problem fixed. In our case the problem was not fixed, much less diagnosed. I kept my tone of voice completely nonjudgmental and calm."

Her response was, "Sir, I fully agree with you that your problem was not fixed, and I'm going to send one of the owners of the company out to your home to repair your problem properly." The company owner came the next day and immediately handed Will his check. He said as soon as he located the problem he would repair it and figure up a new bill. He returned on two additional days (one of which was Sunday afternoon) and went out of his way to make sure the problem was completely remedied. Will said he was pleased he had chosen not to waste any energy by concocting a battle between himself and the company that didn't need to occur.

People do their best, especially when I believe in them.

See if you can bring out the best in others today, by giving them positive attention. Use your heart—especially when dealing with potentially upsetting situations with others—and notice how the outcomes improve.

The world is full of tactile information.

Make decisions today based on your sense of touch. Do the people you meet seem rough, smooth, silky, nubby, electrical, or sharp?

Our bodies are simple and basic like those of animals, yet we're preoccupied by thought and language so much during our waking hours that we forget our bodies are busy perceiving the world directly and instinctively. Our bodies naturally recoil from people who smell bad or odd or who are grating, abrasive, or screechy. Our bodies respond immediately to changes in barometric pressure, shifts in the amount of daylight, and even upcoming earth changes. I remember how my body built up a tremendous charge and I became highly frustrated, even angry, just prior to Mt. St. Helens erupting. After the blast, I was totally calm again.

Lisa went to Venezuela to witness the total eclipse of the sun. As she and hundreds of other pilgrims gathered on a beach awaiting the event, Lisa felt a strange anxiety she couldn't explain. She became nauseous and short of breath and walked away from the camera-laden tourists. Then the eclipse started. The colors gradually became sepia-toned until the sun was entirely black and the sky dark as night. The stars were twinkling—at noon! The breeze stopped. There was total stillness. Then the birds in the air, though still flapping their wings, crashed one by one into the ocean. As Lisa watched, her body had a powerful reaction; she felt terrified for no reason. A moment later, from the side of the platinum corona, the shining sun peeked through, creating a diamond ring in the sky. At that moment, Lisa broke down sobbing. The release of energy was phenomenal. Lisa considers herself a rational, clear person with a scientific understanding of eclipses. She looked around, no one else was crying—most people were chatting noisily, rewinding their film.

It seemed that Lisa's body, like the birds' bodies, became disoriented by the sudden disappearance of light, in spite of the fact that her rational mind had a clear explanation for what was happening. Unlike the other people, she didn't watch the eclipse through a camera; she had switched her mind off. She said, "I did *nothing*. I was not thinking; I was just *being* and *feeling*, experiencing it directly. I felt absolutely connected." What if we let ourselves be more in touch with our animal nature, in tune with nature's rhythms? What if we let ourselves know what our animal selves know? Wouldn't life be more engrossing and revealing?

September 23

Jessie grew up with alcoholic parents who were physically abusive to her and her siblings. As the oldest child, she took on the role of protector and caretaker to her younger sisters. At sixteen, she left home and began to make her way in the world. She became interested in studying psychology, business, the healing arts, and an eclectic spirituality. As her career developed, Jessie rotated through her various areas of expertise, working as a counselor, hypnotherapist, and masseuse; she even had her own spa for a while. But every caretaking job eventually exhausted her. In time she realized it was a carryover from her early years playing the parental role, so she shifted to a career as a bookkeeper and financial counselor. Recently Jessie said that bookkeeping provided her with emotional relief and a kind of neutrality, but she found herself taking care of her clients yet again, teaching them about money and budgeting. Occasionally she'd sing with rock bands at local clubs. It was fun, but she couldn't make a living at it. What was she to do?

Jessie and I were part of a small group exploring the expanded use of intuition, and, during our last meeting, we gave feedback about what we sensed each person needed to move forward into deeper self-expression. For Jessie everyone said passion and playfulness! Someone mentioned that Jessie's innocent child self needed to come out and do whatever she felt like doing. Jessie said, "Actually, in spite of my experience performing, my inner child is rather shy. She never did have a chance to show up during my real childhood because I was either scared or taking care of my sisters." So we gave her some homework— to indulge her innocent self. The next time we saw her, she said she'd had an urge to redecorate her office. She spent a week shopping for accessories and new furniture and had a ball making everything just the way she wanted it. Then someone handed her a brochure for a new kind of vocal training class. She had a shine in her eyes, and we could tell she was on the right track. "I think eventually I could teach this stuff!" she said enthusiastically. Making logical guesses and choices about our life work rarely allows the magical chemistry of the soul to show up.

I enjoy expanding, expressing, and learning.

Notice when you are motivated by enthusiasm and growth today. Follow these urges even if they don't make sense.

**In silence
is my wisdom.**

*Listen for the
silence under
the noise today.
Try a simple
meditation in
which you
entirely stop
your mind's
chatter for as
long as possible.*

Craig claims he's always been physical, impulsive, and emotionally intense. Yet in recent years, he's had a yearning for a spiritual experience—for that extra dimension of life that would help him feel truly satisfied. He began to meditate at the close of each day. He says, "My aim was to slow my mind down and suspend as much of my worldly activity as possible. I set my timer to signal me when one minute had passed. I chose one minute because I'd seen my previous propensity to go head over heels into new things with the results being far below my expectations. I figured I could commit to one minute a day." He did this for a while and had fairly good success at achieving a state of silence.

After he could remain quiet for one minute, he decided to forget the timer and sit as long as he wanted. His new goal was to listen to his inner self and go as deeply into his center of calm as possible. Craig reports, "I began to experience a peacefulness and inner resolve that spilled over into many aspects of my life, especially my relationships with others; I learned to view people through far less critical lenses. I was able to shed self-created soap operas that ate into the quality of my life. I began to develop a keen sense of timing, experiencing regular internal 'prompts' about everything from my professional life to the health or emotional problems of others. My regular sessions of silence solidified my feelings of self-worth and galvanized support from both the physical and nonphysical worlds."

Craig is entering his fourth year of regular meditation now and says he can tell the difference. "The most remarkable thing is that I am completely comfortable with the grand scheme of my life," he says. "When I experience alternating periods of clarity and confusion, I no longer allow my center to shift with the situation. I make better choices; I'm more patient. I am tethered to my place of inner calm with a consistency I've never known before."

September 25

I dreamed I drove to a lake to view the full moon. I parked my Jeep on a steep incline facing east where the moon would rise over the water. When the moon was high, I saw that the lake had flooded and was up to the floorboards of the Jeep. I felt helpless, stranded. When I tried to back out, I skidded in the mud. Then I looked up into the sky and saw a ghostly group of young people floating down a beam of light, lit up in a ghastly way by the moon. They were dressed in baggy clothes, huddled tightly as they surfed across the sky with empty expressions on their faces. When I looked at the moon again, a partially complete triangle was drawn behind it in calligraphic brushstrokes. I meditated later, entered into each main symbol, and spoke as the image.

The lake said, "*I am full of wisdom soaked up from this power spot for thousands of years. Get out of your land vehicle and wade into me, swim in me, change elements, leave the safety of your known world.*" The moon and its incomplete triangle said, "*I am the symbol of the unification of body, mind, and spirit. I am almost complete; it is your faith and attention that will complete the trinity, so continue on your path with determination.*" When I merged into the group of teenagers, I found they couldn't talk. They were lost, caught between dimensions like ghosts. A voice said, "*These people are part of a soul group that has not been able to incarnate all the way yet. They need help from people who understand emotion.*" I realized the group of teenagers symbolized many of today's young people as well as parts of myself that were similarly lost. The message this dream brought was that we must surrender our earthly security and dive into the realms of intuition and feeling so we can reach a state of balanced perception where we can nurture new growth.

The symbols I see hold deeper meaning.

Examine the symbols that float in your awareness today. Is a dream image sticking with you? Did you notice something odd or out of place? Were you arrested by a picture in a magazine? Try speaking to yourself as the symbol to see what it wants to say.

**I trust love
to solve
problems.**

*Today, when
you feel blocked,
frustrated,
or unable to see
the path forward,
ask your heart to
provide a solution
based on trust
and acceptance.
You'll know
when you go
against love's
solution, because
you'll feel that
you're sacrificing
something.*

Erich Fromm said, "Love is the only satisfactory answer to the problem of human existence." Joyce and Barry Vissell, who run the Shared Heart Foundation and teach about the power of love, tell a story about solving a messy problem from their early years. They'd been together for four years and were very much in love but were also struggling with their religious differences. Joyce was Christian and Barry was Jewish. They had become tolerant concerning each other's beliefs but couldn't resolve how they would raise their future children—in fact, they had broken up several times over the issue because they were each so strongly attached to their own heritage. Finally, they decided to trust their love for each other and got married. Though uncomfortable with the unknown religion factor, they hoped that, by the time their first child came, they'd have a sense about what to do. Seven years later, their daughter, Rami, was born. Joyce says, "By that time we had become deeply immersed in the unity of all religions and had found the spiritual truth and essence of each one. Rami was born into that unity of our hearts. Ten years later we told Rami that we almost didn't marry because we didn't know what religion she would be. She looked at us incredulously and simply said, 'But I love God!' "

September 27

About twelve years ago, I experienced a prolonged period of difficulty when I was misjudged and betrayed by colleagues and friends. I had led a vision quest for a Japanese group to sacred sites in Peru. The Japanese were not used to working consciously with their subconscious mind and were not prepared for the emotional intensity that was dredged up. In spite of the clarity many people achieved, when they returned to home, family, and job, many no longer fit into their old ways. Some people left their jobs or spouses, others became depressed.

The organizer of the tour sought out a fortune-teller, who said that everyone had become possessed by evil spirits that I had awakened at Machu Picchu and Nazca. After that I found myself unwelcome in Japan, and a colleague was invited to take my place. To defend myself would have been considered undignified, so I was forced to surrender. In subsequent years, Japan's fascination with channellers, discarnate spirits, and psychic phenomena mushroomed. I didn't fit with that trend—my teachings were more about individual effort. Still, it was hard to accept I had lost hundreds of clients and years of painstaking work.

Several years later, I received an invitation out of the blue from a woman with a prestigious family name who ran a college in Tokyo. Would I come and teach her students and do private sessions for everyone? Could I stay *eight weeks?* My new sponsor was intellectually and psychologically oriented, more aligned with my perspective. By this time, the organizer who had rejected me had lost her reputation in the swirl of psychism, so the fact that I wasn't associated with her now stood to my benefit. At the end of my stay, my sponsor, who was a friend to Japan's royal family, invited Prince Mikasa to a private dinner to meet me and talk about our mutual interests in ancient Egypt and the future of Japan. As I sat there talking to this very special human being over a cozy meal, I realized the betrayals were really a segue to a redirection of my course. Even when life seems crazy, a loving force is at work.

I never give myself more than I can handle.

Are you feeling overwhelmed or caught in a no-win situation? Be fully present with the situation and allow it to be exactly the way it is; it will quickly reveal its hidden benefit.

September 28

I continue
my mother's
lineage.

*Feel your
mother and her
relatives
experiencing
life through
you today.*

James Redfield's *The Celestine Prophecy* introduces an interesting concept. He says that we pick up the unconscious and incomplete desires and beliefs of our parents, and even of their parents, and further them with our own lives. We each have two family lineages that feed us and give us certain leanings. These lineages are alive like streams flowing from high ground to the ocean, picking up new water and remnants of the earth they pass through, growing more complex and broad with time. They want to influence us and want our influence added back into their flow. Make a list of your parents' talents and successes. Then list their disappointments, sacrifices, and the things they didn't finish. Then list the things they didn't like, what they resisted or avoided. List the adages they lived by. Then do the same thing with each of their parents, to the extent you can. This will give you a sense of the raw material you're working with.

In the case of my sister and me, our mother loves to travel, and we both travel extensively in our work. Our mother studied architecture but didn't finish the program and became an interior designer. I became an interior designer, then a graphic designer and art director. Our mother took vitamins and ate health food. My sister became a nutritionist. Our mother was a sculptor, potter, and watercolorist. My sister was drawn to work with clay, I to visual arts. Our mother was involved with a writers group but didn't publish anything; I became a published writer. Our mother was upset by human suffering and didn't like the idea of service work; both my sister and I are in health-related service professions. Our matrilineal grandfather was a pharmacist, and our grandmother was a seamstress who dabbled with many crafts. The predominant themes running through my mother's family are health care and creativity. What are the themes you've picked up from your mother's family?

September 29

In the intuitive counseling I do, I often notice how the generations overlap. Our parents live out certain themes and emotional issues that we probably would have to live out if they didn't. Our parents take some of the pressure off us and give us the gift of the life lessons they learn. For instance, if your father is alcoholic and depressed, you may have a hidden tendency to be alcoholic and depressed also, but because he's doing it, you have been given the chance to feel the pattern from a distance and learn from it without having to act it out. If your father's life is solely about making money, then you get a chance to know how that feels and you probably won't need to use as much willpower to create a good living. We must never resent the choices our parents made because there's always a gift that comes from their experience. What has your father's life triggered in you?

In the case of my sister and me, our father traveled extensively and his job evolved continually, causing us to move all over the country. We have both had evolving careers and have easily embraced change. Our father was bright and went to college at age sixteen but didn't go on to get an advanced degree. My sister earned her M.A. and Ph.D. Our father worked in high-level positions in a large corporation and formed his own recruiting business after he retired. Both my sister and I had organizational experience, then started our own companies. Our patrilineal grandfather was a minister. I became a minister and spiritual teacher, and both my sister and I do public speaking. Our patrilineal grandmother was psychic and came from a line of psychics. I became a clairvoyant counselor. Our great-grandfather was a newspaper editor. I worked on a newspaper and became a writer. The themes from my father's family are spiritual and intellectual development. What themes have you picked up from your father's family?

I continue my father's lineage.

Feel your father and his relatives experiencing life through you today.

**I serve
my future self.**

*Let your
morning self do
something
thoughtful for
your evening
self, and let
your evening self
do something
beneficial for
tomorrow's
morning self.*

I saw comedian Jerry Seinfeld on a talk show late one night. He was doing a hilarious routine about how he sabotages himself. He said that Night Guy likes to stay up late, party, drink a bit too much, and eat pizza. Then Morning Guy has to get up early to be at work and is exhausted, clogged up, and rushing around making lists and getting organized. Night Guy thinks Morning Guy is a wimp, and Morning Guy thinks Night Guy is a jerk!

After Jerry's all-too-true description of our schizophrenic lives, I started to think of myself as Morning Girl and Night Girl. Morning Girl often forgets to exercise and take the vitamins that Night Girl needs; and Night Girl sometimes forgets to brush her teeth and go to bed early, which leaves Morning Girl feeling churlish. So I started pretending that Morning Girl was doing favors for Night Girl; she'd change the bedsheets or take a brisk walk. Night Girl would in turn wash the dishes and leave the sink clean. Morning Girl would make the phone calls and Night Girl would organize the piles by the phone. Night Girl helps Morning Girl by always putting the car keys in the outside pocket of my purse. When your day and night selves, your present and future selves, work for each other's good, eventually you'll know the real self, or soul, that underlies and fuels both.

October

October 1

Pearl is a nonfiction writer who has been working on deepening her writing ability by looking into the underlying patterns in her emotional life. She is pursuing the art of journal writing, using various books such as *The Artist's Way*, *The Intuitive Way*, and *Simple Abundance* to trigger themes in her unconscious. Recent studies have shown that journal writing, especially about stressful experiences and psychological issues, helps keep us healthy. Pearl has learned that her writing takes on greater richness after she's been writing in her journal regularly. She is more tuned in to the inner themes running through her week and to a way of thinking that results from the discipline of a life of inquiry. In this discipline, we continually examine daily experience and look for the correlations between inner motive and belief and the way events occur in our world. So Pearl is ever on the lookout now for synchronicity, omens, symbols, and deeper meanings.

An interesting interweaving of her inner and outer worlds took place recently. She was returning from a writers conference when she noticed a bumper sticker on a pickup truck in front of her. It said something about "telling your story" and gave a website. For some reason, she memorized the website. Over the next few days, she realized she was thinking about a relationship that had ended months earlier that she didn't feel complete about yet. She resolved to do rituals, write in her journal, and do whatever it took to let go. Pearl says, "I woke up the next morning wanting to identify a method for writing about this. I decided I'd look at all my journal-writing books. First, though, I logged onto the computer and looked at that website. It was exactly what I was looking for! It offered a method for examining emotional issues and a way to get at the hidden meaning inside problems. So I sat down and did the writing exercise it suggested. I had my usual doubts such as 'Oh, I didn't do it right, I didn't go enough.' But I found an important insight that showed me that it was truly OK if my ex-boyfriend never called again. I felt at peace. The very next morning he did call and was more communicative than I've ever known him to be. Telling him the bottom line I had arrived at in the writing process led to a revealing discussion that helped me feel new."

I am paying attention to certain ideas, both consciously and unconsciously.

Notice the common themes running through your day. Certain thoughts may cycle through your mind that you gloss over or a certain kind of experience may repeat. These contain key ideas and are not there by accident.

October 2

I am alert to the shifts and changes in my life.

Today, pay attention to small shifts of direction and the larger life changes that are just surfacing. How do you know when to move differently? Practice trusting your impulses; this way you can learn to feel the wisdom that comes from the unknown parts of yourself.

Jana is in her sixties and has had a fascinating life as a businesswoman, a painter, a world traveler, a mother, and a spiritual seeker. I spoke to her recently to see how she was doing; she is recovering from breast cancer and appears to be enthusiastic and healthy again. Before her cancer was discovered, she was living the artist's life in a beautiful adobe home in Santa Fe. She and her husband had an unusual arrangement—they spent much of the year living over a thousand miles apart, pursuing things they loved—he, his job, and she, New Mexico. They wrote love letters, visited often, and came together in the summers. Jana craved privacy and spent many peaceful hours painting landscapes, hiking, and soaking up the Southwest ambiance. She and her husband had been studying Buddhism, and the time alone was perfect for meditation practice. But then she got sick, and it was clear that she needed to be with her husband. He couldn't leave his job, so she made the painful decision to leave her beloved New Mexico and move back to California. As treatment for her cancer progressed, she stopped doing many things: painting, reading, going to seminars, her strict spiritual practice.

As Jana emerged from her ordeal, she committed to stay with her husband and deepen their relationship. She also vowed to give her children the kind of attention she hadn't given them when they were young. What surprised her and everyone else was her sudden interest in Catholicism. To her friends, it seemed she'd gone off the deep end. But missing the earthiness of her New Mexico home, she wanted a new kind of connection. The abstract nature of Buddhism didn't quite meet her need for a rich, sensual experience. She read books and explored the idea of becoming a Catholic in spite of resistance from her friends.

Jana was in the midst of a profound shift in her life direction. She was reinventing many core experiences: home, family, love, connection to the land, connection to herself, connection to God. Each day, she said, she felt oddly nurtured by images of old Spanish-style churches, by reading about the saints, and by praying at her new Christian altar. Each day a new layer of her new self appeared, and there was another nudge forward on her new path to spirit.

October 3

An ancient Zen master, Takuan, describes how the mind of the martial artist functions. In two short essays, "No Gap" and "Mind Like a Spark," he talks about the warrior's fluidity in action, explaining that the spontaneous responsiveness of the warrior is not related as much to speed and quickness of action as it is to immediacy of attention and freedom of mind. He says, "If your mind stops on the sword your opponent is swinging at you, a gap opens up; and in that gap your action falters. If there is no gap between your opponent's striking sword and your action, the sword of the adversary will become your sword. A mind like a spark means the state of mind where there is no gap. When flint is struck, sparks fly at once. . . . There is no interval for the mind to linger. . . . If attention lingers, your mind is taken over by others." I'm thinking here about how many times each day my mind fixates on a thought, a position, a perception.

Dan Millman, who writes and teaches about human potential, says, "You don't have to control your thoughts, you just have to stop letting them control you." Each time we express our likes and dislikes, we create a gap and fixate the mind. Momentarily, creativity freezes around the opinion. Similarly, there is the movement-killing effect of the "yes, but" commentary: *Yes, I'd love to go to the party Friday night, but I don't know anyone. Yes, I'm going to take a vacation soon, but I don't know where to go.* In addition, there's the "what if?" way of thinking: *What if I don't find the right job? What if I go ice skating and fall?* And how about that related phenomenon, your own personal killjoy? Mine just loves to negate any good idea my creative self comes up with. *Take a walk after dinner? No, it's too dark and I'm bored with the neighborhood. Go to a free lecture downtown? Nah, I'll hit rush-hour traffic.* As Takuan describes, even stopping to put a label on your experience prevents direct action. "I'm angry" gives that particular state of contraction too much authority; the experience stays defined too long and takes too much time to reveal its true meaning. Try staying with the contracted energy and see where it wants to flow, what it wants to turn into next. Try acting without commentary.

There's no point in worrying; just do it!

Simplify your life today by acting without hesitation.

**I complete
my day
consciously.**

*Before you go to
bed tonight,
review your day
thoroughly.*

At the end of each day, before you drop into dreams, make a habit of reviewing your day's activity. In this nightly review, you might take stock of what you accomplished and compare that with what your original intentions were that morning. Describe what happened, the way you acted, the feelings you're left with at the end of the day. Be complete and content with what you accomplished today. You can do this mentally or, better yet, make it part of a journal process and write about it briefly. Some questions to ask:

- Did you do everything you set out to do?
- Did you behave in a way you're proud of?
- Did you yell at anyone, or gossip, or think negative thoughts about a friend?
- Were you kind?
- Were you wasteful?
- Were you disciplined?
- Were you playful?
- What are you grateful for that happened today?

TODAY I . . .

Today I felt good about visiting with Mom; we had a great conversation and I really listened to her and she to me. I designed a flyer for my business and it looks good. I took time watering my plants, paying attention to each one, finished the book I'd been reading, walked around the block after dinner.

I feel incomplete about not changing my bedsheets, not cooking up the apples that fell off the tree, not returning the calls from Donna and Masako.

I have a funny, nagging sense of anxiety about the trip to Oregon, about what to say to Robert when I see him.

I regret that I was a bit short with a couple of people on the phone today and that I forgot, once again, to tell people what's good about them. I was judgmental about the way people drive. I didn't meditate and I meant to.

I am grateful for my new car! And for my clients, my friends, my family, and my health. I am grateful that I was offered an opportunity to speak in public.

October 5

At the end of the day, after you've come to a feeling of completion, cast your attention ahead to what you'll do tonight during your dreams. Give yourself a pep talk. "Yes! I'm going to have fun tonight! I'm going to fly, travel, learn, meet new people, and I'm going to remember it all when I wake up in the morning!" What kind of experiences do you want to have? Anything is possible! Here are some suggestions:

- Would you like to visit a distant place or touch base with a relative who's died?
- Would you like to heal psychological or physical wounds?
- Would you like to offer some sort of service to others tonight?
- You could learn about the healing power of plants or how to compose music.
- You could go to the inventor's library and learn about technologies of the future.
- You could have an adventure with one of your guides or meet new friends.
- Ask for some creative insights to solve a pressing problem.

TONIGHT IN MY DREAMS . . .

Tonight in my dreams, I want to go to a new place and meet new people who can teach me about how to be a better counselor and healer. I want to release any negativity I've been holding in my body. I want to wake tomorrow feeling clearer and less jammed up. I will remember my most important dreams in the morning when I wake up. Or, tonight in my dreams I want my soul and my helpers to give me a clear sign and some insight about whether I should take the new job I've been offered. Is it good for me in the long run? What might happen? I will be able to bring this information back with me when I wake up.

When you're finished setting intentions for your dream time, *while you're still vertical*, turn out the light and imagine how you'll feel after you have the new knowledge or experience you want. Quiet your mind and release your dream intentions. Let the thoughts and feelings drift out and up like a huge balloon until they're out of sight, out of mind. Lie down and smile slightly, like the Mona Lisa. Imagine the feelings of total trust radiating everywhere through your body. Go to sleep.

Tonight I set my intentions for the dream world.

Before you go to sleep tonight, decide what you'd like to work on in your dreams.

I start my day intentionally.

Before you launch into action today, take time to list your intentions for the day.

After you summarize your nighttime activities by recording your dreams in the morning, turn your attention to the day. Collect yourself; be centered and calm. Remember what is left from yesterday that you want to complete today. Make your daily list of intentions for the day:

· What impact do you want to have on other people and on the world today?
· What experience and attitude do you want to have?
· What do you want to give?
· What are you interested in learning?

When you've determined your intentions, you may want to make a more specific daily list of things to focus on. Make sure you choose goals that feed your creativity and spiritual growth, not just the tasks that "should" be completed.

TODAY I INTEND . . .

Today I want to make eye contact with as many people as possible and not look away. I want to be more interested in others than I am in myself. I intend to give people genuine compliments.

Today I want to finish updating my mailing list and balance my checking account. I want to dig some weeds out of the front lawn and clean the car.

Today I want to embrace new experiences instead of withdrawing from them. I want to have a positive attitude and think about what's possible.

Today I want to learn a little more about mutual funds.

October 7

Stephanie had been at a corporate job that was toxic to her well-being. She felt she had become soured and out of touch with her true self as a result. Her inner voice told her it was time to leave the job. She writes, "That week I kept thinking about Crestone, Colorado. What I found running through my brain was, 'I'm going to Crestone! I'm going to Crestone!' I'd been to the Carmelite monastery there previously to do a retreat and had experienced it as a vortex of spiritual energy. The monastery was run by both male and female monks who were earthy and accepting of the fact that, while spiritual, I was not Christian. I had found peace and insight there and wanted to return. So I quit my job, and within a week I was off to Crestone.

At the monastery, I met a woman, a friend of the monks, who was going through a divorce and living on the monastery property. It seemed like I'd known her before, and I felt a great affinity with her. For her part, she saw some leadership strength in me that I did not yet see in myself; she helped me find my center again and a new resolve.

"I came home feeling good about my decision and good about myself. I'd been drawn to the concept of 'preservation of soul in the workplace,' something poet David Whyte talks about in his book *The Heart Aroused.* I'd done what I could to spiritualize my last job, but the actions of the company were irrational and based on greed. I saw internal politics that were dysfunctional and plans that were ill conceived. So I let myself have a protracted job search during which I reclaimed my intuitive powers and waited for the perfect opportunity. When the next job came, it was magical. In my new position, I was able to implement programs that were kinder and more spiritually based. I also offered my time to people in job search as a form of community service and became active in two human resource roundtables." Stephanie says that she has continued to listen to her intuition for all the decisions she needs to make. By making that first difficult choice to quit her job and pursue her soul's path, she has continued to grow and find easy connections to better opportunities.

I trust and act on what my inner voice tells me.

Today, listen carefully for messages from your inner voice and, whenever possible, take action on them. How do you know it's your true voice? There will be no "shoulds," and the advice will create a sense of relief and enthusiasm.

I don't need to talk so much.

Be aware when you tire of talking today. In these moments, let yourself enjoy the feeling that is possible with silence, where your awareness can extend out through space and dimensions, bringing you peace and freedom.

Emma is a psychotherapist with a busy practice in a busy city. She talks and listens to people talking every day, and periodically she feels the need for some silence and solitude. So she has started a new habit—every year she takes herself out into the wilderness for some time alone. Her most challenging experience was when she went on a month-long solo journey in the mountains of the Southwest with no books to read, no journal to write in, nothing to distract her from the present moment. "It's amazing how loud the voice in your head is when you enter the quiet of nature," she says. "For the whole first seven days, my thoughts were wildly amplified. 'Why did you come to this place? I'm bored! You're wasting time. What about your responsibilities back home? I'm going to have to be here for twenty-four more days! This day is lasting forever!' But then on the eighth day, I woke up in this immensely comforting peace! It was as if I'd fallen through into the heart of the moment, and the silence had become part of me and me of it. Now I felt full and connected to everything around me. Time itself dissolved. Life started to teach me in this very deliberate way. It wasn't at all like the previous chatter in my head.

"I did a ceremony every morning. Sometimes it would take four hours, and I wouldn't realize so much time had gone by, but when I finished, the sun would be overhead. Then I noticed there was no more past, that all my memories were actually in the moment. I would think of a time from childhood when I was playing on a green lawn, and it was actually happening again, alive in the now. I realized that in the present moment *all time is available; past and future are present.*

October 9

Kari, a healer, says she was honored to have been part of a difficult journey with her friend Cinder. Cinder had come through breast cancer and had done all the right things medically, physically, emotionally, and spiritually. But a year after her mastectomies, the cancer metastasized to her liver. People held fund-raisers to support her and even changed their diets to keep her company. Kari says, "With all the company, though, came the less helpful aspect of people projecting their own fears onto Cinder. I began to see that her journey was not so much her own as it was the community's. She was the first peer in our social circle to be thus stricken. Such an ocean of need surrounded her—it seemed a real barrier to healing. I was called in regularly and, instead of trying to fix her, I just listened to a woman who needed permission to let go of this life. No matter how much we all loved and prayed for her, Cinder's cancer progressed.

"I had a dream during that time that I was an amorphous being like a jellyfish, surrounded by other jelly beings. We were thirsty and hungry and in imminent danger of collective death. We felt a collective pain. But someone found a food source and the food traveled through all of us, comforting us and ensuring our survival. Suddenly I grew out of the jelly skin and became my human self. I looked down on the jelly beings, who were actually a colony of fungus that had just found a happy home between someone's toes. A voice said, 'So you see, disease is completely natural. There is no failure. Life takes many forms.' I told Cinder about my dream, and it reassured her. Cinder was able to let her illness just *be*, continue to love her somewhat misguided friends, and prepare for a conscious death.

"Cinder was in the coma that liver cancer brings, and I was there alone, taking care of her. I felt she needed some privacy, so I cleaned her house, not just of dirt and trash, but also of the fears and needs of the dozens of people who thought they could, or should, heal Cinder. I placed river rocks at the doors of the house and at her feet to ground out all the foreign energy. At ten that night I received a call saying she had passed away quietly. To me her death was a complete triumph of her spirit."

Other people are hurt, fearful, or vulnerable, too.

Forgive others for their unconsciousness or hurtfulness today. You might be in their shoes tomorrow. Forgiveness is really the same as understanding and seeing the vulnerabilities we all have in common.

I release my expectations of others.

Make a list of your unful-filled expectations of others; then let each person be OK just as they are. Expectations of others are often related to our own pride and willfullness.

Robert Fulghum, author of *All I Really Need to Know I Learned in Kindergarten,* tells a story that after Christmas one year he felt he hadn't received very many Christmas cards from his friends. It propelled him into an obsessive inner dialogue in which his various victim voices complained about how little love he was receiving from his friends. Later that year, in August, he was rooting around his attic when he found, in a box with the holiday decorations, all his unopened Christmas cards that he had intended on reading later. So on a hot afternoon, he went on his deck in his bathing suit and sunglasses with Christmas carols blasting from the stereo and read all the loving messages his friends had written, and he cried.

We all have expectations, both reasonable and unreasonable, conscious and unconscious, that the world will provide us with what we need, be it unconditional love from others or acknowledgment about our talents or performances—no matter how well we do. Some of us expect the world to provide us with easy money, a place to live, or an aristocratic lifestyle. When we don't get these things, we pout, we blame, we act petulant. We take, or even steal, what we think should have been ours. How many of us justify absenteeism or padding our expense accounts because we think, "This job doesn't pay me what I'm worth"?

If we are honest with ourselves, we'll see that many of our expectations of others come from the fact that we've never grown up into emotionally and spiritually mature adults who have conscious connections to the divine as the provider, instead of to mommy and daddy. Wherever we are caught in childlike thinking, we will be stuck in ego and false pride. These states of awareness shut down our intuition and inner wisdom. To gain some insight into yourself, complete the following sentences: What do I expect from the people close to me? What do I expect from people I don't know as well? What does the world owe me?

October 11

I have been out of touch with the land in California and feel an urgent need to take a break from the hectic San Francisco area. Where is home? That is my underlying question. I make a pilgrimage to the sanctuary of Chimayo, north of Santa Fe, New Mexico, to pray and connect with the archetypal energy of the divine Mother. I sit down in the little rustic church that is dedicated to healing, close my eyes, quiet myself, and think about my question. And soon I see the powder blue energy of Mary flooding through the church and through my body.

I greet her and I tell her I am feeling separated from others and from the earth. Would she please help me feel connected? Would she please make a good home for me? She answers instantly, "Would you please make a good home for *me*?" I know she means inside me, that my heart and body are the home she wants. I ask, "Will you help me reach more people in my work?" She answers, "Will you help me reach more people in *my* work?" I smile; I suddenly understand that we are versions of each other. Then she asks that I keep the windows clean in my "house," and she will show me the sights I need. I am to keep my windows clean by having no doubts, by feeling her reality and my own essence, by not cluttering the space of my life with negative thoughts. She says, "I am related to your ability to have faith. Whenever you can't feel your connection to your deeper self, the world, and God, it is I who connect you again. I am the function of unity and communion. While there are many other teachers who will give you specific information and skills, I come first, before all of them. I prepare you to *do*. Whenever you are lost, come to me first."

As I'm leaving the church, the priest stops me. "You've been praying a long time," he says. "Is everything ok?" I start to cry. He takes me into his little office, and, though I am not a Catholic and hardly even a Christian anymore, he puts holy water on his hands, makes a cross on my forehead, touches my face and shoulders sweetly, and prays out loud that I may receive what I need.

I receive blessings freely.

Allow yourself to benefit from the world's great compassion today. The presence, help, and generosity of the divine Mother is available to us all the time; we only need to tune in to it.

**The world tells
me a story.**

*Make a list
of images,
animals, symbols,
and sensory
experiences you
notice today.
Then write a
poem, prayer,
or hymn of
thanksgiving
integrating them
all. Let your
writing flow
from your sense
of awe.*

I wrote this after a vision quest, during which I watched the sun and moon make their rounds, and felt the blessed continuity of life.

Thank You, FatherMother, for this day
for the circuit of the sun
for the window in the blue
for the way You move the earth
so slow, so fast
for the way You keep on, and keep on
Thank You for the door in me
that leads me through the dark to You
Thank You for Your rays of dawn and dusk
so soft and safe, that make change beautiful

Thank You, FatherMother, for this night
with its velvet winds of love
for the way You move so close
and breathe upon my eyes
for the panther of the sky
stealthy in the stars
lying over me

Thank You for the purples in the black
for this stillness in my heart
for the humble way You rest
Thank You for making me
and for these tears
that wash me back to Your ocean lap

Thank You for constantly calling me
for vaporizing me up
and raining me anew on parched ground
Thank You, Thank You, Thank You
for reminding me in every way
that We love

October 13

Karla McLaren, author of *Your Aura & Your Chakras: The Owner's Manual,* has been fascinated for years with how people respond to the famous and how the famous respond to fame. So when she herself began to receive attention and acclaim as a writer and healer, she was dropped right into the middle of her own research. How does one handle this change with all the new expectations, pressures, the pain and fear and wishes? It brought up emotional issues and weighed on her heavily. One night, a dream came to her and brought some insight.

Karla says, "I was in a dark valley with no moon, struggling to pick my way through rocks without falling. I felt a light and looked up to find a glowing Jesus ahead of me, illuminating enough of the path for me to see. I kept my eyes on Him and the scene changed to a verdant, sunlit meadow where I could find my way quite easily. Jesus was still in front of me and I knew I was to keep my eyes on Him, even when all around me was lovely and easy. The scene changed again, this time to one of horror. I was walking on thin planking over a malevolent swamp filled with corpses. The not-quite-dead raised their arms up to me, begging and threatening me so I would help. I kept my eyes on Jesus and noticed that though His light shone on many of them, they wouldn't look up. I knew if I reached down to help, I'd be pulled in with them. So, I kept my eyes focused on Him and continued walking.

"The scene changed yet again. Now, there was golden light everywhere, and I was walking on a sea of upraised hands. There were cheers and adulations, and amazingly, the golden light was coming directly from me! But still, Jesus remained in front of me. The crowds disappeared and Jesus and I were alone, standing together as friends. He said, 'No matter what, keep your eyes on me. And, in case you didn't realize it, those hands that held you up in the sunlight are the same hands that reached for you in the swamp.'" Karla was able to relax at last, having found a way to proceed without the confusion of adulation and the fear of attack.

**My imagina-
tion can bring
me insight.**

*Take time to
trust your
unconscious to
give you
guidance about
pressing issues
today. Your
imagination is
your ally. Ask a
question and
let a fantasy
scenario unfold
in your mind.
When it's
finished, look
for the meaning.*

I deserve to be comfortable in the spaces I occupy.

Take responsibility today for improving your relationship to your environment. When your body feels safe and comfortable, you will be more aware. If something bothers you, either change it or change your attitude about it until you feel good.

Marie had rented a fancy condo because it had a heavenly view and lots of open space. She craved a peaceful setting after living in a bustling city for ten years. Her savings had covered the rent for six months, but now she needed to find someone to rent the lower level. It would have to be a special person—they would share the kitchen and the only entrance. Marie needed her privacy and wanted a certain quality of harmony in the house. She put ads in the paper and interviewed many people, but no one quite fit. She tortured herself with thoughts like, "Should I lower the rent? Will I have to live with someone I don't like? Maybe I'll have to sacrifice my quality of life just to pay the rent. Maybe I'll lose this place, which is my dream come true, and how will I find anything else even remotely like it?"

She decided to work with a therapist to clear her negative thoughts. During that process, she had a dream that the lower level of her house was dirty, dark, and overflowing with debris and old junk. In actuality it was light and tidy, so she knew the dream related to her own consciousness. She needed some internal housecleaning! So Marie fasted, meditated, and walked through the open space behind her home to strengthen her connection to the land. She wrote extensively in her journal. She went down to the lower level of her condo, where she hadn't spent much time, and spent some there, even slept there some nights, just to become better acquainted with it. If she didn't feel comfortable there, why would someone else like her want it? Her clearing process turned into a healing process, and it took her mind off her worries. One day the phone rang, and it was a young woman who shared many of Marie's interests, could afford the rent, and loved the view and open space. Marie now saw that she could indeed be supported by the world in what she wanted to do.

October 15

Melanie had left her corporate job and taken some time off to find a new direction. Over lunch with a friend who was a business leader in the city where they lived, Melanie felt compelled to share an odd insight she'd had about the way the two of them were connected spiritually. This was a risk, since the woman was so professional and grounded in the material world. Yet, to Melanie's surprise, her friend responded favorably, telling a story about her own spiritual process and about her astrologer!

One morning Melanie woke up depressed and confused. She walked out on her deck, near tears, and muttered, "I need some comfort!" Immediately she heard a trilling sound and noticed a raccoon in the crotch of a tree. She got her camera and for the next half hour took pictures of the raccoon, who seemed to pose for her. She said, "By the time the raccoon waddled away, I had no desire to cry— but I did have a desire to call that astrologer!" As Melanie spoke with the astrologer, she happened to tell her about the raccoon. "Do you mind if I ask my shaman what the raccoon might signify?" the astrologer asked. Melanie, slightly taken aback, said, "Sure." The astrologer called back and suggested she inquire about studying with the shaman, because he'd said the raccoon symbolized someone in the process of taking off a mask.

Time passed and Melanie didn't call him. Then odd things began to happen. As she'd walk through the house, in her peripheral vision, she'd see the movement of a man in the yard. When she turned to look, no one was there. One day she looked at her wicker rocker and saw a shaman in it. She gave in and called him. They met, and she felt she'd known him before. She became his apprentice.

Simultaneously, she began to receive Reiki energy treatments as part of her spiritual process and decided to become a Reiki Master, but couldn't decide who to study with. One day, Melanie was at a restaurant and the hostess dropped by her table to chat. The conversation turned to spirituality. Melanie confided she was looking for a Reiki Master. "I'm a Reiki Master!" the hostess said. Melanie says her life continues to have this synchronous quality, with one odd thing leading to the next. She says, "There is no going back—and though I have self-doubt, I feel led. I just follow the guidance."

I notice the underlying themes in my day.

Watch for repeating ideas and synchronicities today. The path forward is often marked by unusual omens and connections.

I know when to stop.

Today, notice the times you need to become still. Pay attention to your built-in mechanism that says "Enough!" This way you can start fresh, over and over again, all day.

David Kuntz, in his book *Stopping: How to Be Still When You Have to Keep Going*, defines stopping as "doing nothing as much as possible, for a definite period of time (one second to one month) for the purpose of becoming more fully awake and remembering who you are." He says the purpose of stopping is to make sure "we go in the direction that we want and we are not just reacting to the pace in our lives, but choosing moment to moment what's best. The ultimate reason for stopping is going." Kuntz recommends that we pepper our day with what he calls "stillpoints," very brief pauses in which we do nothing, intentionally and consciously, for just a moment.

We innately know, if we pay attention to the subtle contractions in our body, when we've gone too far, said too much, expected too much, pushed too hard, or eaten too much. When I'm reading a book, watching television, or working in the yard, I know instantly when I'm saturated. When I'm having a phone conversation with a friend and I reach my limit of absorbing information, I hear myself say, "It was great talking to you . . ." When I'm in a creative process and can't write another word or design another brochure, I know that feeling of just going blank. So our body and mind stop many times throughout the day of their own accord, but these pauses and shifts of direction are largely unconscious. What if we became aware of these stillpoint moments when one activity is complete and another has yet to begin? What if we learned to breathe right there, slowly, intentionally, dropping into our moment and finding the simplicity? Could we enjoy the simplicity? Simplicity slows us down, reveals truth. If we could catch and use those natural stillpoints, we could be clearer about which activity wants to come next, instead of leaping forward, propelled by the pressure of our shoulds.

October 17

I went for a hike in the hills one fine spring day with a gay man who was a female impersonator in San Francisco. He had come to one of my seminars, and, though he was wildly dramatic, outrageous, and funny, I could see immediately what an old, wise soul he was. Under the facade was a man who'd known suffering and who had chosen to play instead of go crazy. We formed a close friendship. I learned that he used to be addicted to alcohol and drugs. He'd been labeled as schizophrenic with multiple personality disorder by a psychiatrist, and, instead of trying to get rid of his aspect selves, he'd learned hypnotherapy on his own so he could enter more fully into each one and help them get to know each other! He had found a lifelong devoted partner and was actually balancing his wild inner life with his outer one quite well.

Recently, he had discovered he had AIDS. After a near-death episode, he decided to embrace his life and his illness. He changed his lifestyle, learned to eat simply, walked extensively, and started taking hang gliding lessons because, he said, Peter Pan had always been his hero. What interested me was how he never judged himself negatively—he didn't resist his disease or his "negative" habits, but said he could feel that things were changing naturally and would continue to of their own accord. He let himself do all the things he did in his life—because he wanted to.

Strangely, I had awakened several days before our hike with the words "I am one day closer to my death." I thought, "What am I doing with my time? Am I feeling the purity? Am I in the clear space? Why am I indulging in pressurized, overly electrical, negative thoughts?" I got an overview of my life later that day, as if seeing myself from high in the air—my little body was sitting in cafés, at movies, on hillsides looking out . . . and my mind screamed, "What is she *doing* with her life!??" Another part of me answered calmly, "She is resting. She is retrieving herself." So I took a lesson from my dear friend: embrace everything that comes in life. Embrace the mind buzz, the fear of dying, the warm space of relationship, the fragmentation, the clarity, the action and nonaction. Stop the duality that causes judgment. This is love.

I allow the full range of my experience.

Today, let yourself be happy and sad, peaceful and upset, mature and immature, beautiful and ugly, creative and dull, insightful and blank, quiet and loud, active and passive. When you let yourself have both sides of every equation, you'll become well rounded and flexible.

**Everything
I see is inside
me.**

*Include every-
thing you see
today inside your
personal aura.*

Whenever you think of it, notice your spherical aura. If you extend your awareness out from your body, you'll notice it moves out equally in all directions, always forming a ball of awareness. You can expand and contract this bubble of perception and include more, or less, in it. Focus on clipping your toenails and your bubble is quite small. Focus on finding your way through a maze of city streets to a new destination and your bubble is much broader. Play with this idea today—zoom out and be aware of your house, yard, the street. Zoom in and be aware of just your physical body. Zoom farther in and be aware of your heart beating. Zoom out again and include your whole town. When you notice something, it has suddenly materialized inside your bubble and is therefore not separate from you. It is manifesting out of the very substance of your own awareness. What's inside your bubble is coming from you and *is* you at a higher level. By practicing spherical, inclusive perception, you'll stay in the present moment and will eventually feel the truth that we are all connected and that we are One.

October 19

Jane is highly sensitive with a delicate constitution. Health problems of various sorts forced her, early in her process of self-discovery, to experiment with a variety of healing diets, such as vegetarianism, raw foodism, and fruitarianism. She had developed a persistent, systemic yeast infection that she had fought with, prayed over, eaten around, and tried to affirm away—all to no avail.

She says, "The popular belief at the time was that we create our illnesses through impure thoughts. I tried to purify my thoughts, but it didn't help. One morning, in complete despair, I had a thought that the yeasts were actually little beings with a consciousness of their own. I thought, 'They've been created by a creator as surely as I have and have an equal right to exist.' I decided to speak to them. I got very quiet and asked them, 'What are you doing in my body?'

"The first response I had was a sense of love filling me entirely. Then I imagined they were saying, 'We don't want you to die from diabetes. We're here to keep you well!' This didn't make sense until I realized that my 'spiritual' diets were high in sugars, which keeps the organisms alive and thriving. I began to research blood sugars, more balanced diets, carbohydrate sensitivities, and gluten intolerance. From that point on, I realized the proliferation of yeast in my system occurred whenever I was overloaded on sugar. It became a helpful barometer. Because of my change of attitude about seeing this as a 'problem,' I've been infection free now for over seven years."

I live inside my body as my body.

Focus your attention inside your skin as often as possible today. Your body is not a foreign object; it is simply a dense form of you. Everything inside it is conscious, loving, and purposeful.

October 20

I forgive myself and others.

Look for ways to let go of grievances and find understanding today.

In this aggressive world it's inevitable that we'll clash with other people's personalities. When we make judgments about others based on their behavior, it's a clear sign that there's something under the surface with which *we* have an issue. Something in *us* needs work—not in them. The same thing goes, at a more subtle level, within ourselves— it's possible for one part of our personality to have a judgment about another part—the spiritual, purist part may judge the social, partying part, for example. Forgiveness, then, is the ability to open up around a judgment and look for understanding, even to go so far as to understand the gift that person or personality aspect is giving you.

Adam had for years had a head-to-head rivalry with a coworker. He had been fixated on finding ways to short-circuit her success. Her self-centered actions crushed everyone around her, and it infuriated him to see her break every rule in the book and always come out on top. But Adam had started on a spiritual path and was examining his behavior and thought patterns. He realized he could no longer allow himself to continue to try to cause the downfall of another individual. So he took a bold step—he called his nemesis and invited her to lunch. "We faced each other across the table and spent a few minutes in idle conversation," he began. "Then I looked straight at her and said, 'I am here to tell you that I am no longer your enemy. I sincerely want to help you in any way that will elevate the quality of your life. I'd like to ask for your forgiveness for my acts of unkindness.' She paused, and with a wealth of courage, looked me in the eyes and said, 'Adam, I'm grateful to you for coming forward. Thank you for doing this.'"

Adam says, "In the days that followed, an unbelievable amount of pain and anguish was removed from my life. I saw that the battle had not been with her but with myself all along. I began to meditate on ways to support her and her family. Not long after this, I had an almost psychic dream concerning some health issues her husband was about to face. I called her husband and met with him to share the details of the dream. The dream proved to be accurate, and, because he chose to embrace the information, he was able to offset a major physical calamity that had the potential to end his life."

October 21

Goethe said, "How many joys are crushed underfoot because people look up at the sky and disregard what is at their feet?" Just walking can be a powerful meditation. You can walk far, or not. I used to go hiking on a nearby mountain with a friend who was a Buddhist priest. In his training, he had learned to walk on fire. Walking on mountains was a spiritual practice. We walked slowly and mindfully, sending our attention down into the heart of the mountain and drawing energy back up into our bodies from that core place. With each step we fed the mountain and it fed us. When we got tired, we simply stopped and connected more mindfully, became more peaceful. We paid attention to the leafy, wet, yin places and the sunny, dry, yang places along the trail. This way of hiking was not about speed or conquering or competition. It was about connection.

In an article in the *New York Times Magazine* called "On the Road with God's Fool: How St. Francis Lost Everything and Found His Way," Gretel Ehrlich writes, "To walk is to unbalance oneself. Between one step and the next we become lost. Balance is regained as the foot touches earth, then it goes as the foot lifts. A path is made of dirt and rock; it is also a swath of light cut through all that appears to be solid and unchanging. . . . As it was with Jesus and the Gautama Buddha, the poet Matsuo Basho and the great Ch'an masters of China and Japan, all teachings were given on the move, under an open sky. 'We are not so much traveling as just stopping here and there,' Matsuo Basho said. The divinity of a place rose up through the soles of their feet and went everywhere with them."

Each thing, each moment, has dignity.

Simplify your life today by concentrating on one step at a time.

I allow myself to feel deeply.

Raise your energy level 10 percent as often as you can today, then focus your thoughts on what captivates your attention, what you're strongly interested in. Where's the juice?

Often our passions go underground as we live a rational, responsible, tidy life and try to be consistent and make sense to other people. Passion requires risk. It surfaces when we break habits and act spontaneously. Suzanne, a client, told me that a therapist friend of hers had once described her as "passionate" but didn't mean it as a compliment! She said, "Over the years I've learned about detachment and how to separate my identity from the dramas in my life. I used to apologize for my passion, but not anymore. Now I simply consider myself a maturely passionate person. Lately, I've been journaling about what I call the 'sepia-colored people,' the ones who live some corporate code, or follow a middle-class dream, and have forgotten about Nature, Love, and Art. I've decided I want kindred spirits in my life who can live their passion. I haven't abandoned the sepia-colored people, but I've abandoned the notion that I need to live like that."

There is a place in me, too, that gets fed up with what Suzanne called the sepia world. When I've been fitting in too long, being "nice," I can feel some animal wave just below the surface, like the urge that makes dogs shake water off themselves from head to tail. Things seem so *slow!* Why don't people just *understand* quickly and easily? Why can't we use telepathy instead of talking and writing? Why can't we materialize and dematerialize things instantly? Why can't we be *direct*? Why do we all have to agree on this stupid cause-and-effect rule? Why do things have to move through developmental stages? Why do I have to give my power away to the status quo? Just to feel included in such a poor imitation of true communion? To be appropriate and not offend anyone, why do I pretend to not know, to be incomplete, diffident? Rrrrrrrgh! Part of me wants to be done with this game and not have to struggle against the pain disguising itself as stupidity and bad taste and depression and apathy and reactionary behaviors.

When I get to this stage, if I can take a breath and come back into my body, I realize my passion is back! I'm back in touch with deep feelings. So what do I want to do with all this raw energy? This is the time to ask the childlike, untrained, surprising, illogical, unconscious self for ideas.

October 23

Richard got involved with a high-stakes chain letter game a few years ago. He was successful at it and made several thousand dollars. But, as these things always do, the chain petered out and the people at the end of the line lost money. Some were so upset that they reported the players to the state. An investigation was launched. Everyone who had made money was forced to return it. Richard was the only one who decided to fight the lawsuit, and he embarked on an intensive journey of learning about the law and filing claims and counterclaims. The tax board socked him with a huge bill for monies they estimated he had earned, an amount he hadn't come close to earning. As Richard sank farther into this quagmire, his friends began to abandon him, accusing him of being a victim. Only a few stood by him during the protracted period of legal battling. Eventually he came out the other side, having largely proved himself, but he felt disappointed in his friends for turning away in his time of need.

We talked about the whole misadventure and looked for the inner reasons why he drew this experience into his life. Richard had a dominating mother and a passive father. He himself was sensitive and vulnerable, but also a dynamic, talented hard worker. Unconsciously he felt he was never cared for enough, never quite provided for by his loved ones and by life. So it was logical that he would be attracted to ideas that might make provision easy and effortless. He liked multilevel marketing and get-rich-quick investments. The chain letter money game had appealed to him for that reason. Since the legal hubbub died down, Richard had been working successfully at a variety of things, with no effort spent searching for jobs—everything came to him. He was oddly happy. I said, "Perhaps this whole thing has been to teach you that the provision you need is right here in these ordinary moments, not in some high-falutin' money scheme. That ordinary life loves you and supports you." "Yes," he said, "it's definitely been about faith, and I *have* learned to let go of trying so hard. I feel like I can finally be myself—this has forced me to learn to trust myself, and my life, when no one else would."

It's OK to be vulnerable.

Be totally undefended today. If others criticize you or are rude to you, let the energy pass through you. They're telling you who they are, not who you are. Trust yourself.

October 24

I trust that I am loved.

Choose to feel loving as often as possible today, and notice that, when you do, you also feel loved.

The Dalai Lama said, "If you want others to be happy, practice compassion. If you want to be happy, practice compassion." Yoshie, a friend in Tokyo, is the soul of kindness to others but often forgets to practice the same sweetness toward herself. Thus she sometimes feels unappreciated and lonely. She says she wants a husband, but, in all the counseling sessions we've done, it seems it is a deeper experience of her own soul that she craves.

Yoshie's roommate recently wrote that they have had an unexpected visitor. "A young monkey has made the trees around our apartment her new home. Evidently, this monkey has been spotted in various places, from the Hachioji Mountains all the way to Tokyo, and has traveled on her own about forty miles. For a week or two now, there have been television crews, newspaper reporters, and photographers hanging around outside. No one can catch the monkey (on film or with the net) because she's quick and just appears for a split second before disappearing into the trees.

"Well, Yoshie and the monkey have become friends, and the monkey has volunteered to model for her! Yoshie took more than a hundred photographs of her in various positions and with different expressions from about five feet away and gave them to the newspaper reporter camped outside. Yoshie and I talk about what message the monkey is trying to bring us by making such a long and dangerous journey." I puzzled over the meaning as well. Then I happened to read an article by Lama Surya Das in which he tells the story of Hanuman, the monkey god.

Hanuman is completely devoted to Ram and Sita, the yin and yang aspects of God. He wants to be with them desperately, day and night. Sita has a red mark on her forehead, denoting that she is married to Ram, and thus they may be together all the time. But Hanuman doesn't have the mark. This sends him onto his own spiritual path. He focuses on how he too can unite with God. One night he steals a bag of the powdered red dye used for the mark and dyes his whole body and soul red so he can be with Ram and Sita unendingly. Hanuman represents man's wish to be with God; his animal nature is transformed by a life of service to the divine. My intuition tells me that Yoshie is being reminded of this by Hanuman's little sister, who chose to trust her alone.

October 25

I have had some interesting conversations about death and reincarnation with my niece Julia, who has been highly sensitive to spiritual things from an early age. When she was three, we found a big anthill mounded with tiny quartz crystals the ants had carried up. I told her that the Indians used these crystals in their rattles. She picked up a handful and stared off into space. "I *might have been* an Indian," she muttered. I said, "Maybe you were, in your last life." She popped back to attention and said, "Last life?" "Yes, the one right before this one," I answered. She thought a moment and drifted off again, "Oh, yeaaah . . ."

One year for Christmas she received a see-through plastic person, complete with snap-out internal organs. I said, "Did you know that under your skin you look just like that?" She said, "Yes. When you die, first your skin comes off, and then your muscles come off, and then you're a skeleton. If I died and I was a skeleton, and you were still a real person, I could still see you! If I died, I could be the mom and Paula (my sister) could be me, or I could be you. Usually when you die you get to be a different kid." Then she paused, thinking. "But sometimes when you die, you want to be the same person you just were."

Then, a year later, I showed her an article about the Dalai Lama and his friend the Panchen Lama. I explained to Julia how these special people always come back again after they die and their friends find them. She carefully examined the pictures of the adult Panchen Lama and the boy Panchen Lama, and pronounced they were the same. "You can see it in their eyes!"

If you pretend to be a three year old, how might you describe the state you were in before you were born.

I am conscious of remembering.

Be aware when you project into the past today, then come back to the present moment consciously. What knowledge were you trying to access? Or pick a period from the past. What are your first impressions about what happened then?

**I know
through my
nose.**

*Be aware of
odors today and
how they inform
and affect you.
Smell is our
most powerful,
animalistic sense,
relaying immense
amounts of
information.*

Driving out through the oak grasslands to the Pacific coastline, I roll down my car's windows and am blasted by the crisp, pungent autumn air. The morning and evening fog and occasional afternoon mists have dampened the dry gray grasses, and I can smell the rich underlying mustiness. Cutting strongly through that dull earth odor, there is the sharp, high, sagelike scent of that sticky green plant with the little yellow flowers that peppers the hills from late summer on. I see its lemon-lime color washing across the dry, silvery landscape.

Approaching the ocean, the smells change. Where exactly do I pick up the saltwater in the wind? The cypress trees, coastal grasses, the swampy smells of cattails and kelp? I remember driving to the beach with my old dog, Moon, and how he would start howling and pacing back and forth with excitement at some mysterious point where his nose verified his fond memory of retrieving sticks from the surf.

I recall the agoraphobic client I had last week, who felt she had miraculously survived the path from her door to mine. She had an odd odor of mustiness mixed with panic-saturated sweat. Then there are the various smells of my empty house as I step in the front door each day. I can tell if the house has retained too much negativity from the last day's process of living, or if it is anxiously waiting to send streams of creativity through me. When I take the first breath of inside air, I smell the fresh green plants and whether they need water, or the hint of last night's dinner, or a stagnant no-smell smell that makes me immediately open doors and windows.

Do you smell your clothes to know whether to wash them? Do you remember the smells of your favorite people? Of your dog, cat, or horse? Or of the smoking versus the nonsmoking section of a restaurant? Watch how your sense of smell influences your decisions.

October 27

Do you have assumptions about life that you've carried around with you since childhood? You'll get warts from picking up a toad? You shouldn't pull out the corners of your mouth or it will stay that way? You have to get good grades to be loved? You have to be pretty to be popular? Perhaps you learned that you should put yourself down when you achieved any kind of success, so you wouldn't alienate your friends. Many of these assumptions follow us into adult life and limit how much we're able to perceive and how much we can accomplish. By examining and challenging these hidden beliefs, you can open whole new territories. "I have to follow the instructions? Why? Maybe there's a different way." "I can't do that—it's too dangerous. Wait a minute—maybe it's not!" "This thing I want to do has probably already been done. But I have my own way to do it!"

When I went to design school, I took a furniture design class. The professor told us to design a chair. He had us play with ideas for a while, then asked, "What's the first thought you should have when designing a chair?" We said, "How many legs should it have? How high should it be? Does a chair need a back?" He responded, "No. The first question you ask when designing a chair is 'Why a chair?' " A similar thing happened in my painting class. The professor sent us outside to draw a tree by drawing the empty space around the tree. By drawing the space, a tree magically appeared. It turned my mind inside out.

Keep your eyes open for times when you think one particular thing must be done before another can happen. "I have to lose fifteen pounds before I can wear my new swimsuit." "I have to finish my bookkeeping before I can go to the mall." When you hear yourself making these "if A, then B" statements, look at what limiting assumption is contained in the thought. Perhaps you were taught that things must happen in a prescribed sequence. Why? Use your intuition, make some leaps, and brighten up your creative life. "The only difference between a rut and a grave is the dimensions."

I am aware when I limit or put pressure on myself.

Notice the times today that you say "should" and "have to." Examine the hidden assumptions and the topics you're pressuring yourself about, and why.

When I release struggle and tension, I see the simple way.

Turn contractions and blockages into insight today.

You probably learned, like most of us, that to solve a problem you should concentrate on it, keep at it, and apply a little more effort. Go for it! Something about pain and gain . . . And yes, I admit there is something to this. "Perseverence furthers," as the *I Ching* advises us repeatedly. Yet there are times when using willpower to push through simply creates struggle. The more we force things, the more we get tangled up in a sticky web of variables. When I think I have to solve a problem by myself, and that it is bigger than I am, and that I must use my logic and analytical skills alone, I slowly build tension. Soon I'm chewing on the problem, worrying it to death, and wearing myself out so that I can't concentrate. Then I feel drained and must take a nap. Right after the nap, the breakthrough comes—intuitively, directly, as soon as I stop trying and pushing.

When you're looking for solutions, remember—there's a simple way. It starts with one simple first action that's always doable, always within reach. No problem is bigger than you are, and you are never alone. Even if no people are physically around to help, there are countless beings in the nonphysical realms at your beck and call. Feel them with you, imagine them sending you insights and energy. Next, remember that if the problem has been defined, the solution exists simultaneously. All you have to do is listen for it. Last, try this simple formula—notice the negative beliefs and limiting ideas you're unconsciously holding about how difficult it is. Reverse each one of those thoughts to its positive counterpart. Voice the positive statements out loud. Then, notice the worry you're carrying and how you're working yourself into a fear-based state. Tell yourself, about each doubt, "I don't have to worry about this now." Let go of your concerns. Take the false pressures off. Next, make a clear statement of truth. "I want to solve this problem because it's interesting to me." Next, scan through your physical body and notice the contractions and tension you've been holding. Are you breathing? Relax and shake out your arms and legs, your hips, shoulders, head. Drop your jaw and say "ahhhhh." Reinstate your cheerfulness, remember your innate connectedness. *Now* see what thoughts come to you.

October 29

Have you ever noticed how you can be in a great mood, then deal with an out-of-sorts waiter, and not long after, wonder why you're not feeling good anymore? If we don't pay attention, we can match other people's bad moods. We can just as easily maintain high energy and raise others up through our presence. We just have to stay conscious and in our body and maintain our state of being in the face of other people's storms and difficult energy fields. You probably know the odd feeling of instant wariness that comes when you cross paths with a street person who is talking in a paranoid way to herself and the air. You may also be able to sense people who go on the offensive easily or like to argue, criticize, and humiliate others. There is a prickliness and an edge to them. You may be able to sense people who are habitual liars from the subtle feeling preceding them. I once met a man who made me feel that I was spinning, then falling. It took a few weeks to realize I was not falling in love with him, but that it was a special way he had devised to disorient and distance people. The energy in his aura was spinning.

Some people are highly manic when they come to see me, and by the time they leave, I'm exhausted from trying to keep my body from copying their overly electrical jerking and the flow-reversing their body is doing. As I tune in to someone who is relatively unconscious or out of his body, I may leave *my* body and blank out momentarily, lose my momentum, feel sleepy. I think, "What's wrong with me?" then realize I'm encountering something the *client* is in denial about.

When I first worked with clients who had been sexually abused, they scared me. I wondered why they'd come to see me, because they were sitting with arms tightly crossed in an I-don't-care attitude. As I felt through the layers of energy, however, I could see that it was just a defensive outer layer and under it was extreme vulnerability. Since I work empathically, I tend to match the state of other bodies. By doing that, I understand their life intimately, but I also have to make a conscious effort to return to my own pattern immediately after I've felt theirs. We pick up impressions constantly from other people's energy fields. This is absolutely normal. We must get in the habit, though, of recentering just as constantly back into our own authentic vibration.

I respond to people's energy frequency.

Notice the energy fields of the people you meet today. Our bodies are like tuning forks; they will adjust themselves to whatever energy they come in contact with. Are you raising or lowering your energy level to those of others?

When I experience magical timing, my soul is speaking to me of a higher reality.

Pay attention to synchronicity, coincidence, and subtle time warps today. What is your mind up to? Could you be experiencing a breakthrough from another dimension?

I was driving the ninety-minute journey between my house and a bookstore where I saw clients once a week. I'd made the drive so many times, I knew every segment of the road by heart and how much time each section took. On this particular day, I reached a landmark that normally indicated I was half an hour from my destination, and I glanced at the clock. I was fifteen minutes early! "How did that happen?" I mused. "I'm making great time!" I'd been going full speed with no traffic—but it was a bit too much extra leeway. When I reached my exit, normally fifteen minutes from my destination, I was back on time again. I'd mysteriously gained, then eaten up, a quarter hour.

"Maybe I just made a mistake," I thought. "Did I misread the clock? No. So what just happened to me?" It should have been easy to gloss over this discrepancy, but I couldn't let it go. I suddenly had the thought that I had entered a state of unity somewhere back there on the highway and had collapsed time—in effect, teleported farther along my path. Then, when my conscious mind realized it, my mind dipped out again and changed the reality, so that it lined up again with my normal expectations. "Oh, this couldn't be the real explanation!" I groused. "Why not?" my inner voice responded. "What if you accepted that you are able to travel physically by altering your mind? How would this change who you are?"

If this were true, that would mean we were virtually unlimited in our capacity. In fact, maybe we are doing this very thing now but in a slower, unconscious way—and that is how we actually meet people, how events occur, how we arrive at locations. Maybe what we now take as the ordinary functioning of reality is just a meeting of minds that have not yet awakened to their true potential.

October 31

Maureen lived in a rent-controlled apartment for years, then with a boyfriend who had a mortgage-free house. When it came time to have her own place again, she finally had a good job and could afford something nice. She decided to express herself. "I deserve to live in a place that thrills me!" she declared. The image that came to her was a place overlooking the water that felt like a retreat, with a sleeping loft. She began looking and found one that sounded just right. She made an appointment to see it after work, but the owner said there were many other people looking at it too. "Please don't rent it to anyone until I see it—please?" she begged. As she hurried through traffic to get there, her car started smoking and overheating. She had to stop regularly to cool it off. When she finally arrived, the owner was sitting with a man. As she entered the room, she heard him say, "I'll take it!" Maureen's spirits sank like a stone. Little did she know that her car had helped, not hindered, her.

A mere three days later, a friend of a friend called her. "Lori says you're looking for a place to rent that's on the water, and I'm looking for the same thing. I think I have the place for you! I looked at it the other day and it's not quite right for me." Maureen realized it was a place she had excluded because the rent was out of sight. It had been described as "an enchanted cottage on a private estate." The woman said she'd met the owners, an older couple, and they didn't need the money—they wanted just the right person in their cottage. They had interviewed nearly a hundred applicants and at last had chosen her. When she said it didn't quite suit her needs, they asked, "Do you know anyone else just like you?" So she set up an introduction for Maureen, and the couple liked her immediately and asked what she could afford. She told them and they said "Fine! Done!" And that is how Maureen came to live in an enchanted cottage on the water, nestled cozily among trees, with a sleeping loft.

The world aligns to give me what I need.

What do you really need now? Notice how all your experiences and the people you meet are working together to help you receive what you need, so you can enter a new phase of self-expression. You are entitled to have what helps you develop more wisdom and compassion.

November

November 1

Has this ever happened to you? You're at a seminar or meeting. You've been paying close attention to the speaker, when suddenly you realize you've blanked out and have missed the last few minutes of conversation. Perhaps you've had the even more disconcerting experience of being the speaker, in the flow with your material, communicating clearly, when everything becomes blurry and you lose your train of thought. You were perfectly lucid a moment ago, and now you're a blubbering idiot! Where did you go— and why? Someone in the group was probably triggered by something you said. Without even knowing it, that person became scared, excited, or distracted and left the present moment to explore the thought. And you went along!

We are such telepathic creatures that our bodies are constantly adapting to each other, unconsciously matching levels of energy and awareness to maintain harmony, just as a school of fish changes direction simultaneously. So when one person leaves her body and goes unconscious, the other people in the group often will, too. The plug is pulled, and consciousness goes down the drain. When you notice this, say something about it out loud. "I sense we've just gotten off track here somehow. Are we all on the same page? Has what I said triggered any interesting responses in you?" Or if you've been the one to space out, you might say, "Excuse me! I just realized I drifted. Could you please repeat what you just said—I really want to be here for it all!"

Maybe you're leading a meeting at work and you suddenly feel a wall. You notice people are no longer hearing you. Your intuition tells you that Steve has reached his saturation point and needs to walk around to integrate what he's heard, others need a bathroom break, and Sara has comments and can't pay attention until she voices them. If you speak directly about the hidden dynamics, everyone will come alive again. "Let's stop and take a ten-minute break. I sense we've reached a saturation point, and several of you may have some comments. Let's address those issues as soon as we reconvene." By bringing divergent unconscious issues into the conscious mind, alignment is re-created, and people can relax and pay full attention again.

I bring the hidden to light.

State out loud the hidden factors influencing situations as often as possible today. When you name an undercurrent that might be blocking the flow, it often clears immediately.

My mind can affect the physical world.

Pay attention today to the way your unspoken thoughts can elicit responses from others and can even seem to influence the flow of events around you. You can actually participate actively in the creation of your own reality.

Lynn B. Robinson, a business consultant and author of *Coming out of Your Psychic Closet*, tells an interesting story that stretches our concept of how the world works. She says, "Two young men asked me to come to their rented, restored, historical residence to tell them if I agreed with their suspicion that they might have a ghost." Some unexplained force had been moving various objects in their house. When I tuned in, I encountered a male laborer who I sensed had been hanging around the property for about a hundred years. I then encountered two other males, who seemed to be guides or guardian angels to the owners of the house. When I described them to the young men, they affirmed that the men had actually been part of their lives when they were children.

"After some telepathic conversations with the laborer to help him move on and with the young men and their guides to help them communicate more comfortably, I was getting ready to leave. One of the young men said, 'Oh yes, and could you please tell them that if any one of them knows where my missing ring is, I'd sure like to have it back.' Both the young men had searched the house repeatedly for the ring—one of many small objects that had been mysteriously moved. The next morning, the owner of the missing ring called me, quite shaken up, to report that when he woke up, his ring was clearly in sight on the bookcase across from his bed."

How much power does the mind really have to influence the physical dimension? In the future, we may find that mind and body, thought and form, are simply extensions of one another, not separate at all. If the mental and physical realms are continuous, it's not too much of a stretch to think that a nonphysical force, like focused intention, could move objects.

November 3

A client, a businessman from Korea, had for the past year been on a spiritual quest around the world. He had visited a Native American elder and asked, "What is enlightenment?" The old man said, "The permanent now." So what *is* enlightenment? I encounter quite a few spiritual teachers in my work, and some of them claim to be enlightened. It seems to me that enlightened people wouldn't need to claim they were enlightened; it would be self-evident. Many of these teachers have simply disguised their ego in a new cloak, and I often notice that I don't feel very good when I'm around them.

I've always imagined that enlightened people would make me feel good about myself, because they feel good about themselves. It would be easy to laugh around them. I'd feel that I not only had permission to be great, but that they could already see me doing great things and would naturally convey to me how absolutely probable it was! Enlightened people wouldn't reject me if I said something stupid or self-protective—everything in the present moment would be soulful to them.

Have you noticed how we postpone ourselves or displace ourselves? Our soul or enlightened self is "up there" in heaven or "out there" in the future. We're going to be enlightened—*after* we've meditated enough, paid our dues, worked off our karma, purified our bodies, and given up sex or gotten enough sex. Our model of psychotherapy tells us that the pain we feel in our present moment comes from wounds in our past, and to be healthy we must go back in time, reexperience and heal these traumas. Or that we must locate all our scattered, fragmented parts and reintegrate them all together into one homogeneous self. Remind yourself of this today: "I am my soul, fully present and creating this personality and everything that comes from it. I am enlightened now."

I live inside my soul, my soul lives inside me.

Pretend you are already enlightened. Everything you think, feel, and do comes from your soul. If this were true, how would you change the way you live?

**My intuition is
wide open.**

*Follow your
hunches and
fly by the
seat of your
pants today.
Trusting yourself
implicitly is a
good thing!*

What's the worst thing that could happen if your intuition were wide open? Would you tell someone the awful truth and devastate them, or get punched in the face? Would you give people important insights, and, like Cassandra, be ignored? Maybe you'd get a glimpse of your own future misfortune or find out life had no plans for you. Perhaps you'd be full of self-importance because of your vision, then find out it was mere fantasy. If you were a visionary, would you be a loving one? Nancy Kerrigan said, "Doubt yourself and you doubt everything you see. Judge yourself and you see judges everywhere. But if you listen to the sound of your own voice, you can rise above doubt and judgment. And you can see forever."

What's the best thing that could happen if your intuition were wide open? Would you pick the winning lottery numbers and know which stock was going to quadruple in the next week? Would you have perfect timing? Know what people were thinking? Maybe if your intuition were open, you'd learn that what you feel like saying or doing is exactly what the other person needs you to say or do. Maybe you'd be so in tune with the flow of life that you'd be timely, not always "on time." Maybe you'd be "just right" instead of "dead right." With wide-open intuition, would you be able to change effortlessly from being a trendsetter to a farmer, a homemaker to a doctor or a monk meditating in a cave—if that's what life indicated that you be? What if everything you thought of doing worked? What if along with that came the knowledge that everything you do in the outside world, you also do inside yourself; what you cause others to feel, you must feel as well? What if you couldn't escape the fact that everything you want wants you in the same way? That what you dream really is your path?

What if you learned that when you force your thoughts to take place in the future or the past, you can't feel who you are and your intuition stops? It's hard to misuse intuition, because the intuitive state itself, and the insights it generates, are the result of integrity and connectedness, and that teaches you about being loving. Open your intuition and keep it open, and even the things that seem scary at first, unfailingly turn to gold. Intuition teaches us that everything about life is designed to further our spiritual evolution.

November 5

A friend died yesterday. Now, in late afternoon, I walk up to the hilltop where I can find the sky, where we once walked together. I open the top of my head and send up a beam. Where are you? I sit on the grandmother oak and pray for my friend's easy journey through the heavens. "You knew her, I brought her here. She sat on you, too. Please find her, send my love up your spiral vortex to her." I reach my hands up and release an invisible gift, a drop of love into an ocean of love. Is it noticeable? Can it make a difference? Are you there, dear friend? Do you know?

Immediately I hear a watery noise like a brook flowing merrily; a wind has come up suddenly, shooshing up the hill through the silvery grasses. It curls around me, swirling just here, right where I am, and five feet in front of me it gusts down hard, then bucks up like a wild bronco, gathering dust and debris, swirling crazily. The little twister dances like a dervish around me. It whirls on up the hill, lifting up higher and higher, and finally disperses in space. Then, peace.

I walk back very slowly with baby steps, feeling the quiet. Coming around the bend, I notice the broad hill across the way with its handsome craggy top. Just above, diving through the sky in an arc, curving with the hills— a long snake cloud, a flying dragon with an open mouth, heading west toward the ocean and the setting sun. Is this the reincarnation of my little twister? Now an eye appears in the cloud, an opening to the deep places, and it bores into me, and I enter it to know her path to the beyond. The dragon is diving down now, straight into the hill. I think I see my friend riding just behind the big head, waving gaily.

The sky influences my awareness.

Look for shapes in the clouds today. Exercising your imagination helps open your intuition. Looking for meaning in the sky will make you available to superconscious awareness.

I go toward and away, I focus and dissolve.

Notice how you move through your day via attraction and repulsion, interest and boredom, close focus and broad overview. Life is endless oscillation.

Your mind is like a zoom lens moving from a close focus to a distant one, from a small reality to an extensive one. What you focus on, you become. Notice the times when your attention shifts its focal length from near to far, from physical to mental, from conscious to unconscious to conscious again. Catch yourself in the midst of adjusting your zoom lens, and you'll develop greater control over what you perceive. Ask yourself, "How do I want to feel right now? From what level should I view this problem? Physical? Emotional, Mental? Spiritual? Personal? Collective? What does this situation look like when viewed from one level up?"

SHIFTING YOUR ATTENTION

1. Hold your thumb six inches in front of your nose and stare at it. Then focus on a spot on the wall across the room. Bring your gaze back to your thumb, then back to the wall. Keep shifting back and forth, and feel the size of your aura change.

2. Call to mind a vivid experience in the recent past. Imagine it in detail. Then shift to present time and notice what's happening in the environment around you, in vivid detail. Then shift to a future fantasy and embroider it with vivid detail. Then come back to the present moment again.

3. Think of a friend. Call to mind your physical impressions of that person. How does your body feel when you're near him? Now shift your attention slightly and recall your emotional impressions. What feeling tone characterizes him? How do you feel when you're involved with him? Shift your attention again, and be aware of the kind of ideas that are triggered when you're together. What kind of mental rapport do you have? What's your opinion of him? Stretch your attention now to know who he is in his own heart of hearts. What are the deep qualities of his soul?

November 7

When you find yourself in an unpleasant situation, take a few steps back and ask yourself: "What's *right* with this picture?" Look for:

1. What was I previously unconscious about that is now being brought to my attention?
2. If I trust the process at work here, what can I learn?
3. How is the timing of this event perfect for me?
4. How are other people acting out a role that is an unacknowledged aspect of myself?
5. What might the other people be learning who are involved in the experience with me?
6. How can I flow with this situation and add in my own truth and love?
7. How can I find enjoyment in this situation?

For example, your best friend has buddied up to someone who has treated you badly. In the process, she has listened to gossip about you that is false and seems to have believed it. What's right with this picture? Turn the situation around so you trust that there's wisdom in the process. Perhaps you weren't giving your friend enough attention. Perhaps you need to understand something about your nemesis that you don't want to understand. Why do you need total loyalty from your friends? What are you disloyal to? Maybe you're acting in a way that lacks inner integrity in another area of your life. Solve the problem in yourself instead of in your friend.

Why is the experience happening now? If you could find a way to make peace all around, your nemesis might become your benefactor. Maybe the lesson you gain from this needs to be applied immediately to a similar problem brewing at your job.

If you trust that your friend and your nemesis are connecting for a good reason, how can you feel happier with your role? Maybe your friend needs to be seduced and duped to learn a lesson of discrimination, and you're not the one to do it. Maybe you need time alone to realign with your changing inner purpose. Can you set a good example for everyone and, in the process, flow effortlessly into your next, even better, creation?

Whatever happens, somehow it's just right.

Look for the positive interpretation of the events in your life today.

I expand my present moment.

Your awareness extends spherically beyond your body in onionlike layers through time and space and into higher dimensions. Pay attention today to what you might be doing in these higher levels of yourself.

As you work at the computer, you may lose your concentration without realizing it. Minutes later, you zoom back and remember your train of thought. Where were you? You were in your unconscious, drifting beyond the here and now, not centered and not perceiving with your conscious mind. Therefore, you have no memory of what you were doing. Perhaps you were visiting an emotional reality triggered by something you wrote, or you were dipping into the memory banks of the planet to find inspiration. We travel in and out through the universe's great body of knowledge constantly, yet we discount our other-dimensional experiences as lulls or absentmindedness. There are many zones in the body of knowledge, and all are real, all contain a particular kind of information.

Occasionally, other worlds bleed through into this one. Sometimes as I'm going about my normal routine, I get an overwhelming spacey feeling, and I have to make myself focus on each task three times to accomplish it. I drag on through the day until *finally* I realize something's happening at another level of myself, or my awareness is required elsewhere. So I surrender, lie down, and take a brief nap. This bilocation has often happened just before someone I know has died or before a cataclysmic event, or when a friend is in trouble. The next time you catch yourself being spacey, *stop*. Ask yourself the following questions, and list the first five impressions you get:

1. Is there something from earlier today that I feel incomplete with or preoccupied by?

2. If someone were trying to get my attention, who might it be? What is the message?

3. If I were also in another location right now, where would I be?

4. If I were also in another time period right now, when would it be?

5. If I were also performing another task right now, what would it be?

6. If I were also visiting another dimension right now to retrieve information, which level would it be? What would I be trying to discover or understand?

7. If I were also visiting other people right now, who would they be? What is the purpose of our exchange?

November 9

Spirit that I love
Spirit that loves me
Spirit I dwell within
Spirit that dwells within me
Let us be One
Let us be One
Let us be One
And may the love I carry
Ever in my heart
Be made manifest perfectly
in all the creations of the world
Amen.

Child of God who We love
Child of God who loves Us
Child of God We dwell within
Child of God who dwells within Us
Let Us be One
Let Us be One
Let Us be One
And may the Love We carry
Ever in our Souls
Be made manifest perfectly
in all the creations of Your life
So be it.

I am deeply quiet.

Today, practice entering the silence. Stop talking to yourself and listening to external stimuli for a while. What subtle voices, sounds, or songs are you aware of? Try writing a quiet prayer or song of praise.

I see the hidden lessons I'm working on in life.

Look below the surface of your daily experience for the lesson your soul is trying to teach you today.

You can often tell what your underlying lessons are by the sentences you hear yourself repeating in conversations. What are you complaining about? Jealous about? What points do you make? A few years ago, I heard myself saying ad nauseum, "People don't understand me. No one sees me." My issue was invisibility but, ironically, I couldn't see it! During that period I had a vivid dream.

I'm with a small group. I jump up in the air and show off by doing some complex flying maneuvers. I think I'm cool. Then I notice a South American shaman has arrived, and he's leaning casually against a wall, looking intently at me and communicating telepathically. He looks up in the air and from the upper reaches of the sky, appears a black dot. It becomes bigger and bigger and I see it is a man's fedora, tumbling down end over end. It comes straight at me and bonks me in the head. "See?" he says. Then he says he can dematerialize right in front of me. I watch as he first turns pale; his dark brown skin, hair, and eyes become white, blond, blue, then he begins to shrink evenly all around the perimeter of his body. Soon he is six inches smaller all over and translucent. Then he fills in again and comes back, then fades out and looks like an old man. "See?" he says again.

Days later, I shared the dream with a friend who had recently worked with a real Peruvian shaman. He said, "The hat is an interesting symbol. Our shaman used his hat as a power object; he wore it constantly, gestured with it, and used it to demonstrate points in his lectures. He didn't seem complete without it. I noticed it so much during our training that I actually looked up the hat as a symbol in a book I have. One of the meanings of hat is 'the container of a body of knowledge.' So in your dream, the shaman was basically giving you the Zen stick! 'Wake up and remember!'" "But what about the dematerializing?" I asked. My friend said, "You've been talking a lot about invisibility lately. Have you ever considered that there's a positive side to being invisible? Maybe, like the shaman, you are supposed to remember that you're in control of your visibility and how you appear to others. Maybe you've *wanted* to be invisible—maybe it's suited your purpose." I felt like I'd just been bonked in the head again. See?

November 11

Andrea is a gentle spirit and a talented painter and designer. She is the only child of self-centered parents who never acknowledged her creativity. Every time she did something original, they told her *she* was the one who was selfish. She finally left her home in Europe and came to the United States, where she found success and artistic freedom, but also married a man who didn't acknowledge her. Andrea was a magnet for people who wanted to absorb some of her magical talent and generosity, but who turned on her and put her down after they got what they wanted. For years her parents had been pleading with her to come home, accusing her of abandoning them. Then her father got sick and it seemed he might die. She went back to visit and help take care of him, but he didn't die. In fact, he actually seemed quite strong.

Now the desperate pleas were more intense. "You *must* come and care for your father. Bring the family so they can say good-bye." Andrea knew that when she got to Europe her parents would divide her husband and children against her and have them pressure her to stay. We talked about dealing with victimization. Her parents were victims and had made her into one, treating her statements of need like excuses. If she were going to break the pattern, she'd have to hold her ground and say clearly what worked for her and what didn't. She decided to go, take the family, and practice compassion and firmness.

We formulated a couple of key personal needs that she felt must be upheld at all costs. First, she wanted her husband and children to back her up, no questions asked. Second, she needed to continue the momentum of her life in the States. Making these two declarative statements was frightening to her. "What will I say when they say I'm an ungrateful, bad daughter?" she asked. I said, "You don't need to justify anything, just repeat your statement about what works for you." "But how will I explain that I don't want to take care of them?" I repeated, "You don't need to make excuses; you have a right to have your own life." She repeated it hollowly like a mantra, talking herself into it. No excuses was a wildly foreign concept, but Andrea said she'd try. I ended our conversation with this quote from Elbert Hubbard: "Never explain—your friends don't need it and your enemies won't believe you anyway."

I notice the excuses I make.

Notice your excuses or justifications today. They can show you when you need to stand up for yourself by expressing your truth compassionately.

I notice when I'm speaking words that belong to someone else.

How many of your opinions are really yours? Have you internalized someone else's values? Clear yourself of other people's ideas and emotions today.

Marcus, who practices "dowsing therapy," can measure subtle shifts in a person's energy with a sensitive device called a recording wire. With this method, he can tell if what you say comes from your conscious mind alone, from subconscious fear, or from a place of integration and truth. Lately he has noticed a new phenomenon. Many of the things his clients were saying and taking as gospel just weren't ringing true, so he began to use his recording wire while they were speaking.

Sophie, a therapist, said with a bit of defensiveness, "I am *always* ethical when it comes to my clients. I maintain clear boundaries and never project sexual energy onto them." Marcus started his device spinning. "Are these Sophie's thoughts?" he asked aloud. He got a reading from his wire as it spun left or right. "No, these are not Sophie's thoughts. Whose ideas are these? Her mother's? No. Her father's? Yes!" Then he said, "It's really your father who's worried about you maintaining your boundaries and not being too sexual—what was your relationship with him like?" He discovered that Sophie's father was very puritanical. She had internalized his beliefs so deeply that she thought they were her own. Actually, Sophie had no confusion at all about giving people false impressions; she trusted her appropriateness.

On another occasion, Marcus heard the tinny ring of a statement a woman made about her brother's family being her "real" family. "Are these Ginny's thoughts? No they're not. Whose are they? Ginny's mother's? No. Her father's? No. Her brother's? Yes! How do these thoughts belong to Ginny's brother?" Then he asked a long series of questions. Eventually an interesting explanation surfaced. It seems Ginny's brother was afraid of not getting enough attention, not fitting in, and of being abandoned early in his childhood. He wanted to feel that he belonged. Ginny, as the sensitive older sister, didn't want him to feel scared, so she internalized his idea and acted like *she* belonged with *him*. This took the pressure off him, yet she had lived with a false idea and a strange dependency for many years. He, on the other hand, had been completely at peace!

November 13

Helene leads spiritual and psychological residential retreats in exotic places, from Mt. Shasta to Sedona to Mexico. She takes a small group of people for a week, and they work with meditation, psychological processing, exercise and movement, and ritual. Usually the groups are composed of people from her private counseling practice. On one occasion, a woman Helene didn't know called at the last minute and insisted that she be able to attend. She seemed alternatingly bossy, then needy, firm, then confused and lost. In spite of a strong anxiety signal in the pit of her stomach, Helene acquiesced and allowed her to participate.

When the group arrived at their hacienda in Mexico, the woman began a long series of complaints. She was uncomfortable getting up so early, didn't like the food, didn't understand the meditations, her foot hurt so she couldn't walk with the others, and it was too hot to exercise. She picked a fight with one of the other participants and argued with every point Helene made in the seminars. She worked herself into a snit. Within a few days, she decided to leave early, to everyone's relief. Helene didn't understand why the woman had wanted to come. A month later, she received a phone call from the woman, demanding her money back. Helene had never had anyone dissatisfied with one of her retreats before and didn't know what to do.

She quieted herself and let the feelings of guilt disperse. Then she looked at the inner dynamics of the situation. Why had she attracted such a strong victim? She realized she had had a clear signal from her body but had glossed over it. Her inability to set clear boundaries and her need to be nice had subjected not only her but all the other participants to much needless drama. Then she saw that the woman was taking and controlling but not giving. The retreats were a cocreated experience, an even exchange. Much had been given to the woman, but she had been unwilling to participate. She hadn't even given people the benefit of the doubt. Therefore Helene decided she could not in good conscience give all the money back. She decided this was a time for her to be clear about her parameters, so she called the woman and offered to return one-third of the money. From that point on, Helene always listened to her body.

I pay attention to my truth signals.

Notice how you decide "yes" today. Are you deciding from your body or from "shoulds"?

My heart is a healing force.

Notice when you encounter dark thoughts today, or give power to negativity. Then, simply bring those ideas into your heart. Let the heart's understanding transmute the heaviness and create compassion where there was fear.

David, a talented spiritual healer, just returned from a year working in Germany. He says he's always been able to open his body to the shadow side of people's personalities and let his own energy field transmute some of their pain and darkness without any negative effects to himself. In Germany, however, when he opened to the shadow side, he encountered what he called a "cultural" shadow. "It whomped me!" he exclaimed. "It was a collective subconscious belief in the need to control reality, and it forced me to rethink how healing works. Yet, in spite of it, the German people were clear and serious about healing. They came in saying, 'I am going to heal.' And they'd do the work that was required—so different from many Americans, who just want to be fixed, and quickly!

"In the middle of my work, I took some time and went to India. What was most helpful to me was meeting a group of Tibetan lamas. They were totally joyful and dedicated to compassion. I myself have often protested about the level of pain and suffering on earth, and I've wanted to leave and not have to be here. But the Tibetans told me that their holy men had traveled through the six realms, and the most valuable thing in all the realms was being alive, in a body, in the physical plane. They said, 'This is where you can become free.' So they dedicate every ounce of themselves, all their consciousness, to becoming compassionate.

"If a Tibetan lama gets cancer, for example, he doesn't try to get rid of it. Instead he welcomes it and brings it into the consciousness of his 'heart of compassion.' And not only does he bring his own cancer into the heart of compassion, he invites in all the cancers in all the sentient beings of the world. He knows that the heart eats and transmutes pain and suffering. Some Tibetans even meditate in cemeteries. A Westerner would say, 'Isn't this too overwhelming? How can you be empathic if you're going to suck in all this pain as a result?' The Tibetan would respond, 'You don't know very much about compassion!'" David says he has a new understanding of the power of love to transmute suffering. He hasn't been "whomped" since.

November 15

I had a mid-afternoon snack at a Mexican restaurant the other day, and, for the most part, the waitress and I had the whole place to ourselves. She walked back and forth, doing her waitress tasks and checking on me now and then, while I wrote in my journal. Suddenly I had an urge to ask her about her intuition. "Excuse, me," I began, "but could I ask you a personal question?" She was game. "I'm writing a book, and I was wondering if you've ever had any unusual experiences with your intuition that convinced you there was more to life?" Her eyes widened for a split second, then she blithely said, "Sure. I have dreams that come true. Like, I'll dream something and, in about six months, it happens. I just had one this week that my car was going to be stolen, that I was going to walk out of work and it would be gone. So now I lock up real good, and I take my CD player out and put it in the trunk."

"How do you know if it's one of *those* kinds of dreams?" I asked.

"Well, they just feel *real*. I just know. And they always wake me up between two and four A.M. I had one about five months ago, about me and my mom fighting really bad, and now it's starting to happen. My real life feels just like my dream now."

"So how does this make you feel?" I asked.

"It kind of scares me. It's freaky, 'cause how could I know these things so far ahead?"

"Well, you know, it's really the most natural thing in the world," I said. "In my work, I find that it's actually normal to know about the future, especially if it's going to affect you in some dramatic way. In fact, it's probably harder to pretend you don't know!"

"Yeah," she quipped, "come back in six months and see if I'm still driving!"

My body knows the truth.

Notice when you sense truth/safety or lying/danger today. We often sense lies easily because we know our warning signals well. Truth is sometimes less obvious, but it evokes an equally powerful body response.

Objects have consciousness, too.

Feel the presence and awareness in inanimate objects today. When you tune in and sense extremely subtle kinds of consciousness, you stretch your intuitive capacity.

It was the day after a week of heavy rain. The sun had come out and the air was sparkling and brisk. I decided to put on rubber boots and hike through the redwoods on Mt. Tamalpais near my home. The trails were sopping and muddy, and at mid-morning I still had them mostly to myself. The vibrant green mosses were standing up at attention—growing almost visibly—and tree trunks were steaming as the sun warmed them. I smelled mushrooms, rotten logs, bay laurel, and eucalyptus. And then, as I rounded a bend on the trail, I saw something that stopped me dead—three large redwoods had fallen during the storm. There was a strange stillness in this area of the woods, as though someone had literally died, and I knew it was the trees. Even the birds seemed quiet. I stood and meditated. Here in the middle of a forest, where no one might ever know, three trees gave up their lives, and it seemed to me that their act was one that may have saved the lives of potential earthquake victims in South America, or prevented a jet plane from crashing, or helped premature babies all over the world survive difficult births. The trees had been growing in a perfect triangle and now they lay like arrows, sending their love out to the world. I sobbed. And I thanked them for the gift they gave.

three noble redwoods
in divine triangle
fell all at once
in rain-soaked forest,
gave up their grip
on this watery earth
crashing away from center
and far away from those
they saved,
now in silent sacrifice
they lie, cradled
in the arms of their friends,
pointing out

A client in Japan had brought her autistic teenage son with her to her session. She, her son, the interpreter, and I squeezed tightly into my tiny hotel room. The boy sat cross-legged on my bed, rocking back and forth, and occasionally groaned loudly. I went into a deep intuitive state in spite of the commotion, and, as I began to tune in to the mother, her son became agitated, got up, and stood in front of the mirror. He made even louder sounds and periodically clapped sharply. I could see that the mother was emotionally tied to the boy in a way that seemed like a servant to a master. She had absolutely no freedom. Even the small amount of attention I was giving her seemed threatening to her son, whose actions became increasingly dramatic and demanding. Finally, I opened my eyes and watched him. I knew very little about autism, and perhaps it was good that I had no previous biases. I simply perceived him intuitively.

He was staring at himself in the mirror, then zooming forward until his nose hit the glass, then backing away abruptly, staring, then clapping ceremonially and making a kind of karate yell. He seemed content to do that, so I went back into my altered state. Again having difficulty concentrating on the mother, I found myself receiving information about the boy; it was as if I were looking out through his eyes. As he stared into the mirror, I could sense he had the impression that it was an opening. He'd begin to go through the "doorway," only to realize it was solid as his nose hit the wall. The shock of it disoriented him severely, and he got very frustrated.

In his confused state, the boy's energy field was like an open door for discarnate entities. I could sense them hovering around him like mosquitoes, crowding into his space to voyeuristically experience something of the emotional and physical realms. When he realized he was being crowded, he'd clap and yell, which would disperse the cloud of beings temporarily. Then he'd forget what had just happened and repeat it all again. Because he had little sense of personal self, he had no real boundaries either, and was constantly open to psychic disturbance. Since observing the boy and his mother, I've tried to look below surface explanations for the more subtle spiritual and energy dynamics in various mental and behavioral disorders. There is always a good reason for what seems chaotic.

My shadow self is rich and full of knowledge.

Be aware of shadows today, of what is barely seen or on the edge of memory. Can you sense what's behind you? Our dark side and the things we avoid because they lack clarity contain amazing amounts of helpful information.

**What I say
shows who I
am.**

*Listen fully
to what you say
today. How often
do you say yes,
how often no?
Are you speaking
from soul or fear?*

Saying yes and no to people and possibilities can come from fear or it can be a way to permit your soul optimal expression. Many spiritual seekers have at some point tried to be positive and nonjudgmental by saying yes to everything. Someone told me once that God has only one word—*yes!* Trying out more yeses can be beneficial as a practice—for a little while. Eventually, we learn to stay focused on what's authentic and appropriate for us in each moment, knowing that we can't do and like and permit everything, all the time. Perhaps God-in-the-body has three words: *yes* and *not now!*

A friend who is blossoming into a successful writer has been saying yes to just about anything that comes along, and her career has developed in a very meandering way—this talk leading to that person, those contacts maturing into this offer, that book leading to this seminar. She says she has moved "like a leaf on water." As she entered the rapids of being self-published, then was picked up by a minor publisher, then became an in-demand speaker, her "leaf" state became less fun. She says, "After almost three years of promoting, touring, and gaining recognition, I was being buffeted along at greater and greater speeds, away from the center of my heart. Finally, I said no. No, I won't tour anymore. No, I won't plan for the future. No, I don't care what happens. I'm taking time off and letting the whole thing, and all its worked-for and slaved-over momentum, fade away. It was terrifying. I thought the entire spirit world would gather itself together to smack me upside the head for being unappreciative and uncooperative!

"Then, not twelve hours after my tantrum, I got a call from a premier publisher in the field I really want to be in. But the books I'd written branded me as something else. I was in the terrible position of having to say that I wasn't available to do anything like the books I'd become known for. Before I could explain, however, the publisher asked what my dream project would be. I told her, she loved it, and we're going ahead with it right away. I realized that my *no* was my soul telling me that the path I was on didn't have enough heart. The minute I could feel that my dream project might happen, the real yes popped out of me unequivocably. Ah, the healing power of tantrums!"

November 19

Michael was meditating one evening and saw a quick flash of himself sitting there meditating. In that fraction of a second, he could see a large, orange-yellow flame burning brightly up from his lower abdomen through his torso, ending a foot above his head. The scene was peaceful, and, after a few short moments, the image dissolved. No other thoughts accompanied the vision. He finished his meditation and retired for the night.

"The next morning," he says, "I arose and headed to work. As I entered the office, I passed a woman whose clothes looked dowdy and askew. My thought was, 'This person needs some help selecting her wardrobe!'

"Immediately, the image of me sitting in meditation from the night before came back into my mind's eye. This time, the flame was the size of a thimble. It was clear that the image had something to do with my judgment of the woman's superficial appearance. I said to myself, 'This person's clothing has absolutely nothing to do with her spiritual worth or who she really is.' With that, the flame shot back up and out the top of my head.

"As I sat at my desk, I couldn't help but realize the jaded lenses through which I habitually view others. No doubt, these are the same opaque filters I have also used to view myself." Michael said that from that day on he began to see others and himself differently, and much more deeply. He says, "There is no enlightenment without looking at our opinions and habitual patterns of thought."

I can relax my hold on my adamant beliefs.

Notice the times you hear yourself make a strong declarative statement today. You've probably invested extra energy in the idea because you're avoiding another possibility. What might that be?

I am aware of the power of my words.

Take inventory today of how you channel power through language. Do you wound or heal? Beautify or denigrate? Do you vitalize or flatten the experiences you describe? Words are catalytic, the building blocks of our reality.

We all know how words we use every day become pale. "I love you," the husband intones to his wife every time he finishes a phone conversation with her, mind already on his next task. "Amen," we drone at the end of saying grace, little realizing the original punctuating, manifesting power of that word. Language is something into which meaning has to be put as well as something from which meaning has to be drawn out. In talking about spirituality and intuition, it's easy to use words that have either faded from overuse or sound like jargon. Yet some of the most commonly used words have amazingly potent origins. *Courage* comes from the word for heart, *essence* means being, *enthusiasm* means "to be full of God." So when I say the word *spirit*, I think "breath of life." I think "Why did the ancient people link spirit, breath, life, and the divine?" I try to feel the underlying experience that generated the original name.

I'm reminded of the words invented by Koko the gorilla, *baby drink* for milk, for example. Similarly, I make up *direct knowing*, my gorilla name for intuition.

Where a clearly defined universal vocabulary doesn't exist, why not use a variety of parallel terms to describe a concept? Each word has a slightly different nuance, and, by grouping and overlapping them, we may become saturated by the synthesis and catapulted into a deeper understanding. We are forced to integrate. Does *satori* equate with *nirvana*? Is *karma* the same as a *psychological block*? Is a *plane* the same as a *planet*, a *level*, a *dimension*, a *realm*, a *body*? In Japan, there is no word for love. Instead, they focus on the concept of *harmony*. Describing the *fourth-dimensional reality*, or the *spiritual experience*, or the *intuitive process*, or the *diamond light*, or the *Pure Land* is like the blindfolded men describing the elephant. It comes down to an exercise in poetic artistry. No words can ever match or reveal the intensity and clarity of the universal, divine world. We can only swirl and spiral around it, worshipping it with our little sounds.

November 21

Every day we look for signposts to help us gain our bearings. There are many voices calling out directions; some are loud, some silent. We must learn to listen in new ways. There are answers seeking to be asked for and questions seeking to be heard. If we pay close attention, there is quality guidance everywhere, from a casual conversation over lunch, to the inspiring words of great spiritual leaders, to country-and-western song lyrics. The divine wisdom speaks to us in every cloud, every tree, every ant carrying a crumb, every face we see on the street. Yet each of us looks at the cloud and sees a different shape. One person interprets a hawk as an omen of good fortune, another sees it as a warning. How do we make sense of this glut of meaning?

We each live by an individualized system of personal truth, and revelation is given accordingly. For each person, place, and moment in time, the divine says only one thing. All forms that occur in our momentary reality echo that one appropriate idea. The voice of Spirit speaks simply and gives only the piece of truth we need next. If I ask what the hawk means, what the cloud means, what the ant with the crumb has to say, what the stranger on the street corner is secretly telling me, they all give their version of the same truth, like instruments in an orchestra playing to the same conductor. We may each hear a different message, but every clearly perceived message brings us closer to each other and to a universal understanding.

We hear the One Voice in many ways. Whether it's our own words, the words of a friend, or the words of a discarnate entity, it is the One Voice. Whether the words sound Christian, Hindu, Jewish, Sufi, or Buddhist, it is the One Voice. Whether it comes as a question or an answer, it's all part of the divine wisdom teaching us through revelation. The Voice speaking to me speaks to part of you, and what awakens you awakens me in some parallel way. The still Voice we hear eventually reveals that speaker and listener are the same, that there is no That or Them—only This, We, and Us.

The unknown is speaking to me.

Notice messages in song lyrics, random phrases, and license plates today.

I really do know!

Let's not feign ignorance. Today, notice when you say, "I don't know" or "I don't know why I . . ." Stop and reverse the comment by saying, "What I do know about this is . . ." You always know something about everything.

One of the writing exercises in my "Writing Direct from Intuition" workshop is to complete the sentence "I don't know . . ." in as many different ways as possible. Then concerning each item write: "What I already know about this is . . ." Here are some of the results:

I don't know why I'm drawn to powerful people.

What I already know about this is that powerful people are courageous in some way; they express themselves without apology. They know how to manifest goals, be seen, be helped, release energy—and these are things I'm working on in myself.

I don't know whether I'm egotistical.

What I already know about this is that I can just be true to myself and I won't be egotistical. If I'm passionate, the passion does a lot of the work of getting things recognized, and I don't have to worry so much.

I don't know why I can't find a good relationship.

What I already know about this is that I have thought a man could interfere with my freedom to be myself, and I also know that's a lie. I know I am learning to recognize a new kind of man who I can be comfortable with, and that when I'm ready, someone will come.

I don't know where I go at night.

What I already know about that is that, in my dreams, I go to places where large groups meet at gatherings and conferences and I visit people, some of whom I haven't met in my waking life. I know I go to foreign countries and into hospitals to help people or get operations on parts of myself.

November 23

Your body will give you reliable insight about what is healthy and unhealthy for you, either through a truth or anxiety signal in the moment or through dreams. When you experience a contraction of thought, emotion, or physical energy, take it as a sign that whatever you're considering may not be in your best interests. An expansion, on the other hand, probably indicates something beneficial. Dr. Marcia Emery is a psychologist, a physician's daughter, and the author of *The Intuitive Healer: Accessing Your Inner Physician*. Many years ago, she had a dream in which a doctor was telling her she had cancer, but she clearly didn't believe him. She called him a quack and walked out. Months later, she noticed a growth on her nose and went to another doctor, who took a biopsy. He insisted she prepare herself for immediate cancer treatment. Remembering her dream, she went for a second opinion and discovered that the first doctor's suspicions were false! Marcia has learned to trust the inner voice she calls the "inner physician" and to tune out the distracting "cocktail party" voices of our societal conditioning.

According to Marcia, it is through dreams and symbolic imagery, even daydreaming, that we tap into the intuitive knowledge that we each carry within for our own healing. She reports the example of an obstetrician who nodded off during a meditation and received vital health information about one of her pregnant patients. She dreamed that the expectant mother could no longer write from left to right but instead wrote right to left. In her dream, a dream therapist told the doctor that it would be dangerous for her patient to write forward. Amazingly, the patient's grandfather had the same dream.

Upon waking, the doctor realized that the dream related to a breech birth. She planned to turn the baby for a normal delivery but discussed this first with her patient and opted for the more difficult breech delivery, which turned out to be the right medical decision.

I am aware of my anxiety signals.

Notice how you decide "no" today.

I trust and listen to my conscience.

Make a conscience list of things your heart wants to do, and start acting on the items.

I want to look up my old friends from college and drop them a note. **I'm grateful to my neighbor for helping me water my garden while I was on vacation—I think I'll bake her a cake.** My body would like to walk down by the water at sunset. *I want to send a thank-you note to my secretary for the extra time she put in on the big project.* I'm going to take my friend Kay to lunch, just because she's always there for me when I need someone. **I need to apologize for a thoughtless remark I made to my brother—I let it slide by and felt badly about it.** I'm going to do the extra chore that will save my spouse some worry. *I need to pay Lisa back for those three dollars she lent me for dinner last week.* I want to send birthday cards to friends this year. **I want to rerecord my answering machine message so my voice sounds friendlier.**

You probably have thoughts like this every day, but how often do you do something about them? You might keep a list by your phone and jot down conscience list ideas whenever you get them. Then make a point to act on one per day. Acting from your heart will bring you into the present moment and help you develop compassion and mindfulness. It is also one of the easiest ways to feel good about yourself. Near the end of the movie *Always*, Richard Dreyfuss's character, who has died and become a spiritual guide, says of being on the other side, "I know now that the love we hold back is the only pain that follows us here."

November 25

Neil spoke idealistically, even romantically, about spirituality and God. He was fascinated with practices and ceremonies that would help him merge into spiritual awareness. On the surface, his devotion seemed admirable, but underneath lurked an interesting pattern. Neil actually wanted to be saved and taken care of by "Spirit"; he wanted an experience to come to him from outside that he didn't feel within.

In his personal life, Neil was also obsessive about romantic love. He talked about how much he loved and appreciated women, how they were like goddesses. He gave his girlfriend an inordinate amount of attention, anticipating her needs, giving her thoughtful gifts, and telling her constantly how much he loved her and how beautiful she was. If she didn't call to let him know she'd be late, or if she wanted to spend time with other friends, he worried he was being rejected. Neil confessed that his ideal was to totally merge with a woman. He felt that if he could bond entirely with a woman, he'd feel complete and connected.

Neil had been largely ignored and rejected by his parents, especially by his mother, as a young boy and never felt the safety of reliable and consistent nurturing. As most children do, he had unconsciously projected his parents' patterns onto God and had assumed that God was distant and didn't love him and that he would never get the sustenance he needed. He couldn't relax and feel safe and had become needy as a result—but in a way that seemed noble to him. What's ironic in situations like Neil's is that, though he professed undying devotion to God and women, he was angry at them underneath for not being there for him. All his energy went into getting, then keeping, external sources of love. It's tricky to see through the illusion sometimes, but there is truth in the Christian adage, "Seek ye first the kingdom within, and all else will be added." It is difficult to know God when we project the divine into the outer world and objectify it in form. The divine is a personal experience that is inherent in our nature and cannot even be given by a doting mother. It is ours to recognize, eventually, on our own. It's what we already have.

I use what I have.

Be content with what you have today. You've already been given the love, talent, tools, and opportunities to do what you want to do, feel the way you want to feel, and be who you want to be.

357

My creativity and intuition open when I become round and curvy.

Take time today to be soft and surrendered. Let your thoughts and energy flow freely and wander. There's no need to pin yourself down with definitions.

Wanda is young, soft, round, and big. Big body, big heart. She radiates warmth and generosity, yet her eyes seem sunken and gray around the edges, as if she's lost and can't quite tell who she is. She is worried about her weight. "I need to control myself but I can't." Then she says, "I like to help people, and I wonder if I have any healing ability, because people always seem to feel better after they've been with me." Wanda, in her feminine body and vulnerability, has a quality I sense will occur in more of us in the future.

At first glance, it seems Wanda is naive, even nondiscriminating. In truth, she needs a personal identity much less than the rest of us, but, because it's such an odd thought to be egoless, she has tried to fit in with prevailing beliefs by identifying herself somehow. Am I a healer? An artist? A minister? Should I work with suicide prevention? The homeless? Abused women? Do I look OK?" She's in a kind of partnership with the essential, nonphysical world and has a clear perception of the collective consciousness. She is aware when she receives impressions, instructions, urges, guidance, and healing energy from beyond. She is also good at relaying those resources through herself, giving freely to others and the world. She doesn't need to stop that flow, name it, or identify with it. She is an opening through which riches pour. Who is she? On any given day, she is what is flowing through her. Her identity is in the joy she enters into as this collaborative motion proceeds. And yet this kind of freedom is so foreign as to be nearly unrecognizable.

The missing piece for Wanda is that her centering device is not an ego but her expansive, sensitive body. If she can let it regulate itself and love it and live in its responsiveness, that feeling will become her identity. Then, if she embraces her role in her partnership with the invisible forces, she'll see that her body shapes the unending flow of divine force in specific ways that are fun for her and beneficial and influential for others. As she dives into the enjoyment of it, her eyes will light up, and she won't feel like a misfit but will become a teacher and role model instead.

November 27

I am a process and my life is not separate from me. Life is no longer an unordered array of disjointed experiences; it is becoming a moving continuum of consciously created revelations. My life and I are a single unified experience, punctuated only by varying focuses of attention. Perceptions fit into an ever-expanding puzzle now, constantly synthesizing and creating new wholes within wholes. There is nowhere to go, no arrival point on this path— only unceasing oscillation and the illusion of stillness as I become one with the flowing. Frustrations give way to satisfactions, satisfactions to new curiosities—and everything folds over and into itself to be known anew. The process is exciting, incredibly simple yet astoundingly complex. There are moments of pure understanding and times I am overwhelmed by the sheer volume of input wanting to be known in a conscious way.

I notice that my perception varies if I move my body differently. For instance, if I sit in the garden and tune myself to flowers, dragonflies, and fresh dirt, the writing in my journal takes on a minimalist, Zen quality. If I put on rock and roll music and leap around the living room, then write, the words come out with a staccato rhythm, the attitude raucous and more audacious. If I walk faster, I feel perkier, more in my head and eyes, alert like a hawk. If I walk slower, I merge more with what's around me and feel alert through a telepathic communion that comes mysteriously through my ears and skin. If I'm sedentary too long, thoughts easily turn morbid and sad. If I am overbooked with too many appointments, thoughts can move toward hostility, anxiety, and desperation. If my feelings are cold and hard, my body contracts and gets sluggish. When I entertain warm feelings and open my heart, my body wants to reach out, move, travel, dance. My body, emotions, and logical mind are simply viewpoints along a continuous spectrum of awareness, and they affect each other intimately, immediately. They are fed by a much greater, higher sensibility and, in turn, feed this world back to heaven.

My awareness shifts with my speed.

Walk faster or slower than you normally do today. When you shift your pace, notice that you may think different kinds of thoughts and feel different emotions.

I say what I mean.

Listen and feel for the unspoken words behind the spoken words you hear coming from yourself today, and name the discrepancies. Practice speaking with absolute intention, using only the words you can "get behind."

Mitch is a young entrepreneur who sold his successful business and took a few years off to develop himself spiritually. He was ready to be productive again, and, though he sensed something big was about to happen, he felt blocked. When we spoke, I noticed a few phrases that innocently slipped out of his mouth and would have dropped into the abyss, but I grabbed them and fed them back to him. "I heard you say you feel like you've walked up to a door but aren't opening it," I said. "What's on the other side of the door, and why aren't you opening it?"

"What's on the other side is this big future I think is coming. In it I'm getting a lot of recognition and money and doing something at a national level." "That sounds good," I said, "so why aren't you stepping through?" "I guess I'm reluctant, because I fear that people will think I'm just selfish and materialistic." This was important— Mitch didn't quite understand that his new venture would be created from his new spiritual values, not his old will-based ones, and would be based on enthusiasm, respect, flow, and sharing. And that people would therefore have a positive response.

Several minutes later, he described how he had undertaken a program of transforming himself physically and had been intensively working with a personal trainer in carefully designed twelve-week periods. He recently looked at himself in the mirror and said, "I'm almost there." I fed this back to him too, because I sensed he was waiting to be perfect before he'd allow himself to have the life he wanted. I said, "It sounds like you're an expert at using 'male energy,' at being focused and disciplined and achieving your goals. But perhaps you are learning to use your 'feminine energy' now, so that, when you move into your next creative venture, you'll be truly balanced. And the feminine awareness would have a totally different take looking at your body in the mirror. It would say, 'What a great, responsive body! Look how sensitive it is and how much pleasure it gives me right now! I love this body and I love to move it.'" It was then that Mitch realized he wasn't letting himself be fully present and that his great life actually *was* now. With that, he stepped through the door.

November 29

I was visiting some friends who have a horse ranch. While I was there, a phone call came from a couple on the other side of the valley—their five-year-old gelding had come down with colic and died early that morning. My friend John acted as the "horse coroner" for the valley and said he'd be right over. I asked if I could come along and help. I'd had horses and lived on a farm growing up but had never seen a dead horse. So we got the truck with its winch and headed out.

The dead horse was in an awkward position—he had to be pulled across the paddock where he'd fallen against a fence, then around a wall, through a narrow stall and barn, and into the truck. The men were all business and physics, figuring out the best angles and places to tie the body for the best traction. The wife and I walked to the horse's head. She acted tough and matter of fact, explaining how he got the colic and what happened in the horse's intestines to kill him. I stroked his head and looked at his open eyes—the life had just barely left him, and a powerful stillness was around his body. She went on, "Yeah, he was actually pretty cantankerous, used to bite . . ." After much hauling, pushing, heaving, and maneuvering, we got the gelding to the truck, and, just as he was about to be winched up the ramp, the woman ran into the tack room and came back with a pair of scissors. She bent down and snipped off a hunk of his mane, then looked nervously at me. "Something to remember him by," she said, still trying to be tough, but I saw she was near tears. Now I knew why I'd come. I stepped closer and smiled at her, touched her arm. "John will be really good to him from here on, you know," I said. She sniffled. "Yes," she whispered.

On the drive home, John said he'd seen many touching scenes like this and many that had made him cry. Once he had waited for forty minutes as a woman knelt next to her horse, crying, talking to it, saying good-bye. On another occasion, when he arrived, the fallen horse was surrounded by a circle of the family's children. When he came closer, he saw the horse was covered entirely in rose petals. The children were performing their own special ceremony of blessing and release.

I am empathic.

Pretend you're inside the body of the people you meet today, and feel the world through their sensibility. Empathy is a powerful way to expand your knowledge base and understand just how many realities are possible.

November 30

We are all actors in a grand stage play, and I chose the cast.

Today, notice what roles other people play in teaching you about yourself and life.

Curt was the manager of a health club that catered to affluent, conservative families. The club was unusual in that it encouraged a policy of emotional openness and forthright sharing. Many of the staff members thought this was odd, even a bit threatening. Though they went gamely along, Curt often found himself moderating misunderstandings brought about when the sharing caused emotional wounding. He would never have guessed that he'd be forced to examine his own psychological limits and belief systems when he took the job, but after several years he had to admit he'd learned a lot and grown. Each troubled staff member had served as a mirror for his own hidden issues. Now he saw the power of emotions to either motivate or sabotage a team's effectiveness. The only problem was that the staff had become so involved in each other's life processes, there was a constant stress level just below the surface. It was hard to leave work at the door at the end of the day. Curt realized he'd received what he could from the situation and decided to move on.

The next job Curt found was managing a club in a big city. The new urban culture was racially diverse and emotionally colorful. Here the drama was not a tense undercurrent but a playful part of each day. Curt could introduce new programs and the staff was enthusiastically behind him. Instead of being caught in the middle between people who felt misunderstood, he now saw that the people in his life acted as triggers to activate new aspects of his expressiveness. Curt learned new rhythms and ways to communicate and discovered a talent for humor and performing. He was learning to see himself as creative and spontaneous. When he looked back over the past few years, he felt like he'd been in a dream, that his daily reality had had a surrealistic quality. Yet he was amazed. Some part of him had engineered a highly concentrated and rapid period of emotional growth, then used his newfound ability to feel more fully to open him to even greater varieties of human interaction and the potential for endless innovation and enjoyment. He knew the people in both situations were the real gift—they unwittingly drew forth the qualities from him that he needed.

December

December 1

Suzie Daggett, now a business coach and public speaker, was training to become a flight attendant in Kansas City when she was twenty-two. She was having a grand adventure on her own and far from her southern California roots. One evening she and her roommate went to a local bar for some socializing. She says, "As I rounded the corner to enter the bar, I looked up, and for a millisecond I saw a waiter standing above the crowd serving beer. In that instant, my inner voice said, quite clearly, 'Oh, there he is, the man I am going to marry!' I had no idea that I would find my husband in a bar in Kansas City. I had always imagined I would marry a tall, blue-eyed California boy from a Catholic family. Instead I was looking at a brown-eyed Kansas boy from a Baptist family!

"I sat in his section all night and even wrote a check with all my vital information on it, so he could address me by my name. It had no impact on him. At one A.M., I was still there, and the band was packing up. Finally, the waiter looked over at me casually and asked, 'Would you like to go to breakfast?' It didn't take long after that for his knowing to catch up with mine. We were engaged not long after our initial meeting and married within three months. We've remained very compatible, growing together spiritually, emotionally, and mentally for thirty years." Suzie now includes intuition as an important component of her coaching and teaching, based largely on her experience of synchronicity and trusting her own instinct, or what she calls "instant knowing."

I trust my gut instinct.

Pay attention to your visceral urges today— how you act based on your sense of safety and danger, attraction and repulsion. Your body knows what's real and true long before your mind does.

December 2

My communications are cohesive.

Align your words, intentions, feelings, and pictures when you communicate today. Misunderstandings occur when one or more of these are out of alignment. When your words describe the telepathic pictures in your mind, there will be immediate rapport.

My niece Valerie has always been on the go. She started walking early, especially into uncharted territory. She was just toddling, still hauling herself up via a wall, chair, or someone's pantlegs, then planting her steps tentatively, when one morning I heard her screaming. I ran over and saw her swaying back and forth on wobbly legs, standing at the top of the stairs down to the basement. Tears were running down her cheeks as she sucked on one fat little finger. There was an intense look in her eyes—was it fear? Had she tried to go down the steps and realized she might fall?

I quieted myself and let my body tune in to her little body. I could immediately feel that she wasn't in the least bit scared—she was frustrated. Instead of saying, "That's OK. Stop crying now," I said, "Oh, are you frustrated because you can't get down the steps by yourself?" She immediately stopped crying and her eyes widened a bit. The finger came out of the mouth. "Do you want me to hold your hand and help you go down?" I continued. She turned to face me. I took her hand and we worked our way down, one big step at a time. I realized that she had a perfectly functioning brain inside her toddler's body and was thinking quite clearly. She just couldn't get her desires into ideas into words. And she couldn't get this tiny little body to do what she wanted it to do! From then on, I noticed that whenever I took the time to feel what was going on under the surface in her and to state it out loud, Valerie relaxed and released her frustration. Now I realize it's the same with everyone, no matter how old we are.

December 3

When I work in other cities counseling a river of people, many insights come because I meet people with whom I would not normally be close, and my usual capacity is pushed beyond its comfort zone. On one such trip to the Midwest, following on the heels of another long trip to Japan, I became uncomfortably aware of my own voice giving people insight. As it spoke, I wondered, "Who am I to do this? Where are all these words coming from?" There was a strange dissociation with my ego—I could barely stand to be with myself and the known rhythms of my mind, speech, and body. As this occurred, my throat tightened and my voice began to give out.

And yet, from my slightly disembodied viewpoint, I could see that each person, each new experience of a human life, was a great gift. I wrote, "All the people I meet are my past or future selves—the ones who don't feel recognized, who don't feel motivated though they are overflowing with talent, the ones who rely on illness to provide temporary structure and help them learn about healing, the ones who feel like misfits and are hanging by a thread. The millionaire worrying about being judged, the sex- and drug-addicted warrior, the dance-hall girl with the heart of gold, the courageous housewife enduring abandonment—all these live in me, too, and help me be whole. Each is original and gorgeous."

Decompressing on the plane going home, I wrote, "I don't even want the stewardess to say anything personal to me! I don't want to know another detail that would make me journey into someone's reality, that would make me become her . . . as if my body might blow apart at the immensity of human and planetary diversity. I need to find the universal, calming vibration." When, days later, I finally digested the experience, I clearly saw that when we become too aware of a sense of self that seems false, it is because we are cut off from the holy spirit, the comforting, connecting, revealing, teaching function of the divine. My throat tightened and I felt overwhelmed because I perceived myself to be doing my work alone. I had forgotten that when we give, we are simultaneously receiving. One word cannot come out of my mouth unless an equal amount of sustenance is flowing in. So to give the cleanest, best service, we must bless ourselves as we bless others.

I receive as much as I give.

When you give today, whether it be your time, money, talent, or intellect, remember that you are receiving as you send. Nothing can come out of you unless something else is coming in, pushing it out. There is never a gap between inflow and outflow.

I live in my heart.

Be grateful to your heart for its incredible loving perspective. The heart can help you see death as life, tragedy as success. Often when reframed from the heart's view, the worst things in life become the best.

Allan, a computer company executive, was in his early sixties when his son died in an automobile accident. Trying to find peace of mind, he came to see me for a reading. He brought photographs and his son's wallet, which had been on him when he died. Allan radiated an odd combination of pain and vulnerability, along with the arrogant authority of someone who is used to giving orders. His mind was sharp, and he wanted answers! He asked if I could connect with his son and relay any communications the son might have. Though I am not a spiritualist medium, I can often feel the emotional/mental state of people who have just died. I told Allan that his son seemed amazingly peaceful, as though he'd succeeded at a complicated task and was pleased with himself.

Allan said, "But can you give me some kind of *proof* that there's life after death? Can't you ask my son to tell me something like 'I hid the key behind the book in the library'?" And he thrust the son's wallet into my hands. I was suddenly filled with an intense energy from the object. When it spread out more evenly, I had a better sense of the son and why he had died. I got an image of a broad, positive vision the son had held about life, and I sensed his death experience was a test he had set up for himself. Could he maintain his positive view, even when confronted suddenly with a frightening, disorienting experience, even while passing from one level of awareness to another? If he could maintain it through sudden death, the positive view would become a permanent part of his consciousness. This is what I sensed he had succeeded at doing, and I was very happy for him. His father, however, would not be consoled without *proof.*

I told Allan that even if there were a key behind the book, it wouldn't be proof of the continuity of existence—I could just be psychically pulling facts out of the air. The important lesson here was for Allan to shift from his head to his heart. Then, from that more open place, to intuit his son's presence and love. If he could feel the essence of his son's love and soul, they would be connected immediately. And he would know subjectively that spirit is eternal. Allan left disgruntled, still in his head, unable to release his need for physical proof. Meanwhile, his son waited patiently.

December 5

Renee has been studying many kinds of spirituality—
Christianity, Buddhism, esoteric metaphysics, transpersonal
psychology, the Kabbala. She's worked with many kinds of
teachers, from trance mediums to Native American
shamans, to Tibetan lamas, to Hindu gurus, to Philippine
psychic surgeons. One theme has prevailed throughout—
Renee has been looking for the answers outside herself. As
a result, she has sometimes been buffeted about by seductive teachers and strange explanations of psychological and
psychic phenomena. Presently she is involved in an in-
depth, year-long apprenticeship program with a mystic.
One tenet of the new teachings is that all problems must
be solved with God's love and compassion, not via personal
will or cleverness. She is beginning to recognize the hidden ego and distortion in certain spiritual teachers and cos-
mologies. She's been asking, "What is real?"

Last week, Renee had a powerful dream that helped
answer her question. In it, she is involved with a young
boy who can materialize objects of great beauty—things
that are components of her secret dreams. He leads her on
until she realizes he is a magician. She calls him on it. He
deflects her words, and she decides to use magic against
him in self-defense. She performs a few adroit maneuvers,
and he turns himself into a rabbit and flattens out to the
thickness of a pancake, then slips through a crack in the
floor. She thinks she must talk to his mother and tell her
what her son has done. The mother is an obese woman
who is talking to several other people and seems scattered.
No matter what Renee says to her, she makes an excuse
about her son, changes the subject, acts stupid, or loses her
train of thought. Suddenly it dawns on Renee—here is the
master magician! The mother is controlling everything!
When Renee can't penetrate her ruses, she thinks she must
use magic on the mother as well—that it's going to come
to a showdown. She gathers herself for the onslaught.
Then she wakes up, shaking. Within minutes, she is embarrassed that she has not thought to use compassion and
understanding instead of the magician's power play.

The dream made Renee think deeply. She learned to
recognize the signs of magic and the will orientation and
to see through seductions and distractions. Now she can
practice dealing with people in real life who employ subtle
forms of illusion and temptation.

**I bring the
core issues into
the open.**

*Ask the
courageous ques-
tions today.
Whether you're
alone or in a
group, cut to
the chase.
Try being the
facilitator of
greater truth
by being
more direct
than usual.*

**I can have a
positive impact
on others.**

*Touch others
physically,
emotionally, and
energetically
today.*

One of my clients has kept a diary for several years, in
which he writes from his heart to his young children. He
intends to give it to them when they are grown. He has
been kind enough to share some of his entries:

Dear Hannah and Ian,

Each day we create the lyric and story line of our lives
through choice. It is the most powerful ability we possess.
If a particular need or problem continues to circulate
through your life, know that you are experiencing a
moment that affords you the opportunity to choose again.
Choose again, as often as you need to, until the results
you obtain produce loving consequences for yourself and
others. The greatness of your life will be measured by
your loving acts toward others; there is no separation
between yourselves and others. When in doubt, pause and
consider the power you possess through choice.

Dear Hannah and Ian,

This past week, grandpapa's sister passed away. Since his
mom died in childbirth, she became the caregiver for the
whole family. She was a special spirit. Four days before she
died, I had picked up a fallen oak leaf and put it on my
dashboard in tribute to her. All the memories of family
reunions in her backyard come streaming back when I see
oak leaves falling, as her backyard was full of them. For
the next few days I kept the leaf on my dashboard not
consciously knowing she was in her last days. This is an
example of how the universe communicates with us via
the ineffable sacred spirit of life, without our being fully
aware of it. Never underestimate or overlook the subtle
communications from spirit.

Dear Ian and Hannah,

Sometimes you'll be in a quandary or confused about
something or someone. But many times things we classify
as a mystery find a way of working themselves out without us forcing them. It's important to be quiet and listen.
How do you listen? When do you listen? Who do you
listen to? How do you discern the correct choices? How
do you know when to listen and when to act? There must
be a balance between the moments you listen for direction and moments you act. Inactivity does not imply a
lack of resolution or progress.

All my love, Your Dad

December 7

In the pursuit of spiritual clarity, an entire practice can be made of meditating on the power of the word. In ancient times, priests knew the words of power, those that, when filled with intention and entered as literal experiences, could bring walls crashing down or materialize angels out of thin air. Merlin wove his spells with magical words. Entire armies have been filled with battle-winning power by the inspired words of their generals.

I have noticed how, when I'm engrossed in the writing process, intimately connected with seeking a feeling of reality, then allowing the appropriate words and rhythms to flow out to describe it, the words on the page seem deep and dimensional, taking me into a vibrating, living state of understanding. When I go back later to read over what I wrote, the words appear to lie flat on the surface of the paper, and my mind speeds across them. They sound different. I too feel flat—until, as I take more time, concentrate and feel into each phrase and sentence, I once again sink down and enter the living inner experience under the sound, beneath the pattern of letters. It's as if I read with my chest then, not with my eyes alone.

Let's remember that words are names. In all traditional cultures, naming is a sacred art, and names are given very carefully, after much meditation. People typically have names used only in childhood; names for common, public use; and other inner, secret names to be uttered only by high priests. A person's name originally was meant to describe the qualities of his or her soul and to guide the personality in developing certain character traits. The words we so unconsciously skim over and throw around were once meditated upon and carefully chosen to convey exact experiences. Let's slow down and honor language, bring language into the present moment, put our attention into it and feel its power.

I am intentional about the words I use.

Refrain from using ugly or meaningless language today.

December 8

My left and right sides both have value; I nurture them both.

Pay attention to your nondominant side today and use it more consciously.

Roberta had had a variety of accidents. When she inventoried her traumas, she discovered the majority were to her left side. She had broken her left ankle, had chronic infections in her left elbow, left ear, and left tonsil, and had surgery to remove a tumor in her left breast. All the scars from cuts and scrapes were also on her left side. Through therapy, Roberta discovered that she'd been programmed early by her parents to believe that self-sufficiency was of primary importance. No one was coddled in her family. All the children were expected to be ambitious and hardworking and to make their own way in the world.

The health and functionality of Roberta's right, doing, manifesting side was therefore sacrosanct. Unconsciously she could not risk injuring it, since the approval of her parents and her very survival depended on it. So when Roberta had physical problems, she unconsciously shifted them to her receptive left side. As a result, she had difficulty even understanding the concept of receiving freely. Over the years, her trust and intuition eroded to a point where she felt disconnected, unappreciated, and alone. She needed to activate her left side and learn to receive love. How can you balance and nurture both sides of *your* body? (If you're left-handed, right is your receptive side.)

INVENTORYING YOUR LEFT- AND RIGHT-SIDE TRAUMAS

1. Think back through your life, and list all the major injuries and surgeries you have experienced. Were they on the left or right side of your body?

2. Examine your body. Do you have more scars on the left or right side?

3. Describe what you know about the relative strengths and weaknesses of your left and right sides.

4. Where does your tension usually lodge: left or right side?

5. Look at your face carefully in the mirror. Is your left or right eye bigger? Does one side of your face seem more open or closed? Does one side of your mouth tip up or down? When you smile, which side appears more relaxed and happy?

6. Ask the left and right sides of your body, "Why did this trauma occur here?"

7. Ask the left and right sides of your body, "How can I love and heal you?"

December 9

Have you ever stopped to notice how you know what you know? How does something register as real for you? How do you know something is true or appropriate, or that a certain course of action will work? Patrick is a management consultant and trainer who is fascinated with perception. He remembers being five years old, sitting at his desk looking at a book, while simultaneously aware of a gaping hole on the other side of the room. He called it the "eye of God," and he experienced being inside the eye of God, looking at himself at his desk *and* being in his body. It wasn't coming from his inner imagination, he said, but felt physical, real. Later, in his teenage years, he ran his car off a road at high speed, and saw a figure sitting on the front fender as everything went into slow motion. Was it Death waiting to take him? Or a spiritual guide? Whoever or whatever it was, he saw it plain as day.

Today, Patrick has an uncanny ability when consulting with companies to see an entire picture of how everything fits together and how different combinations of variables will work. He says, "It's as though a huge paintbrush comes out of my center and makes a broad arc, painting a whole panorama. It's like a video—a movie of energy. First it comes as a knowing, then it translates into pictures. I feel the flow of the pattern and how the energy would shift if different things happened, even what kinds of intentions must be held by each person for a plan to work, and when someone is a poor fit. If one variable changes, the entire canvas adjusts itself immediately! Sometimes I can slide into the way one of the participants is feeling and quickly understand how he or she thinks the process will work, then I compare that to what my body knows—and I know how to communicate the nuances of the process."

You, too, regularly use visioning skills, but you may not pay much attention to the mechanics of your perceptual process. For instance, when you meet someone you feel might be a partner or a best friend, your mind probably paints the panorama of your potential life together and watches how it unfolds. You no doubt know right away whether situations have a good chance of working or not. You probably even know ahead of time exactly what will cause problems. What are you involved with now that you already have a panorama about?

I pay attention to how I know.

There are many unusual ways that your mind creates perceptions. We are not informed by logic and words alone. Today, pay attention to your odd knowings, the ghostly images between you and what you see with your eyes.

I ask clearly for what I need.

Today, be precise about what you ask for, and notice how what you receive may relate to an inner, unexpressed need. Life always responds to what's most real for you.

Sherry found Luna, a wolf-dog mix, half dead under a porch with her pups. Sherry was single and wanted a dog for companionship and protection, so she nursed the mother back to life and managed to save some of the puppies. As the two began to bond, however, Luna became less obedient and more protective. She also would only obey Sherry's boyfriend. This made Sherry feel like Luna didn't want to be *her* dog. She called her friend Becky, an animal communicator and medical intuitive, and asked her to tune in to Luna. Becky, who hears animals talking to her telepathically, says, "I asked Luna what was important for me to know. She told me that three of her puppies were now dead and she missed them, that her stomach hurt, and that her owner had fed the surviving puppies a muddy brown fluid but wouldn't allow her to have any because it gave her diarrhea. Then she talked about being a fisherman and showed me images of her diving underwater to catch fish. I relayed this to Sherry, who confirmed each detail—even the fact that Luna swam underwater to catch fish!

"Luna explained that Sherry had said she wanted companionship, but because she lived in a marginally safe area and her boyfriend worked in another city during the week, she really wanted a protector. Luna picked up on this and was primarily being a protector. Luna was just being the alpha female, the primary protector of the "pack" that consisted of herself and Sherry. When Michael was in the house, he became the alpha male and Luna deferred to him, not Sherry. She felt she was qualified to be the alpha female because of her mothering and hunting skills. It seemed that Luna was teaching us all some important lessons. First, be clear about what you ask for, because the true request is the one that will be answered. And second, don't judge others negatively— they are probably trying to help you the best way they know how."

December 11

Allen Hicks, a designer, actor, and poet, recently married. He and his new wife went hiking in the deserts of the Southwest, where time is commonly known to slow and even stop and the long tale of the earth is quietly told. He wrote this on the journey:

Hermit shale ground
to pink trail powder, laid
down 2-hundred 80-million
years ago now recompressed by
patterned soles of boots (squares,
circles, chevrons, diamonds, Nikes,
Reeboks) passing layers of limestone,
sandstone, vishnu schist, zoroaster granite
past hoodoo pillars, volcanoes, cinder cones
("Five-thousand-foot mountains inside this hole!"),
lava flows, travertine falls, into the grand canyon
of the Colorado.

We pause
to soak our feet
in bright angel creek
pick 3 stones for souvenirs
and ascend, shod again, two bipeds
both fifty, celebrating this delicate, eternal
blink of an eye.

The ground is precious.

Notice the soles of your feet on the ground as you stand, walk, and sit today. What do they know?

**I let go of
a dependency
and make
space.**

*Give up an
attachment or
fixed idea today,
and see what
your soul substi-
tutes instead.*

Melvin Morse, author of *Closer to the Light: Learning from Children's Near-Death Experiences,* has written movingly of how children experience dying and returning to life. There is a reassuring quality to the child's innocent view of the other world that, if used properly, can inspire us all to let go more easily of the tight grip we hold on our daily lives and our ego-based belief systems. For instance, one child said, "There was a beautiful Light that had everything good in it. For about a week, I could see sparks of that Light in everything." Another reported, "When I came out of the coma in the hospital, I opened my eyes and saw pieces of the Light everywhere. I could see how everything in the world fits together."

My little friend Malina, who was blond and blue-eyed, died at age four, but during her short life she regularly spoke of her "other family" and her "sister." She described how they all had black hair and wore towels around themselves for clothes. She left them before, she said, "because I could. I flew away." Her parents asked her if her other family wanted her back. Yes. Was she going to go back? "Naahhhh . . ." she said. But a week before she died, she started to glow and became extremely joyful. She said her "sister" was talking to her a lot. After she died, I had several dreams about her. In one, I had also died and was undergoing a strange sort of autopsy. Doctors were removing the systems of my body—organs, then blood, then muscles, one layer at a time—on an operating table. In between procedures, I stood on the sidelines watching, with a small girl with black hair at my side. We were chatting. I knew it was Malina, reverted to her "other self." As the doctors began to chop up my bones, I panicked. I wouldn't be able to get back in my body after that, and I wouldn't be my old self. I'd have to totally disengage. The little girl said, "But, Penney, you're already dead! It won't hurt!" And we walked over to look out a picture window at a beautiful green park that extended far into the distance, dotted with people strolling about peacefully. Soon we would go out there. Today I truly believe I have less fear about dying because Malina paved the way for me and gave me firsthand guidance from the other side.

Lani, a friend who lives a quiet life close to the earth, found herself confronted with the electronic age last year. She writes, "I just got a new CD player, a credit card terminal for my home business, a new modem, and I got on the Internet! Suddenly I'm swimming in a tangle of cords and complexity, trying to figure out how to hook one thing through another. I've made a jump into hyper-cyberspace, diving into my monitor like it's a swimming pool. I have to reorganize something in my body now to match the World Wide Web—and it's stretching me beyond what I can imagine. At night, I can feel myself being 'rewired' like my house, and I sense I am soon to be bursting at the seams with all these new sources of information that I'm not sure I need or want. There's nothing to do but surrender!

"In contrast, I just spent a week watching Jane Austen movies and sinking into the more 'proper' morality of those times. That way of living, though very slow, was also very real, especially in contrast to today's speed and shallowness. Some odd nostalgia gripped me. It's not that I want to live back then, but I'm missing the sincerity of that age. I want to pull out all the plugs and incoming lines of data that are making me feel so complex and electrified. Our world seems increasingly inhuman, in the volume of information we must consume like food and in the diet the media chooses for us. At least no one can reach me in my car unless they come directly into the center of my head as a thought! Maybe, if I could develop my intuition, I'd realize the data I dread digesting is already in me."

I live inside my electro-magnetic center.

Stay focused in the center of your head—an electro-magnetic center of your body— as often as possible today. Perceiving from here will bring clarity. When you become distracted by outside stimulation, simply return to your center.

I am a better person because of the attention of others.

Thank others today. Take time to give people feedback on the contributions they've made to your life. Keeping your gifts in the front of your mind helps you stay healthy, even lucky.

Tobias was sixty-three when he had a stroke. As a psychotherapist, he had been very analytical and mental for most of his career. He had evolved a precise system of assessing his clients' problems and helping them methodically clear their subconscious blocks. Just as he dealt with his clients, Tobias was relentless about analyzing details from his own repressive childhood.

For several weeks after his stroke, he lay unconscious in the intensive care unit at the hospital while his many friends prayed, meditated, visited, and held out hope that he would come back. He did finally reemerge, unable to speak but more in touch with a humanitarian love and a childlike spirit. In a short period of time, he was talking, walking, learning again to button his shirt and write his name. Life was new again, and he had almost forgotten his desire to dissect things mentally. Now Tobias was softer, sweeter, more intuitive. Soon he was ready to work with clients again. This time he wanted to touch people more and balance the energies in their body. But, inexplicably, Tobias returned to his old ways and to the safety of his habitual mental patterns. He pushed his otherworldly experience to the back of his mind, and, whenever one of his friends talked to him about what a valuable teaching it had offered, he brushed it off.

Now, years later, he is taking a tentative peek at what really happened to him and how he'd overtaxed the linear, controlling, masculine part of his awareness and underused the nurturing, allowing, feminine part. He is letting himself fully understand what an outpouring of love was showered on him by his friends. It had been too much to integrate before, and instead it'd been easier to return to old feelings of being unloved by his parents and to his proven methodology for living with that pain. Now Tobias is seeing he has been offered a chance to release his tight worldview, along with the old pain, and substitute a new experience of being more spontaneous and highly valued and loved for who he really is. Making room to feel the love that is given—this is what heals all of us, of everything.

December 15

My colleague Larry was working with a woman to help her clarify why she felt blocked concerning her work. She had written a book about women and money and was having trouble making it visible. As he worked with her, it became apparent that her main issue was that she felt stupid, especially with men. She actually used the word several times. Her father had started a well-known financial institution, and the whole time she was growing up it was the men in her family who were allowed to know about money, not the women. She had written the book to discover her own power and truth. Yet, as Larry asked her various questions to elicit her personal insights, she answered "I don't know" to each. As a man, Larry realized he was triggering her pattern as he worked with her.

As he described the situation, I thought, "We have to assume that she knows exactly what she needs, and that, by identifying herself as stupid, she is trying to get at something deeper that really *is* close to her essential nature. What if *stupid* is just the mind's shallow interpretation of a beneficial experience? If we look deeper for what the soul is trying to activate, *stupid* would become *beginner's mind* or *innocence*. And that is a true gift of the soul—it means that she is able to see with fresh eyes." So this woman had something valuable to offer—her fresh perspective on money—developed precisely because she had been treated as stupid and thus had been buffered her whole life from being programmed by her father's dominant view. Now, if she could reframe what she considered her main flaw and see that it was actually her main gift, her purity and innocence would turn immediately to wisdom, the expression of which was her soul's intent.

I see the advantages in my challenges.

Notice what you complain about today. If each thing that bothers you were really giving you something, what might the gift be?

December 16

I can see the vision that guides me.

Imagine the space around you and inside you is filled with a glossy light today. Imagine the light is loaded with all the energy, wisdom, and assistance you need. Let it help you; look for the visions it contains.

I led two vision-quest tours to Egypt, five years apart. We journeyed down the Nile, visiting the temples that punctuate the river like chakras along a spine, finishing at the Great Pyramid. We were able to enter the King's Chamber in the early morning before the tourists arrived, to have individual meditations inside the granite sarcophagus. Each person was allowed seven minutes in the powerful crystalline box. Though Egyptologists believe the Great Pyramid is a tomb, metaphysicians sense it was used for spiritual initiations. Knowing about the conductivity of crystal and the focusing power of pyramids, it was reasonable to assume that the sarcophagus would amplify one's consciousness.

My seven minutes inside the sarcophagus were astonishing. No sooner did I lay down than a spontaneous vision began. My body and the box seemed to dissolve. I was surrounded by a field of rich indigo light that was distorted by a plethora of insistent black dots. My attention was drawn away from the indigo light to deal with the black dots, which were extremely irritating. I knew the indigo light was coming for me, and I wanted it to get me and take me into it. If I could keep my attention focused on the indigo, the dots would dissolve and the light would come faster. I was just getting the hang of it when someone gently touched my foot. I came back to my body with a jerk and a deep internal moan. If I'd just had five more minutes! Nevertheless, the vision persisted, and in subsequent years I continued to focus on the indigo light in meditations to dissolve my subconscious blocks.

Five years later, I lay down again in the sarcophagus. As before, a vision began instantly. This time I became aware that I'd entered the sacred container with an unconscious question: "What am I to do in my life and am I courageous enough to do it?" A voice answered, "There is nothing left for you to do. No mission." I saw myself as a small girl sitting on God's lap, pointing to a man, saying, "Let's help *that* person!" God instantly sent out a ray to help him. Then I'd survey all the possible things to do and say, "Let's do *this* project!" And we would. There was no more work, only accepting and playing with the partnership we all have with God, doing my part—which was picking things, anything! To this day, these two seven-minute experiences are indelibly engraved in my memory.

December 17

It is a popular belief that angels can take human form and walk among us. Metaphysical teachings, however, deny this. Officially, angels are entities who serve as messengers between the human kingdom and the divine. They do not materialize physically but can "overshadow" us or flow through us, helping to raise the level of our thoughts and feelings. Certain animals—particularly dogs, horses, dolphins, whales, elephants, and birds—are considered especially attuned to the angelic realm and often are used as vehicles for angelic assistance. I heard Matthew Fox and Rupert Sheldrake once muse that angels probably embody the morphological fields of aligned energy that are created through ceremonies. So many people sense angels and see inexplicable angelic forms that it's difficult to deny that *some* force of consciousness is present with us, affecting us in ways so subtle that we normally gloss over the resulting "good works."

Donna, a friend in Tokyo, was driving her son to school one day in rush-hour traffic. She stopped at a red light and glanced in her rearview mirror to see a huge Mercedes speeding forward in the lane to her left. The driver either didn't notice the red light or was intending to run it. There was a piercing screech as the car slammed on its brakes and came to a jolting halt. Just at that moment, two yellow beanie caps came into view across the big car's hood. Two tiny boys on their way to school dashed across the pedestrian walk, giggling and chattering, unaware of any danger. Then Donna gasped at what she saw. Pressed up against the front of the Mercedes was the transparent shape of a huge angel. "It was almost formless," she said, "more like a thin veil, but the image was totally clear to me." The man actually got out of his car and walked around to the front to examine his bumper as if he'd hit something. Shaking his head, he got back in his car and drove on carefully as the light turned green.

I walk among friends and helpers.

Pretend that everyone you meet today is an angel or enlightened master in disguise. How does this change your behavior and your experience of what you receive?

I can extend myself a little bit farther.

Include more of the past, the future, and the environment in your present moment today.

By making a practice of being focused in the present moment, you will soon see that the present is like a bubble of awareness around you, and it can expand or contract with the intention of your conscious mind. As your present expands, your "here" includes more space, and your "now" includes more time, and that means more knowledge as well. When the past and future come into the now, you have a broader view of how events are coordinated, how the process of your life evolves. New insights become available—knowledge you had cut yourself off from because you defined the past and future as separate from you. Perceiving from the present moment produces intuition, and *intuition cuts through the normal limitations of time and space.* You can know the past and future as if they were *now.* Or you can be in other locations as if they were *here.*

We expand and contract our focus all the time, moving out to check the longer view, which is like a blueprint for daily reality, then zooming back in to take a specific action that comes from that larger pattern. You might zoom in to concentrate on setting your watch. The next instant, you straighten up, take a breath, and look out the window. Your mind drifts out, moving through space and time, and, without realizing just how, you know how your day will go, how you'll handle a tricky phone call, and what you'll cook for dinner. Then you return to a tighter focus again, combing your hair or opening the mail.

When we extend the present moment, we often see visions. This is how we plan and set goals. We are simply observing the "blueprint" of our lives and basing our actions on it, though we may not be consciously aware of what we're doing. It's important to remember that this "blueprint" evolves continually—so the view you saw yesterday may not be the one that exists today. By extending your now to include, let's say, a three-year time period, then describing it, coming back and taking one appropriate action, then extending again to the same focus, checking again, describing again, acting again, and so on, you will stay aligned with your own life purpose and in synch with the world.

December 19

I talk with thousands of people every year about their innermost lives, and it seems people are becoming excruciatingly sensitive. I see an increase in complaints about being out of control, that negative emotions can no longer be ignored, suppressed, or contained. This rise of emotion is healthy, because in the long run it helps us become free, fluid human beings, helps us learn to receive and release energy, ideas, and creativity. But as denied feelings begin to stir, we experience resistance, retrenching, struggle, overindulgence, and reactionary behavior. It is important now to let go of things that have provided security but are now too limiting. Some people might call this "ego death," others might call it the practice of nonattachment. Wherever we've been holding on, or holding to, or holding forth, we are now being asked to examine our reasons for doing so. Do we really need such a big income? Do we feel safe being a housewife, or having a full-time job at the post office, or being addicted to smoking or drinking? Do we have to be nice to be loved, or audacious to get recognition, or angry to get our way? We must let go where our habits are too strong and develop adaptability.

In addition, many people today have a lower tolerance for seeing others being victimized. We are affected much more intimately by current events than ever before, even if they're on the opposite side of the world. Somehow, we just can't pretend that it's none of our business; we can't seem to keep ourselves separate. Whether it's ethnic cleansing, a shooting in one of our schools, the tragic loss of a young hero, or a hurricane that devastates an entire coastline, what used to be impersonal is now personal. Some say the world is getting smaller, but, in my view, *we* are getting bigger, including more in our present moment. Perhaps we're getting so used to having vast quantities of information that we can no longer process it all intellectually. Perhaps our minds have become saturated, and the truth is seeping through into our feelings and bodily sensations. Perhaps we are starting to experience our interconnection with others and the planet, emotionally and physically. If so, we're on the road to becoming global citizens.

I sense underlying currents in the world.

Pay attention to the deep patterns you see and feel today— in the news, in conversations, in your own subliminal thoughts.

December 20

My posture influences the way I perceive the world and the way others perceive me.

Keep your head level and your chest up and open today. Look at life equally through both eyes; hear through both ears; reach out with both hands; stand equally on both feet.

When I teach workshops I often lead guided visualizations. Participants close their eyes and become centered, then allow their imagination to bring them pictures or sensory information as they follow along with the words. It's fascinating to watch what happens to their bodies. People who have unconscious resistance to allowing the unknown to make an impression on them will cross their ankles, legs, and arms as though to cut off a flow or protect their belly, diaphragm, or heart. Other people tilt to the left or right or their heads drop back or droop forward, chin to chest. "Keep your head level," I repeatedly intone, "and remember to breathe!" My intuition tells me that people tilt and dip to gain access to information from the part of the brain they are tilting toward. In a similar vein, neurolinguistic programming teaches that when people are asked a question and they look up and to the right, they are seeking the answer from the right brain, and when they look up and to the left, from the left brain. When you keep your head level, your perception can flow evenly from all directions into your center.

When you converse with others, do you cover any part of your body? If you find your hand over your forehead, you may not want to see something. When your hand covers your throat, you may feel hesitant to express yourself honestly or to allow input that makes you doubt your certainty. Cover your chest or heart, and you may not want to be hurt or to feel vulnerable. Cover your stomach or solar plexus, and you may be trying to control your fight-or-flight response. Covering the lower portion of the body may indicate feeling overwhelmed, that you want to protect yourself from other people's neediness and fear. Do you twist your body away from the person you're interacting with? You're probably protecting the side that's farthest from the other person. By positioning yourself so your chest is wide, flat, horizontal, and open, and you're "straightforward," you'll have the best chance for perceiving clearly and neutrally.

December 21

It was the Christmas holiday season and I was waiting in an airline's lounge area for a delayed flight that would take me to visit my family. It had been a trying autumn, with many emotional ups and downs and losses of friends, all of which had left me drained and slightly depressed. I was hoping a little Christmas spirit would cheer me up and help me find renewed meaning in life. While we waited, a Santa Claus strolled into the lounge area, belting out a hearty "Ho, ho, ho!" and a "Merry Christmas, everybody!"

"Who here has a Christmas wish?" he continued merrily. I looked up from the book I was reading and, following Santa's line of sight, turned my head to look back over my left shoulder. The timing was perfect. Just at that moment I saw a tiny boy turn toward the booming voice. I watched the expression on his face shift from surprise and caution to a realization of who had just entered his world. His eyes lit up like sparklers; he raised his chubby little arms straight up in the air and, without a moment's pause, broke into a full-tilt gallop down the length of the waiting area and leaped directly up into Santa's warm embrace.

The power of his instantaneous joy just about knocked me over. Here was a role model for me if there ever was one. This is the way I should run to God! Turn my head, notice who's present in my world, and seamlessly, without debate or comment, raise my arms and start running!

I am innocent and fresh in all that I know.

Whenever you say "I" today, pretend your innocent child self is speaking. Your innocence is directly connected to a higher, inspired knowing.

December 22

I am overflowing with creative ideas.

Do something that stimulates and thrills your inner artist self today.

What we can dream, we can make real. If a vision comes to you through imagination, it's just a transparent, preliminary version of a potentially solid reality. Hold it in your mind just a little bit longer and add in all the sensory experiences of it. How does it look? How does it sound? How does it feel? How does it taste? How does it smell? Your vision will flesh out and eventually happen. Sometimes this process is blocked by subconscious beliefs: "It's too much for me to do alone." "As soon as I get it, life will take it away." "If I want it too much, it won't happen." Here are some ideas to keep in mind when making your dreams and visions come alive. They can help counteract your "yes, buts."

I don't do anything alone. All creation is collaborative. We are linked to innumerable beings, and they are as real and valuable as we are, whether they are physical or nonphysical. We constantly participate with others, even if we don't see them. Start having a more conscious relationship with those you haven't seen yet. We live to support each other and to expand; if we didn't we'd all die.

I remember to invoke help. It is the natural condition of all beings to cooperate and help energy flow into and out of form. Call in and connect with those who come before you and those who come after you to set up a continuum for the flow of creativity. We are all always receiving and always giving. Make a ceremonial offering.

I state my intended result and leave room for happy accidents. You may only have part of the creative vision in your conscious mind; the rest comes with the flow, out of your deeper self and from the world. Just start, and let go of the outcome.

I jump-start the creative flow by acting "as if." Make a symbolic act. If you want to travel in France, take a French class. Start a trickle of what you want so your body will know it's real. If you want to change careers and be a freelance artist, carry a sketchbook and draw every day.

The end product of creating something is gratitude, love, and the joy of feeling the dance of creation. The results in form don't matter that much; it's the process that counts. Think of creating, not so much as making or getting, but as a way of freely giving.

December 23

Peter Martin writes, "At an Al-Anon meeting, when we were debating the existence of the 'higher power' mentioned in the twelve steps, one person said, 'I think if God did exist He would manifest Himself in other people.' These Christmas stories bear that out.

"The first story involves a big-hearted friend who took a delinquent teenage girl under her wing and into her home. My friend's generosity often went unappreciated, and frequent altercations took place between them. A few days before Christmas, the girl took the family's only car, without permission, to go 'Christmas shopping.' This led to a serious argument that resulted in the girl's being grounded for the holidays. The day before Christmas my friend peeked into the girl's closet. There lay a yet-unwrapped package that contained a top-of-the-line Cuisinart. My friend realized then that the girl had saved all the money from her job at Burger King to buy the gift.

"The second story comes from another friend who, shortly before Christmas, helped move his daughter to a new apartment in upper Manhattan. While unloading the car in front of the apartment, they temporarily left a box of shoes and boots on the curb. When they returned, a pair of boots was missing and a homeless man was about to leave with a pair of shoes. When accosted by my friend, the man explained that since the box had been left on the curb, he assumed it was to be discarded so he had helped himself. He returned the shoes, and said he thought he knew where the boots had gone. A few minutes later he returned with another homeless man, who appeared even more down on his luck. The man carried the boots, now wrapped as a Christmas gift, and offered to return them. Touched, my friend offered to buy back the boots from him. 'No,' the man said. 'Give the money to my friend here. He needs it more than I do.'

"The third story occurred at a recent pre-holiday white elephant sale. A man walked up to one of the saleswomen and handed her two twenty-dollar bills. 'What are you buying?' she asked, noticing that he had nothing in his hands. 'Last year I bought a camera here for ten dollars,' he said. 'I didn't know if it was going to work, but I decided I'd risk the ten dollars to find out. Well, it works fine and I've been using it all year, so I just wanted to come back and pay you what I think the camera is worth.'"

I trust in the goodness of others.

Today, look for ways to trust people and to demonstrate your trust. Trust is the force that most enables us to experience love, accurate intuition, and inspired cocreation. Trust is not gullibility but an affirmation of the true nature of things.

**Peace is all
around me.**

*Notice the
natural order of
life today, the
harmony that
exists even
within the chaos
of thought.
Peace is a
quality of con-
sciousness that
attunes you to
a sophisticated
wisdom.*

This message came through direct writing many years
ago; it came slowly, deliberately, word by word. "Peace is
all around you. Look. Feel. Peace is in every cell within
you; the order of the body itself is peace. The order of
nature is peace. You are woven together by peace, by love,
and there are no seams by which you are sewn into the
tapestry of your life. You are not held in place forcefully,
but come together with everything else voluntarily to live
in a perfectly blended way. Do you see the many finite
forms and personalities being themselves, yet all belonging, cooperating, coming from one source, made of one
energy? Their coexistence and interplay is peace.

"Make it your daily living prayer to act from this
awareness. Then you create the constant opening, the
portal of light you truly are. Yet, through forgetfulness
and flashing attention, your personality becomes an incon-
stant expression of this and you lose touch with peace.
Focus on your constancy. Stay open and connected. Smile.
The smile is the first step in aligning yourself to know
peace. All learning comes through peace of mind and
being one with the rhythms of the world; lessons are not
conquered but integrated into the fabric of your being.
Integration is an act of peace. There is a changing yet
nonmoving quality to life that, when internalized and
identified with, leads you straight into the divine. Be this
peace and the power of grace will bring miraculous
expansion in your creativity, understanding, and ability to
serve. Make it your highest priority to find and choose
the harmonious way. Be aware of the quiet inside confusion, the voice inside the quiet. It is always there; truth is
always waiting in the peace."

December 25

When Alberta was young, she led a wild life. At one low point, she decided to try prostitution. A friend arranged for her to meet a pimp in a dirty apartment. She showed up early and no one was there yet, but the door was open so she went in. As she waited, she became more and more nervous. She didn't feel safe. She was about to bolt out the door and call it off when she heard two men arguing hotly in the hallway. She knew it was the pimp and sensed impending violence. She got cold chills all over her body. In her imagination, she saw a knife, and she immediately prayed fervently for help. She ran into the bedroom and locked the door. There was no way out except the window.

Desperate, Alberta opened the window and looked out—she was on the fourth floor, too high to jump. Her only hope was a ledge that extended toward the ledge of the window of the next apartment. Still praying, she decided to take her chances rather than stay where she was. She climbed out and inched toward the other window. As she reached the end, she heard the pimp yelling insanely in the apartment. She was so terrified that he would find her and drag her back that she contemplated leaping to the other ledge. The distance seemed too great to cross. But the pressure crescendoed to an excruciating focus, and she knew with every fiber of her being that she must jump. Clutching at the building, she reached her leg out and pushed off with great force. At that moment, she says, her legs stretched like rubber bands, and she was transported miraculously through space, as though by angels, to the other window ledge. "Thank you, God!" she moaned.

Now she just had to get inside and escape. But the window was locked! She could see a man inside, doubled over and drowsy—he'd just shot up with drugs. She banged on the glass. He looked up to see a strange figure spread-eagle across his window, and his glazed-over eyes widened with terror. She kept banging. Finally, he staggered over and reluctantly let her in. "Are you the Angel of Death?" he asked. "Have you come for me?" "No," she said, "I'm Alberta, and I think the angels brought me— and I think I love you!" And she hugged him as hard as she could.

I love and keep my heart open, no matter what.

Love uncondi- tionally today. Make your top priority keeping your heart open, your chest soft and wide, no matter what slings and arrows come your way.

December 26

**I can choose
what I think
about.**

*Catch yourself
when your
thoughts take
control of you
today. Stop and
change your
mind.*

Everybody wakes up in the middle of the night some-times. Those wakeful moments can often turn into anx-ious inventories of what has to be done, relationships that seem off-kilter, problems that are resistant to solutions. Sandy, a busy self-employed woman who was prone to these restless hours in the middle of the night, began to observe what happened when she woke up. At first, a small daytime thought would creep in and she'd think, "Right, I have to remember to do that tomorrow." That would lead to another item on her to-do list. Within minutes her one thought had cascaded into many. As each one spilled into her consciousness, her anxiety rose—a slightly elevated heart rate, a tightening of her stomach, a sinking feeling that failure lurked right around the corner. Soon her body was aching, she was mad at herself, and she was exhausted but wide awake.

One night, in the midst of her self-induced spiral into anxiety, Sandy thought, "I'm doing this to myself. It does no good to think all these things now. They're not even real! The anxiety doesn't reflect anything I truly need to fear. I'm just hashing over the usual stuff and the ongoing problems that happen to be part of my life." She realized she could use simple meditation techniques to defuse the anxiety.

The next time it happened, Sandy said out loud to her-self, "I don't have to think about this right now, and I don't have to do anything about this now. I can think about it tomorrow when I'm vertical!" Then she began to breathe deeply, counting each breath and focusing on it as she drew it in and sent it back out. Each time a trouble-some thought returned, she'd start back over at step one. Sometimes she started over again and again as her thoughts insisted on pushing themselves back to the fore. But she persisted. Not only did the counting and breath-ing take her hamster-on-a-treadmill mind off its track, it also calmed her body. Eventually, she found she could go back to sleep. It was a great way of breaking free of the bonds of anxiety that gripped her in the deepest part of the night. Now when she wakes up she isn't afraid that those moments will be the beginning of another bout of self-torture.

December 27

I was in Japan, preparing for a talk on "Predictions and Future Trends." I went into a deep meditation and asked to feel, then see, what might be coming in this part of the world. Oddly, nothing came. Nothing at all! I had the distinct impression that I was hitting a wall. "What is this?" I asked myself. "Why can't I see anything?"

My inner voice responded clear as a bell, "Because the future isn't out there anymore. The future isn't separate from you; it's in the now." Huh? My voice continued. "Time has been accelerating because the gap between the present and the future has been closing. Think of doing something and it happens almost instantly. *The decisions you make in your present moment are your future.* If you repeatedly make decisions based on feeling like a victim, your future is now one of victimhood. If you make decisions based on provision your future is now bright. There is no longer the luxury of thinking there will be time to change your ways. There is no more time lag. What you choose now is what you live, period. There is no 'later.'

"Along with the realization that time is coalescing into only one category, not three, comes the awareness that your choices affect not only yourself but everyone else. You will soon see that any act of projecting responsibility for the quality of your life onto others is detrimental to the fabric of the world itself. For example, if you say to your husband, 'You make me happy,' that is an act of *oppression.* He does not make you happy, *you* make you happy, and for him to live with that false responsibility creates a burden for him. If you say you are unhappy because of your boss, that is an act of *violence,* because projecting responsibility for your pain onto her attacks the core of who she is and places undue burden on her life. Imagine the number of projections, both positive and negative, placed by one person on another the world over. If you could see these as lines, the world would seem to be covered by a thick spiderweb, and the true flow of soul force and light would be dimmed throughout. Now imagine people expressing themselves without these false responsibilities and illusions. The planet shines brightly! So, for the health and safety of the planet, people must now learn to live entirely in the moment, which actually is the consciousness of the soul."

My thoughts— right now—are my future.

Entertain the idea today that there is no future. Live like you'll never do anything else but what you're choosing to do now.

December 28

I practice conscious communion.

Today, put your attention on the oneness of life. Feel your connections, your kinship with others, and your permeable nature, which shares and receives easily.

Whether you use the term "God," or "the Creator," or "the Divine," or "the Oneness," or "the Us," or "the Buddha Nature," contemplate its compassionate power and omnipresence.

Everything inside me is made of God,
and made by God, the way God wants it to be.
I trust my body.
I trust my life.
I trust my destiny and that I am going to God,
that I live with God every day,
that I came from God.
I trust that everyone is made of God,
even the hate-filled ones, even the most hardened ones.
I trust that every thing is made of God, and every thought,
I trust that what I notice will become my reality—
and it is what God *causes* me to notice.
I trust that if I follow my noticings
they lead me to truth and greater love.
God guides my mind and my motives.
I trust there is really no inside or outside,
just a continuous variety of densities
of God-Us-Me.

December 29

I hear myself eerily now whenever I make a false statement. This sensitivity has come as the result of a resolution I made to identity myself as my soul, present here
and now in its full wisdom. I vowed to give my soul a
chance to take over my body, emotions, mind, creativity,
and self-expression, to do with me what it would. As I
practice this, I have moments of giddy excitement as I
glimpse what the unimpeded soul is capable of knowing
and doing. These clear insights then inexplicably collapse
into my habitual way of perceiving, where I am imbedded
in limitation and victim thoughts or in patterns of hostility, irritation, or impatience. I realize with a deep, private
embarrassment that every time I choose to get juice out of
feeling maligned or unappreciated, I am stalling being my
true self. "This is not the way I want to spend my short
time on earth!" I yell as I drive along in my car.

I have been investing my life force and attention in ideas
that block the flow of my soul, just as I might invest my
savings in a loser mutual fund! How many times have I
chosen to close my heart just because someone else's heart
was hard or cool? Why do I cause myself pain like that?
Just to have some kind of connection? I'm drawing the
line! I'm investing in soul-serving, soul-freeing thoughts
from now on.

I list the ideas I've held unconsciously that pertain to:

1. doubt, worry, lack of confidence
2. self-sacrifice, victimization, unfairness, helplessness,
rescue, overwhelm
3. scarcity, fear of loss
4. denial, avoidance, procrastination, postponement
5. rebellion, stubbornness, complaining
6. feigning ignorance
7. envy, resentment, indignation, betrayal, stealing
8. violence, retribution, punishment, judgment,
vengeance, aggression, domination.

These are mistakes of perception. I ask to catch myself
now every time I start in on these themes or hear those
platitudes we're all hypnotized into repeating: "Well,
everybody does it." "I'm not too bad." "Oh, I don't
know." "I'm no expert." "It could be worse." "I can't."
"Maybe . . ." Patiently, I ask my soul to reeducate me
about who I really am.

**I recognize my
soul-blocking
thoughts.**

*Catch yourself
when you block
the natural
expression of
your soul today
with life-negating
ideas. Replace
these limiting
thoughts with
soul-freeing
behaviors instead.*

December 30

I release what is toxic for me and claim what is healthy.

Today, make an inventory of people who drain you, activities that don't serve your growth, habits that pull you down, and objects that have too much importance or are in your way. Examine your list carefully and decide what you will let go of for the new year.

When the Princess of Amen Ra died around 1500 B.C., her mummy was buried deep in a vault at Luxor to rest forever. In the late 1890s, four Englishmen visiting the excavations at Luxor were invited to buy an exquisite mummy case containing her remains. They drew lots and the winner bought the mummy. A few hours later, he was seen walking toward the desert. He never returned. The next day, one of the remaining three men was accidentally shot by an Egyptian servant. His arm had to be amputated. The third man found on his return home that the bank holding his entire savings had failed. The fourth man suffered a severe illness, lost his job, and ended up selling matches in the street. Nevertheless, the coffin reached England where it was bought by a London businessman. After three of his family members were injured in a road accident and his house damaged by fire, he donated the mummy to the British Museum.

As the coffin was being unloaded at the museum, the truck suddenly went into reverse and trapped a passerby. Then, as the casket was being lifted up the stairs by two workmen, one fell and broke his leg. The other, apparently in perfect health, died unaccountably two days later. Once the Princess was installed in the Egyptian Room, other exhibits in the room were often hurled about at night. One watchman died on duty, causing the other watchmen to quit. Finally, the authorities had the mummy carried down to the basement. Within a week, one of the helpers was seriously ill, and the supervisor of the move was found dead at his desk.

Soon afterward, the museum sold the mummy to a private collector. After continual misfortune, the owner put it in the attic and tried to find a new home for it. The fact that almost twenty people had met with misfortune, disaster, or death from handling the casket, in barely ten years, was now well known. Eventually an American archaeologist, who dismissed the happenings as quirks of circumstance, paid a handsome price for the mummy and arranged for its removal to New York. The new owner escorted the ornate casket aboard a White Star liner about to make its maiden voyage to America. On the night of April 14, 1912, the Princess of Amen Ra accompanied 1,500 fellow passengers to their deaths at the bottom of the Atlantic. The name of the ship was the *Titanic*.

394

December 31

Einstein said, "Tell me what you pay attention to and I will tell you who you are." What did you pay attention to this year? Better yet, *how* did you pay attention? Did you place your awareness on things, or in things? Were you separate from what you perceived, or did you learn to join it, know it, and respect it? Did you grant life and dignity to what you perceived? Did you hold still with what you were perceiving, and did you keep paying attention just one second longer, then another second, then another—past the point where your mind said it was bored? Did you find surprising, humbling revelations that way? Were you able to be so focused in the present moment that it expanded like a ripening fruit and began showering you with riches? We hold the world in our gaze, just as we are held constantly in the gaze of God. Some greater force keeps us in focus, and in existence, by being aware of our every move and thought. That Perceiver penetrates us and actually creates us with its perception. If that great gaze were to perceive us shallowly or get bored and distracted for a second and look away—we would poof! And so, there is an attention on us that teaches us how to use our attention to create our lives and our world.

I would place my glittering perception on you
and welcome you to the space
of my knowing
and if you step in
everything you know
and everything I know
will dissolve in diamonds
and fire

Angeles Arrien, a crosscultural anthropologist, describes four important steps to living a successful life: show up, pay attention, tell the truth, and don't be attached to the results. I would add "love others as you would be loved," or "feel yourself in others and them in you," or "experience God in you and you in God." As you complete this cycle of a year's opportunity to perceive life more fully, take a present moment to contemplate the gift, and the giver, and the giving. As you contemplate, sink in, feel deeply, become and embody what you perceive.

I complete things consciously and get value from what I do.

What did you learn this year? What life lessons were you concentrating on? How is your perception different now than it was at the beginning of the year? Take time to congratulate yourself on your successes and feel deeply content today.

Notes

To the Reader

Intuition: Knowing at the Speed of Light
"The Soul Is a Verb," by Phil Cousineau, from *Handbook for the Soul*, edited by Richard Carlson and Benjamin Shield (Little, Brown, 1995).

Return to Beginner's Mind
Wild Mind: Living the Writer's Life, by Natalie Goldberg (Bantam, 1990), page 9.

"Zen Mind, Beginner's Mind," by Shunryu Suzuki, from *Entering the Stream*, edited by Samuel Bercholz and Sherab Chodzin Kohn (Shambhala, 1993).

Embrace "Nothing Special"
"Soul Work," by Jon Kabat-Zinn, Ph.D., from *Handbook for the Soul*, edited by Richard Carlson and Benjamin Shield (Little, Brown, 1995).

Keep Thine Eye Single
Sri Aurobindo, or The Adventure in Consciousness, by Satprem (Institute for Evolutionary Research, 1993).

Express Loving-Kindness
"The Soul's Legacy," by Dr. Brian Weiss, from *Handbook for the Soul*, edited by Richard Carlson and Benjamin Shield (Little, Brown, 1995).

Awakening Loving Kindness, by Pema Chödrön (Shambhala, 1996).

Live a Life of Inquiry
Writing Down the Bones: Freeing the Writer Within, by Natalie Goldberg (Shambhala, 1986), page 86.

Trust Your Body: Home of Your Soul
The Joyous Cosmology, by Alan Watts (Vintage Books, 1962), page 31.

January

2   *The Purpose of Your Life: Finding Your Place in the World Using Synchronicity, Intuition, and Uncommon Sense*, by Carol Adrienne (William Morrow, 1998).

13   Haikus contributed by Lorraine Anderson, Pat Hukill, Kelley Peters Floyd, and Susan Smith, M.D.

28   *Sacred Journeys in a Modern World*, by Roger Housden (Simon & Schuster, 1998).

February

22   *How Much Joy Can You Stand? How to Push Past Your Fears and Create Your Dreams,* by Suzanne Falter-Barns (Wellspring/Ballantine, 2000).

April

13   *Timeshifting: Creating More Time to Enjoy Your Life,* by Dr. Stephan Rechtschaffen (Doubleday, 1997).

15   *BrainStyles: Change Your Life Without Changing Who You Are,* by Marlane Miller (Simon & Schuster, 1997).

16   *Do I Have to Give Up Me to Be Loved by You?* by Margaret Paul and Jordan Paul (Compcare, 1993), and *Do I Have to Give Up Me to Be Loved by God?* by Margaret Paul (Health Communications, 1999).

May

5   *Desert Solitaire: A Season in the Wilderness,* by Edward Abbey (Ballantine Books/Random House, 1968).

9   *The Artist's Way: A Spiritual Path to Higher Creativity,* by Julia Cameron (Jeremy Tarcher/Putnam, 1992).

18   *The Alchemist: A Fable About Following Your Dream,* by Paolo Coelho (HarperSanFrancisco, 1995).

June

2   *Life, Paint and Passion: Reclaiming the Magic of Spontaneous Expression,* by Michell Cassou and Stewart Cubley (JP Tarcher, 1996).

5   *Mr. God, This Is Anna,* by Fynn (Ballantine Books/Random House, 1974).

9   "Lama Brought Out the Buddha in Me," by Christine Wicker, Religion Section, *Dallas Morning News,* September 4, 1999.

19   *The Relaxation Response,* by Herbert Benson (Avon, 1990).

21   *About This Life: Journeys on the Threshold of Memory,* by Barry Lopez (Vintage Books, 1999).

23   *Bird by Bird: Some Instructions on Writing and Life,* by Anne Lamott (Anchor/Doubleday, 1994).

July

12   "Teach Me Tonight," by Sammy Cahn and Gene De Paul; copyright Cahn Music Co., rights administered by Warner Bros. Music Corp. and The Hub Music Co. (ASCAP).

13   Inuit song, from *Earth Prayers from Around the World*, edited by
      Elizabeth Roberts and Elias Amidon (HarperSanFrancisco, 1991),
      page 41.

August

13   *Thank You God: The Prayers of Children*, compiled by Fiona Cor-
      bridge (Beyond Words Publishing, 1997).

14   Excerpted from Congregation of Abraxas, from *Earth Prayers from
      Around the World*, edited by Elizabeth Roberts and Elias Amidon
      (HarperSanFrancisco, 1991), page 140.

24   *Grow Yourself a Life You'll Love*, by Barbra Garro, M.A. (Thomas
      More, 1999).

September

28   *The Celestine Prophecy*, by James Redfield (Warner, 1994).

October

10   *All I Really Need to Know I Learned in Kindergarten: Uncommon
      Thoughts on Common Things*, by Robert Fulghum (Fawcett Books,
      1993).

13   *Your Aura & Your Chakras: The Owner's Manual*, by Karla McLaren
      (Samuel Weiser, 1998).

16   *Stopping: How to Be Still When You Have to Keep Going*, by David
      Kuntz, Ph.D. (Conari Press, 1998).

21   "On the Road with God's Fool: How St. Francis Lost Everything
      and Found His Way," by Gretel Ehrlich, *New York Times Magazine*,
      1999.

November

2   *Coming out of Your Psychic Closet: How to Unlock Your Naturally Intu-
      itive Self*, by Lynn B. Robinson, Ph.D. (Factor Press, 1994).

23   *The Intuitive Healer: Accessing Your Inner Physician*, by Dr. Marcia
      Emery (St. Martin's Press, 1999).

December

12   *Closer to the Light: Learning from Children's Near-Death Experiences*,
      by Melvin Morse (Villard, 1990) page 181.